7-SYNDROME
Healing

ALSO BY MARCIA ZIMMERMAN

——

Eat Your Colors
The A.D.D. Nutrition Solution
The Anti-Aging Solution
7-Color Cuisine™

7-SYNDROME Healing

*Supplement
Essentials for the
Mind and Body*

MARCIA ZIMMERMAN, CN
& JAYSON KRONER, CSN

NUTRITION SOLUTION PUBLICATIONS
Chico, California

DISCLAIMER

LIMIT OF LIABILITY/DISCLAIMER OF WARRANTY ✦ The information contained in this book is not intended to serve as a replacement for professional advice. Any use of the information in this book is at the reader's discretion. The authors and publisher specifically disclaim any and all liability arising directly or indirectly from the use or application of any information contained in this book. A health care professional should be consulted regarding your specific situation.

NUTRITION SOLUTION PUBLISHING
700 Serrano Ct., Chico, CA 95928-8414
www.thenutritionsolution.com

EDITOR AND PROJECT MANAGER: Virginia P. Ray
COVER AND TEXT DESIGN AND PRODUCTION: Jeff Potter/Potter Publishing Studio

Printed in the United States of America by Central Plains Book Manufacturing.

Set in Adobe Jenson and Linotype Univers.

ISBN 0-9721740-2-8

10 9 8 7 6 5 4 3 2 1

Dedication

7-Syndrome Healing is dedicated to those who have served the public to help make natural healing something that everyone can understand.

They are the unsung heroes who have fought for the right of consumers to choose more healthful products and dietary supplements to support optimum wellness. They are practitioners who have risked being ostracized by their peers as they recommend dietary change and use of nutritional supplements.

They are the scientists who have worked to explain how dietary supplements work and what they are useful for.

And they are the retailers and manufacturers who have dedicated their lives, and companies, to improve the health of millions.

Because of these dedicated people, we now have the freedom to choose complementary medicine as the best route to long and healthy lives.

This book contains the best of what these people have accomplished.

Contents

What Is a Syndrome?

SYNDROME… It's a word that we hear frequently. It's also one that's often confused as a synonym for other words, such as disease, illness and trauma. In fact the word *syndrome* has a different nuance entirely. Webster's defines it as "a group of signs and symptoms that occur together to characterize a particular abnormality."

Not every sign or symptom related to sluggish health is indicative of a true syndrome. Unfortunately, too often today we tend to over-generalize and use the term syndrome almost as a cliché to indicate poor health. From there it follows that we become a little too comfortable asking for a drug of choice to "cure" whatever "syndrome" we think we're experiencing.

And that's where the big mistakes start.

In the business of health and medicine, *syndrome* is a term that's used carefully as a way to identify an umbrella of related health challenges that can lead to chronic disease. It's a particularly appropriate term for this handbook, as we've worked hard to examine some of the most common "little" things that we notice about our bodies. Many are harmless and may never graduate past embarrassing nuisance levels of worry. But just as many have the potential to snowball and feed off the compromised conditions of other systems. When left unaddressed, this situation can spell biological human disaster.

Regardless of where they rank on the severity scale, it's the collective accumulation of little things that often leads to the development of a legitimate syndrome. By listening to your body, considering genetic and lifestyle risk factors, and taking appropriate dietary and supplement actions, your chances of experiencing a legitimate health-challenging syndrome will be tremendously decreased.

Of the many points that you'll want to remember from *7-Syndrome Healing* three are key.

First, we wanted to set the standard to identify and describe each of the body's major biological syndrome categories. This is our modest attempt to eliminate the high redundancy rate that often accompanies the use of the word. For example, high blood pressure is not a syndrome, but rather a condition. By contrast, high blood pressure coupled with irregular heart rate, clogged arteries and chest pain would unquestionably fall under the umbrella of the *cardiovascular syndrome*—one of seven that we'll be discussing in great detail throughout the book.

Next, we wanted to paint a clear and accurate picture of the health network that connects within our bodies, as well as to delineate the connection among corresponding major syndromes. As you'll learn, there is an amazing biological link that defines us. The conditions associated with the *stress syndrome*, for example, can have a direct impact on cardiovascular, structural and hormonal health. Rarely do we think about it, but some of our most common (and seemingly insignificant) physical anomalies often serve as stepping stones to much more serious conditions.

Finally, we want to enlighten you to the countless measures that can be taken when trying to attain and preserve good health. By this we're referring to lifestyle adjustments, dietary consciousness, nutrition and supplementation and many others that will be covered in great detail throughout. Because regardless of who you are, where you hail from, and what your life's work entails, you alone are responsible for improving your health by taking appropriate measures that acknowledge your needs.

7-Syndrome Healing is the result of our shared passion for everything that we now have at our health-seeking disposal. Dietary supplements are more than just pills that line the shelves of health food stores. They're gifts of immeasurable worth, many of which come to us in a nearly unadulterated fashion from the soil we share. Henry David Thoreau once wrote,

In wildness is the preservation of the World. Every tree sends its fibers forth in search of the Wild. The cities import it at any price. Men plow and sail for it. From the forest and wilderness come the tonics and barks which brace mankind...

Of course, Thoreau penned these words of wisdom at a time when health-seeking individuals didn't have access to the science and knowledge that we do today, but he makes a good point. We have been blessed with everything we need to become and remain healthy. The primary purpose of *7-Syndrome Healing* is to educate you about the specific health benefits of dietary supplements, the potential risks in combining them with medicines, and how to use them effectively and responsibly. You may be one of 46 percent of Americans who use dietary supplements regularly, or one who wants to close the gap between scientific knowledge, accurate information, and the urban myths that surround their use. While easy-to-read and straightforward in style, this book is based in scientific fact. We hope that you'll find it interesting and helpful and feel assured knowing that our research is extensive. In *7-Syndrome Healing* you'll find information about more than 100 dietary supplements that explains:

- How supplements work within the body.
- Their benefits for seven common syndromes.
- Companion (synergistic) supplements for each.
- Brands to look for.
- Medications that interfere and contraindications for use with medications.

As many Americans will agree, dietary supplements play a valuable role in promoting health and preventing illness, and 6 out of 10 adults currently use them on a regular basis, according to a 2001 survey conducted by the Natural Marketing Institute. During the same survey period, it was determined that another 25 percent of adults took supplements, although not regularly. If you're like most people, you're probably familiar with multiple vitamins and other popular supplements such as vitamin C, garlic and ginseng. But these better-known supplements merely scratch the surface of what is currently at your disposal.

Sadly, fewer than half of supplement users discuss their supplement choices with their doctors, leaving a gap between using supplements responsibly as a complement to conventional therapies. Many of today's most skilled physicians now recommend the use of dietary supplements, although just as many have voiced concerns about the interactions that they may pose with prescribed medicines or inappropriate dosages. This handbook provides guidelines that can strongly benefit physicians and their patients.

One of the biggest problems in taking prescription drugs is that their activity may deplete essential nutrients. Unfortunately, this information is often not conveyed to the patient and so he or she can ultimately experience unnecessary and otherwise avoidable side effects.

According to the Dietary Supplement Information Bureau, the following are among the most commonly prescribed medications that have the potential to deplete nutrients[*]:

+ Atorvastatin (Lipitor®)
+ Azithoromycin (Zithromax®)
+ Combined Estrogens (Premarin®)
+ Inhaled Corticosteroids (Nasacort®)
+ Lansoprazole (Prevacid®)
+ Omeprazole (Prilosec®)
+ Oral Corticosteroids (Prednisone®)
+ Pravastatin (Pravochol®)
+ Pisperidone (Risperdal®)
+ Simvastatin (Zocor®)

As we proceed, you'll find the specific nutrients that these medicines deplete as well as important information about how to design a supplement program that may offset many common side effects.

---

[*] Source: Dietary Supplement Information Bureau 2005

Similarly, we'll examine which supplements can actually enhance the effects of medications, and which ones to discuss with your doctor. They include:

- Vitamin A
- Vitamin K
- SAM-e
- Vitamin E
- St. John's Wort
- 5-HTP

Ideally, we want you to use this handbook as your personal guide to select formulas for specific indications. Condition-specific formulas have surged in popularity and when choosing them you should look for those that contain the specific nutrients we've listed. They'll help you in your quest to prevent and manage the seven syndromes that we'll be exploring. Keep in mind that "combination formulas" can provide a synergism of action and many include amounts that vary from formula to formula. You can use the amounts given in this handbook to gauge whether or not the formula you choose contains a reasonable amount of each nutrient.

The dietary companion to this handbook is *7-Color Cuisine: A Nutrition Guide and Cookbook*. With this two-volume set, you'll have all of the tools necessary to take charge of your life today and enjoy years of vitality and good health.

Foreword

THE FIRST AND SECOND EDITIONS of *Pharmacology: Essentials of Basic Science*, written in 1992 and 1996 (Little, Brown & Co.), contained groundbreaking information about drug nutrient interactions, which was written by Marcia Zimmerman. At the time that my colleagues and I wrote the books, there was little appreciation for the interference of medications with vitamins and minerals. Of equal importance was the lack of information about how certain dietary supplements could enhance or inhibit the action of prescription and over-the-counter medicines. Moreover, the lack of required information on the source and purity of many supplements introduced the possibility of interactions with impurities or byproducts. Little did we know back then how vital this information would be as more and more consumers have turned to dietary supplements (nutraceuticals) as the first line of defense against numerous medical conditions.

Today, more than half the population is seeking alternative remedies for practically every disease known without informing their physicians. The demand for dietary supplements has led to an explosion in products—often bearing unfounded claims—with little supporting scientific evidence. While dietary supplements have a long history of safety, guidelines about what consumers should look for are clearly needed. Moreover, for every 5 years after age 50, a person is diagnosed with one disease for which two drugs are prescribed on average; for every two drugs, there is a 20 percent chance of drug interactions, without taking any drug-supplement interactions into account. A definitive guide on interactions between dietary supplements and drugs is, therefore, of the greatest importance. Many reputable companies, including those based on my own research (www.algonot.com), offer products that conform to the highest pharmaceutical standards and this book suggests brands to shop for in the Appendix. The information in this handbook is pre-eminent for anyone using dietary supplements, as well as for physicians who want credible information upon which to base supplement recommendations.

Marcia Zimmerman has been on the cutting edge of nutraceutical technology for many years. She has formulated hundreds of products, been a popular speaker, and written extensively on the health benefits of nutraceuticals—natural compounds with medicinal properties. My own research spanning the past 25 years offers strong evidence for incorporating these natural compounds to mediate inflammatory conditions. The applications presented in this handbook include stress, cardiovascular disease, immune disorders, inflammatory conditions, allergies, chronic infections, and cancer.

The information in *7-Syndrome Healing* is well organized by Marcia Zimmerman and her co-author, Jayson Kroner, and presented in an easy-to-read style. I have found the information contained in this book extremely credible and useful, not only for consumers, but also for my health-providing colleagues.

T.C. THEOHARIDES, PH.D., M.D.

Professor of Pharmacology
Internal Medicine and Biochemistry
Director, Laboratory for Molecular
Immunopharmacology and Drug Discovery
Tufts University School of Medicine
Tufts-New England Medical Center, Boston, Massachusetts
www.mastercellmaster.com

Acknowledgments

W E ARE DEEPLY GRATEFUL for Dr. T.C. Theoharides's critical review of the medical and pharmacological information in this book. Dr. Theoharides's work to validate the effectiveness of several nutraceutical compounds discussed in this book lends tremendous credibility to it. Readers and medical practitioners can have confidence that the material presented is well researched.

You can read more about Dr. Theoharides's work and download his publications at www.mastercellmaster.com.

7-Syndrome Healing has brought together an extraordinary team of talented and dedicated individuals. Our editor and "chief of operations" is Virginia Ray, who has worked tirelessly to pull together all the components of this project. Jeff Potter's design and artistic talents have made this book truly outstanding and a delight to read.

We both owe a debt of gratitude to Clare, Jay, Dan, and Neil for their friendship, faith, and advice during this project. Jayson also acknowledges the love and support of his parents, Michael and Elizabeth Kroner, and his sister, Shannon Kroner.

CHAPTER ONE

The Basics of Healthy Living

IVING IN THE TWENTY-FIRST CENTURY is fraught with challenges—work responsibilities, family needs, social obligations—and a mind-numbing list of many that can't even be categorized. Individually, each one can be demanding. But when you collectively cram them all into the blender of life, add a few major ups and downs for flavor, and then frappé the thing for five, ten, and even twenty years, things have a tendency to get messy. Good health, sadly, is almost always one of the first areas to suffer.

There is, however, good news.

We are living in an age of exceptional science and brilliant minds. The past decade has been one of the most exciting to date. As a result of great advancements, we've discovered hundreds of new ways to cope with many of the most common diseases and health challenges. There is a catch, however. In order to reap the benefits of all that we now know, we must first learn to embrace and understand the basics of healthy living, stress reduction, commitment to lifestyle, and sound diet.

If you're like most people, you've probably at some point turned to any number of products to improve your quality of health and well-being. If you have, you already know that there's certainly no shortage of offerings when it comes bettering human health. Each one of us has access to a worldwide

1

supply of promise, and throughout each chapter of this book we'll be reviewing many of what we consider to be the best.

It's no secret that the business of health and wellness is doing very, very well. As we speak, 7 million baby boomers are refusing to follow their parents by simply going quietly into advanced middle age. Instead, they're fighting back with every healthy and natural tool they can grasp. Fueling this passion for prime health are incomes that are higher and more disposable than ever before in history. At the same time, there has been unprecedented growth in the senior population. Much longevity may be attributed to medical advances that have made it possible to lead longer, more active lives. And, as it turns out, this year's freshman class of senior citizens is far more likely to use supplements than any of their predecessors. And why not? In many cases, dietary supplements are much more benign and far more affordable than prescription drugs. Plus, there's an expanding environmental awareness that continues to drive health-conscious consumers toward natural products. Americans are seriously concerned about the quality of the air they breathe, the water in their faucets, and the foods they serve and consume. Many have made the decision to avoid pesticides, hormones, and extensive food processing. Consequently, there's been a 17 percent growth rate in the sale of natural and organic foods, not to mention a 7 percent increase in the overall market for health-related products in just the last year.

The Demand for Dietary Supplements

Sixty percent of Americans now use dietary supplements on at least a periodic basis. This makes the natural products industry one of the fastest growing categories in the human health arena. But with that popularity comes a dilemma: choosing the best supplements for *you* can be confusing. Are you one of the growing number of Americans who sincerely wants to take charge of your health, but is disturbed about conflicting news regarding the use of supplements? And what about the mantra sung by supplement critics—that supplements are "unregulated" and therefore of questionable safety? Before we pass judgment, let's sort out the facts about dietary supplements, beginning with their origins.

The Birth of Health Foods and Dietary Supplements

The dietary supplement industry grew out of the need to supply "super foods" for those with special dietary needs. It all started with the first ready-to-eat, dry, whole-grain cereal produced in 1894 by W. K. Kellogg and his brother, Dr. John Kellogg, for use in their sanitorium in Battle Creek, Michigan.

The popularity of "health foods" didn't really catch on until the 1930s and 1940s. Several companies emerged, including California's Hain Health Foods, which produced supplemental garlic and parsley tablets, and Bragg Health Products, which offered liquid amino acid formulas. At the same time in the midwest, Gaylord Hauser launched Modern Health Products, while Fearn Soya Foods began catering to crowds that preferred the natural, organic, and wholesome.

The first natural vitamins were produced in the early 1940s. One of earliest pioneers in this new and profitable line of business was Eugene Schiff. Anabolic Labs, Kal, NOW Foods, Plus, Solgar, and Thompson products soon joined him. These products were sold in health food stores, which began cropping up around the country. At the same time, the first supplements supplied for the military were commissioned during World War II.

Quality and Regulation

In the early days, food supplements were produced using the same standards that governed food products. They were also regulated as foods by the newly formed Food and Drug Administration (FDA). Doing so tightened the reins on qualified health claims, and only recently has the FDA allowed health claims that are supported by scientific evidence. Still, at the time this writing, that agency has approved fewer than a dozen claims for foods and dietary supplements. Foods that *can* make these claims are referred to as *functional foods*; they contain specified amounts of an ingredient that has been shown to alter the course of disease.

The production of dietary supplements has come a long way since the early days. Reputable supplement manufacturers now produce vitamins and other products according to meticulous pharmaceutical standards. Today, strict controls must be in place to:

- Quarantine raw materials until their identity and freedom from contaminants and toxins can be confirmed.
- Operate an in-house laboratory that offers biochemical analysis and microbiological testing capabilities.
- Maintain sanitary standards for workers, equipment, and filling and production chambers.
- Test for potency, stability, product uniformity, production, and packaging.
- Retain samples of each product batch for future testing.
- Verify what was done and who signed off on each step of the manufacturing process.
- Submit to unannounced FDA inspections and render labels for scrutiny from the agency.

In addition, most manufacturers submit their products to third-party testing facilities administered under Good Manufacturing Practices (GMP) or United States Pharmacopoeia (USP). Designation for these programs appears on the labels of products regulated by these organizations.

The National Nutritional Foods Association (NNFA) and American Herbal Products Association (AHPA) have created codes of ethics that their respective members must adhere to. Both organizations insist that their members ensure that products actually contain what labels claim and that all proper manufacturing procedures are followed. These associations will also issue alerts upon discovering adulterated products.

The FDA maintains strict rules for supplement labels. Products must specify the percentage of the recommended dietary or daily allowance (RDA) for essential vitamins and minerals. In the case of herbs, the agency requires manufacturers to disclose the product's Latin name as well as the specific parts of the plant used and the percentage of active components in standardized herbs. Finally, the ingredients used to encapsulate or tablet the product and facilitate disintegration in the gastrointestinal tract must also be listed.

When looking for dietary supplements there are many factors to consider. Aside from the quality and science behind the companies that provide them, there are other questions you'll want to ask. Does the company use environmentally friendly packaging? If it manufactures supplements, does it offer a Web site with access to scientific papers or literature that support the product's claim? Is the company committed to promoting product integrity and advocacy issues? These, along with quality products, are usually good indicators that the manufacturer has done the homework.

In 1994, Congress passed the Dietary Supplement Health and Education Act (DSHEA) allowing the unrestricted sale of vitamins, minerals, herbs, amino acids, and semi-vitamins—as long as manufacturers don't make medical claims for these products. Manufacturers can, however, relate the use of their products to particular body functions, such as promoting vitamin A for healthy vision or calcium for bone health. Moreover, the following disclaimer must accompany any structure/function claims on product labels, advertisements, specification sheets, etc.: "*These statements have not been evaluated by the FDA and are not intended to diagnose, treat, cure, or prevent any disease.*"

The Federal Trade Commission (FTC) is responsible for regulating such claims and the FDA has been fully empowered by Congress to remove any supplement deemed harmful. This power was demonstrated when the FDA made a bold move to ban the sale of ephedrine-based products in 2004. Although regulation of dietary supplements is a herculean task, it comes in handy when some unscrupulous characters attempt to sneak products into the public domain with the intention of cashing in before they get caught.

That said, it's important to investigate claims that seem a little too good to be true. When shopping for supplements, do so at reputable stores and through credible online providers. Use this handbook to guide you and read labels carefully, paying special attention to guarantees and extravagant promises.

Now, let's move onto putting your personalized supplement program together.

Why Supplement?

The craziness of living in these times and our increasing exposure to environmental toxins has driven millions of people to seek better health protection with dietary supplements. A good place to start is with a daily multiple vitamin and mineral. Even the ultraconservative Harvard School of Public Health included a daily multiple in its suggested food pyramid in 2004. According to Harvard researchers, "a daily multivitamin, multimineral supplement offers a kind of nutritional backup." Several large studies have shown that healthy adults who supplement with multiple vitamins and mineral formulas can reduce their risks of heart disease and cancer while enhancing immunity and brain function.

Advantages of a Daily Multiple

It's easiest to begin with a daily multiple because in it vitamins and minerals are kept in balance, which avoids depleting any of them. B vitamins, for example, work as a team and seem to work more effectively when supplemented together. And, like B vitamins, *antioxidants* afford greater protection against a wide range of conditions when combined.

The safe track record of multivitamin and multimineral formulas is another good reason to base your nutrition regimen on a basic multivitamin. It can be difficult to choose which individual vitamins, minerals, or herbs to use as supplements, especially given conflicting reports that find their way into the evening news. This handbook will take the mystery out of making the right decisions for you.

Essential Vitamins and Minerals

Vitamins and minerals with demonstrated abilities to reduce the symptoms of a nutritional deficiency are considered essential. The Food and Nutrition

Board of the National Academy of Sciences is charged with reviewing the latest scientific research to determine the level of essential vitamins and minerals needed on a daily basis to prevent disease. This level is referred to as *Recommended Daily Allowance*, or RDA. Current RDAs are very conservative and

Vitamin	RDA	Function and (Deficiency Symptoms)
A	5,000 IU	• conversion of neural signals into visual images (night blindness) • integrity of epithelial cells in skin, lining of organs, body cavity (rough, scaly skin) • genetic expression, embryonic development (impaired development) • immune function (reduction in immune cells)
C	60 mg	• collagen formation (skin wrinkling, poor wound healing) • capillary walls (easy bruising) • amino acid metabolism (muscle wasting, fatigue) • neurotransmitter function (nervousness, anxiety) • iron absorption (anemia)
Carotenoids	none established	• vitamin A (some) • intercellular communication (cancer) • protects vitamins C and E; DNA (immune function) • antioxidant (chronic disease, aging)
D	400 IU	• calcium absorption (bone thining, cavities) • growth and development (rickets) • skin (psoriasis, acne) • cell growth (colon, prostate, breast cancer)
E	30 IU	• prevents LDL oxidation (cardiovascular disease) • platelets (adhesion, thrombosis) • neutralizes superoxide radicals (cellular damage) • anti-inflammatory (peripheral neuropathy, neurological symptoms, muscle weakness, absent tendon reflexes)
K	80 mcg	• blood coagulation (increased bleeding time) • bone formation (bone thinning)

FIGURE 1-1 **Vitamin Functions at a Glance**

serve as the basis for governmental regulation of dietary supplements. Figure 1-1 lists the RDA, function, and deficiency symptoms of each vitamin.

The RDA can help the consumer gauge the quality and balance of his or her diet. As mentioned above, you will find the percentage of the RDA for each nutrient listed on the supplement panel. The Food and Nutrition Board also sets optimum and upper limits of intake. In many cases, these more closely reflect the potencies included in today's supplements. The list of essential nutrients keeps growing as new scientific evidence reveals the need for particular nutrients. Still, many of the most effective supplements are not considered essential.

Nonessential Nutrients

Nonessential doesn't always equal not important. To make this distinction clear, scientists have proposed the term *semi-essential* to describe nutrients that don't have RDAs, but are helpful in overcoming metabolic bottlenecks. A growing body of scientific evidence supports the use of semi-essential nutrients, and they have become the darlings of complementary and alternative medicine.

What You Will Find in This Chapter

Significant detail about each of the essential vitamins and minerals is included in this chapter. Throughout this book, you'll find a cross-reference for many essential nutrients. These are coenzymes or cofactors for semi-essential nutrients, herbs, or amino acids—each recommended for the particular syndrome under discussion. The essential vitamins and minerals included in most multiple formulas function in several specific categories, and have been grouped accordingly in this chapter.

- Growth and differentiation factors
- Antioxidants
- Nutrients for building and maintaining
- Nutrients that regulate metabolism

Growth and Differentiation Factors

VITAMIN A

MAJOR APPLICATION OF VITAMIN A ✦ Vitamin A is most often associated with vision, but there's more to it's effectiveness than just maintaining a healthy set of eyes. Vitamin A has a direct impact on the integrity of the immune system, digestive function, cellular growth and differentiation, nervous system function, brain development, and skin.

AN OVERVIEW OF VITAMIN A ✦ First isolated in the 1930s, vitamin A (or retinol) was the first fat-soluble vitamin ever to be discovered. Until then, we were at the mercy of our diets to get adequate amounts of this ultraimportant nutrient. Back then, yellow and dark-green vegetables provided carotenes that could be converted into vitamin A and oils from fish livers were a common tonic during winter months. Then again, that was 75 years ago—a time when vitamin A deficiency was not much of an issue. When you fast-forward to modern times, however, the situation is vastly different. Fast food, days riddled with stress and deadlines, long working hours, increased exposure to toxins, and a host of other elements catapult vitamin A supplementation to the rank of necessity.

Symptoms associated with low vitamin A intake are so rampant in third-world countries that the scientific community has proposed a widespread enrichment of native foods, rice included. Closer to home the increasing incidence of obesity, along with certain metabolic and malabsorption syndromes, continue to fuel the rise in vitamin A deficiency.

HOW VITAMIN A WORKS ✦ Vitamin A, a nutrient found only in animal-derived foods, is produced in the intestines from its dietary precursors—the carotenoids (natural pigments) alpha and beta carotene and beta cryptoxanthin. Vitamin A is stored in the liver until needed, then dispensed to many of the body's vital systems. These include the eyes, where vitamin A is required for photoreceptors to function. Vitamin A is also essential to the integrity of epithelial tissues, including those lining internal organs, the body cavity, the mucus membranes, and the skin. If your daily diet doesn't include 5-10 servings of red, orange, and yellow fruits and vegetables, this is one supplement you won't want to neglect.

Therapeutic Uses for Vitamin A

- *Cancer.* Certain types of cancer, most notably breast, lung and skin, may respond well to vitamin A supplementation. Scientists at the Temple University School of Medicine in Philadelphia, Pennsylvania, have proposed that vitamin A may curb ovarian cancer by blocking telemerase activity in cancer cells. Telemeres are found at the end of chromosomes in normal and cancer cells, and are often described as molecular clocks. They shorten each time a cell divides in order to keep cellular reproduction in check. However, cancer cells have devised a system to overcome this. They contain telemerase, an enzyme that prevents telemeres from shortening while allowing the cells to proliferate. Because vitamin A has the ability to block telemerase, it may be a useful adjunct to chemotherapy, but this is definitely something to discuss with your doctor.

- *Clear skin.* Use of vitamin A is one of the most basic and natural ways to encourage healthy skin. In fact, it serves as the foundation for some very popular prescription formulas. If you're already using one, it's important to always remain cautiously aware of your oral vitamin A intake. An overabundance of vitamin A commonly results in excessive redness, drying, and flaking skin and lips. These are red flags that you're taking more than your body needs. As an alternative, try dabbing a tiny amount of vitamin A on the occasional blemish. It really seems to help the healing process.

- *Crohn's disease.* This puzzling disease is becoming more and more common among young adults and adolescents. While there's still much to be learned about its cause, researchers have determined that vitamin A levels are low among those afflicted. Vitamin A deficiency is common among those who have chronic digestive disturbances, such as celiac disease (gluten intolerance), and those who have had gastric bypass surgery. French researchers have focused several studies on reversing vitamin A deficiency in Crohn's patients as one method for reducing inflammation.

- *Healthy vision.* The retina, mucus membranes, and tear ducts rely on vitamin A to function properly. And because visual adjustment from bright to dark light depends upon photoreceptor function, vitamin A deficiencies have been known to result in the condition most commonly known as night blindness.
- *Minor burns and wounds.* The combination of topical vitamin A ointments and oral supplements has been shown to expedite the healing of minor burns, scrapes, cuts, and abrasions.
- *Upper respiratory infection.* Upper respiratory infections can wreak havoc on healthy mucus membranes. By stimulating the immune system, vitamin A helps support these delicate, vulnerable tissues and may even assist to repair damaged lung tissues. Researchers in Mexico have determined that the combination of vitamin A and zinc can help reduce oxidative stress and may even be an effective way to curb the inflammatory response associated with lung disease. A new study by Harvard researchers proposes that vitamin A supplementation for children may decrease the risk of several diseases, including diarrhea, measles, HIV infection, and malaria. Some physicians have further proposed that vitamin A supplementation among infants may improve their antibody responses to some vaccinations, including tetanus, diphtheria, and measles.

TIPS FOR TAKING VITAMIN A

- Vitamin A is a fat-soluble nutrient and should be taken with a meal that contains some fat to enhance absorption.
- Most, if not all, multivitamin formulas include vitamin A as a primary nutrient. Always factor this in when deciding how much will be needed from separate supplementation.
- Under *no* circumstance should pregnant woman ingest more that 5,000 I.U. (international units) of vitamin A per day. Serious birth defects have been linked to high doses during pregnancy.
- While vitamin A offers a wide range of life-enhancing benefits, taking more than you need won't offer greater protection. Doing so can lead to some very undesirable health problems including hair loss, physical weakness, bleeding gums, nausea, and dry, flaky skin.
- IU (international units) is the most common unit of measurement for vitamin A. In some articles, you may come across the letters RE (or retinol equivalent). A simple conversion is 1,000 RE = 5,000 IU.
- Keep in mind that if higher doses of vitamin A are required for an acute condition, those dosages should be continued only for 3-4 weeks, or as specified by a physician.

NATURAL COMPANIONS FOR VITAMIN A ✦ Antioxidants, B vitamins, zinc and iron (from daily multiple vitamin and mineral formulas).

ANTIOXIDANTS

MAJOR APPLICATIONS OF ANTIOXIDANTS ✦ The term *antioxidant* is so prevalent and so widespread that one can't help but wonder if every supplement is an antioxidant and question which are truly needed to live at our pinnacle. Antioxidants, the defensive team for plants, come in many different categories. How they protect plants varies according to their specific chemical structures. Fortunately, plant antioxidants also protect us and are readily available from diets that contain a wide variety of fruits and vegetables. Many scientists, including those at Yale

University's School of Medicine, have determined that antioxidants such as beta carotene and other carotenoids, vitamins C and E, and selenium protect against many chronic diseases.

An Overview of Antioxidants ✦ Antioxidants are indeed plentiful, but it's important to realize that many different kinds are needed to protect the body against aging and age-related conditions. The major groups of antioxidants include more than 600 carotenoids and more than 4,000 polyphenols. Carotenoids, being oil-soluble, protect cell membranes as they post themselves at specific duty stations within those membranes. Polyphenols are water-soluble and free to roam about the body in blood, lymph, and tissue fluids. Scientists refer to the cooperative action of carotenoids, polyphenols, vitamin A, vitamin C, vitamin E, and selenium as "the antioxidant network." Dr. Lester Packer of the University of California at Berkeley was the first scientist to describe the interdependent role of antioxidant vitamins, along with the semi-essential nutrients alpha lipoic acid, glutathione, and CoQ_{10}.

How Antioxidants Work ✦ In short, antioxidants seek out and neutralize free radicals. Those unstable molecules have unpaired electrons and are able to compromise the structure and activity of healthy cells. In some instances, those extra electrons can weigh down the antioxidant, transforming it into a radical. The antioxidant system that Dr. Packer identified uses the talents of several antioxidants to shuffle electrons back and forth until they can be safely eliminated from the body.

Supplement Companions for Antioxidants ✦ Natural carotenoids include alpha and beta carotene, lutein, lycopene, zeaxanthin, beta cryptoxanthin, the vitamin E family (including tocopherols and tocotrienols), and the vitamin C family (including flavonoids and the mineral selenium). Although CoQ_{10} and lipoic acid are important players in antioxidant recycling, just a select number of multiple formulas contain them. Those that do are definitely worth your consideration.

NATURAL CAROTENOIDS

MAJOR APPLICATION FOR NATURAL CAROTENOIDS ♦ Have you ever wondered why fruits and vegetables display such a fascinating spectrum of color? It's not by chance. In fact, these colors represent much more than a pleasant array of nature's beautiful possibilities. The specific shade of each fruit and vegetable, be it red, orange, yellow or green, is determined by its *carotenoids*, natural pigments that possess strong antioxidant properties.

Despite thousands of years of consuming these carotenoids, only recently have we truly begun to understand what a comprehensive role they play in human health. From cardiovascular and immune support to healthy vision and respiratory function, carotenoids are bursting with natural compounds that can have a profoundly positive effect on our quality of life.

AN OVERVIEW ♦ To date more than 600 different carotenoids have been identified. Ironically, only a small percentage of these are thought to be useful in human nutrition. The following six are the most abundant in today's diet and offer the widest range of health benefits. They include alpha and beta carotene, lycopene, lutein, zeaxanthin, and beta cryptoxanthin. Let's take a closer look at each one's source and specific method of action.

- ♦ *Alpha carotene.* This predominantly orange pigment can be found in pumpkins, carrots, winter squash, and sweet potatoes, among other foods. As one of the most common of all carotenoids in typical U.S. diets, alpha carotene is also one of the 50 "pro-vitamin A" carotenoids, meaning that it can be converted to an active form of vitamin A known as *retinol.* From a functional perspective, alpha carotene is a powerful antioxidant able to promote a more responsive immune system, protect cells from free radical damage, and help prevent abnormal cellular growth and activity.
- ♦ *Beta carotene.* If your diet doesn't include fresh fruits and vegetables such as kale, spinach, sweet potatoes, thyme, squash, collard greens, and fresh cilantro, you'll definitely want to get to know beta carotene. Traditionally beta carotene produces the yellow and orange colors in

fruits and vegetables. But its ability to easily merge with other phyto-nutrients often results in foods bearing shades of red and pink. Like alpha carotene, beta carotene is equally capable of being converted into vitamin A and possesses strong antioxidant properties. Additionally, it's been shown to play an integral role in human reproduction, making it ideal for couples trying to conceive.

- *Lutein and zeaxanthin.* Unlike the two previous carotenoids, lutein and zeaxanthin cannot be converted into the retinol form of vitamin A within the body. But that doesn't make them any less important. Despite having predominantly yellow pigments, lutein and zeaxanthin are no strangers to dark green and leafy vegetables such as broccoli, spinach, kale, collard greens, and peas. Others such as corn, bananas, zucchini, and Brussels sprouts also contain robust amounts of lutein and zeaxanthin. With their ability to filter many of the sun's harmful UV rays, both are of great value to human eyes and have become staples in the prevention of macular degeneration and cataracts as well as in promoting all-around ocular integrity.

- *Lycopene.* Lycopene isn't just one of the most popular members of the carotenoid family, it's also one of the most beneficial. Red in color, lycopene is essentially what provides tomatoes with their rich, ruby appearance. It can also be found in fruits such as watermelon, papaya, and pink grapefruit. Although it's primarily stored in the lungs and prostate, lycopene offers many health benefits ranging from cardiovascular and prostate support to cancer prevention and increased fertility. Most impressive, lycopene is able to eliminate one of the most damaging of all free radicals, *singlet oxygen radicals.* These highly reactive byproducts of oxidation are formed during the metabolism of polyunsaturated fatty acids and can be devastating to healthy cell membranes.

- *Beta cryptoxanthin.* This slightly yellow-orange "pro-vitamin A" carotenoid is most commonly found in oranges, peaches, cantaloupes, carrots, mangoes, sweet potatoes, and nectarines. From a wellness perspective, it has seen the most popularity as an effective and natural anti-aging, anti-cancer agent.

Beta cryptoxanthin is a relentless free radical fighter, quite capable of quenching massive amounts of oxidation throughout the body. Many researchers believe that this unique activity best serves the respiratory tract and the colon—two regions of the body where free radical activity and oxidative stress is especially high. This thought is supported by studies suggesting that elevated levels can encourage the production of the *RB gene*, a natural guardian of healthy, uncompromised cells.

THERAPEUTIC USES OF NATURAL CAROTENOIDS

+ *Cancer.* Harvard researchers have found that among men enrolled in their health professionals' study, high lycopene intake was protective against prostate cancer, especially among those who didn't have a family history of the disease. Beta carotene intake among younger men was also associated with a lower incidence of prostate cancer. Canadian scientists have reported that lutein and zeaxanthin may help prevent colon cancer.

+ *Immune system support.* High blood concentrations of carotenoids appear to protect against upper respiratory infections. Researchers in the Netherlands found that patients with the highest beta carotene levels in their blood had the lowest incidences of acute respiratory infection. The other five carotenoids tested—alpha carotene, beta cryptoxanthin, lycopene, lutein, and zeaxanthin—appeared to offer no additional protection.

+ *Cardiovascular health.* Cholesterol levels are an important risk factor in cardiovascular disease. Low-density "bad" cholesterol is vulnerable to free radical oxidation and, once oxidized, it may recruit inflammatory mediators that damage the interior wall of arteries—a process known as atherogenesis. Dietary antioxidants may reduce cardiovascular disease, particularly if both carotenoids and polyphenols are included.

- *Healthy vision.* Age-related macular degeneration (AMD) is the leading cause of vision loss among people over 50 throughout the world. Lutein and zeaxanthin are the only carotenoids found in both the macula (a yellow area in the center of the retina) and the lens of the human eye. They have dual functions in both tissues, acting as powerful antioxidants as well as filters for blue light. A 2003 review of several large trials found that supplements containing lutein and zeaxanthin appeared to prevent and treat AMD. Researchers at the National Eye Institute found that giving 5,000 patients supplements of vitamins A, C, E, and beta carotene reduced early stage AMD by 19 percent.
- *Age-related memory.* Clearly, episodes of high stress and the fact of growing older can increase our forgetfulness. So it's normal for us to occasionally forget where we put our keys. Forgetting what keys are used for, however, can be an early sign of Alzheimer's Disease. Both simple forgetfulness and Alzheimer's result from free radical damage to the brain. Several studies have shown than an antioxidant cocktail containing the carotenoids zeaxanthin, beta cryptoxanthin, lycopene, lutein, and alpha and beta carotene may ameliorate some of the symptoms and slow progression of this disease.
- *Diabetes and blood sugar.* Diabetes is another disease that's commonly linked to an increase in free radical activity. Many of the complications associated with it result from damage to the blood vessels and other tissues. A study recently completed in Queensland, Australia found that among 1,597 adults with type 2 diabetes, the blood levels of five carotenoids including alpha and beta carotene, beta cryptoxanthin, lutein/zeaxanthin, and lycopene, were low. The lowest levels of carotenoids were found in those with impaired glucose metabolism.

Tips for Taking Carotenoids
- If you're one of the handful of people who actually consume 5-7 servings of fresh fruit and vegetables daily, good for you. If you're not, there

are plenty of carotenoid formulas to choose from. Look for one with a broad, well balanced profile that includes the carotenoids mentioned in this chapter.

+ Carotenoids are fat-soluble and should be taken with a meal that includes some fat. Some users opt to take their essential fatty acids (EFAs) with their carotenoids to increase assimilation.

+ Make sure that the formula you choose provides a minimum of 5,000 IU of vitamin A activity. The antioxidant properties of beta carotene must be considered as separate from its function as a precursor of vitamin A.

+ Individuals who smoke or frequently consume alcohol should use caution when taking carotenoids, especially those high in beta carotene. Several studies suggest that doing so may increase the chance of cardiovascular or lung disease.

+ Look for a complex that includes the six natural carotenoids.

VITAMIN E

MAJOR APPLICATION OF VITAMIN E + Vitamin E was first discovered in the early 1920s by a team of University of California researchers studying the chemical breakdown of green, leafy vegetables. Today vitamin E is universally accepted as one of the most beneficial nutrients ever made available. It's made up of two closely related compounds, including four tocopherols and four tocotrienols. Recent studies have led researchers to believe that tocotrienols may be more important, for instance to cardiovascular function, than tocopherols.

AN OVERVIEW OF VITAMIN E + Despite a history that boasts 80-some years of proven safety and effectiveness, a very recent study had the audacity to suggest that moderate-to-high doses of vitamin E might increase a person's risk of heart attack. It's worth noting, however, that after careful review of said "research," not only does it appear to be severely flawed, but also inconsistent, having focused only on less-expensive, synthetic vitamin E supplements. In addition, it was reported that some of the participants were elderly and that a number had serious medical conditions. What wasn't disclosed: natural vitamin E supplements are 50 percent more powerful than synthetics, and they are easy to identify as they're labeled "d" tocopherols. By contrast, less expensive synthetic vitamin E can be recognized by a preceding mark of "dl" on the supplement.

How Vitamin E works ✦ Stored in the body's fatty tissues, vitamin E is a versatile, multitasking nutrient which plays a number of roles. It's best known, however, for its vigorous attack on free radicals. Aside from its daily duties to protect cell membranes, it scours the body to eliminate unstable, free radicals' oxygen. In addition, vitamin E has been shown to help prevent and fight infection by stimulating the immune system.

Therapeutic uses for Vitamin E
- *Age-related memory.* Free radicals are notorious for damaging nerve fibers, including the neurotransmitters that carry thought impulses from the brain to the rest of the body. Some studies suggest that the antioxidant properties of vitamin E, especially those of d-alpha tocotrienols, may help protect the cells that make up these fibers. American and German scientists have shown that tocotrienols suppress the neurotoxic effects of both the brain and the nerve stimulant glutamate. Brain neurodegeneration is associated with age-related memory loss.
- *Cardiovascular support.* Vitamin E prevents the oxidation of LDL cholesterol, a prerequisite to the development of circulation-robbing plaque buildup in the arteries (atherosclerosis). It also supports normalized blood clotting, improves blood flow, and reduces some of the inflammation associated with heart disease. Doctors from the Harvard School of Public Health, as well as those at Brigham and Women's Hospital in Boston, have determined from large epidemiological studies that vitamin E, vitamin C, and carotenoid supplements appear to reduce the risk of stroke.

- *Cancer Prevention.* When the body has low levels of vitamin E, cells may become vulnerable to various types of cancer, especially in the lungs and prostate gland. For potential cancer and general DNA protection, look for vitamin E formulas that include tocotrienols, as they've shown the most promise to reduce cell abnormalities. Several studies have reported that tocotrienols may be more effective in preventing cancer than tocopherols. They slow cancer cell growth by blocking the proliferation of blood vessels—a process that supports tumor growth known as *angiogenesis.*
- *Clear skin.* Vitamin E has proved useful to alleviate the effects of many skin problems. Taken internally or applied directly to the skin, it can be helpful in the treatment of acne and eczema, and its antioxidant properties make it beneficial to promote recovery from minor wounds, scrapes, abrasions, and burns. Vitamin E ointment applied to scars appears to help encourage the healing process.
- *Fertility.* Early research has shown promise for vitamin E's ability to protect the delicate membranes that encase sperm cells and protect them from damage caused by free radicals. Some researchers propose that the vitamin may also increase the likelihood of fertilization by protecting the sperm cells which are most capable of conveying their precious DNA package to the egg.
- *Healthy vision.* Studies continue to suggest that vitamin E may help prevent the formation of cataracts, the cloudy film that gradually infiltrates the lens of the eye and can eventually lead to vision loss. Low levels of vitamin E have been found among adults who suffer from age-related macular degeneration.

TIPS FOR TAKING VITAMIN E
- Vitamin E is fat-soluble and should be taken with a meal that contains some fat. If you take vitamin E without a meal, flaxseed

and Omega-3 fish oils are ideal companions and will not compete for absorption.

- Multiple vitamin formulas include a water-dispersible form of vitamin E, d-alpha tocopheryl succinate or acetate. Vitamin E in softgels and capsules typically includes a vegetable oil to help disperse it.

- Vitamin E is made up of eight different forms: four tocopherols and four tocotrienols. To get the most out of your vitamin E, look for mixed formulas that include all eight.

- When deciding how much vitamin E to take, keep in mind that you may find as much as 200-400 IU already included in your multiple. Taking more than 1,000 IU daily is not advised. Consider a separate mixed tocotrienol and mixed tocopherol supplement to avoid having alpha tocopherol deplete the other isomers.

- Vitamin E may be most effective when taken at the same time each day.

- Once vitamin E has made its rounds eliminating free radicals, it actually becomes a very weak free radical itself. This can be easily resolved by taking plenty of vitamin C, which is usually supplied in a good multiple. Vitamin C has the unique ability to restore vitamin E's oxidation-fighting capabilities.

- Vitamin E serves as a mild, natural blood thinner and should be used cautiously if you're taking anticoagulants or aspirin.

- Very high doses of vitamin E may interfere with the blood's natural clotting properties. If you're preparing to undergo surgery, advise your physician that you are taking it.

NATURAL COMPANIONS FOR VITAMIN E • Selenium, in addition to vitamins A and C, is generally included in most multivitamins. In certain applications, you may wish to consider supplementing with CoQ_{10}, lecithin, alpha lipoic acid, or omega-3s.

VITAMIN C

MAJOR APPLICATION OF VITAMIN C ◆ Vitamin C (ascorbic acid) is unquestionably one of the most popular nutritional supplements ever introduced. While it plays many roles within the body, its popularity can be attributed to its healing, cell-protecting, and immune-boosting properties. Natural vitamin C from citrus is still considered one of the best sources, although vitamin C supplementation can be equally effective. Many forms of vitamin C are now available, including tablets, capsules, powders, liquids, and drink mixes.

AN OVERVIEW OF VITAMIN C ◆ Vitamin C offers proof that God definitely has a sense of humor. We rely on vitamin C to maintain life. We use what we have almost instantaneously and are incapable of manufacturing our own supply. Without delving too deeply into the history of this popular antioxidant, let's just say that vitamin C supplementation has come a *long* way since its discovery in 1928. In those days British sailors, at sea for months at a time, devoured raw limes to reap the antiscorbutic extract that mysteriously prevented scurvy—hence their nickname of "limeys."

HOW VITAMIN C WORKS ◆ Vitamin C travels throughout the body in search of free radicals, rendering them ineffective to healthy cells. With fewer unstable, cell-damaging molecules to worry about, the immune system is free to concentrate on more threatening microbes and infectious agents. One of the most interesting facets of antioxidants is that after they successfully complete their job to eliminate free radicals, many become free radicals. Vitamin C helps recycle "spent" antioxidants and should therefore be taken with others, such as vitamins A and E, alpha lipoic acid, CoQ_{10}, and grape seed.

THERAPEUTIC USES FOR VITAMIN C

- *Collagen.* Collagen is the most abundant protein in the body. It makes up tendons, which attach muscle to bone, and the ligaments that attach bone to bone. Most formulas designed to reduce joint stiffness and osteoarthritis include vitamin C, which is required for collagen synthesis due to its synergism with glucosamine, chondroitin, and the amino acid proline.

* *Healthy skin.* In its fat-soluble form, ascorbyl palmitate, vitamin C can be quite effective when applied topically to the skin. It's now found in many personal care products, especially those that target wrinkles, scars, and aging skin. Taking vitamin C internally appears to help reduce wrinkles, particularly in smokers who typically have low levels of the vitamin. Some estimates have suggested that each cigarette smoked depletes 10 mg. of the body's vitamin C pool. So quit, already!

* *Healthy vision.* Vitamin C is concentrated in the fluid portions of the eye and helps prevent the formation of cataracts. It may also reduce the incidence of glaucoma, an increase in ocular pressure that may be a complication of diabetes. Sadly, age-related macular degeneration (AMD) is the most common cause of blindness among people older than 50. A large study at the Massachusetts Eye and Ear Infirmary has determined that consuming more lutein and zeaxanthin (from yellow and deep green vegetables rich in vitamin C) may offer greater protection against AMD. Researchers at the National Eye Institute have also used vitamin C supplements in their studies and many have shown some rather impressive results.

* *Allergies.* Allergies are essentially the immune system's overreaction to foreign invaders such as dust, mold, pollen, and pet dander. Ascorbic acid has strong antihistamine properties capable of inhibiting the inflammation that causes distress in allergy sufferers.

* *Cancer prevention.* Studies have shown that by helping to safeguard human DNA, a diet rich in vitamin C may be able to help prevent certain types of cancers. This is possible for one reason: Vitamin C helps regulate white blood cells in addition to other immune-centric components. Everyday the human body produces cancerous (abnormal) cells: Vitamin C has a penchant for ensuring that they don't get out of control.

- *Cold and flu symptoms.* Vitamin C won't eliminate the possibility of catching a cold or coming down with the flu, but when taken during the very early stages of what feels like a cold or flu, it may be able to help prevent the infection from fully maturing by boosting immune power. This may ultimately shorten the duration of symptoms.
- *High cholesterol.* One of the most beneficial aspects of vitamin C is its ability to prevent LDL cholesterol and lipoproteins from oxidative damage. This in turn helps prevent plaque build-up in arteries. Many people who suffer from high blood pressure tend to exhibit unusually low levels of vitamin C.
- *Minor cuts and burns.* Vitamin C can help expedite the healing of minor cuts, bruises, and burns by strengthening the tiny blood vessels (capillaries) surrounding the wound. This helps assure that nutrients needed to facilitate the healing process make it to the injury site unscathed.

TIPS FOR TAKING VITAMIN C

- Remember that vitamin C is water-soluble and does not store in the body. It's very difficult to get too much, especially during times of high stress. Your body will excrete what it doesn't need in a matter of hours.
- Vitamin C works very well when taken in conjunction with other antioxidants, especially the carotenoids, vitamin E, selenium, CoQ_{10}, grape seed extract, and a long list of others. Flavonoids (or bioflavonoids, as they're often labeled) can increase the overall effectiveness and bioavailability of ascorbic acid.
- If you have a sensitive stomach, you may want to consider buffered C, Ester-C® or calcium ascorbate. These gentler versions are just as effective and may offer less stomach discomfort.
- Megadoses of vitamin C can interfere with the body's ability to absorb certain minerals, especially selenium, zinc, and copper. This is one reason why most multiple formulas contain amounts that may be

lower than what is needed for acute conditions. Short-term use of high doses, in addition to taking vitamin C separately from your multiple formula, can help avoid any interference with mineral utilization.

+ Abruptly discontinuing vitamin C intake can be very stressful on the immune system. If you must go off vitamin C for any reason, do so gradually.

+ Vitamin C can be taken with or without meals. Be sure to take it with a big glass of water, however.

+ Vitamin C has a half-life of approximately 30 minutes. This means that 50 percent of the vitamin C you take right now will be out of your system in half an hour. For this reason, it's wise to take smaller doses throughout the day.

NATURAL COMPANIONS FOR VITAMIN C ✦ Vitamins A and E, selenium, astaxanthin, flavonoids, polyphenols, anthocyanidins, lutein, zeaxanthin, zinc, copper, CoQ_{10}.

Polyphenols and *bioflavonoids* belong to a family of compounds that includes more than 4,000 members. Among them are some of the most plentiful water-soluble antioxidants in plants. These powerful antioxidants roam feely throughout body fluids. Perhaps the most amazing characteristic of anthocyanidins is their propensity to bind to proteins. In the mouth, they prevent oral bacteria from adhering to teeth, gums, and other tissues. They also have an affinity for collagen and help protect it against oxidative damage.

Bioflavonoid is a loose term that's often used to describe a specific family of polyphenols, some of which are natural partners of vitamin C. This family includes the flavon-3-ols and anthocyanidins that were just discussed. Other members are flavones (apigenin), flavanones (hesperedin), chalcones (phloretin), and flavon-3-ols (quercetin, kaempferol, myricetin). Some of these may be familiar to you, but each has a different mode of action, while all are classified as antioxidants. It is very common to see bioflavonoids listed in multiples and vitamin C formulas.

Astaxanthin is a red carotenoid found in many aquatic species. One of the most powerful carotenoids, it helps protect fish and other aquatic animals from the intense light that penetrates the water's surface. Like other carotenoids, astaxanthin embeds itself between the two fatty acid layers that make up cell membranes. But unlike other carotenoids, astaxanthin possesses the unique ability to recycle free radical electrons instead of holding on to them, and it doesn't become useless after picking off extra electrons.

SELENIUM

MAJOR APPLICATION OF SELENIUM ✦ Selenium is one of eight essential trace minerals, most of which are required in microgram amounts. This particular trace mineral has piqued the interest of many researchers as they continue to uncover how vital a nutrient it truly is. Biologically, it's active in many of the body's most basic cellular functions, most notably producing internal defensive enzymes capable of neutralizing harmful toxins. Selenium is often overlooked as a mineral and widely regarded as a staple antioxidant.

AN OVERVIEW OF SELENIUM ✦ Committing to a diet rich in nuts and grains is one of the best ways to ensure an adequate selenium reserve. However, the content of selenium in the soil varies greatly from one area to another, making it tough to gauge how much selenium might be in the foods you consume. Supplementation is a sure-fire and inexpensive way to be confident that you're getting the amount you need to live well.

How SELENIUM WORKS ✦ This eager trace mineral teams up with its natural partner, vitamin E, and gets right down to business. Selenium travels throughout the body in search of free radicals and renders them useless and easy to expel. Along the way, selenium caters to several special "target" zones, the thyroid gland being one of the most crucial. By encouraging the production of iodine, selenium can assist the body to produce thyroid hormones which regulate the speed of metabolic reactions. It's also concentrated in the macular regions of the eyes to ward off oxidative damage. Finally, selenium helps maintain the balance between LDL (bad) cholesterol and HDL (good) cholesterol.

THERAPEUTIC USES OF SELENIUM

- *Anti-aging.* Selenium is an all-star among antioxidants and works hard to protect cells from being ravished by free radical-induced oxidation. We age from the inside out, putting a new spin on the integrity of the 100 trillion-plus cells of the body. Keeping cells flexible and permeable, so that they can use vital nutrients, while inhibiting harmful molecules can help ensure that we don't grow too old, too fast. One of the best things you can do to pre-serve the lifespan and normal activity of your cells is to supplement modest amounts of selenium every day. Most multiple formulas contain selenium, but additional amounts are suggested for some of the 7 syndromes.
- *Cardiovascular health.* Those who suffer from heart disease and high cholesterol often have low selenium levels, and they seem to benefit most from supplementation. Based on this result and selenium's ability to help promote good cholesterol and lower bad cholesterol, supplementing selenium can be a wise move for anyone concerned about keeping his or her ticker in tiptop form.
- *General health.* It's important to remember that the minute selenium enters your body, it's immediately confronted with a biologically over-whelming to-do list. Your immune system will have no reservations when it comes to rounding up all that it needs to prevent you from going into a state of toxic overload. A weak reserve of this high-demand trace mineral leaves the body no choice but to ignore (in some capacity) other selenium-demanding systems such as the eyes, heart, thyroid, and skin. Selenium supplementation, even in modest amounts, is a very wise move that your body will thank you for in the years to come.
- *Immune system support.* Research continues to indicate that people with compromised immune systems have one thing in

common: frighteningly low selenium levels. Not only is this condition unhealthy, but it also puts a tremendous strain on the immune system. Selenium is a key component in the production of T-cells, microphages, and other "killer" cells that target toxins and foreign microbes. When the body doesn't have a well-stocked reserve, it loses the ability to produce these immune-supporting cells.

Additionally, high intake of selenium is associated with a one-third lower incidence of colorectal cancer. Scientists at the University of Arizona Cancer Center in Tucson, Arizona, found that among 1,763 individuals who participated in polyp-prevention trials, those with the highest selenium levels had the lowest cancer risk. Many researchers believe that this is possible because selenium is a known component of *glutathione peroxidase,* an extremely potent detoxifying enzyme.

- *Inflammation.* Daily living can be a grueling task in itself. But when you throw in a dash of inflammation, even the most basic activities can become more challenging. The combination of selenium and vitamin E (see our chapter on inflammation) boasts strong antiinflammatory attributes and has become a staple for those who suffer from chronic joint pain and other conditions.

Tips for taking Selenium

- Selenium and vitamin E are the Bonnie and Clyde of nutrients. They have a strong synergy and, when taken together, each seems to complement the functional potential of the other.
- Try to avoid taking more than 600 mcg. of selenium in a 24-hour period. If your diet is already high in grains, nuts, and seafood, don't forget to factor those sources in, too.

- Antioxidants work well on their own, but even better in groups. To get the most out of your selenium supplementation, try to get in the habit of taking senenium with other antioxidants.

NATURAL COMPANIONS FOR SELENIUM ✦ All other antioxidants, including vitamin E, alpha lipoic acid, N-Acetyl Cysteine, and CoQ_{10}.

Nutrients for Building and Maintaining

VITAMIN D

MAJOR APPLICATION OF VITAMIN D ✦ The first thought that comes to mind when we mention vitamin D is a grade of milk that most adults quickly abandon after reading the label's fat content. But there's no arguing how much we need vitamin D in order to live long, healthy lives. While most of us have been made well aware of how crucial it is for strong, healthy bones, our relationship with vitamin D is *much* more diverse.

In addition to its structural role, vitamin D also supports the immune system, protects against certain types of cancers, and has been shown to help reduce the symptoms of psoriasis.

AN OVERVIEW OF VITAMIN D ✦ If you spend your life working or playing outdoors, live in a warm, sunny climate, or just happen to drink plenty of milk, you're probably in the clear for needing more vitamin D. But let's be realistic; many of us don't have that lifestyle or drink a lot of milk. Long hours in fluorescent-lit cubicles coupled with laughable diets and the caloric terror of drinking whole milk can quickly deprive a person of his or her vitamin D reserve, but that won't change the fact that some of the body's most basic functions are at vitamin D's mercy.

HOW VITAMIN D WORKS ✦ We've been taught that vitamin D is a requisite for healthy bones, although most people don't fully understand why. Nicknamed the "sunshine vitamin," vitamin D is manufactured in the body after being exposed to the sun's UVB rays. As we age, however, our bodies become less capable of manufacturing the amounts that we could during our younger years. As we lose the ability to produce adequate reserves of vitamin D, we subsequently become less capable of absorbing calcium. This is why many calcium supplements also contain vitamin D.

THERAPEUTIC USES FOR VITAMIN D

- *Healthy bones and teeth.* Have you ever noticed that just about every calcium supplement you've ever seen includes Vitamin D? This is more than just some clever marketing ploy. A vitamin D deficiency makes it virtually impossible for the body to properly absorb calcium and phosphorous. When the body can't find the calcium it needs, it uses the calcium from bones to do its job. This is just one of many reasons why it's so important to pay close attention to whether you're getting enough vitamin D in your diet. Without it, the body can become accustomed to slowly and gradually chipping away at the calcium that we rely on for structural support.

- *Skin disorders.* A growing number of skin disorders have been linked to inadequate vitamin D levels. One of the most concerning is psoriasis, a condition that leaves sufferers with itchy, flaky, bumpy, red skin that causes both discomfort and painful embarrassment. Supplementing with higher levels of vitamin D has been shown to help mitigate the symptoms of psoriasis, primarily because it helps develop new skin cells. It's also been shown to help diminish acne blemishes and a number of other minor skin challenges.

- *Abnormal cell development.* More and more researchers are focusing their studies on the potential impact that vitamin D may have against some forms of cancer, especially those that affect the prostate, colon, and breasts. While it's still unclear why, some studies have determined that there is an unmistakable pattern of low vitamin D levels in those with these types of cancer. Some researchers believe that this can be attributed to the role that vitamin D plays in the growth, development, and activity of healthy cells. Research is ongoing and continues to show promise.

Tips for Taking Vitamin D

- Vitamin D is fat-soluble. To ensure proper absorption, always take vitamin D with a meal that contains some amount of fat, preferably healthy mono- or polyunsaturated fats.
- When selecting a vitamin D supplement, look for one that's sold as "D-3 from cholecalciferol." This is a very potent and effective grade, and has been used in some of the most well respected studies. It's also one most easily absorbed.
- There seems to be growing confusion surrounding how much vitamin D should be consumed from supplementation. The current RDI ranges from 200 IU to 600 IU, depending on age. Most experts agree that larger doses (1,000 IU) can be taken safely and may offer more beneficial effects.
- If you're taking multiple supplements, make sure that you've accounted for all that may contain vitamin D so that you don't get more than your body can use. These include multiple vitamin/mineral formulas, calcium supplements, and other bone-supporting specialty formulas.
- If you regularly take magnesium-based antacids for heartburn, avoid taking them with additional high doses of vitamin D. This can interfere with the body's normal regulation of magnesium.

VITAMIN K

Despite being one the least known of all basic nutrients, there's no denying the role that vitamin K plays in human wellness. A team of Danish researchers stumbled upon this natural clot-forming compound while trying to prevent excessive bleeding in newborn chickens on fat-restricted diets. Today vitamin K is commonly used to help insure normal blood clot formation and, as a result, many multiple formulas now include it. Vitamin K can also be found in a number of foods, especially leafy, green vegetables.

Sara Booth and colleagues from the Jean Mayer Human Nutrition Research Center on Aging at Tufts University have identified three vitamin K–dependent enzymes involved in bone mineralization. Several studies have found that the risk of a hip fracture is greater among men and women with low levels of vitamin K. Bone-mineral density is also inversely associated with low blood levels of vitamin K in women.

Harvard researchers have identified a vitamin K–dependent growth factor in the development of the brain, thus emphasizing the increased need for vitamin K during pregnancy. The emerging role of vitamin K for bone health and nervous system development makes it an important compound to look for when choosing the right daily multiple.

THE MINERALS

Minerals account for about 4 percent of typical body weight and are vital to healthy cellular function. Even the slightest fluctuation can be extremely detrimental to health. Eighteen of the 92 naturally occurring mineral elements are considered essential and just two remain classified as semi-essential. This means that they haven't been proven useful for humans, although animal studies strongly suggest that they may be essential under certain conditions.

Essential minerals fall into three groups: macro minerals, trace elements, and ultra-trace elements. *Macro minerals* are those required in 100-mg. or greater amounts. These include calcium, phosphorus, magnesium, sodium, potassium, chloride, and sulfur. *Trace elements* require 1 mg.-100 mg., while ultra-trace elements are needed in only microgram amounts. Trace elements include iron, zinc, copper, manganese, and fluoride. *Ultra-trace elements* are selenium, molybdenum, iodine, chromium, boron, and cobalt. Vanadium and silicon are the two semi-essential elements.

Each mineral has an important function in each of the 7 syndromes, and a more complete discussion of those individual functions will be fully explored as you read on. Earlier in this chapter, the role of selenium as an antioxidant was discussed. Its function in several syndromes will be highlighted later on as well. Figure 1-2, which summarizes the primary function of each mineral,

Mineral	RDA	Function
Calcium	1,000 mg	Bones and teeth; blood clotting; cell membrane permeability; neuromuscular activity
Phosphorus	1,000 mg	Bones and teeth; buffer; metabolic intermediary (high in diet, not generally found in supplements)
Magnesium	400 mg	Bones and teeth; energy production; neuromuscular sensitivity
Sodium	2,400 mg†	Acid/base balance, cell membrane permeability, muscle activity (from diet only, not supplements)
Potassium	3,500 mg†	Acid/base balance (opposes sodium), cell membrane transport, neuromuscular excitability
Chloride	3,400 mg	Electrolyte, gastric acid, fluid balance (from diet, not supplements)
Sulfur	2,000 mg*	Joint lubricants, proteins, biotin, lipoic acid (generally not found in multivitamin and minerals)
Iron	18 mg	Hemoglobin, myoglobin, detoxifying enzyme catalase, energy production, enzyme cofactor
Zinc	15 mg	Constituent of insulin, cofactor for more than 300 enzymes
Manganese	2 mg	Detoxifying enzymes, joint lubricants, glucose metabolism
Copper	2 mg	Hemoglobin, cofactor for 11 enzymes
Fluorine	1.5–2 mg*	Bones and teeth (perhaps toxic in high amounts)
Selenium	70 mcg	Detoxifying enzymes, inhibits oxidation of fats
Molybdenum	75 mcg	Enzyme cofactor, sulfur amino acid metabolism, protect steroid membrane receptors
Iodine	150 mcg	Thyroid hormone, cellular respiration
Chromium	120 mcg	Carbohydrate and fat metabolism; facilitates insulin function
Boron	1 – 3 mg*	Bone calcification, increases vitamin D levels, glucose metabolism (often included in multiples)
Cobalt	‡	Constituent of vitamin B_{12} (not found in multiples)
Vanadium	‡	Bones and teeth; collagen synthesis, mimics action of insulin in diabetes
Silicon		Possible genetic expression (generally not in multiples)

† Amount for dietary recommendations, not supplement labeling.

* Amount suggested but not required.

‡ Amount not established.

FIGURE 1-2 **Minerals at a Glance**

can be helpful in choosing a multiple vitamin and mineral formula that best suits your specific needs.

Nutrients that Regulate Metabolism

B-COMPLEX VITAMINS

MAJOR APPLICATION OF B-COMPLEX VITAMINS ✦ B vitamins, a series of 10 individual nutrients, listed below, are essential for many of the body's most basic cellular functions including energy production, metabolism, and reproduction. As co-factors for more than 3,500 metabolic enzymes, B vitamins play a weighty role in keeping us alive and healthy. For this to happen, specific B vitamins must activate these specific enzymes. A deficiency in even one B vitamin can ultimately compromise any number of the body's core functions.

More serious and widespread B-vitamin deficiencies are an entirely different story and can snowball to affect every system of the body. The most typical symptoms are anorexia, weight loss, apathy, difficulty with short-term memory, confusion, irritability, cracks around the mouth and lips, seborrhea, elevated homocysteine levels, nervousness, numbness, restless leg syndrome, sleep disturbances, and a host of digestive challenges.

If you're taking a potent multiple-vitamin formula, you're more than likely getting the B vitamins that you need, but you should make sure that all of them are included in balance. However, you don't necessarily want them to be in the same amounts. In some situations, higher levels of individual B vitamins are best, and you may add them to your supplement program to help support specific deficiencies due to poor diet, stress, and other situations.

AN OVERVIEW ✦ The B family of vitamins is made up of 10 individual nutrients: B-1 (thiamin), B-2 (riboflavin), B-3 (niacin), B-5 (pantothenic acid), B-6 (pyridoxine), B-12 (cobalamin), folic acid, biotin, choline, and inositol. B vitamins unquestionably make up one of the most important nutrient classes as evidenced by their inclusion in just about every multiple formula on the market today. Individually each one serves a unique purpose in the body, although many are commonly used to treat a wide range of ailments. Figure 1-3 lists the functions and deficiency symptoms of each. You will also find the coenzyme forms listed because they're included in some select dietary supplements.

An important consideration in determining one's need for B vitamins is their potential interaction with certain pharmaceutical drugs. Table 4 in the Appendix contains a list of drugs which may interfere with or deplete the body's supply of B vitamins.

Attempting to balance each B vitamin individually would be a task rivaled only by hopping down a flight of stairs on one hand. Fortunately, most manufacturers offer multiples that include all the B vitamins, offering an excellent way to supply these vital coenzymes when they're needed. Although few individuals are deficient in all B vitamins, many health conditions can be improved by supplementing with them individually. Higher amounts may be needed due to drug-nutrient interactions (figure 1-3).

THERAPEUTIC USES
- *Neurological symptoms*
- *Cardiovascular support*
- *Anti-aging*
- *Muscular support*
- *Chemical dependency*
- *Fertility*
- *Hair, skin and nails*

NATURAL COMPANIONS FOR B-VITAMINS • Nutritional protocols often combine B vitamins with other nutrients for more balanced benefits. These include

B- Vitamin	RDA	Function and (Deficiency Symptoms)
Thiamin, Cocarboxylase and Thiamin Pyrophosphate (B-1)	1.5 mg	• growth and development (impaired growth, cellular reproduction) • carbohydrate and amino acid metabolism (carbohydrate sensitivity, alcohol syndrome) • cardiovascular, muscular, nervous, and gastrointestinal function (impaired function)
Riboflavin and Riboflavin 5-Phosphatae (B-2)	1.7 mg	• immune function (infection, diabetes) • oral and mucus membranes (lesions, periodontal disease) • healthy skin, visual acuity • collagen formation (poor recovery, osteoarthritis, cardiac disease)
Niacin, niacinamide and hexanicotinate (B-3)	20 mg	• cholesterol management (lipid dysfunction) • blood sugar control (diabetes, loss of memory) • carbohydrate metabolism (apathy, fatigue) • neurological (tinnitus or ringing in the ears, depression)
Pantothenic Acid and Pantetheine (B-5)	10 mg	• cholesterol metabolism (high cholesterol/triglycerides) • fat metabolism (gastrointestinal complaints, nausea, vomiting, abdominal cramps, alcohol syndrome) • sugar metabolism (hypoglycemia and increased insulin sensitivity) • nerve transmission (irritability, restlessness, fatigue, malaise, sleep disturbances, headaches, personality changes, numbness, muscle cramps, burning feet sensation, impaired motor coordination)
Pyridoxine (B-6) and pyridoxal phosphate (P-5-P)	2.0 mg	• amino acid metabolism, including several neuro-transmitters (depression, confusion, convulsions, vertigo) • cardiovascular (elevated homocysteine impaired platelet function, clotting mechanisms, microcytic anemia) • epithelial tissues (seborrhea, acne) • brain and nerves (premenstrual syndrome, carpal tunnel syndrome, nerve damage) • carbohydrate metabolism (alcohol syndrome)
Cobalamin and methylcobalamin (B-12)	6.0 mcg	• nervous system (neurological symptoms, numbness and tingling in hands and feet, nerve damage, ataxia, shingles) • brain (memory loss, dementia, fatigue, depression, moodiness, poor memory, confusion, agitation) • blood cell formation (anemia)
Folic Acid and Tetrahydrofolate	400 mcg	• cardiovascular (elevated homocysteine, megaloblastic anemia, palpitations, cerebrovascular disease) • brain and nerves (weakness, fatigue, difficulty concentrating, irritability, headache, shortness of breath) • reproduction (birth defects) • DNA synthesis (cancer) • protein, carbohydrate, and fat metabolism (malabsorption syndromes)

CONTINUES

B- Vitamin	RDA	Function and (Deficiency Symptoms)
Biotin	300 mcg	• protein metabolism (dermatitis, thin hair and nails, conjunctivitis) • energy metabolism (neurological symptoms, loss of sensation, anorexia, nausea, weight loss, depression, hallucinations)
Choline	445, women; 550 men*	• structural integrity of cell membranes (cellular dysfunction,cancer) • fat, cholesterol metabolism, pancreatic function (digestive disturbances, gallstones) • neurotransmission (poor memory, dementia)

* Suggested.

FIGURE 1-3 **B-Vitamin Functions at a Glance**

essential fatty acids, antioxidants, protein supplements, amino acids, and digestive support aids such as probiotics, enzymes, and fiber.

Choosing a Multiple Vitamin

Serving Size
Most complete formulas will require 2-6 capsules or tablets per day. Two-capsule or tablet formulas will contain lower amounts of the macro minerals calcium and magnesium. Chances are you'll probably need to add a mineral supplement. Six-capsule or tablet formulas are generally all-inclusive, however the amounts of calcium and magnesium in them may not meet the daily required intake (DRI). It's easy to get additional amounts from dietary sources or calcium supplements.

Specific Formulas
MALE-SPECIFIC FORMULAS • Male-specific formulas are generally iron-free and contain more zinc as aspartate, picolinate, and monomethionine. These formulas are also often higher in vitamin E and may contain higher levels of other vitamins needed to support a man's larger frame. Men's formulas should

ideally contain at least 500 mg. of calcium, as that amount has been shown to help protect healthy men against heart attack and colon cancer. Otherwise a separate mineral formula would be recommended. Some of the best men's formulas also contain potent male-supporting compounds such as saw palmetto, nettle, lycopene, grape seed extract, ginseng, L-carnitine, and CoQ_{10}.

FEMALE-SPECIFIC FORMULAS · These contain a number of specific amino acids as well as chelated iron, the best formula being Ferrochel®. Calcium and magnesium are extremely important and, if at least 500 mg. of each is not included in the formula, should be added separately. Soy isoflavones and ipriflavone are often included to help balance hormones and retain bone mineral density. Many women's formulas also contain higher levels of vitamin B-6 and herbs such as vitex, grape seed extract, dong quai, eleuthero ginseng, and wild yam extract. Bioflavonoids, especially rutin, are an important addition to women's formulas.

PRENATAL FORMULAS · These formulas rarely contain herbs, but do contain more conservative levels of vitamins that help counter stomach upset. Folic acid is included at 800 mcg., the RDI for pregnant women. Despite how important both are, pregnant woman should never consume more than 5,000 IU of vitamin A or beta carotene. Calcium is usually in the range of 1,000 mg. and is often complemented by 400-500 mg. of magnesium. With regard to iron, look for multiples that use Ferrochel® as their primary source. It's nonconstipating, well tolerated, and very easily absorbed.

Best Time to Take a Multiple Vitamin Formula

Multivitamins will work at their greatest potential when taken with a meal, which can help eliminate any potential stomach discomfort. Ingesting vitamins with food also facilitates effective absorption. It's not necessary to take a multi every day. We suggest that you take your multiple five days a week and take a two-day break. This gives your body a chance to properly process nutrients and a rest from taking pills.

CHAPTER TWO

The Stress Syndrome: Mind, Body, Spirit

U
NRESOLVED CONFLICTS AND PROBLEMS that are unique to the twenty-first century have profound effects on the mind and body and can ultimately lead to premature aging and chronic conditions. The everyday stressful situations that we're exposed to have no precedent in human history, and we haven't evolved a more appropriate response to today's threats. Our response,acute stress,is the same to potentially life-threatening situations—whether we're being faced with being eaten or late for an important appointment. The so-called "fight or flight" mechanism kicks in by flooding the brain and body with chemicals that ready us for a fast getaway. While this might be appropriate when confronted with a predator, it doesn't help when stuck in traffic. What do these stress chemicals do and how can we reduce the common effects of a stressful lifestyle?

Most stressful situations today come from what we *perceive* to be a threat, whether it's dissatisfaction with our jobs or with our personal lives. Noise, crowding, isolation, and extreme heat or cold are all examples of perceived threats. Even hunger can be perceived as a threat, although few people in modern societies are faced with starvation. Many, in fact, satisfy hunger pangs not with foods that nourish, but with comfort foods that appear to reduce stress, at least momentarily.

	ACUTE STRESS EFFECTS	CHRONIC STRESS EFFECTS
Brain	• Increased alterness • Decreased perception of pain	• Impaired memory • Risk of depression
Immune System	Ready to fight injury, infection	Decreased immune response
Circulatory System	Increased heart rate	• Elevated blood flow to muscles • Increased blood pressure risk of CVD
Adrenal Glands	Mobilized energy supplies	High cortisol levels lessen response to acute stress
Reproductive Organs	Functions temporarily suppressed	Increased infertility and risk of miscarriage

FIGURE 2-1 The Acute and Chronic Effects of Stress

(adapted from Scientific American, December 2005; 293:97)

If any stressful circumstance can be quickly resolved, it doesn't pose any long-term harm—discounting, of course, the health effects of poor diet. It's the things that repeatedly get under your skin that spell trouble, and that's called *chronic psychological stress.*

Chronic psychological stress, by definition, is one that persists for extended periods of time and causes most chronic health problems. Anxiety disorders, depression, headaches, sleep disturbances, poor memory, and fatigue have all been identified as stress-related disorders. Moreover, chronic psychological

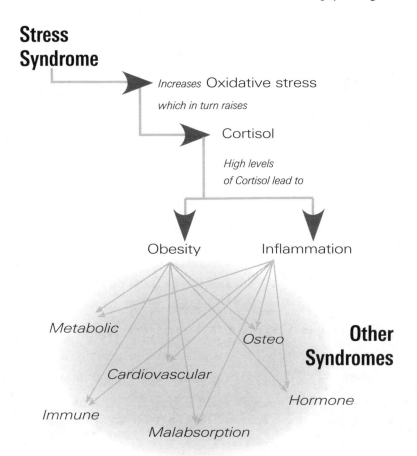

FIGURE 2-2 **Chronic Stress and Its Consequences.**

stress can lead to obesity, diabetes, heart problems, high blood pressure, high cholesterol, cancer, arthritis, pain and inflammation, infection, skin disorders, ulcers, gastric reflux, thyroid and adrenal gland disorders, and reproductive dysfunction—all conditions that are discussed in subsequent chapters. Scientists at the University of California, San Francisco, found that chronic psychological stress actually damages DNA, causing cells to malfunction and age prematurely. To highlight its importance, the *stress syndrome* is positioned at the pinnacle of the 7-syndrome hierarchy.

What You Will Find in This Chapter

Learning to deal with stress is primarily up to you. Chronic stress is not a disease per se, but it heads the list from which the other mind and body syndromes emanate. Effectively managing stress, eating a healthy diet, exercising frequently, and using dietary supplements are all needed to reduce chronic psychological stress and, with it, your risk of chronic disease. In this chapter we will address:

- Effective stress management
- Mood, memory, and attention span
- Cortisol and its hormonal effects
- Oxidative stress and aging

Effective Stress Management

Reducing stress is the first and most important measure that must be taken to derail aging of the mind and body. Nutritional psychiatrist Hyla Cass, M.D, provides an excellent questionnaire for determining your stress levels and what long-term effects stress will have on your body in her book, *8 Weeks to Vibrant Health*. Four steps in effective stress management frame the platform for healing the other six syndromes.

Eliminate the Stress

Eliminating stress may seem evident, but often this step involves some hard choices. Are you trying to do too much? Can you shift some work to another? Families may have to prioritize activities children are involved in.

There are two important times of the day for reducing stress. The first is early morning, when you have the chance to nip pending concerns in the bud before they become full-blown aggravations. Get up a little earlier to leave time for this important stress-relieving tactic. The second time is in the evening, particularly as the family gathers for the evening meal. Dinnertime can be a very stressful time and many families miss this opportunity because they are either shuttling children back and forth or staying late at work.

As for stress during the day, if you are dissatisfied with your job, it might be time to join the growing number of people who are making mid-life career changes. Some return to school to learn new skills, and others switch to another department or company. Some may even be forced to change jobs because the job has left them. While such change can be extremely stressful, it may lead to a more fulfilling opportunity. Whatever the reason, you must do everything you can to help your body cope with such changes.

Exercise to Keep Body and Mind on an Even Keel

Exercise stimulates the mind and body by improving communication among its psychological, neurological, and physiological functions. The same chemicals that course through the brain and nerves stimulate cells to release hormones, tone the cardiovascular and digestive systems, and heighten immune response. *You can direct these chemicals.* Exercise calms the mind, improves respiration, and tones the body. One of the best ways to do this as we age is to practice the ancient antiaging arts of yoga, Tai Chi and Qi Gong. Yoga is helpful to reduce sleep disorders, especially among older adults.

"No pain, no gain" is not a suitable mantra for those entering later mid-life. If you still have the mindset of a 20-year-old, it's time to readjust your sights. According to the U. S. Consumer Product Safety Commission, the highest number of sports-related injuries come from bicycling, basketball, baseball, and running. Skiing is high on the list, but, because it's a seasonal sport, not as many injuries are reported. Getting older means being more vulnerable to knee, ankle, lower back, and shoulder injuries. Enjoying these sports means being smarter and not pushing the envelope. We'll go into greater detail about how to protect your body from sports injuries in Chapter Eight.

Be Mindful, Meditate or Pray, and Relax

Numerous studies have shown that taking time daily for meditation, prayer, and relaxation reduces the severity of chronic ailments. The late Norman Cousins, former editor of *Saturday Review* and faculty member at the University of California, Los Angeles, specialized in applying the biochemistry of emotions to physical ailments. He showed in the early 1980s that conquering panic and hopelessness with laughter could reverse crippling illness. The body has an amazing capacity to heal itself, and it begins with using the mind and emotions to heal.

The role of spirit in reducing stress and promoting healing is increasingly recognized in the medical community. Michael Samuelson, M.D., has been practicing mind/body/spirit medicine for twenty-five years. He uses many art forms to alleviate the pain and suffering of cancer patients, and he relates his experiences in *Creative Healing*, one of fourteen books he has written.

We have enjoyed the privilege of watching Dr. Samuelson practice Native American healing rituals on a friend. His work was being taped for ABC-TV during an interview about alternative healing with the network's then–medical correspondent, Nancy Snyderman, M.D. Locking into the universal force that regulates nature through meditation and prayer is a powerful tool in taking change of your stress-reducing program. As Dr. Samuelson writes, "prayer, art, and healing come from the same source—the human soul."

Relaxation techniques include listening to music, taking a walk in a beautiful place, and watching the breakers on a beach. Tapes and CDs with relaxation techniques are also helpful. Some of these tools provide guided imagery, helping you create in your mind a peaceful, relaxing occasion or scene. You may recall a recent vacation that was especially relaxing, and you can train yourself so that every time you think about it, you can feel your body relax. Guided imagery does the same thing. Use beautiful vacation scenes as screen savers on your computer to remind you to relax and take a few deep breaths before moving on.

Eat Well and Supplement Your Diet with Appropriate Nutrients

A good diet rich in fruits and vegetables is loaded with antioxidants to combat the dangerous free radicals released during stressful periods. Much of the physical damage to the body that occurs from stress is due to oxidative damage. Oxygen-free radicals are produced in copious amounts within the body as byproducts of acute or chronic stress. While the body has a powerful internal antioxidant-defense system, the number of free radicals produced overwhelms it.

Consequently, outside sources of antioxidants from diet and supplements must be supplied to preserve health. The culinary companion to this book is *7-Color Cuisine: Making healthy, colorful foods a lifestyle for nutrition and good eating*, and it provides an easy, four-step plan that takes even the most inexperienced person through the process needed to use food to heal the mind and body.

The daily vitamin and mineral program outlined in Chapter One is the basis for healing the *stress syndrome* and each of the six other syndromes described in this book. Each of the seven syndromes requires additional supplements to ease the symptoms resulting, at least in part, from chronic stress. In this chapter we'll concern ourselves with the effects of both short-term and chronic stress on the brain and body.

Short-term, or periodic, stressful situations occur in everyone's life. How you respond to these events determines your degree of discomfort. Memory recall issues (brain glitches), forgetting to do things, periodic sleep disturbances, and minor mood swings are all common signs of stressful overload and can be dealt with easily. Using the herbal aids suggested here can help you get through short-term stressful situations so that your stress doesn't become chronic.

Supplements for Periodic Stressful Periods

Herbal remedies have been used since antiquity to calm nerves, overcome injury-related stress, and improve strength, stamina, and sleep. A popular name for these herbs is *adaptogenic*, meaning that they help the body better cope with stress. Russian scientists have established three criteria for adaptogenic herbs. They must:

+ Provide nonspecific increase in resistance to physical, chemical, or biological agents.
+ Help normalize physiological effects of stress.
+ Neither stimulate nor relax beyond normal levels.

Adaptogenic herbs have been used in Asia, Russia, and India for centuries, and we are presenting three with an outstanding record of reducing stress and improving mental performance and memory. Two of these herbs come from Asia and Russia and one is from India.

Rhodiola rosea is a plant that lives at high altitudes in Eastern Europe and Asia. Its roots have been used in traditional medicine to improve resistance to physical stress. Although there are several species of Rhodiola, the rosea species appears to be the most effective to improve endurance, speed recovery, and resist cold weather—which is why it was very popular with Russian soldiers and athletes. In the U.S., Rhodiola has gained popularity for its dual ability to improve memory and cognitive performance while also producing calmness. It does all this by enhancing the effects of brain chemicals called *neurotransmitters*. Rhodiola's active components, known collectively as *rosavins*, also appear to enhance "feel-good" and pain-killing chemicals (peptides) in the brain.

Studies published in 2000 and 2001 documented the amazing adaptogenic and psycho-stimulant properties of *Rhodiola rosea*. The first study was conducted during final exams among 40 healthy male medical students, and the second included 56 male and female physicians working night shifts. Both groups demonstrated antifatigue benefits without any adverse effects. The physician group had a measurable increase in perceptive and cognitive cerebral function, while the supplemented student group showed a 50 percent increase in psychomotor function and reduction in mental fatigue as compared to a placebo group.

These studies used a *Rhodiola rosea* extract standardized for salidrosides only, which are found in other species of Rhodiola, not just rosea. Today extracts are standardized to rosavins, which are unique to Rhodiola rosea and may also be standardized to salidrosides. This assures the proper identity of the herb and its major constituents.

Eleuthero senticosus, also known as Siberian ginseng, is an adaptogenic herb that has been shown to increase energy and stamina and help the body resist viral infections, environmental toxic exposure, radiation, and chemotherapy. Eleuthero has been used in traditional Chinese medicine for more than 2,000 years and, according to the *Clinical Guide to Herbs* from the American Botanical Council (ABC), is used today primarily to boost immune competence, fight fatigue, and treat memory disturbances. ABC also lists reduction in total cholesterol, LDL cholesterol and triglycerides, insomnia, chronic inflammatory conditions, and visual disturbances as important potential areas of use.

Eleuthero dry extract (300 mg./day) was given to 10 seniors who were experiencing fatigue and weakness for four weeks. Another 10 patients were given a placebo. Within the treated group, 70 percent noticed an increase in strength and a reduction in fatigue. In another study of healthy people, a liquid extract produced a significant increase in short-term memory, and the effect was most pronounced among those with high nervous activity in the evening. Fifty healthy volunteers also took eleuthero tincture (25 drops, three times daily) for a month. Laboratory blood analysis revealed increases in cellular defense, oxygen utilization, and lipid metabolism.

In vitro studies have shown how eleuthero works. In one study, the herb blocked reproduction of all RNA viruses, including human rhinovirus (HRV), respiratory syncytial virus (RSV), and influenza A virus. In another study to explain the biphasic action of eleuthero, it was found that the herb occupied the receptors for stimulating and calming neurotransmitters. This caused a redistribution of the body's energy reserves from regeneration to activity, resulting in the physiological balancing effect experienced with this herb. The last study showed that eleuthero could reduce allergic response by inhibiting the allergic response to environmental triggers.

Ashwagandha (Withania somnifera) is also known as winter cherry and incorrectly as Indian ginseng. It is an Ayurvedic (eastern Indian) herb with more than 3,000 years of use in traditional medicine. Historically it has been used for many conditions, including bronchitis, asthma, ulcers, insomnia, and senile dementia. Animal research and clinical trials support its use for anxiety, neurological disorders, inflammation, and Parkinson's disease. It has also been useful as an adaptogen to reduce nervous exhaustion, insomnia, and sexual debility due to stress.

A clinical trial of ashwagandha involving more than 100 men aged 50-59 found that 71.4 percent reported improvement in their capacities for sexual performance. The same study found a decrease in cholesterol levels. Cardio-protective effects, including reductions in total and low-density cholesterol levels (LDL) and blood lipids, have also been reported. In addition, ashwagandha has been shown to lower blood glucose levels, scavenge free radicals, reduce tumors, and normalize hormone balance.

Of particular interest in battling stress, ashwagandha appears to block the breakdown of acetylcholine, a neurotransmitter involved in cognitive function and memory. Ashwagandha also appears to protect the brain during periods of increased oxidative stress. Since ashwagandha contains natural steroids, its use during pregnancy is contraindicated. Ashwagandha is available in several forms, including dried root, standardized extract (1.5 percent withanolides) and 1:2 fluid extract.

Refer to Table 8 in the Appendix to help you select appropriate herbs.

Supplements for Chronic Stress

Chronic stress generates copious amounts of free radicals that the body attempts to neutralize. Internal antioxidant systems are the first line of defense, and antioxidants from food and supplements provide additional support. Unfortunately, during periods of high stress most people don't feed themselves properly. That's why a high-quality multiple vitamin and mineral formula with high levels of natural carotenoids and vitamins A, C and E becomes extremely important. Ultimately, chronic stress depletes energy, raises the hormone cortisol, and leads to insulin resistance and weight gain. Chronic stress can lead to anxiety, mood swings, depression, and poor cognitive function. Moreover, chronic stress inevitably causes aging.

Oxidative Stress and Aging

The free radical theory of aging, first proposed by Dr. Denham Harman in 1956, is considered by many experts to be the most important factor in how we age.

Pro-oxidants are compounds that interfere with normal metabolism by oxidizing various parts of the cellular machinery, chemically altering a cell at the molecular level. If DNA happens to be the molecule that's damaged, a mutation will be the likely result. If the molecule is an enzyme, the enzyme's effect will be reduced or lost entirely. Since metabolic enzymes (3,870 in all) are vital for health maintenance, an accumulation of damaged enzymes will inevitably lead to loss of tissue and organ function.

Most pro-oxidants are generated in the energy-producing factories of the cell known as the *mitochondria*. These pro-oxidants accumulate in the most energy-demanding organ of the body, the brain, and are implicated in memory loss, anxiety, depression, poor attention span, and Parkinson's and Alzheimer's diseases. In addition to the specific dietary guidance you'll find in *7-Color Cuisine*, the following supplements may be helpful to reduce oxidative stress and aging and to improve mood, memory, and attention span. They may also help reduce the effects of stress on cortisol and insulin, topics discussed in Chapter Three, the *metabolic syndrome*.

SUPEROXIDE DISMUTASE (SOD)

MAJOR APPLICATION OF SOD ◆ SOD is short for *superoxide dismutase*, one of the body's three built-in antioxidants. As a major part of our body's biological armor, the substance is capable of destroying enormous amounts of free radicals throughout the body.

Researchers tried for years to prepare an oral version to enhance the body's reserves, but they were unsuccessful in preventing SOD from being attacked and denatured by natural acids in the stomach. That quickly changed when a group of French researchers determined that by combining *Cucumus melo* (a melon high in SOD) with a wheat protein called *gliadin* as a stabilizer, it was possible to prevent SOD from deteriorating in the digestive tract. Thus it was absorbed and available to attack free radicals for extended periods of time.

AN OVERVIEW OF SOD ♦ The supernutrient SOD protects us from a particular class of nasty free radical: *Superoxide anion* and *peroxynitrite* free radicals, which pose the greatest threat to the 100 trillion cells that compose the human body. These highly reactive, merciless molecules are major factors in oxidative stress and are capable of wreaking havoc on healthy cells. When cells are left unprotected and vulnerable to superoxide free radicals, the results can be disastrous. Respiratory problems, premature aging, memory loss, cardiovascular challenges, vision failure, and joint-structure damage may ensue.

HOW SOD WORKS ♦ SOD is one of the body's most powerful built-in lines of defense, and clearly it's important to keep these reserves as high and functional as possible. Once the stomach-acid denaturing process has been overcome, SOD can be absorbed by the digestive tract and transported through the bloodstream to where it can be utilized. It scours the body in search of the highly reactive superoxide free radicals and, when it finds them, neutralizes them before they can damage cellular structures and their functions. Simply put, SOD hinders the chain of events that cause cells to age.

THERAPEUTIC USES OF SOD

- *Anti-aging.* Since the dawn of time, people from every corner of the earth have been trying without much success to find the proverbial "fountain of youth." SOD may offer users a way to significantly control the pace at which their cells age. Its ability to effectively quench superoxide free radicals makes it unique in many ways, and anyone concerned with living a long, healthy life should definitely consider supplementation.

- *Immune system support.* When the body becomes overrun with oxidation, the immune system is forced to work much harder than it should be required to ideally. One of the reasons why this is so common is because we're constantly exposed to billions of invisible toxins. Over time they collect in the system and, as a result, the immune system becomes less effective in fighting them before damage is done. SOD shoulders a huge portion of this burden by targeting the most potentially destructive types of free radicals. Ultimately, this leaves the immune system free to tend to its job without interruption.

Tips for Taking SOD

- Stomach acid is a sworn enemy to SOD. Avoid consumption of highly acidic foods when taking SOD, thus helping prevent its being destroyed before it has a chance to serve its purpose.
- Taking SOD throughout the day in divided doses is one of the best ways to ensure that the body is constantly fueled with what it needs to eradicate highly reactive free radicals.
- Always take SOD as recommended, as these doses have been carefully researched to determine the most effective method of delivery and utilization. Taking more than you need could result in an upset stomach or indigestion.
- If you're allergic to wheat products, consult your physician before using SOD supplements.
- Taking SOD in combination with other antioxidants such as grape seed, green tea, and alpha lipoic acid may provide greater antioxidant support throughout various systems of the body.

Cofactors and Contraindications for SOD · Refer to Table 5 in the Appendix for more information.

ALPHA LIPOIC ACID (ALA)

MAJOR APPLICATION OF ALA ✦ Alpha lipoic acid, or ALA, is arguably one of the most potent free radical fighters ever to be discovered. Unlike most other antioxidants, which are either fat- or water-soluble, ALA is unique in that it has the ability to target both fat- and water-based organs and tissues. This versatility has made ALA extremely popular for those concerned with heart, nervous-system, skin, and liver health as well as overall energy level.

AN OVERVIEW OF ALA ✦ Believe it not, this supercharged antioxidant was originally discovered in the 1950s and initially classified as a vitamin. Thirty years later, however, researchers were able to determine that this vitamin-like compound was actually capable of quenching free radicals with high efficiency. Today it's become a favorite among top researchers such as doctors Bruce Ames and Lester Packer of the University of California at Berkeley.

The body does manufacture a small amount of ALA each day. Unfortunately, these amounts are tiny in comparison to what is needed to properly address some of the most applicable health concerns. Certain foods, including liver, rice bran, and dark-green, leafy vegetables such as spinach and broccoli, contain very modest milligram amounts of this antioxidant—hardly enough to provide the antioxidant and antiaging protection you can get from dietary supplements. In his book, *The Antioxidant Miracle*, Dr. Packer calls ALA "the universal antioxidant," due to its diverse antioxidant effects and ability to protect and restore other antioxidants.

HOW IT WORKS ✦ It comes as no surprise that ALA has been appropriately nicknamed the "universal" antioxidant because, while all antioxidants function by scouring the body for oxidation-causing free radicals, ALA takes that role to a level that others simply cannot. Here's why. For the most part, antioxidants are either fat- or water-soluble, but not both. That means that some antioxidants can be used by tissues composed of fat, such as the nervous system and brain, or of water, such as the heart and lungs. ALA doesn't follow the rule. Its unique structure and activity allow it to quickly eradicate free radicals in any area of the body, making it incredibly versatile.

Equally impressive, ALA can actually recycle other antioxidants. Once a free-radical scavenger, such as vitamin C, CoQ10, or glutathione, has pulled the damaging and oxidizing electrons from a free radical, the scavenger itself becomes a free radical. ALA has been shown to recharge these compounds back to their active antioxidant state, freeing them to continue on their missions.

THERAPEUTIC USES OF ALA • ALA has many therapeutic actions, detailed and listed below. In this chapter, we're going to focus on the ability of ALA to reduce oxidative stress in the brain and alleviate stress-related conditions. In future chapters, we'll discuss the role of ALA in other syndromes.

- *Age-related memory.* Preliminary animal research has indicated that ALA may be able to help prevent damage that leads to age-related memory loss. ALA can pass through the discriminating blood-brain barrier because of its unique chemical structure. Consequently, it can fight free radical-induced oxidation before certain regions of the brain are corrupted. This keen area of ALA research continues to show promise.

- *Fatigue.* Aside from protecting cells, another key function of ALA is to encourage the production of energy within the mitochondria region of the cells. This is greatly important, especially when you take into consideration how quickly the body uses up the very small amount of ALA that it produces on its own. Supplementation creates a "pool" of free lipoic acid. This reserve not only provides the added protection that cells need, but it also helps spark the energy that the body requires for metabolism and a long list of other biological activities.

- *Healthy vision.* The optic nerve is actually an extension of the brain and, as such, is sensitive to free radical buildup there. In addition, the eyes are exposed to glare and environmental factors throughout life that leave them extremely vulnerable to free radical damage. Europeans have been using ALA to help prevent the formation of cataracts for years. This early popularity was based on several successful animal studies suggesting that ALA could reduce or prevent the cloudiness associated with the disease. While research is ongoing, what we do know is that ALA helps boost the effectiveness of vitamins C and E, two antioxidants that help to naturally block out harmful ultraviolet rays of the sun.

- *Healthy skin.* Topical applications of ALA have also been found to reduce aging effects on the skin.

TIPS FOR TAKING ALA

- Although ALA is very safe, diabetics should always consult their physicians prior to supplementing with it, as insulin doses may need adjustment.
- ALA can be taken with food or on an empty stomach.
- Taking ALA in divided doses throughout the day is recommended for greatest effectiveness.
- Some users have experienced mild stomach upset after supplementing with ALA. If this occurs, try lowering the dose or taking it with food.

NATURAL COMPANIONS TO ALA ✦ A basic antioxidant, multivitamin and mineral formula, ashwagandha, SOD, N-acetyl-L-carnitine, and pomegranate seed extract.

ABOUT THE COMPANIONS ✦ *Acetyl-L-carnitine* and *L-carnitine* are both used to improve mitochondrial function. When both forms of carnitine have been supplemented in animals, blood and brain levels of the nutrients have been increased. However, only acetyl carnitine was found to be effective in lowering oxidative damage in the brain. Dr. Bruce Ames analyzed 21 double-blind clinical trials using acetyl carnitine to treat mild cognitive impairment and mild Alzheimer's Disease. The studies showed significant improvement in cognitive ability.

An analysis of two placebo-controlled trials in which 1,257 people with diabetic neuropathy were enrolled showed that acetyl carnitine alleviated symptoms, particularly pain, and improved nerve fiber regeneration and feeling in their extremities.

Pomegranate seed extract is a concentrated source of ellagic acid, anthocyanidins and trans resveratrol. Pomegranate has been a medicinal food in the Middle East since biblical times, but has only recently been studied in the United States. A March 2003 article published is the *Journal of the National Cancer Institute* touted pomegranate as "nature's power fruit." Scientists believe that pomegranate may bind to DNA, thus preventing damage that leads to aging. Pomegranate may also protect natural detoxifying enzymes such as SOD, catalase, and glutathione peroxidase that detoxify the body and help extend antioxidant activities.

POSSIBLE CONTRAINDICATIONS TO ALA ✦ One reported. Refer to Table 5 in the Appendix for more information.

Mood and Anxiety

Among the most profound results of chronic stress is its effect on brain function. The following section of this chapter deals with the various kinds of mental stress, including mood swings, anxiety, depression, poor memory, and reduced cognitive function, that may result.

5-HTP (5-HYDROXYTRYPTOPHAN)

MAJOR APPLICATION OF 5-HTP ✦ This natural byproduct of the amino acid tryptophan has only surged in popularity. Many 5-HTP users have reported that it's one of the most effective, natural ways to help combat pain, induce peaceful sleep, and promote a positive mood. It's also been shown to help control panic attacks and anxiety.

AN OVERVIEW OF 5-HTP ✦ The body can manufacture its own supply of 5-HTP—a substance that is converted into serotonin, an ultra-important peptide in the brain that wears a number of biological hats—provided that there's ample tryptophan in the diet. Thanks to the ritualistic overeating that many engage in every November, the term *tryptophan* has become familiar, but it's more than just a chemical that naturally occurs in turkey. Aside from its ability to induce a much-needed post-football nap, it's also an essential amino acid which offers an impressive array of health benefits.

Many protein-rich foods, such as turkey, chicken, beef, and fish, contain tryptophan. Unfortunately, most food manufacturers don't list an amino-acid profile on their labels, making supplementation ideal for anyone taking it to address a specific health concern.

How 5-HTP WORKS ✦ One of the distinguishing aspects of the 5-HTP molecule is its incredibly tiny size, which makes it able to manoeuver its way past the protective blood-brain barrier that blocks out most substances. Once inside the brain, 5-HTP is converted into serotonin.

Serotonin serves as a neurotransmitter, and as a vasodilator, enabling the brain to send and receive messages throughout the nervous system more effectively. It also helps to prevent inflammation in blood vessels. Unfortunately, bizarre eating habits and unceasing to-do lists have a way of making this more difficult than it appears.

THERAPEUTIC USES FOR 5-HTP

✦ *Aches and pains.* Life is challenging enough when one is well. Add chronic pain, and living can become unbearable. Those who suffer from these daily struggles have been found to exhibit surprisingly low levels of serotonin. By increasing the body's production of this natural chemical, some researchers believe that it may be possible to improve their pain tolerance. While that won't eliminate the root disorder, anything that makes it more possible to enjoy life is a definite improvement.

- *Depression and anxiety.* In addition to helping the brain communicate with the body, serotonin also has a way of keeping emotions in check. Many types of depression, anxiety, and panic attacks have been linked to consistently low levels of this mood-supporting neurotransmitter. This has served as the inspiration behind a number of clinical studies, suggesting that 5-HTP's knack for boosting serotonin production can be beneficial to counter the effects of depression and anxiety.

- *Insomnia.* Anyone who's ever devoured an enormous serving of Thanksgiving turkey can testify to the inevitable drowsiness that's almost sure to follow. This happens when tryptophan-rich proteins produce high levels of 5-HTP. It then scurries its way to the brain, crosses the border, and stimulates the production of serotonin. This (not the overload of boring family stories) is what induces sleep and promotes deep, prolonged rapid eye movement (REM) periods. Many users report feeling refreshed upon waking.

- *Migraine headache.* An agonizing migraine headache can be triggered by something as simple as a bright light, a steady noise, or even by staring at a passing train. As both a vasodilator and a powerful neurotransmitter, 5-HTP may help lessen the severity and regularity of these brutal attacks when used as a supplement. It's worth noting that, once triggered, migraines tend to have wills of their own. The key here is prevention. For added support, try taking the herb feverfew, as well.

- *Weight loss.* A 1989 clinical study published in the *Journal of Neurotransmission* claimed that when taken prior to eating 5-HTP, it appeared to induce greater feelings of fullness in those taking it. It was also noted that 5-HTP may also be helpful to reduce the desire to consume sweets and starches. Shedding excess pounds is not only a smart health move, it may also make trips to the beach less stressful.

• *Psychological disorders.* Chemical dependency, depression, anxiety, panic attacks.

Tips for taking 5-HTP

• To improve absorption, take 5-HTP 30-40 minutes before a meal, on an empty stomach.
• Many medications for depression, anxiety, and panic attacks work in the same manner as 5-HTP. If you're already taking one of them, check with your doctor before starting 5-HTP.
• Make sure that the formula you choose is derived from *Griffonia simplicifolia.*
• Depending on your specific condition, it may take some time to fully realize the effects of 5-HTP, so it's recommended that you start with a smaller dose and gradually increase it.
• It's strongly advised that you avoid taking any other medications or chemicals that cause drowsiness, including certain allergy medications, sleep aids, muscle relaxants, alcohol, and prescription narcotics when you take 5-HTP.
• Drowsiness is common. If you find yourself nodding off at inappropriate times or too frequently, reduce your dose to one that's more agreeable.

Natural Companions for 5-HTP ✦ Basic antioxidant, vitamin and mineral multiple, SAMe, feverfew, calcium and magnesium combination, melatonin.

Cofactors and Contraindications for 5-HTP ✦ Refer to Table 6 in the Appendix for contraindications and more information.

S-ADENOSYL METHIONINE (SAMe)

MAJOR APPLICATION OF SAME ✦ S-adenosyl methionine (SAMe) is created within the body when the amino acid methionine teams up with energy-producing molecules called *adenosine triphosphate*, or ATP. The result is an aggressive chemical substance that the body uses liberally to provide raw materials for its systems and organs, most notably the liver, brain, and articular cartilage. In Europe SAMe sales topple those of Prozac®.

AN OVERVIEW OF SAME ✦ SAMe was discovered in 1952 by Italian researchers. Word of its discovery swept through Europe and, by the 1970s, it was one of the most widely prescribed medications there. In current-day U.S., SAMe has become a staple in the lives of millions. Touted as a wonder supplement for everything from back pain to Alzheimer's disease, SAMe has gained a following that only seems to swell as the supporting research grows increasingly positive.

HOW SAME WORKS ✦ As you're reading this, your body is doing everything in its power to produce SAMe, the substance that's absolutely essential for the billions of chemical reactions that take place every second within human cells. Without getting unnecessarily technical, this process—more formally known as *methylation*—occurs when a compound (such as SAMe) lends its *methyl group* to another group of cells trying to carry out a bodily function. Hence SAMe is what we like to call a methyl "donor," a crucial element in cellular development.

SAMe also extends its biological generosity to many of the body's most vital components, including the brain, joints, liver, and neurotransmitters.

THERAPEUTIC USES OF SAME

- *Age-related memory.* While the research that surrounds SAMe's role in brain health is still relatively new, there appears to be promise. SAMe molecules assist the brain in creating both dopamine and serotonin, the chemical compounds that directly affect reasoning, memory, learning capacity, and mood. Some studies have shown that those who suffer from age-related memory disorders typically have low levels of SAMe. These statistics have led many researchers to believe that it may be possible to mitigate the severity of these conditions through supplementation.

+ *Depression.* Believe it or not, your day-to-day activities, encounters, and stress factors are only a fraction of your mood puzzle. How your body adapts chemically is what regulates how apt you are to emotional display. SAMe helps spark production of the brain's key neurotransmitter, serotonin. This mood-regulating chemical is what essentially allows you to cope with bad drivers, tight deadlines, and a house full of loud loved ones. Research has shown that low levels of serotonin are often common among those who become easily depressed, fatigued, and angry.

+ *Fatigue.* By upping the body's store of healthy neurotransmitters, mainly dopamine and serotonin, the process of sending and receiving chemical messages (neurotransmission) throughout the body can be greatly improved, helping you remain energetic and alert. Keep in mind that fatigue is a separate condition from exhaustion. Exhaustion is what the body experiences after running a 26-mile marathon. Fatigue is the weariness, tiredness, and lack of endurance more closely associated with stress and mental overload. SAMe makes it possible for the body to produce an ample reserve of the chemicals needed to compensate for both exhaustion and fatigue. When it comes to battling the feelings of depression and hopelessness that often occur with fatigue, SAMe may be able to help.

+ *Healthy joints.* Once SAMe has donated its methyl group, the body breaks down what remains of the molecule to helpt form cartilage and the viscous fluid matrix that cushions joints. This action, coupled with its ability to alter the way that the mind copes with pain, has made SAMe one of the most popular joint-supporting supplements ever introduced. Some studies suggest that SAMe is just as effective as many NSAIDS (non-steroidal anti-inflammatory drugs) and less challenging to the kidneys, stomach, and urinary tract.

- *Liver health.* SAMe encourages the formation and activity of the metabolic superhero, glutathione. This hard-working antioxidant is absolutely essential to help keep the liver healthy, clean, and free of toxic buildup. When glutathione surrenders its biological authority, the liver is typically one of the first organs to feel the effects. And when the liver suffers, the entire body suffers. Supplementing SAMe, even in modest amounts, is a smart way to ensure that the liver is getting everything it needs.

- *Pain management.* Have you ever wondered why no two people in this world of billions deal with pain in the same way? Or why some label pain as a "state of mind?" They may be right. Each one of us has a number of built-in mechanisms that make it possible for us to deal with pain rationally. Coincidentally, many of those mechanisms are regulated by one of the chemical peptides that SAMe produces, serotonin.

Tips for Taking SAMe

- Certain foods can limit the body's ability to use SAMe. For best results take SAMe on an empty stomach. If nausea or heartburn occurs, take it with a bland meal or lots of liquids.
- Avoid taking SAMe too close to bedtime, as it's been known to provide a slight-to-moderate energy boost.
- SAMe appears to work well with other mood-enhancing supplements, especially 5-HTP, phosphatidylserine, and St. John's wort.
- Look for formulas that offer an enteric, or intestinal-friendly, coating. This will ensure that the SAMe you purchase hasn't lost its stability and potency.

- If you're not taking a daily multiple, make sure that you're not neglecting your intake of B vitamins, especially B-12, B-6 and folic acid. They help prevent the buildup of homocysteine, a toxic methionine byproduct linked to different forms of cardiovascular disease.
- *It is strongly recommended that anyone suffering from manic, bipolar, or schizophrenic conditions consult his or her physician before using SAMe.*

NATURAL COMPANIONS FOR SAMe ✦ Basic antioxidant, vitamin and mineral multiple, DHA, phosphatidyl Serine, St. John's wort, valerian, and ginkgo. Several other supplements targeted specifically for joint pain are Celadrin®, glucosamine sulfate, and MSM. These will be fully discussed in Chapter Eight.

COFACTORS AND CONTRAINDICATIONS FOR SAMe ✦ Refer to Table 6 in the Appendix for contraindications and more information.

ST. JOHN'S WORT (*HYPERICUM PERFORATUM L.*)

MAJOR APPLICATION OF ST. JOHN'S WORT ✦ Long before America caught word of St. John's wort, Europeans had been using it for years as a way to keep calm, support positive outlook, and enjoy night after night of deep, uninterrupted sleep. St. John's wort continues to be one of the top-selling herbal supplements in the world. In the eyes of many loyal users, it's one of the most effective as well. While it's most commonly used to help alleviate mild to moderate depression, this fascinating herbal extract continues to show promise to help make life much more enjoyable for those who once relied on many popular prescriptions.

AN OVERVIEW OF ST. JOHN'S WORT ✦ Many experts believe that German researchers were among the first to use St. John's wort to counter the effects of depression and anxiety. While that may be true with respect to early clinical applications, the herb actually has a rich history. Limited documentation suggests that St. John's wort was used centuries ago to drive out evil spirits, protect the soul from spiritual corruption, and heal battle wounds.

Over the years, St. John's wort seems to have shed its mystical persona. To date it has been the subject of more than 30 clinical studies, all carefully examining the role the herb plays to stimulate the production of serotonin, a powerfully influential brain chemical that ultimately determines the quality of human mood and emotion. Results have been astonishing. Many of these placebo-controlled studies have suggested, and continue to suggest, that St. John's wort works as effectively as many of the most popular prescription medications. It is also far more affordable and readily available to just about anyone interested in using it.

How St. John's Wort Works • Researchers still don't know precisely *why* St. John's wort works as well as it does. What they do know, however, is that the shrub's bright, yellow flowers contain abundant amounts of a dark red pigment known as *hypericin*. Accordingly, some of the most convincing studies continue to presuppose that hypericin essentially allows St. John's wort to increase the brain's production of mood-enhancing neurotransmitters by blocking their breakdown by the enzyme monoamine oxidase in the neural synapse. This theory has been so universally accepted that some of the most trusted St. John's wort formulas are now standardized in accordance to how much active hypericin they contain.

There's more to this mood-supporting herb than just hypericin. It also contains respectable amounts of *hyperforin*, flavonoids, and naturally occurring essential oils. Many of these compounds are currently being studied to determine what, if any, role they might play to combat depression, anxiety, panic, and other disorders. These constituents have also demonstrated antiviral activity.

Therapeutic Uses of St. John's Wort
  • *Depression.* Based on its history and the overwhelming success rate among European users, St. John's wort has inspired millions of users

to reconsider their needs for some of the most popularly prescribed mood-enhancing medications. In Germany alone, sales of St. John's wort now topple those of Prozac® and Zoloft®. This is not by chance. It's far less expensive, virtually free of any concerning side effects, and has the potential to offer precisely the same results as those higher-priced medication counterparts. St. John's wort is effective for mild depression, but not major depression.

- *Insomnia.* Some of the most loyal users of St. John's Wort take the herb just to help encourage sound slumber, although it seems to be equally helpful to alleviate the insomnia that traditionally accompanies mild to moderate depression. Unlike some sleeping pills and other nighttime medications, St. John's wort appears to be nonhabit-forming. Many users claim that by achieving a greater-quality night's sleep, they awaken more refreshed, are more alert throughout the day, and less fatigued in general.
- *PMS.* Although more research is clearly needed, a growing number of women continue to hail St. John's wort as one of the most effective natural compounds to help manage the seemingly endless mental and physical symptoms associated with premenstrual syndrome (PMS). Some researchers attribute this to hyperforin, another powerful, active constituent found in the plant's dried, yellow flowers.
- *Infection.* A number of in vitro studies have suggested that St. John's wort may exhibit strong antiviral properties against herpes simplex types 1 and 2, influenza strains A and B, and Epstein-Barr virus, a primary cause of mononucleosis. This area keenly interests researchers, as all three viruses are incurable.

Tips for Taking St. John's wort

- Standardized extracts are the only way to go. Look for a formula that is standardized to a minimum of 0.3 percent hypericin.
- It's advisable to take St. John's wort with a meal to avoid any unwanted stomach discomforts.

- Be patient when taking St. John's wort for the fist time. It can take up to several weeks to fully absorb into the system. Once it has, there's no need to cycle on or off.
- Some users, especially those with fair skin, have reported an increased sensitivity to sunlight. Using a stronger SPF-rated sunscreen, especially in high-UV climates, is strongly advised when using St. John's wort for the first time.
- If you're considering using St John's wort and are already using a prescription antidepressant, it is strongly advised that you consult your physician first.
- It is advisable to avoid tyramine-containing foods such as red wine, cheese, yeast, and pickled herring while using St. John's wort.

NATURAL COMPANIONS FOR ST. JOHN'S WORT ✦ For depression and anxiety, St. John's wort may be used with other herbs such as valerian, hops, skullcap, and passionflower.

COFACTORS AND CONTRAINDICATIONS FOR ST. JOHNS WORT ✦ Refer to Table 8 in the Appendix for contraindications and more information.

Memory and Attention Span

"To the dull mind, nature is leaden. To the illumined mind, the whole world burns and sparkles with light." — *Ralph Waldo Emerson*

PHOSPHATIDYLSERINE (PS)

MAJOR APPLICATION OF PS ✦ Human cells are incredibly complex structures and, although microscopic, are made up of many compounds, among them a group of fats called *phospholipids*. Present in the membranes of every living cell, their highest concentrations can be found in the brain. PS is a phospholipid most actively involved in the brain's ability to communicate with the rest of the body. Its primary function is to support the successful transfer of electrical impulses across the synapse of the brain to their respective destinations. Although the body can manufacture PS, its ability to do so gradually declines. This is just one of many reasons why PS has continued to fascinate researchers with regard to age-related memory conditions.

AN OVERVIEW OF PS • The brain is nothing close to the solid, shiny organ that we often imagine it to be. In fact it's made up of approximately 60 percent fat, and PS accounts for approximately 15 percent of its total phospholipid supply. From a functional perspective, phospholipids are important in the formation of cellular membranes, and play an active role in fat metabolism.

HOW PS WORKS • PS is unquestionably one of the busiest compounds in the body and is actively involved in the billions of neurotransmissions occurring every nanosecond within it.

Its unique size and structure allows PS to cross the blood-brain barrier, transferring nutrients and facilitating waste removal. Like every other organ in the body, the brain needs specific nutrients to function at its best. PS makes it possible for these nutrients to reach their destination, because it's the chief architectural feature for securing nutrient and neurotransmitter receptors. PS thus improves the efficiency of transfer by clearing paths for uptake and, at the same time, it protects brain cells from structural damage. As the body ages, the amount of PS that's naturally produced declines. This relationship has led many researchers to believe that PS can be an effective weapon in the war against memory deterioration.

THERAPEUTIC USES

  • *Age-related memory and mental clarity.* According to a bevy of clinical studies, PS has shown amazing promise to prevent, and possibly reverse, many memory-related conditions. Every impulse, thought, action, reaction, movement, emotion, and desire that we display results from the body's neurotransmitters in action. PS plays a weighty role in the support of these actions. Based on these findings, PS supplementation can help promote the body's ability to think more clearly and recall memories more easily.

- *Stress.* Every time you get stressed out, whether emotionally or physically, your body responds by releasing a troublesome adrenal hormone known as *cortisol.* While cortisol does serve a purpose within the body, overproduction of this steroid hormone can result in emotional imbalance, depression, metabolic interference, and immune system suppression. PS supplementation has been shown to help limit the amount of cortisol that's released during these trying times, making it once again possible for you to live and work without smacking your computer monitor.

- *Depression.* Based on its ability to help control excess cortisol production, PS has become very popular among those who suffer from various forms of depression. Research has taught us that phospholipids, including PS, play a clear-cut role to help support healthy and positive moods.

- *Post-workout recovery.* Immediately following strenuous activity, the body responds by releasing *adrenocorticotropin* (ACTH), a hormone that discourages testosterone production and encourages the release of cortisol. By limiting ACTH production, PS can reduce the amount of muscle tissue breakdown that occurs during exercise. A common misconception is that muscles grow during exercise—wrong. In fact, muscles are bulldozed during exercise and grow *in between* workouts, hence the term *recovery.* During recovery, PS helps prevent the activity of growth-inhibiting hormones. This may allow athletes to recover faster, so that their exercise gains are realized more quickly.

Tips for Taking Phosphatidylserine

- Some users report a mild energy increase while supplementing with PS. If this happens to you, it's nothing to be alarmed about. Simply avoid taking it close to bedtime.
- PS should be taken before meals with lots of liquid to help facilitate absorption.
- It can take time for the body to recognize the effects of PS, especially when taken for depression and other mood-related ailments.
- Don't take PS with any medications known to produce a stimulant effect.
- If you decide to make PS part of your exercise regime, take it about an hour prior to beginning your workout.

Natural Companions for Phosphatidyl Serine

Natural Companions for Phosphatidyl Serine • Basic antioxidant, vitamin and mineral formula, should include choline and inositol, or add it separately. Huperzine A, Vinpocetine, Docosahexaenoic acid (DHA), Acetyl L-Carnitine, GABA, SAMe.

About the Companions

- **Choline and Inositol.** *Choline* and *insositol*, considered semi-essential members of the B-vitamin family, were discussed in the Basics Program in the Preface.

  Choline is a precursor of Phosphatidyl choline (lecithin), the most abundant structural component in cell membranes. A form of choline known as alpha glycerylphosphorylcholine (alpha GPC) has shown considerable promise to improve memory and reduce loss of brain function in the suffering from Alzheimer's Disease.

  Phosphatidyl inositol (IP_3) is the third member of the important phosphatidyl team, which includes phosphatides of choline, serine, and ethanolamine. IP_3 serves as an anchor in cell membranes for the omega-6 fatty acid, arachidonic acid, and is an important signaling molecule in the brain and central nervous system.

- **DHA.** *Docosahexaenoic acid* (DHA) is converted within the body from alpha linolenic acid (flaxseed oil). Apparently in its dedication to energy conservation, the body evolved using the same set of enzymes to produce DHA and omega-3 fatty acid from its precursors as it did to produce arachidonic acid, an omega-6 fatty acid.

  This was not a problem as long as we depended on eating primarily fish, range animals, and vegetables rich in DHA—which we did for many thousands of years. However, as we have depended more upon grains and other cultivated foods for sustenance, precursors of arachidonic have locked on to the majority of these enzymes, leaving the production of cognition-enhancing DHA waiting in the wings. In its absence, arachidonic acid and its pro-inflammatory descendents have proliferated. Impressive results in treating learning and cognition deficiencies have resulted from DHA supplementation.

- **GABA.** Gamma aminobutyric acid (GABA) is the most important calming neurotransmitter in the brain. The late Carl Pfeiffer, M.D., referred to GABA, glutamic acid, and glutamine as the "three musketeers of the brain," meaning that they are vital for energy and smooth-running brain reactions.

  GABA's role is to help reduce anxiety and improve memory. It has been used clinically to treat depression, seizures, hypertension, and alcoholism. GABA also has a profound affect on sympathetic nervous responses in the pancreas, thymus, and duodenum, and so plays an important role in immune and digestive function.

- **Vinpocetine.** Vinpocetine is derived from *vincamine,* an extract of periwinkle (*Vinca minor*). Vinpocetine stimulates memory by increasing blood flow to the brain and improving its use of glucose and oxygen. This is particularly useful for memory impairment due to reduced blood flow to the brain.

  With increased cerebral circulation comes enhanced energy production in the brain and a resultant aid to recall, concentration, short-term memory, and learning. Other possible actions of vinpocetine include reducing dizziness (vertigo), tinnitis or ringing in the ears, Meniere's syndrome, sleep disorders, and some forms of impaired hearing.

Hundreds of studies have been made about the safety and effectiveness of vinpocetine. In one overview of 882 patients with neurological disorders who used it, significant improvements were found in 62 percent of those patients. Since vinpocetine enhances the action of other brain enhancement nutrients discussed here, you will usually find it in combination formulas.

+ *Huperzine A.* This herbal extract of club moss (*Huperzia serrata*) has been used in Chinese medicine for centuries to treat fever and inflammation. But the herb doesn't actually contain anti-inflammatory compounds. Its activity is due to Huperzine A, an alkaloid and strong acetyl-cholinesterase inhibitor. Acetylcholine is responsible for communication among brain cells. In brain abnormalities such as Alzheimer's Disease, acetylcholine has an unusually high breakdown rate. Huperzine A prevents this breakdown, and thus helps improve memory, focus, and concentration. Huperzine also appears to protect brain cells from damage by glutamate overstimulation. Like vinpocetine, huperzine is generally used to enhance other brain nutrients.

COFACTORS AND CONTRAINDICATIONS FOR PS + Refer to Table 8 in the Appendix for contraindications and more information.

Age-Related Memory Loss

GINKGO BILOBA

MAJOR APPLICATION OF GINKGO + The oldest living species of tree on earth, ginkgo is the premier herbal aid for age-related memory loss.

Taken in China and Japan for centuries, ginkgo has been revered for its ability to enhance circulation to the brain and extremities. It helps improve memory, concentration, circulation to feet and hands, recovery from stroke, and hearing loss.

AN OVERVIEW OF GINKGO • Ginkgo's activity is due to several groups of constituents: *ginko flavone glycosies* and *ginkgolides bilobalides*. Ginkgo products are prepared from the green leaves of the ginkgo biloba tree as standardized extracts that contain 22-27 percent ginkgo flavone glycosides, including quercetin, kaempferol, and isohammetin. In addition they contain 5-7 percent of the *terpene lactones*, ginkgolides and bilobalides. The leading liquid extract in Germany contains a 50:1 level of herb to alcohol.

HOW GINGKO WORKS • Ginkgo increases blood flow to the brain and nerves and also to peripheral circulation. It's also a powerful antioxidant due to its flavone constituents. Ginkgo increases serotonin release and blocks brain chemicals that slow neurotransmission. It also enhances choline uptake in the hippocampus area of the brain. Ginkgo crosses the blood-brain barrier and exerts its effects directly on brain centers. It helps improve blood flow to the legs and is a useful adjunct to therapy in cardiovascular and diabetic regimens.

Since ginkgo is the premier herb for age-related cognitive disturbances, it deserves special recognition. It takes 240 mg. of standardized extract, taken in two divided daily doses, to achieve the desired effect. Consequently, ginkgo is generally taken with, and not added to, formulas. Normally it takes about two weeks for benefits to be realized.

THERAPEUTIC USES
- *Neurology.* Ginkgo improves circulation to the brain and nerves. It protects the brain from oxidative damage and slows formation of nitric oxide, further protecting the brain.
- *Vascular problems.* Ginkgo helps prevent platelets from sticking together in a process that can lead to blood clots. Ginkgo also relaxes

blood vessel walls so that the plaque-building process is thwarted. Its ability to improve circulation to all parts of the body gives ginkgo the ability support normal reproduction and sexual performance, improve hearing when poor circulation is the basis, and help the body adapt to extreme cold.

Tips for Taking Ginkgo

- For best results, take ginkgo before meals and in smaller doses throughout the day.
- Some users report mild headaches the first day or two of taking ginkgo. We suggest that you reduce the dosage and then gradually increase it over two weeks.
- Although rare, some users may have an allergy to ginkgo and should avoid it.
- Ginkgo may enhance the effects of medications that increase circulation or prevent clotting. Check with your doctor if you are taking these medications.

Natural Companions of Ginkgo ✦ Vitamin C, Phosphatidyl serine and DHA.

Cofactors and Contraindications of Ginkgo ✦ Refer to Table 8 in the Appendix for contraindications and further information.

Gingko Biloba.

7-SYNDROME HEALING

To Sum It All Up

The *stress syndrome* is the basis of ailments that plague us throughout life. Stress can be acute, meaning that it poses a real danger to our survival. This kind of stress is helpful in that it allows us to escape serious injury, illness, and even death. Stress can also be chronic, as when the stressor is physical, environmental, or psychological. Whether the stress is acute or chronic, the body's response is the same: the adrenal glands, brain, immune, reproductive, and cardiovascular systems prepare for a fight.

Obviously, if the condition of heightened alert continues for an extended period of time all systems involved will be affected. Oxidative stress is a normal byproduct of acute and chronic stress.

In an acutely stressful situation, immune cells produce free radicals aimed at viral or bacterial targets. These accumulate at the injury site and must be neutralized. In a chronically stressful state, the heightened emergency generates greater amounts of free radials as a byproduct of enhanced energy production within mitochondria. The body again meets the challenge with its internal antioxidant systems such as SOD, catalase, and glutathione enzymes, drawing additional support from exogenous antioxidants.

In this chapter we have focused on the effects of stress on the brain, highlighting steps that you can take to alleviate them before they get out of hand. We also gave an overview of normal aging and methods to deal with problems unique to older people. Now that we have fully explored the *stress syndrome*, it's time to move on to the other six.

CHAPTER THREE

The Metabolic Syndrome

M ETABOLIC SYNDROME, formerly known as "syndrome X," describes a cluster of abnormalities including obesity, high blood pressure, and disturbances in blood lipids and glucose metabolism that can increase a person's risk for coronary heart disease, stroke, and Type 2 diabetes. The syndrome itself has no specific treatment strategy and, because of this, some researchers question the validity of the title. Nevertheless, by addressing more than just one of the conditions present, a more effective disease-preventing strategy can be undertaken. For example, a person might be treated for high blood pressure alone when he or she also has high triglycerides and high cholesterol. Both other existing factors should be addressed in order to effectively alter the risk of cardiovascular disease. Fortunately, the maladies grouped under the *metabolic syndrome* umbrella are easily modified by diet, supplements, and lifestyle changes.

Five criteria have been established to identify a person with *metabolic syndrome* and three out of the five must be present for it to exist.

- Waist circumference > 102 cm (40.16 inches) in men and > 88 cm (34.65 inches) in women (apple shape).
- High serum triglycerides ≥1.7 mmol/l (150 mg/dL).
- High blood pressure ≥130/85 mm Hg.

- Low HDL cholesterol <1.04 mmol/l (<40 mg/dL) in men and <1.29mmol/L (50mg/dL) in women.
- High fasting serum glucose ≥6.1 mmol/l (110mg/dL) [National Cholesterol Education's Adult Treatment Program (ATPIII) criteria].

What You Will Find in This Chapter

- Obesity
- Insulin resistance
- Glucose balance and eeight loss
- Diabetes, Type 2 (Noninsulin-dependent diabetes mellitus)
- Hypoglycemia

Role of Obesity

The criteria listed above create a mental picture of a 50-something person with a layer of fat around the middle—a couch potato with a lousy diet. While this is an accurate description, it isn't the complete picture of a person with the *metabolic syndrome*. Being overweight or obese and physically inactive pose serious threats to health that lead to insulin resistance, impaired glucose tolerance, elevated blood pressure, increased triglycerides, and decreased HDL cholesterol. Left untreated, these risk factors will likely lead to diabetes and cardiovascular disease. But location of body fat is an important consideration, and a person with fat around the hips and thighs (pear-shaped) is at lower risk than someone with fat deposits around the visceral area.

It's not surprising that abnormalities in *metabolic syndrome* reveal a hierarchical order in which some occur more often than others. A Miami study of 517 people with *metabolic syndrome* established this model. Insulin resistance was found to be the primary factor, followed in order by obesity, lipid disorders, and disturbances in blood factors. The group included Caucasian, African, and Cuban Americans of both genders, so the order was well established among a diverse group of individuals.

There's little doubt among experts that the obesity epidemic is driving the metabolic syndrome by decreasing cellular responsiveness to insulin. Insulin resistance and its related deviations in glucose metabolism have reached pandemic proportions. One hundred-fifty million people worldwide currently have Type 2 diabetes. In the United States, 43 million people have been identified as having the *metabolic syndrome* and, because it's still largely undetected, it has been estimated that 70 million Americans could actually be involved. Alarmingly, it's younger Americans who are being increasingly diagnosed. Type 2 diabetes now affects children under the age of 10, which explains why it is no longer called adult-onset diabetes.

Insulin Resistance

Experts have identified insulin resistance as the cornerstone of the *metabolic syndrome*. Insulin is a hormone secreted by the pancreas gland, which regulates the flow of glucose (blood sugar) to cells. Once inside the cell, glucose is converted into the energy currency known as ATP. One molecule of glucose is converted into 36 molecules of ATP, which supplies energy for all metabolic processes. Consequently, a steady supply of glucose is needed for healthy metabolism.

Insulin facilitates the passage of glucose into cells by docking on to receptors located in the cell membrane. With insulin resistance, the receptors don't function correctly and insulin can't dock and pass glucose into the cell. As a result, glucose continues to circulate throughout the system and rising levels become life-threatening, triggering the storage of excess glucose as fat. Meanwhile, the pancreas pumps out more insulin, which can also lower glucose by promoting its storage as fat and glycogen, a type of stored glucose. Coupled with an insulin molecule that has become insensitive to the coaxing of receptors, this is a recipe for disaster.

Hormone Effects

Insulin is a hormone and its levels are increased by the hormone cortisol. A pattern now becomes evident. The *stress syndrome* increases cortisol, which in turn increases insulin and decreases its opposing hormone, glucagon. More glucose is stored as fat and less is burned for energy. Most of the fat is stored in the visceral area near the liver, which releases glucose into the blood.

It isn't surprising that cortisol and insulin affect other hormones, including those that control sexual function and fertility and those that help us stay youthful. It lowers DHEA (dehydroepiandrostone), glucagon, and growth hormone while raising IGF-1 (insulin-like growth factor). Glucagon, as we've seen, is of particular importance because it increases fat burning—the opposite of insulin's action. IGF-1 has been implicated in cancer, particularly when estradiol and testosterone are high. In women, polycystic ovary syndrome, infertility, immune dysfunction, and chronic inflammation are all associated with insulin resistance.

Insulin resistance has been associated with Alzheimer's Disease by some investigators. Two theories on the association have been proposed. Toxic glucose metabolites may be involved in beta plaque formation, a key deformity in Alzheimer's Disease. There may also be incongruity in the insulin-signaling pathways in the brain, which would tend to garble information being processed. Since cerebral vascular disease can result from blood vessel anomalies known as endothelial dysfunction, memory loss and poor cognitive function could certainly be anticipated. Erectile dysfunction might also be a result of insulin resistance as a mechanistic byproduct of blood vessel abnormalities.

Advanced Glycation End Products (AGEs)

In addition to increasing fat storage, insulin resistance causes a profound imbalance in glucose metabolism. Glycation is a progressive process in which glucose attaches to proteins, causing them to change shape. The shape of proteins is critical to their function, as these huge and otherwise unwieldy molecules fold and curl themselves into manageable shapes.

The nooks and crannies created in folded proteins are extremely important because the reactive sites are tucked into those folds. When glucose binds to proteins, it reshapes them so that they're no longer able to function correctly and form useless *glycosylated end products*. Additionally, these glycosylated proteins cause mischief such as clouding the lens of the eye (cataracts). AGEs are involved in many aging conditions including what you see in the mirror—wrinkled skin. That's why dermatologists will tell you that eating sugary foods is the worst thing you can do to your skin.

Metabolic Syndrome Consists of Modifiable Risk Factors

The *metabolic syndrome* consists of several modifiable risk factors for disease and is the perfect place to begin dietary intervention. Begin with the stress reductions as suggested in Chapter Two, follow the nutrition guidelines in *7-Color Cuisine*, and use the specific supplements suggested in *7-Syndrome Healing* to form an appropriate strategy.

The Center for Disease Control's Third National Health and Nutrition Examination Study found that people with *metabolic syndrome* had lower levels of antioxidants, particularly all of the carotenoids (except lycopene), and vitamins C and E. This study of 8,808 adults highlighted oxidative stress as the underlying cause. Given the results of this and other studies with similar results, it would be prudent for those with the *metabolic syndrome* to take a natural multi-carotene formula in addition to a daily multiple such as the one suggested in Chapter One.

Supplements for Cortisol and Insulin Resistance

There are other specific supplements you should consider that address the five qualifying conditions of the *metabolic syndrome*. Discussion of the *cardiovascular syndrome*, the topic of our next chapter, naturally flows from the conditions pecular to the *metabolic syndrome*.

RELORA®

MAJOR APPLICATION OF RELORA® ✦ Perhaps you are one who has made repeated attempts to lose weight, all without success. Let's also assume you now know that cortisol is involved in gaining weight around the middle of your body, as described above. The herbal formula Relora® has been designed specifically to address stress and cortisol-related weight gain. In just the past year, this remarkable, proprietary blend of plant extracts from *Magnolia officinalis* and *Phellodendron amurense* has become immensely popular, based primarily on its unblemished history of safety, clinical merit, and its track record with thousands of extremely satisfied users.

AN OVERVIEW OF RELORA® ✦ When we make the conscious effort to embark on a diet, the body is forced to react to the sudden shift in metabolic and physically enduring changes to which it's subjected. While this may seem well and good, the internal signals that control metabolism suddenly get the impression that we're starving to death. Consequently, the body responds by slowing metabolic rate and increasing appetite. It does this for one reason— protection.

HOW RELORA® WORKS ✦ Trying to overcome this inherent metabolic defense mechanism by continuing the weight loss diet puts a tremendous amount of stress on the human system. In the response with which you are now all too familiar, the body increases production of hormones such as cortisol,the stress hormone that has been linked to abdominal fat, depression, and explosive bursts of appetite. Relora® was developed specifically for stress management without sedation and stress-related appetite control.

Relora® has been shown in a number of clinical studies to help combat stress associated with dieting as well as weight gain resulting from chronic stress. It helps regulate the body's production and activity of stress hormones. This includes maintaining healthy hormone levels, moderating the stress response, and altering eating behavior associated with stress. All of these actions aid in a successful weight loss program.

+ *Reduction of stress-related symptoms.* In a recent open trial, 50 adults took 200 mg. of Relora® three times daily for two weeks. Participants reported their responses to stress-related symptoms such as irritability, mood swings, restlessness, muscle tension, poor sleep, and difficulty concentrating. Seventy-eight percent of the respondents reported being more relaxed and sleeping better. Some drowsiness was reported in 24 percent of the subjects. None of the trial participants experienced stomach upset or any other side effects. Relora's® ability to reduce anxiety and stress response in 8-day-old baby chicks temporarily placed in solitary confinement helps support its stress-reducing activities.

+ *Stress hormone normalization.* A second open trial checked for elevated cortisol and reduced DHEA levels in 12 adults. As discussed above, these hormones are affected by stress. After the 2-week regimen of taking Relora®, morning cortisol levels were lowered by 37 percent, while salivary DHEA levels were 27 percent higher. Meanwhile, patients living at Cincinnati's Living Longer Clinic reported after three months taking Relora® that it helped alleviate fatigue.

+ *Eating behavior in response to stress.* Scientists at the Miami research group conducted a double-blind, placebo-controlled trial of 28 overweight women who reported stress-related eating behavior. All of the participants in the placebo group gained weight during the trial, while those in the Relora group experienced some weight loss.

Cofactors and Contraindications for Relora® + See Table 8 in the Appendix for more information.

CHROMIUM

Major Application of Chromium + Chromium is one of the most popular and widely used essential trace minerals in the world. While its popularity can be attributed to some wildly far-fetched weight loss claims, it's actually vital in the metabolism of carbohydrates, fats, and proteins. In addition, chromium has been shown to help increase the body's sensitivity to insulin. This has been very helpful to many Type 2 diabetics, and shows great promise for anyone concerned with taking control of his or her blood-sugar levels.

AN OVERVIEW OF CHROMIUM • Saying that chromium is popular is like saying that water is wet. The truth is that the only mineral to outsell chromium here in the United States is calcium. This is remarkable when you consider the difference in historical availability between the two. Regardless, chromium is now used by millions of Americans every year.

But make no mistake—chromium is also one of the most misunderstood of all supplements. This can be chalked up to some of the outrageous advertising claims made during the chromium revolution of the mid to late 1990s. For a time, some manufacturers actually suggested that it could melt fat away during sleep, quadruple the metabolic process, and build Arnold-esque physiques in very little time. By 1997 the FTC had heard enough, and slapped a restriction on what claims could and could not be made.

HOW CHROMIUM WORKS • Here's a simple metaphor that will make it impossible to forget chromium's role in the body. Think of your bloodstream as a superhighway for nutrients, one of which is glucose, or blood sugar. During its commute to the office (the cell's mitochondria), glucose gets a flat tire. Witness to this is insulin, a hormone produced by the pancreas. Being the good biological Samaritan that it is, insulin immediately offers glucose a lift to the center of the cell. Upon arrival, glucose nails its presentation and is promoted to the rank of energy. Simple enough, right?

Unfortunately, the pancreas doesn't always produce the amount of insulin needed to transport blood sugar to the cells. And even when it does, there's really no guarantee that glucose is going to accept the ride. This is where weight gain, diabetes, and hormone imbalances get nasty. Chromium helps facilitate the transfer of glucose to the cells when the pancreas fails to produce enough insulin, as well as when glucose gets stubborn.

- *Healthy blood sugar.* Anyone concerned with blood-sugar levels, especially those living with diabetes or hypoglycemia, should talk to his or her physician about supplementing with chromium. A wealth of research continues to show that it is one of the best natural ways to help decrease insulin resistance while increasing GTF, or glucose tolerance factor, as evidenced by the low chromium levels common among Type 2 diabetics.

- *Weight loss and metabolism.* If you're one of the very few who actually eat well on a consistent basis, you should be commended for your efforts. Sadly, there aren't many people who fall into this rapidly diminishing category. The reality is much more concerning. In 2004, a year of record profits for major fast-food chains, we also heard that one-third of all Americans are obsese. If fast food is your diet, pay very close attention. Processed foods have little to no chromium content. Over time, your body will eventually become resistant to insulin, making the process of converting glucose into energy a grueling one.

Myth: Chromium melts away fat quickly.
Truth: No, it won't. But without adequate chromium, the body will have a very difficult time burning fat.

Myth: Chromium will help me build muscle without working out.
Truth: Not a chance. But it will help you use glucose more effectively, instead of immediatly storing it as fat.

Myth: Some forms of chromium are easier to absorb than others.
Truth: It makes very little difference which grade you choose. Your body will be grateful with whatever grade you supply.

- *General health.* If you have any reservations that you're getting enough chromium from the foods you eat, don't wait until it's too late. Supplementing even the most modest amount of this trace mineral is a smart move, any way you choose to look at it.

+ *Controlling cholesterol*

TIPS FOR TAKING CHROMIUM

+ If you're diabetic, always consult your physician before supplementing with chromium.
+ Taking chromium with a small meal can help prevent unwanted stomach discomforts.
+ When taking chromium specifically for blood sugar management, we suggest using GTF (glucose tolerance factor) chromium to help increase insulin sensitivity.
+ Many multiples now contain notable amounts of chromium. If you're trying to be very specific about the dose you take, read the labels carefully.
+ When taken in high doses, chromium can inhibit zinc from being properly utilized. Adding 15-30 mg. of zinc is an easy solution to this concern.
+ To avoid complications do not take chromium when pregnant or nursing.
+ Consult your physician before mixing chromium with antidepressants.
+ Milk, dairy, and other calcium-rich foods should not be consumed at the same time as chromium. They can make it very difficult to absorb this trace mineral.

COMPANIONS TO CHROMIUM + Vitamin C, niacin, amino acids (especially glycine and cysteine), hydroxyl citric acid (HCA).

COFACTORS AND CONTRAINDICATIONS FOR CHROMIUM + See Table 3 in the Appendix for more information.

Weight Loss

CLA (CONJUGATED LINOLEIC ACID)

MAJOR APPLICATION OF CLA ✦ Conjugated linoleic acid is an extremely popular omega-6 essential fatty acid more commonly known by its initials, CLA. Since its introduction in the mid 1990s, CLA has developed one of the most loyal followings among supplement users, especially those concerned with their figures. That's due to how well CLA seems to help people of every shape and size reduce the amount of body fat they tote around. In addition, CLA has become a smash in the bodybuilding community and continues to be one of the most trusted supplements to help increase and preserve lean muscle mass.

AN OVERVIEW OF CLA ✦ An explosion of supplemental innovations that started in the 1990s continues today to shape the way health-conscious people live.

CLA is one of the best examples. Although it was initially marketed to athletes and bodybuilders, it didn't take long for the general weight-conscious population to become interested in this remarkable supplement. Within a relatively short period of time, people who had never reached for anything other than a multivitamin were using CLA religiously.

Some foods, especially milk, cheese, beef, and lamb, do contain varying amounts of CLA. Over the years, however, the actual amount of CLA in these foods has steadily diminished. Many experts believe the decline has a great deal to do with the diets of the animals that provide CLA-"rich" foods. Clearly it would be very difficult to obtain the suggested 2-4 grams of CLA from our diets.

HOW CLA WORKS ✦ Mere mention of the word "fat" can send most would-be dieters running away in horror. Most people do everything they can to avoid fat by whatever means necessary. This is one of the biggest mistakes a person can make. The fact is that the body needs certain good fats to carry out a long list of biological tasks. Metabolism is among the most imperative.

To date, CLA remains one of the most thoroughly researched of all dietary supplements and nutritional science has taught us that CLA helps improve body composition in three unique ways. They are as follows:

- *Discouraging the activity of lipoproteins.* Lipoproteins are protein carrier compounds that transport fat and cholesterol throughout the body. CLA helps restrict this activity, making it possible for the body to metabolize lipids before they can be deposited in cells.
- *Converting stored fat.* In order to burn fat, the body must have the right tools to increase its overall energy expenditure. CLA has been shown in a number of studies to dramatically increase the body's cellular metabolic rate, making it much more possible (and likely) to burn stored fat.
- *Preservation of lean muscle mass.* CLA only targets fat as a source of energy and will not promote muscle-related weight loss. When the body begins to burn fat as a primary source of metabolic energy, muscle tissues gradually become more physically toned and visibly defined.

THERAPEUTIC USES OF CLA

- *Improved body composition, with body-fat reduction and lean muscle mass preservation.* You may have noticed that we're not referring to CLA as a "weight-loss" supplement. This isn't by accident. As unconventional as it may sound, CLA might not help you lose weight. But that doesn't mean that it won't positively improve your body composition. On your quest to look and feel better, keep in mind that a pound of fat and a pound of muscle vary greatly in size. Many CLA users have reported dramatic changes in their appearances despite having lost just several pounds. This is easily explained by understanding CLA's unique ability to help burn fat for energy while preserving and increasing lean muscle tissue.

- *Cardiovascular health.* CLA has been shown in a number of studies to help reduce LDL cholesterol and triglycerides. Based on the role it plays in mining away at the body's reserve of stored fat, the ratio of good cholesterol to bad cholesterol can be steadily improved. When this occurs over time, there's simply less fat available to clog the heart's arterial walls.
- *Immune system support.* The number of people taking CLA to improve body composition is remarkable. Yet very few of these same people are probably aware of the antioxidant and immune system support they're gaining in the process. Like other omega-6 fatty acids, CLA also has the ability to safeguard healthy cells from the devastation that can be caused by unstable free radicals.

TIPS FOR TAKING CLA

- Keep in mind that CLA is in no way an overnight wonder pill. Many users report positive success, but this success takes time. If you're considering making CLA a part of your diet, do so with the understanding that it might take several months before you begin to see results.
- Don't be alarmed if you start to notice improved physical changes with no lost pounds to show for it. This happens for one reason; CLA preserves muscle mass and muscle weighs more than fat.
- Supplementing with CLA requires a certain amount of discipline, and it should be taken consistently at the same times throughout the day. Many experts agree that taking it 45-60 minutes prior to a meal can yield the best results.
- CLA is not typically known for giving people tremendous bursts of energy, but if you do find yourself initially restless or anxious, avoid taking it too close to bedtime.
- The most successful studies continue to suggest that 3-4 grams daily in a divided dose can be the most effective.

NATURAL COMPANIONS OF CLA ✦ Chromium, L-Carnitine, green tea.

COFACTORS AND POSSIBLE INTERACTIONS OF CLA ✦ See Table 7 in the Appendix for more information.

MILK THISTLE (SILYBUM MARIANUM)

MAJOR APPLICATION OF MILK THISTLE ✦ A complex of potent flavonoids known as *silymarin* fuels milk thistle, one of the most historically used and trusted herbs. It has become synonymous with liver health and is a key factor in the production and activity of bile, one of the body's primary digestive fluids and, ultimately, a precursor of hormones. How much bile the liver produces ultimately determines how efficient the body is in breaking down fats, eliminating toxins, and absorbing nutrients. In a nutshell, milk thistle helps keep the liver clean, nourished, and, for lack of a more technical term, unclogged.

AN OVERVIEW OF MILK THISTLE ✦ Milk thistle has been around for a very long time. Since its earliest applications to modern day, millions have used the herb's standardized extract worldwide to encourage good health and sound liver function. What's even more reassuring is that this bold claim is backed by a plethora of scientific evidence. As research intensified throughout the decades, it has become obvious that there's something very special about this prickly, purple shrub.

HOW MILK THISTLE WORKS ✦ In order to appreciate just how important milk thistle is, it's important to know a bit about the liver. Inside your abdominal cavity is a large, reddish-brown, football-shaped organ that can best be described as a metabolic filter. It spends every second of every day trying to make sense out of the often bizarre things that enter your body. This is an unceasing task that far too many of us take for granted. And that's a big mistake because, like all filters (pool owners will appreciate this), it gets clogged. When this happens, things have a tendency to go terribly wrong. Milk thistle comes to the rescue.

Therapeutic Uses of Milk Thistle

- *Alcoholism and other chemical dependency.* One of the first steps in recovering from a chemical addiction such as one to alcohol or narcotics is to completely rid the body of these toxins. Supplementing milk thistle can expedite the process by producing more of the compounds (bile and glutathione) needed to expel stores of toxins that have accumulated over the years. As these toxins are safely swept from the system, milk thistle works to replace them with fresh, healthy cells.
- *Skin disorders.* The reoccurrence of acne, blemishes, cold sores, and other skin ailments is essentially the body's way of telling you that it needs a good cleanse. One of the most important things to remember about the liver is that it must answer for every element it's subjected to. And, let's be honest, not many of us reside in a completely sterile environment, have flawless health, and consume nothing but organic foods.

  So it's important to know that as toxins collect, the liver eliminates what it can and deposits the rest throughout various cells in the body. The skin is no exception to this rule. Supplementing milk thistle is a simple way to eliminate toxins before they have the opportunity to make an appearance.
- *Digestive support.* Sluggish digestion is often the result of a liver that's being forced to work harder than it should be. A lifetime of poor dietary choices can eventually clog the liver, creating a buildup that restricts its natural flow of bile. Over time, the entire digestive process can suffer.

Milk thistle helps support healthy digestion by stimulating digestive fluid production.

- *Liver health and hepatitis.* Milk thistle is liver-friendly in many regards. One of the most significant rests in its influence on glutathionea, the tripeptide protein that helps neutralize toxins and waste. Studies have shown that milk thistle not only preserves glutathione concentrations, but also helps stimulate its production by as much as 30 percent.
- *Detoxification.* Additionally, milk thistle helps shield liver cells from toxins and other harmful agents. Over time, these toxins gradually damage the liver, making even the most basic tasks more arduous. And milk thistle encourages the regeneration of damaged liver cells, a remarkable quality that has allowed many people to take charge of metabolic health.

TIPS FOR TAKING MILK THISTLE

- Quality is of the utmost importance when shopping for milk thistle. Always go with an extract that's standardized to a minimum of 80 percent silymarin.
- Milk thistle appears to be most effective when taken on an empty stomach prior to meals.
- If you suffer from diarrhea, keep in mind that milk thistle increases bile flow. This can be a very unpleasant combination, especially if taken at inappropriate times. A little caution will spare you both discomfort and potential embarrassment.
- Always drink plenty of water when taking milk thistle supplements to stimulate the flush of toxins and chemicals.
- Taking milk thistle before a night out or social event can be very helpful to prevent that unwanted throbbing that inevitably follows the day after. Moderation is key, however.

- When detoxifying, look for a formula that contains at least 300 mg of milk thistle per serving.

NATURAL COMPANIONS FOR MILK THISTLE • Lysine, NAC, glutathione, molybdenum, soluble fiber, turmeric, acidophilus, digestive enzymes, antioxidants, essential fatty acids.

Let's be frank, when we hear the word *fiber*, most of us immediately think of constipation, bloating, and thick, gritty concoctions taken by actors in heart-warming television commercials. But make no mistake—while fiber *is* a critical part of the digestive processes, its actions extend far beyond maintaining digestive regularity. All fiber is the same, right? Not quite. There are actually two types of fiber, soluble and insoluble. Both are undigested and are therefore not absorbed through the digestive tract into the bloodstream. As a result, neither genuinely assists in energy production and both are eventually excreted from the body. Although physically similar, they function very differently within the body. This makes it important to understand which one is better for your specific biological needs.

- *Insoluble Fiber.* The first form of fiber is the one with which most Americans tend to closely identify although few of us know its namre—insoluble fiber. Insoluble fiber bulks and grinds and scurries its way throughout the digestive tract, making sure that things are "moving along" in a normal, unfettered fashion. It also keeps tabs on the pH levels of the intestines to ensure that microbes and other foreign invaders aren't taking over. Food sources of insoluble fiber include whole wheat, bran, fruits, and vegetables.
- *Soluble Fiber.* Unlike insoluble fiber, which characteristically blasts its way through the intestines, the soluble form of fiber is detail-driven. It dissolves in water and gels in the intestines and colon. As a result, soluble fiber is able to travel throughout the GI tract in a much more controlled and productive manner.

A growing number of researchers believe that this slow, unhurried passage may help control blood sugar and LDL cholesterol levels while conditioning the digestive tract along the way. This makes soluble fiber absolutely essential for anyone concerned with metabolic, cardiovascular, and digestive health. Food sources in which to find it include nuts, flax, dried legumes, carrots, apples, and bran. Psyllium seeds and husks are among the best sources of soluble fiber and can be found at most health food stores.

+ *Molybdenum.* This element has a difficult name to pronounce. Try "molly be denim" to help remember. Regardless of its funny moniker, molybdenum is required for three oxidase enzymes to function. These enzymes are involved in liver detoxification or processing of sulfites, xanthines, and sulfur amino acids. Additionally, molybdenum may be involved in stabilizing the steroid-binding capacity of glucocorticoid receptors. The latter function may be important in cortisol metabolism. Although no specific molybdenum deficiency in healthy people has been identified, the Food and Nutrition Board of the National Academy of Sciences has established a recommended daily intake (RDI) for molybdenum of 45 micrograms per day. It is included in comprehensive daily multiples.

Cofactors and Possible Interactions of Milk Thistle + See Table 8 in the Appendix for more information.

Diabetes, Type 2 (Noninsulin-Dependent Diabetes Mellitus)

Noninsulin-dependent diabetes mellitus (NIDDM), or Type 2 diabetes, is a long journey and one that begins long before symptoms appear, as as we have shown. Once you get diabetes you'll have it the rest of your life. And, make no mistake about it, this is a life-threatening condition that must be treated by a doctor.

Twenty million Americans are now thought to have diabetes, a disease that stems from either an under-production of insulin (Type 1), or from an insulin supply that's not functioning as it should (Type 2). Type 1 diabetes occurs when the pancreas becomes unable to manufacture a sufficient amount of insulin and insulin injections are needed to help control abnormal glucose levels.

People with Type 2 diabetes produce limited amounts of insulin, but the body is unable to use it properly. Approximately 30 percent of those with this type of diabetes also need insulin injections.

The remaining group does not depend on insulin and is typically diagnosed with a condition more formally known as noninsulin-dependent diabetes mellitus, or NIDDM. Instead, this group seems to be the most affected by making the right lifestyle changes. Physicians who practice complementary alternative medicine commonly recommend many of the supplements that we'll be discussing later. But before we do, a strong word of caution. If you have NIDDM, take these suggestions to your doctor. Do not, under any circumstances, attempt to treat yourself or change your medications.

> **If you have NIDDM, take these suggestions to your doctor. Do not attempt to treat yourself or change your medications.**

GYMNEMA SYLVESTRE

MAJOR APPLICATION OF GYMNEMA ✦ India's traditional practice of medicine, Ayurveda, has relied on this tropically grown vine for more than 200 years to help balance blood-sugar levels and treat diabetic conditions.

As far back as the 1920s, researchers have been studying *Gymnema sylvestre* to determine if there is a genuine link among its active components and their potentially joined caabilities to help make living with diabetes a more manageable reality.

Fast-forward 80 years. As it stands now, more and more practitioners of alternative medicine are optimistically recommending it to their glucose-sensitive patients.

An Overview of Gymnema ◆ Appropriately nicknamed "the sugar de-stroyer," gymnema leaves, when placed on the tongue or chewed, can deaden the sensation of sweetness. Accordingly, many health-conscious individuals have turned to it as a means of shutting the door on sweets, losing weight, and rediscovering a much more favorable dietary agenda. It was this simple property, however, that inspired some of the most preliminary scientific studies that took place in the early 20th century.

How Gymnema Works ◆ Based on some of the more promising studies, gymnema appears to moderately lower blood-sugar levels in people with Type 1, or insulin-dependent, diabetes. After taking the extract internally for several months, many participants in one study reported more normalized blood-sugar levels and a drastic increase in pancreatic insulin production.

Type 2, noninsulin-dependent diabetics, are, however, most likely to benefit from gymnema. Several clinical trials report that the extract was able to im-prove blood-sugar levels, making it possible to gradually reduce the amount of medication participants needed on a daily basis.

As cautioned earlier, this is by no means an invitation for diabetics to completely abandon their testing, treatment, and medications. Diabetes is a very serious disease that requires strict medical supervision. What we do know is that *Gymnema sylvestre* shows remarkable promise in managing blood sugar.

Therapeutic Uses of Gymnema

◆ *Diabetes.* This is without question one area of interest that continues to fascinate some of the world's most respected nutritional research-ers. Since the 1920s, studies ranging from small, placebo-controlled trials to full-blown university-led clinical studies have suggested that *Gymnema sylvestre* may be able to improve blood-sugar levels and the way that diabetics produce and use insulin.

- *High cholesterol.* More research is clearly needed to determine how effective it may actually be, but some researchers believe that there are clear links in the extract's ability to curb sugary snack cravings, which might be able to reduce LDL choleserol levels.
- *Weight loss.* If you're like most people, you probably have a very special place in your heart for sweets. While there's nothing at all wrong with this, excess sugar consumption is one of the worst things a person can do when trying to lose weight or maintain a lean physique. If this is your downfall, chewing gymnema leaves (or simply placing a few on your tongue) has been shown to drastically help curb the cravings.

TIPS FOR TAKING GYMNEMA

- If you're living with either Type 1 or 2 diabetes, we can't stress enough how vital it is *not* to abandon your medications or insulin. Gymnema may be able to help you manage your blood sugar and insulin, but it is by no means a "cure" for this very serious disease.
- Always look for standardized extracts that contain no less than 25 percent gymnemic acid.
- There are no clear-cut rules on when to take gymnema sylvestre, although many nutritionists recommend taking it twice daily, approximately 20-30 minutes before meals.

NATURAL COMPANIONS OF GYMNEMA • *Mormordica charantria L.,* vanadium, cinnamon, pantetheine, *Stevia rebaudiana,* Fenugreek (*Trigonella foenum-graecum*)

- *Mormordica charantria L. (bitter melon or gourd).* Bitter melon can be found in the Asian produce sections of many supermarkets because it has long been a popular culinary and digestive aid among Chinese and eastern Indian people. The fruit is light green, about six inches long, with tapered ends and deep, longitudinal grooves. It is served as a vegetable and spice to stimulate the appetite.

Unripe fruits have been prepared for medicinal purposes dating back to 1,000 B.C. Chief among them is its use as an anti-diabetic agent since bitter melon has been shown to lower blood glucose levels in humans and animals and has been reported to influence insulin's efficiency and to support general well being. Bitter melon is often added to formulas for *metabolic syndrome*, but it's seldom found as a standalone supplement.

• **Cinnamon.** This historically cherished Asian spice is better for you than you might imagine. In fact a wealth of research has been conducted over the years and findings are very promising. For openers, science has taught us that cinnamon is a wonderful digestive aid. And its oils and extracts contain a number of natural compounds that have been shown to help stimulate the digestive process, making it beneficial for those occasional and uncomfortable bouts with constipation.

Cinnamon also has strong antifungal, antiparasitic, and antibacterial properties. Based on these unique qualities, many have used it successfully to combat *Candida albicans*, the fungus responsible for yeast infections. It's also proven its worth in countering *Helicobacter pylori* (*h. pylori*), a common stomach lining bacteria that's been liked to the development of peptic ulcers.

Additionally, cinnamon has piqued the interest of many researchers with regard to the role it seems to play in controlling blood-sugar levels. This has made it of keen interest to the diabetic community, not to mention anyone concerned with keeping blood-sugar levels within the healthy, normal range. This was evidenced by a 2003 double-blind, placebo-controlled study that evaluated the blood lipid changes of 60 people for 6 weeks. The results were nothing short of remarkable. On average, blood-sugar levels improved by 18-29 percent, LDL cholesterol levels improved by as much as 27 percent, and triglyceride levels dropped as much as 30 percent.

- *Vanadium.* An essential role for vanadium in human nutrition has not been established, but numerous biochemical and physiological uses have been suggested, primarily its ability to mimic insulin. It is thought that vanadium assists the glucose transport into the cell and may have a stimulating effect on insulin release in the pancreas. That property may make it a useful adjunct in treating diabetes. Vanadium attaches to enzymes and presumably activates them in a manner similar to that seen with chromium, copper, iron, iodine, sulfur amino acids, and zinc. It has been proposed that vanadium has stimulatory effects on cell growth and differentiation, transfer of phosphorus in cellular energy reactions, and is a co-factor in hormone, lipid, glucose, bone, and tooth metabolism. Vanadium appears to interact with iodine and may be important in moderating the action of thyroid hormones, particularly in stress-induced, subnormal thyroid conditions.

  Mushrooms, parsley, dill seed, black pepper, seafood, cereals, and liver are the best sources of vanadium. The Food and Nutrition Board of the National Academy of Science reports average intakes from food to be 6.5-11 micrograms per day. The upper limit for total vanadium intake has been established at 1.8 milligrams per day. (One milligram is equal to 1,000 micrograms.) Vanadium supplements can be difficult to retain in the body. A new amino acid-chelated form called bis-glycinato oxovanadium (BGOV) is better retained than inorganic forms such as vanadyl or vanadate. Natural partners for vanadium include vitamin C, chromium, iodine, riboflavin, pantethine, sulfur amino acids, and protein.

- *Pantethine.* This coenzyme form of pantothenic acid is an important addition to supplement programs in *metabolic syndrome* primarily because of its ability to lower triglycerides. In those with microvascular constriction—including diabetics—pantethine's well-documented benefits on lipid metabolism may help prevent oxidation of fatty acids and narrowing of microvascular walls in the brain and extremities. Much more on pantethine will be found in the *cardiovascular syndrome*, the topic of our next chapter.

Hypoglycemia

PROTEIN POWDER

MAJOR APPLICATION OF PROTEIN POWDER ✦ We're fascinated by how many people still regard protein as some sort of "power" supplement, appropriate only for bodybuilders and serious athletes. While it is true that athletes who train on a regular basis do require it to repair muscle tissues, there's much more to protein supplementation than just muscles and mass. In fact, protein is one of the most essential of all supernutrients, and works throughout the body to ensure that many of our most basic biological requirements are being met. For those who live with hypoglycemia, getting ample amounts of quality protein is of especially great importance.

AN OVERVIEW OF PROTEIN POWDER ✦ Once ingested, protein is at the mercy of the body's metabolism. Ideally, the protein from diet and supplementation is broken down to provide the body with amino acids and other compounds. In addition to tissue repair, these vital chemical building blocks are responsible for producing many of the neurotransmitters, enzymes, and hormones needed for day-to-day function. Depriving the body of protein is the metabolic equivalent of spooning cement into a blender—things just have a way of "slowing down." This is especially true in the case of hypoglycemia or, for that matter, any low blood glucose (sugar) levels.

HOW PROTEIN POWDER WORKS ✦ The metabolic process is governed by a number of chemical components, one of which is blood glucose. Hypoglycemia is a condition in which the body exhibits abnormally low levels of glucose, making it very difficult to spark some basic metabolic actions, including normal protein absorption. For this reason protein consumption is something that those with hypoglycemia must monitor closely.

Fortunately, it's not that difficult to find protein these days. Determining which one to take, however, can be a daunting task as there are literally hundreds to choose from. For people living with hypoglycemia, we recommend a high-quality whey protein. Whey is easy on the stomach and contains an impressive profile of amino acids and other essential nutrients in addition to being easily and rapidly absorbed.

THERAPEUTIC USES OF PROTEIN POWDER

- *Hypoglycemia.* Protein intake is of dire importance to individuals living with hypoglycemia because it helps produce many of the chemicals needed for some of the body's more fundamental functions. Supplementing a quality whey protein is one of the best ways to ensure that the body is well nourished and using glucose in an effective, normalized manner. It can also motivate the body to use insulin more effectively and help prevent glucose levels from crashing after a meal in the way that many simple carbohydrates tend to cause.

- *Healthy metabolism.* Depriving the body of protein is arguably one of the worst things you can to for your metabolism! It's also one of the best arguments for never skipping meals, especially those high in protein. Here's a simple way to look at it. Your metabolism is like a team that relies on protein to produce many of the chemical "coaches" needed to get the job done. When the coach doesn't show up, the team slacks, panics, and fails to perform. The same is true of protein. When the body doesn't have the protein it needs to create the essentials of metabolism, it compromises by using muscle tissue. Not only does this rob the body of strength and tone, it also increases the ratio of fat to muscle to a level that can be dangerously unhealthy.

- *Fatigue.* A body that lacks protein will inevitably become a body that lacks energy. There's just no clever way around it. This happens gradually, eventually becoming a part of everyday life that many simply chalk up to "getting old." Not true. Many of the chemical and hormonal compounds supported by protein's presence help provide energy for functional metabolism. When they're not there, neither is the vigorous payoff. And when you consider how much of the body's energy reserve is inspired by metabolism, it simply doesn't make sense not to provide it with the protein it needs.

- *Tissue repair.* We could easily dedicate an entire chapter to repairing muscle tissue, but let's just say that protein is vital to healthy tissues. During strenuous physical activity muscle tissues, along with other structural tissues, are broken down. The amino acids in protein are essential in repairing these tissues. This is where the term "building block" begins to make the most sense. But make no mistake—strenuous activity extends far beyond the walls of health clubs and gyms. Carrying groceries, picking up your children, opening a heavy door, and thousands of other activities fall into this category. If you're not meeting your daily protein requirements, you're gradually leading your body down a path of metabolic confusion.

- *Immune system support.* Aside from its high concentration of amino acids and low sugar and carbohydrates, one of the biggest perks of supplementing whey protein is the effect that it seems to have on the body's ability to produce and utilize *glutathione.* This ultra-important antioxidant is actually a combination of glutamate, glycine, and cysteine, and is vastly important for people with low blood-sugar levels, such as those inherent to hypoglycemia.

Tips for Taking Protein Powder

- People with hypoglycemia and other metabolic challenges stand to benefit greatly by supplementing protein intake with glutamine, a nonessential amino acid that helps prevent muscle tissues from "wasting."

- The body is in a constant search for protein. Supplementing small to moderate amounts throughout the day is a great way to keep nitrogen balance positive.
- Never forget that the digestive system can only process so much protein at a time. To prevent waste, try to limit your protein intake to no more that 25-30 grams per serving.
- If you've grown accustomed to skipping breakfast, a protein shake in the morning is an outstanding way to fire up your metabolism while keeping well nourished in the process.
- Look for a quality formula that contains a high ratio of protein to carbohydrates.
- Many protein formulas contain sweeteners. Read the labels carefully to ensure that yours is either unsweetened, or sweetened with one that's suitable for your specific needs.

Natural Companions for Protein Powder

- *Glutamine.* This nonessential amino acid is extremely important for those living with hypoglycemia. Aside from the role it plays in preventing many common catabolic reactions within the body, glutamine can also be converted to glucose when blood-sugar levels begin to drop at a pace that the body cannot contend with. While even the healthiest people rely on ample reserves of glutamine, hypoglycemics stand to benefit greatly from supplementing it in their everyday diets. Doing so may ultimately result in more balanced blood-sugar levels, less tissue wasting, more energy, and a host of other benefits.
- *ZMA.* This patented combination of zinc and magnesium has established itself as one of the best all-around supplements for anyone who lives with low blood sugar. Here's why.

  Magnesium is a mineral that plays a number of biological roles within the body, one of which happens to be glucose metabolism. When the body loses its ability to effectively use glucose, the effects and conditions of hypoglycemia can become even more threatening to the metabolic system. Magnesium has also been shown to help protect vulnerable organs such as the eyes from the damage caused by Type 2 diabetes.

Part two of the ZMA equation is zinc, an equally important mineral that helps the pancreas synthesize, regulate, and properly store the body's insulin supply. Zinc has been shown to help support healthy glucose metabolism, an area of key concern to those living with low or compromised blood-sugar levels.

Individually, both magnesium and zinc contribute greatly to the unique nutritional requirements of hypoglycemics. When combined they work synergistically to help each other carry out metabolic tasks in what appears to be a much more effective manner.

+ *Stevia.* Stevia isn't a dietary supplement per se, but rather a natural extract from the leaves of *Stevia Rebaudiana* plants native to South America. It is incredibly sweet, has a very low glycemic index rating, won't cause cavities, and has next to no calories. When added to beverages, desserts, and in other applications that call for sugar, stevia serves as one of the smartest alternatives available. Today more and more health food stores carry a diverse selection of stevia products, including liquid extracts and pure powders.

COFACTORS AND CONTRAINDICATIONS FOR PROTEIN POWDER + See Table 6 in the Appendix for more information.

To Sum It All Up

How the Metabolic Syndrome Leads to Other Syndromes

Metabolic syndrome stems from chronic stress and stress-induced obesity and encompasses several risk factors for other syndromes. These factors increase the risk for diabetes and cardiovascular disease, yet they can be modified through dietary change, exercise, and supplement use. *Metabolic syndrome* in adolescents is of particular concern.

Adolescents and Hormone Imbalances

The *metabolic syndrome* begins to develop during adolescence. In a large study conducted at two European centers, 9- and 10-year-old girls were followed for 10 years. Only one 10-year-old girl had three of the qualifying risk factors for *metabolic syndrome* present at the beginning of the study. Yet by ages 19 and 20, 3 percent of the girls showed at least three of its qualifying criteria.

This means that the *metabolic syndrome* may have a devastating effect on hormone balance and bone growth and that it might be wise to screen overweight young girls with severe PMS for it. Peak bone density is developed during the adolescent years and a poor diet, along with *metabolic syndrome*, could well have a negative effect on bone metabolism, thus increasing later risk of bone-thinning and hip fracture.

Obese adolescent boys and young men with metabolic syndrome may have a future poorer outcome if ultimately diagnosed with prostate cancer. Swedish scientists found that among 320 men with prostate cancer, those with *metabolic syndrome* were more likely to die. They further proposed that irregularities in insulin metabolism might serve as useful markers for prognosis and tumor aggressiveness among men with prostate cancer.

The Metabolic Syndrome and Cardiovascular Disease

Anomalies associated with *metabolic syndrome*, but not listed among the qualifying criteria, help create a more complete individual profile. Tiny sub-fractions of LDL cholesterol are particularly dangerous because they contribute to arterial blockage. Irregularities in blood clotting factors and high uric acid and homocysteine levels are also important markers. Apolipoprotein B-100 (Apo-B100) is a type of protein that attaches to very low-density lipoprotein (VLDL) and is associated with atherogenesis, or plaque buildup, in blood vessels. High levels of Apo-B100 are often found in those with *metabolic syndrome*. Blood vessel abnormalities coupled with low antioxidant levels are also common. All of these factors represent a heightened risk for cardiovascular disease. They also place special emphasis on the need for us to adopt colorful diets and add full spectrum antioxidant formulas to our daily nutritional regimens.

Now it's time to progress to the *cardiovascular syndrome* and see how *metabolic syndrome* risk factors might be expressed.

CHAPTER FOUR

Cardiovascular Syndrome

MOST OF US TAKE our hearts for granted, assuming that they'll continue their steady, reliable beating of 72-80 beats per minute. Over each of our lifetimes, our hearts will beat about three billion times, increasing the number of beats per minute during aerobic exercise or times of stress. Achieving the desired increase in heart rate is, in fact, the goal of cardio-training and can also help doctors detect abnormalities during stress testing. It takes years before telltale signs that the heart is in trouble first appear—signs that warn of heading down a dangerous path. But, if we heed these early signals, we can determine the direction our heart-health will take.

High blood pressure is often the first sign of trouble, but high levels of total cholesterol and LDL cholesterol, and low HDL cholesterol levels are also early warning signs. The ratio between LDL and HDL cholesterol is also important because HDL indicates cholesterol is being cleared from the body, while LDL represents a possible buildup of fat in arteries. These symptoms usually show up during routine physicals and are treated with lifestyle modification, weight-loss regimens, and medication—if the numbers are seriously off-base. Yet, as you read in Chapter Three, these symptoms represent just part of the total picture of metabolic imbalance that leads to cardiovascular

Blood Pressure	Boost HDL Cholesterol
1. Engage in moderate physical activity.	1. Engage in aerobic exercise at least 30 minutes most days of the week.
2. Maintain normal body weight.	
3. Limit alcohol consumption.	
4. Reduce sodium intake.	2. Moderate-fat diet with primarily mono- and polyunsaturated fats (olive oil, fish). Avoid trans fats (processed foods, snacks).
5. Maintain adequate intake of potassium.	
6. Limit cholesterol intake to 300 mg/day or less.	
7. Eat lots of fruit, vegetables, whole grains, oats.	
	3. Reduce intake of high glycemic foods.
	4. Moderate alcohol intake, 1-2 drinks/day. If you don't drink, don't start.
	5. Discuss other options with your doctor if your HDL is below 50 mg/dl.

FIGURE 4-1 **What You Can Do**

disease. It's up to you to work with your doctor to determine if other risk factors are present.

Risk factors for *metabolic syndrome*, including obesity, altered glucose metabolism, high waist-to-hip ratio, low ratio of lean body mass-to-fat, and body mass index should all be assessed. Other tests that are important for gauging cardiovascular risk are serum levels of triglycerides, homocysteine, Angiotensin II if blood pressure is high, and C-reactive protein or CRP levels. The latter test is a nonspecific measure of inflammation and, according to recent research, is the most revealing test, with cholesterol profiles, to detect early atherogenesis, particularly in women.

Cardiovascular — a Man's Disease?

Cardiovascular disease (CVD) is still considered by many to be primarily a man's problem and is often overlooked in women. Yet an equal number of women are afflictedand they are more likely to die from it, particularly if they have diabetes, which significantly increases the risk of dying after an acute myocardial infarction (MI). Moreover, as compared to men, women display a different set of symptoms that precede a MI. In a recent study of 512 women, 70 percent experienced unusual fatigue, sleep disturbances (47.8 percent), and shortness of breath (42.1 percent) at least one month before a heart attack. Very few women reported chest pain, the primary symptom when men have heart attacks. Furthermore, the more severe the preheart attack symptoms were in women, the more severe the heart attacks that followed.

Mortality from CVD is the leading cause of death in industrialized nations and the second leading cause of death worldwide. It's expected that by the year 2020, CVD will be responsible for 36 percent of all deaths in the U.S. and the leading cause of death in the world.

The good news is that early stage risk factors for CVD, such as elevated blood pressure and cholesterol level, are modifiable in both men and women by changing diet, exercising, and using certain dietary supplements. Figure 4-1 summarizes what heart experts advise their patients.

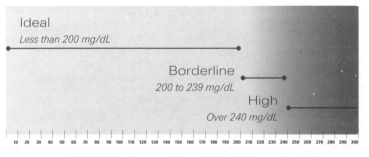

FIGURE 4-2 **Total Cholesterol Level Guidelines**

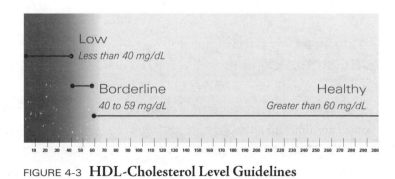

FIGURE 4-3 **HDL-Cholesterol Level Guidelines**

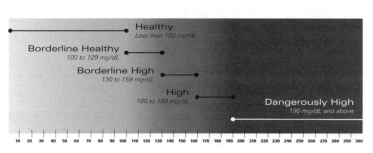

FIGURE 4-4 **LDL-Cholesterol Level Guidelines**

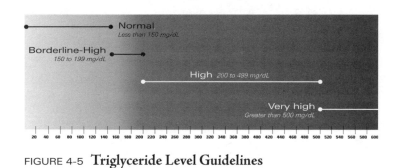

FIGURE 4-5 **Triglyceride Level Guidelines**

Atherosclerotic plaque buildup, the first stage of CVD, can begin during the teen years. This makes it extremely important to begin risk assessment and preventive measures in younger Americans.

What You Will Find in This Chapter

This chapter is a little different from others in this book because the recommendations are arranged in a hierarchal order. The various steps group related risk factors that make up the cardiovascular syndrome.

+ Step One: Managing blood lipids
+ Step Two: Inflammation and artery protection
+ Step Three: Homocysteine regulators
+ Step Four: Heart energetics
+ Step Five: Peripheral veins and restless legs

Step One: Managing Blood Lipids

Abnormality in blood lipids is a significant marker for metabolic syndrome, as you read in Chapter Three. These deviations in lipid metabolism are the primary links between the metabolic and cardiovascular syndromes. Consequently, stage one includes supplements that are effective for managing blood lipids.

POLICOSANOL

MAJOR APPLICATION OF POLICOSANOL ✦ High cholesterol is big business these days. Each year more than 30 million American consumers spend billions of dollars on prescription drugs with the high hope of lowering life-threatening LDL cholesterol levels. What many of these collective big spenders don't know is that the effect of a simple, waxy extract from sugar cane and certain vegetables continues to leave some of the world's best researchers speechless. Since its discovery in the 1990s, a completely natural substance called policosanol has been giving some of the most popular cholesterol-lowering medications a close run for the money.

AN OVERVIEW OF POLICOSANOL ✦ As mentioned, policosanol is a waxy, natural extract made up of eight unique and unusually long-chain fatty alcohols including octacosanol, the primary active component. It was initially believed that these extracts could be obtained only from sugar cane. But as interest grew, research intensified, and it is now well accepted that the same grade of policosanol extracts can be found in beeswax and certain vegetables. Today it's not uncommon to hear cholesterol-centric success stories from people who have watched their LDL levels drop by close to 30 percent in a matter of weeks after using beeswax and other vegetable forms.

It gets better. One of the biggest concerns with statin drugs is the enormous strain they can place on the liver. This is well documented and, if you listen closely to the commercials touting them, you'll almost always hear the phrase, "may complicate liver function," or "please notify your doctor if you have a history of liver problems" as part of the advertisement. This is not the case with policosanol extracts. Not only is policosanol absolutely free of any potential liver complications, but some studies have determined that it can reduce levels of two liver enzymes, CPK (*creatine phosphokinase*) and AST (*aspartate aminotransaminase*). When these two enzymes are out of normal range, it can spell trouble. Since policosanol appears able to modify that problem, it may actually improve liver function.

How Policosanol Works ✦ A surprising number of studies, given the recent discovery of policosanol, have suggested that it can be very effective in supporting the cardiovascular system by several methods. First, it's been shown to significantly decrease the amount of LDL cholesterol in the blood while simultaneously increasing the ratio of HDL-to-LDL. According to a number of these studies, policosanol decreases the amount of cholesterol manufactured in the liver. This is a significant finding because low cholesterol diets don't address the problem of cholesterol overproduction. Moreover, policosanol works in a different way than statin drugs do to reduce cholesterol production in the liver.

Policosanol prevents oxidation of LDL cholesterol which, as we have seen, is a necessary step to atherosclerosis. It also reduces excess buildup of smooth muscle in artery walls, which prevents narrowing of the artery. Policosanol was more effective in this action than the drug Lovastatin® when tested. It reduces platelet adhesion (stickiness) and thus helps prevent clotting.

Research has also suggested that the substances in policosanol can have a positive impact on triglyceride counts. This was evidenced by a 2002 study that pitted policosanol against one of the leading prescription statin drugs. After eight weeks of treatment, both groups (prescription users and poli-cosanol users) equally reported a 15 percent decrease in total triglycerides. This is incredibly good news when you consider that some statins can cost as much as $150 per month versus approximately $20 per month for the natural, completely side effect–free alternative.

- *Cardiovascular support and cholesterol management.* Policosanol encourages healthy cardiovascular function by using the unique properties of pure wax extracts from such plant sources as carnuba, candilla, and rice bran. Naturally rich in triacontanol, octacosanol, and hexacosanol (three long-chain fatty acids), policosanol has been proven in several studies to raise HDL cholesterol while reducing LDL cholesterol. It has also demonstrated significant anti-oxidant protection of lipids and prevents their attachment to artery walls.

TIPS FOR TAKING POLICOSANOL

- Despite how safe policosanol has been shown to be, anyone currently taking statin medications or coagulants for blood thinning should consult a physician about using policosanol supplements.
- Women who are pregnant or nursing should not take policosanol.
- To avoid any potential nausea or upset stomach we recommend taking policosanol supplements with a light, balanced meal, preferably in the morning.

NATURAL COMPANIONS FOR POLICOSANOL ◆ CoQ$_{10}$, hawthorn, omega-3 essential fatty acids, TMG, natural vitamin E and selenium.

COFACTORS AND CONTRAINDICATIONS FOR POLICOSANOL ◆ See Table 7 in the Appendix for more information.

PANTETHINE

MAJOR APPLICATION OF PANTETHINE ◆ In order for the body to effectively produce peptides, enzymes, and other chemicals needed to metabolize fat, carbohydrates, and amino acids from the diet it must have the right mesh of co-factors. One of the most vital is pantothenic acid, or vitamin B-5. Pantethine, a biologically active form of pantothenic acid, is an important precursor to coenzyme-A and prerequisite to a long list of metabolic and chemical reactions.

AN OVERVIEW OF PANTETHINE ♦ Pantethine's biological to-do list is in no way limited to metabolism oversight. Aside from the role it plays in the helping the body determine what to do with everything it consumes, it's also involved in the production of enzymes, hormones, and chemical messengers known as neurotransmitters. When the body is deprived of this multi-tasking compound, a chain reaction takes place that can cause stress to the entire system. Ultimately, this can result in fatigue, increased LDL cholesterol and triglycerides, digestive challenges, and a host of other problems.

HOW PANTETHINE WORKS ♦ Once absorbed by the body, Pantethine's first order of business is to help it produce coenzyme A, a biochemical metabolite that helps metabolize (burn) fat within the muscles and a number of other cells. This is accomplished (ideally) when the body's reserve of pantothenic acid, or B-5, teams up with another important metabolic co-factor, adenosine triphosphate (ATP).

Unfortunately, the body doesn't always have access to the amount of pantethine it needs to make this happen. Remember, pantethine is involved in much more than just the metabolic process. Other systems rely on it, too, and when supplies run short something is bound to suffer. As time passes, this can result in high triglyceride counts, insulin resistance, dangerously unhealthy LDL cholesterol levels, mental cloudiness, poor circulation, and a steady decline in metabolic integrity.

THERAPEUTIC USES OF PANTETHINE

+ *Cardiovascular health.* Researchers continue to be fascinated with pantethine's influence on the overall integrity of the human cardio-vascular system. Although it's still not crystal-clear why, a growing number of studies indicate that it seems to help not only prevent but reduce plaque build-up within the arterial walls, a serious medical condition known as *atherolosclerosis.* Over time, clogged arteries make it increasingly difficult for the heart to circulate blood throughout the body. If left unattended, this can have a dangerous impact on many basic daily functions.

+ *High cholesterol and triglycerides.* Maintaining healthy cholesterol and triglyceride levels isn't just smart, it's literally a matter of life or death. Pantethine has been shown in a number of studies to help improve blood lipid levels when taken by those who enjoy a healthy lifestyle. If you haven't already done so, try to get in the habit of having your cholesterol and triglycerides checked at least twice annually. Figures 4-2 through 4-5 list healthy and not-so-healthy blood lipid levels.

+ *Insulin resistance.* An equally important characteristic of pantethine is its ability to contain triglyceride levels, a common characteristic in those with metabolic syndrome. Triglycerides are a kind of lipid (fat) that is carried throughout the bloodstream in protein "carts" known as lipoproteins. They're typically stored and used for energy when needed. Consequently, too many of us are carrying around more stored fat than we'd like to admit and, as a result, our bodies become less and less responsive to insulin.

TIPS FOR TAKING PANTETHINE
+ For optimal results, pantethine should be taken as part of a healthy lifestyle that includes a well balanced diet, cardiovascular exercise, and plenty of rest each night.
+ Look for products that use Pantesin®, as studies have shown it may be more effective than other forms of pantethine.
+ Have your cholesterol and triglycerides checked at least once every six months.

NATURAL COMPANIONS FOR PANTETHINE + CoQ$_{10}$, red yeast rice, natural vitamin E, and B-vitamins

COFACTORS AND CONTRAINDICATIONS FOR PANTETHINE + See Table 4 in the Appendix for more information.

GARLIC (ALLIUM SATIVUM)

MAJOR APPLICATION OF GARLIC ✦ As perhaps the most medicinally recognized member of the lily (*Liliaceae*) family, garlic continues to be one of the most popular ways to promote cardiovascular health by reducing various risk factors. High alliin concentration within the plant's pungent bulb is responsible for all of garlic's health-promoting actions. Crushing, chewing, slicing, or grinding the bulb releases an enzyme that transforms alliin into a potent chemical called *allicin*. It is the allicin from garlic that has made it such a favorite among the heart-conscious, and in kitchens worldwide. Allicin is further transformed into a number of biologically active components including ajoenes, various sulfides, and scordinin. You will sometimes see these specified on garlic supplement labels.

AN OVERVIEW ✦ Simply saying that garlic is versatile is a gross understatement. Unlike many supplements that specifically target one region or system of the body, garlic's healing portfolio is one of the most impressive. It also has a rich history that has been traced back to biblical times.

Today garlic is used by millions to improve cardiovascular health, prevent stroke, lower blood pressure, manage cholesterol, and to fight infection, among other uses. In light of its ability to successfully target so many common health concerns, garlic's true claim to fame centers on the role it plays in supporting a healthy heart and blood vessels.

HOW GARLIC WORKS ✦ Based on the mountains of research that continue to investigate garlic's role in human health, it's become clear that this odiferous extract has a special fondness for the heart. Allicin chemicals have been shown to stop blood platelets from becoming sticky and clogging within the arterial walls of the cardiovascular system. Additional support is provided by *ajoene*, a natural derivative of allicin, that can be very effective in breaking up clots that may eventually lead to arterial plaque. Over time, atherosclerosis can make it dangerously difficult to pump adequate amounts of blood throughout the body.

Garlic also seems to have an influence on how effectively the liver metabolizes cholesterol. A number of clinical studies have shown that several of the active components in garlic (allicin and ajoene) may be able to discourage the liver from metabolizing cholesterol into forms which are released into the bloodstream. This can ultimately result in lower levels of LDL cholesterol and triglyceride. While there's still much to learn about the potential cholesterol-lowering effects, we believe that garlic may be helpful, especially when taken with supplements such as CoQ_{10}, red yeast rice, niacin and policosanol.

Some recent studies suggest that garlic may be able to increase the flexibility of the heart's aorta, the primary organ responsible for carrying blood from the heart to the rest of the body. As we age, this hard-working organ has a natural tendency to harden, making it much more difficult for the heart to return to a normal resting state after each beat. Garlic has also been shown to protect artery walls from oxidation.

THERAPEUTIC USES OF GARLIC

- *Infections.* The active chemical components in garlic have unusually strong antiseptic, antiviral, and antifungal properties and have been used for thousands of years to help fight a number of microbial ailments. Many of today's most common viruses require specialized enzymes before they have the opportunity to set up camp in the body's healthy cells. Some smaller studies have shown that the allicin in garlic may prevent the production of these enzymes, making it difficult for viruses and other infectious agents to run rampant throughout the body.

- *Cancer prevention.* In addition to being a wonderful supplement for the cardiovascular system, garlic has also been touted as a potential cancer preventative. This is based on its naturally occurring antioxidant and diverse nutrient profile, which includes vitamin C, trace amounts of vitamins A and E, bioflavonoids, calcium, phosphorus, potassium, magnesium, zinc, manganese, selenium, germanium, and most other trace minerals. These powerful antioxidants and nutrients help protect healthy cells from free radical damage and support all metabolic processes, including normal growth and differentiation.

- *Wart removal.* Okay, so warts don't quite make the list of life-threatening conditions. But there's no denying that they can be bothersome, embarrassing, and just plain ugly. When garlic is taken internally, there's not much hope that a wart will disappear. However, many people swear by garlic's ability to help remove them quickly when used as a topical press or wrap.

  For topical applications, make a tincture of garlic from allicin or slice off a thin section of the bulb. Before going to bed, apply either to the affected area and wrap it with a breathable gauze or cloth. You can add a drop of tea tree oil to help expedite the healing process.

Tips for taking Garlic

- Garlic supplementation is notorious for causing bad breath, and can be extracted through the sweat glands as well. Some companies offer enteric-coated capsules to help reduce the odor.
- Contrary to popular belief, garlic does not work to dispel vampires. However, taking garlic before spending time outdoors is an outstanding way to keep those pesky mosquitoes from getting too close.
- Garlic is a natural companion to many other supplements and has strong synergistic properties.
- Do not take garlic before surgery as it may interfere with normal clotting.
- Garlic should be taken throughout the day in divided doses for optimal effects.

Garlic.

* If you currently use medication to treat high blood pressure, depression, high blood sugar, or clots, consult your physician before supplementing with garlic.

NATURAL COMPANIONS FOR GARLIC • Hawthorn berries, cayenne, CoQ$_{10}$, selenium, vitamin E, and probiotics such as acidophilus and bifidobacteria.

COFACTORS AND CONTRAINDICATIONS FOR GARLIC • See Table 8 in the Appendix for more information.

Step Two: Inflammation and Protecting Arteries

For many years physicians considered cardiovascular disease to be primarily a plumbing problem. In atherosclerosis, fat-laden gunk gradually builds up inside arterial walls and impedes blood flow. Combined with reduced elasticity in vessel walls and clot formation, tissues robbed of blood eventually die. When cardiac muscle or the brain is involved, a heart attack or stroke occurs. However, new evidence has shown that only about 15 percent of heart attacks occur this way. It's now recognized that the cells making up arterial walls are involved in an inflammatory process in which our own immune cells bombard us with friendly fire.

In the first stage of inflammation, white blood cells, sensing that a bacterial attack is underway, reconnoiter at the threatened site. They secrete an array of chemicals, including oxidants, and signal molecules called cytokines whose intent is to limit infection. Excess LDL cholesterol passing by in the bloodstream sticks to arterial walls, and the destructive process begins. The fatty and protein layers of LDL are readily oxidized and the proteins also attract glucose molecules to form glycation end-products. These destructive molecules were described in Chapter Three.

Next, the vessel walls secrete adhesion molecules that latch on to passing inflammatory cells, called monocytes. These cells stick tightly to artery walls and signal additional inflammatory cells to gather. Meanwhile, the monocytes are transformed into larger immune fighters, known as macrophages, and they begin gobbling up LDL particles. They become so engorged with fat that they appear bubbly and are aptly named "foam cells."

T-cells, another type of immune cell, now arrive and begin penetrating the arterial wall to fight the infection that now includes engorged foam cells and inflammatory agents. A fatty streak in the vessel wall is formed as the earliest form of atherosclerotic plaque. The vessel then builds a fibrous wall to encase the infection and prevent further damage. Meanwhile, foam cells are going about their business secreting a tissue factor that weakens the protective wall. Eventually the plaque ruptures and spews dead cells and inflammatory mediators into the vessel, among them clot-inducing chemicals. This mess releases clot-forming elements in the blood and a clot is formed. Large clots block blood flow to the tissue the vessel is feeding. Smaller clots may cause transitory in ischemic events (TIAs) that resolve spontaneously.

Factors that Contribute to Inflammation

Although the process just described is one way in which inflammation occurs, there are other conditions that promote it. Angiotensin II, a hormone partly involved in hypertension, incites inflammation. Obesity and diabetes both contribute to inflammation, as noted previously. Smoking has long been associated with risk of CVD, in part because it hastens oxidation of LDL. HDL cholesterol offsets the oxidation of LDL by transporting antioxidants to fight free radicals. These factors all contribute to atherogenesis, but infections are also involved.

Infection and Atherosclerosis

Herpes viruses and the bacterium *Chlamydia pneumoniae*, a frequent cause of respiratory infections, are two potential contributors to atherosclerosis. Streptococcus group A bacteria, the cause of acute rheumatic fever, has been associated with cardiovascular disease since 1976. It may take years for CVD to develop after initial infection. Other agents that have been implicated are

Helicobacter pylori, involved in stomach ulcers, and *Cytomegalovirus* (CMV) and *Coxsackievirus* (CV), which cross-react with cardiac muscle proteins and institute structure changes.

Periodontal disease harbors bacteria such as *Porphyromonas gingivalis* that invade gingival tissues and cells in the aorta, the great vessel that carries oxygen-rich blood from the heart. Since more than half the adult American population displays some sign of gingival disease and 70 percent have periodontitis (inflamed gingival tissues), the chance of systemic infection from oral bacteria is significant. Evidence includes finding immune proteins against periodontal bacteria in the blood of those who had heart attacks or died from cardiovascular disease. Periodontal bacteria have also been found in atheromatous plaques. Furthermore, periodontal disease and its toxic by-products may contribute to autoimmune and joint diseases. We will discuss periodontal disease as part of the *osteo syndrome* in Chapter Eight.

Macrophages can ingest infectious agents and transport them through the bloodstream to the site of plaque buildup. As the macrophage burrows into the arterial wall, it transfers the infectious agent into neighboring arterial cells and, as the infection spreads, attracts its own cascade of immune mediators.

Supplements for Inflammation

We begin our discussion of anti-inflammatory supplements for CVD with a supplement that lowers cholesterol and also tames inflammation. It is especially appropritate for those who have elevated cholesterol *and* inflammation.

RED YEAST RICE

MAJOR APPLICATION OF RED YEAST RICE ♦ This popular and somewhat maligned extract is produced when red Chinese yeast (*Monascus purpureus*) is fermented over rice. The herb has a long history of use in Traditional Chinese Medicine (TCM) to promote blood circulation. It was also used as a dietary staple to make rice wine and as a food coloring and flavoring agent for fish and meat. Today red yeast rice, also known as cholestin, is immensely popular among heart-conscious people concerned with improving cholesterol and triglyceride levels.

An Overview of Red Yeast Rice ✦ There's no shortage of drama when discussing the history of this supernutrient, also known as *cholestin*. At about the same time that Americans were discovering the potential benefits of this statin-like natural compound, some of the nation's top drug manufacturers were doing everything in their power to prevent supplement manufacturers from selling it. That makes sense when you consider that *mevinolin*, one of the active components (monacolins) in red yeast rice, was developed and patented as Mevacor® by a major pharmaceutical company. However, as a natural extract, red yeast rice contains other active ingredients, including a family of nine monacolins, plant sterols, isoflavones, and monounsaturated fatty acids. The action of monacolins is virtually identical to the cholesterol-lowering statins in many of today's most popular and pricey prescription drugs, but it isn't clear if the family of components in red yeast rice is possibly responsible for its lipid-lowering and anti-inflammatory effects. After a long court discussion, it was eventually decided that red yeast rice could be sold as a dietary supplement and it is currently available at most independent health food stores.

How Red Yeast Rice Works ✦ Some of the most encouraging studies indicate that the active compounds in red yeast rice seem to prevent the liver from producing cholesterol in addition to helping manage triglyceride levels. This can have a snowball effect on the cardiovascular system over time, as high cholesterol and triglycerides often serve as gateways to many forms of heart disease. As the body gradually loses the ability to manufacture cholesterol, blood lipid levels may be able to improve to a more normal range over time. Anti-inflammatory action has been demonstrated with red yeast rice, as well, and this is important to reduce fatty streaks and help prevent arterial damage.

- The extract's active compounds function in the liver in somewhat the same way as most prescription statins. Consequently, those currently using prescription statins to treat high cholesterol should not use red yeast rice until first consulting with their physicians.
- To avoid any unwanted stomach discomforts red yeast rice should be taken with a full meal and plenty of liquids.
- Children, women who are pregnant or nursing, those with liver disease, and those who have recently scheduled or undergone surgery should NOT take red yeast rice.
- When using red yeast rice make a conscious effort to limit consumption of alcoholic and highly acidic beverages as they may interfere with the activity of the extract's compounds.
- Despite its safe history, there is limited research on the long-term effects associated with red yeast rice supplementation. For this reason, many experts agree that its use should be limited to short-term cycles.

Natural Companions for Red Yeast Rice ✦ Red yeast rice has a natural synergistic effect with a number of antioxidants and supplements. Some worth considering are CoQ_{10}, alpha lipoic acid, natural vitamin E, milk thistle, niacin (B-3), and omega-3 fatty acids.

Cofactors and Contraindications for Red Yeast Rice ✦ See Table 7 in the Appendix for more information.

OMEGA-3 FISH OILS

Major Application of Omega-3 ✦ In September of 2004 The Food and Drug Administration authorized the use of a qualified label claim for omega-3 fatty acids. It states that, *"supportive, non-conclusive evidence shows that consumption of EPA and DHA Omega-3 fatty acids may reduce the risk of coronary heart disease."*

An Overview of Omega-3 ✦ While studying Greenland's Inuit population in the 1970s, two Danish researchers (Bang and Dyerberg) discovered that in spite of the Inuit diet, which consisted of little more than seal, whale, salmon, and other fatty fish, that population appeared to be in stellar health. It was only a matter of time before the connection was made between the Inuits' apparent well being and the diet that seemed to support it.

What researchers found was that coldwater fish are high in unique, long-chain polyunsaturated (LCP) fats, or omega-3 fatty acids—one of the good fats required by the body. Omega-3 can be obtained from a number of sources, but fish offers high concretions of the two most potent LCP omega-3 fatty acids, DHA (docosahexaenoic acid) and EPA (eiscosapentaenoic acid).

How Omega-3 Works ✦ We refer to essential fatty acids as "essential" for a reason. For starters, the body needs them to carry out a dizzying list of biological functions that range from basic to vital. Here's the catch: As human beings, we are incapable of producing them on our own. That's because as we evolved, these fats were plentiful in our diets and in our bodies, and this saved our bodies the metabolic expense of having to create them. Consequently, it's vital that we get adequate amounts from our diets. But, as far too many of us already know, that's not always as easy as it seems.

The generous EFA content in fish oil has a positive influence on many of the body's most vital systems. Numerous studies have shown that EFA helps to lower cholesterol, support immune system function, reduce inflammation, promote healthy skin, and may be beneficial in treating many mental and neurological disorders.

Therapeutic Uses of Omega-3

- *Cardiovascular support.* When the body's saturated-to-unsaturated fat ratio is off balance, things can go terribly wrong. Through extensive research, researchers have been able to determine that when the body becomes deficient in omega-3 fatty acids, it relies on unhealthy saturated fats and cholesterol to build new cellular membranes. Over time a once healthy heart will be forced to work harder, because saturated fats and cholesterol are less flexible in structure and function.

Omega-3 fatty acids also have natural blood-thinning properties, making them beneficial to help prevent blood clots that can eventually lead to stroke. Those who consume fatty fish or supplement with omega-3 tend to have noticeably lower blood pressure and LDL cholesterol levls than those who don't consume DHA and EPA on a regular basis.

+ *Clear skin.* Conditions such as eczema, acne, and psoriasis tend to respond very well to omega-3 supplementation. Many common skin disorders stem from inflammation and so consuming adequate amounts of essential fatty acids from DHA and EPA may help reduce inflammation that often leads to skin disorders.

+ *Healthy joints.* Omega-3 fatty acids can be very helpful to alleviate the pain and degeneration associated with arthritis and other joint disorders. Studies have shown that EFA reduces inflammation which, in turn, helps reduce the rate at which articular tissue deteriorates. As a result many researchers strongly recommend that those suffering from these disorders supplement with EFA as a natural treatment.

+ *Neurological health.* The brain is not as solid as you might imagine. In fact, it's approximately 60 percent fat. Without ample amounts of omega-3 fatty acids, such as those found in fish oil, it simply cannot function at its peak.

A now-famous 1999 Harvard study was conducted to determine whether or not omega-3 fatty acids could reduce the effects of manic depression and bipolar condition. One of its most significant findings was that a majority of subjects had low levels of EPA and considerably low levels of DHA. This has lead many researchers to believe that omega-3 fatty acids can be of great benefit to those suffering from many forms of depression. DHA treatment, in particular, has been found to alleviate many behavioral and attention-deficit symptoms in both children and adults.

Tips for taking Omega-3

- The most common dose for fish oil is 3 grams (3,000 mg) daily. Taking it throughout the day in divided doses can help prevent flatulence and belching.
- Higher doses of omega-3 have been shown to be more effective in treating inflammatory conditions such as arthritis, Crohn's and Raynaud's diseases, lupus, and psoriasis.
- Individuals with sensitivity to acid reflux may have difficulty taking fish oil supplements. Some companies now offer molecularly distilled formulas that are enteric-coated to prevent a gag reflex and nausea.
- If you're diabetic, it's strongly recommended that you consult your physician prior to taking fish oil supplements.
- Keep fish oils supplements away from sunlight or high heat. Refrigeration is highly recommended for liquid forms, but not soft, gelatin capsules.
- Omega-3 fatty acids are natural blood thinners. If you're taking aspirin or other prescription blood thinners, check with your doctor before using omega-3 or fish-oil supplements, particularly over extended periods of time.

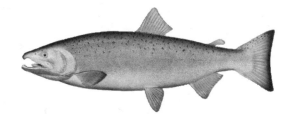

Salmon, one of the many sources of omega-3.

NATURAL COMPANIONS FOR OMEGA-3 ✦ Omega 6- and -9 essential acids, garlic, vitamin E and other antioxidants, hawthorn, lecithin, phosphatidyl serine, 5-HTP.

COFACTORS AND CONTRAINDICATIONS FOR OMEGA-3 ✦ See Table 8 in the Appendix for more information.

VITAMIN E (TOCOPHEROLS AND TOCOTRIENOLS)

Vitamin E is a potent antioxidant that inhibits the oxidation of LDL cholesterol. Two large epidemiological studies published in the 1990s showed that among 40,000 male physicians and 90,000 female nurses, intake of vitamin E from supplements was associated with a lower risk of coronary heart disease. The doses taken were between 100 and 249 IU (International Units) of natural vitamin E daily, and participants were healthy at the start of the four-year study. A later placebo-controlled study involving 2,000 patients *with heart disease* showed that those who took vitamin E supplements (400-800 IU daily) had a 77 percent lower rate of death from MI. A 2005 report of the same women studied in the 1990 study showed that while vitamin E (600 IU every other day) reduced incidence of MI by just 7 percent, it reduced cardiovascular mortality by 27 percent.

There are additional factors to keep in mind when considering supplementing with vitamin E for cardio-protection. For instance, natural d-alpha tocopherol is fifty percent more potent than synthetic dl-alpha tocopherol. Not all published studies take this into consideration.

Moreover, vitamin E is a complex of four naturally occurring tocopherols and four tocotrienols. Recent studies have shown that tocotrienols, particularly gamma tocotrienol, may be better at protecting the cardiovascular system than alpha tocopherol. Additionally, large doses of alpha tocopherol may crowd out the other beneficial tocopherols and tocotrienols. The best kind of vitamin E supplement to take to protect your heart is one with efficacious amounts of all eight members of the vitamin E family, in bio-balanced ratios.

Finally, vitamin E works best when other antioxidants such as vitamin C, carotenes, selenium, lipoic acid, and CoQ_{10} are also available. That's why we recommend a multiple vitamin and mineral formula as the basis for your cardiovascular program.

Vitamin E may enhance the anticlotting effects of certain medications, such as Coumadin®. Be sure to check with your doctor if you are taking blood-thinning agents. For more discussion on indications for vitamin E, please refer to Chapter One.

Supplements for Protecting Arteries

PYCNOGENOL

MAJOR APPLICATION OF PYCNOGENOL ✦ It would be unfair to assume that Pycnogenol's beneficial effects are in some way limited to just one realm of human wellness. That's because post-1990s researchers have discovered a wealth of potential uses for this unique extract. Its active components have become legend for their ability to provide antioxidant support and improve circulation and respiratory challenges and heal wounds, but Pycnogenol's role in cardiovascular health is where it seems to shine brightest.

AN OVERVIEW OF PYCNOGENOL ✦ Pycnogenol is a water extract derived exclusively from pine trees that grow in France's southwest maritime region. In 1951 a small study was conducted at the University of Bordeaux and is believed to be the first to determine that the extracts contain *oligomeric proanthocyanidin complexes* or OPCs. What makes these compounds unique is that they possess antioxidant activity superior to even vitamins C and E.

As scientists continued to learn more about the healing properties of OPCs, Pycnogenol research has skyrocketed. As a result it's been suggested that Pycnogenol may be able to improve conditions associated with varicose veins, PMS, allergies, hemorrhoids, skin disorders, wound healing, asthma, and impotence.

Some of the most impressive studies, however, have focused heavily on the role that Pycnogenol seems to play in cardiovascular and circulatory health. Many of the findings are nothing short of remarkable, as some claim that Pycnogenol can provide beneficial effects within five critical areas of cardiovascular health. We'll examine each briefly.

THERAPEUTIC USES OF PYCNOGENOL

- *Platelet aggregation.* Ideally, the body responds to a simple blood vessel tear by producing a clot. This is a normal and nonconcerning part of the biological process. But poor lifestyle habits, such as smoking and using narcotics, can encourage abnormal platelet activity, potentially resulting in the formation of clots capable of becoming embedded in arteries throughout the body, including in the heart. Under these circumstances it becomes incredibly difficult for the heart to pump blood throughout the body. Pycnogenol has been shown to reduce abnormal platelet activity.
- *Protect blood vessels.* The OPCs in Pycnogenol are considered by many experts to be among the most potent and effective of all antioxidants.

  This is great news for your blood vessels, because they're constantly under free radical attack. When not properly quenched, free radicals can damage blood vessels, causing inflammation that can interfere with normal circulation. Pycnogenol's strong concentrations of antioxidants may help prevent free radical damage to blood vessels.
- *Reduce high blood pressure.* High blood pressure is an early warning sign for many forms of heart disease and should in no way be taken lightly. Many of the cardiovascular-centric studies conducted on Pycnogenol have universally agreed that it appears to help reduce high blood pressure to a more healthy level.
- *Support healthy cholesterol levels.* High cholesterol is one of the most common gateways to heart disease, as we have seen. But it's important to keep in mind that there are two types of cholesterol: HDL, or high-

density lipoprotein, is "good" cholesterol, while LDL, or low-density lipoprotein, is the "bad" cholesterol that has been linked to a long list of health concerns. Pycnogenol has repeatedly demonstrated its ability to reduce dangerous LDL levels while boosting the body's HDL reserves.

* *Improve circulation.* Poor circulation can rob a person of the ability to live well due to its negative impact on many parts of the the body.

  The most obvious signs are also the most frustrating and include fatigue, headaches, cold hands and feet, impotence, varicose veins, itchiness, and tingling. While these may sound benign, it's important to remember that if left untreated these "simple" conditions can mature into life-threatening conditions that include potential heart attack, atherosclerosis, and stroke. A growing number of experts believe that Pycnogenol can be effective to help restore healthy circulation throughout the body.

Tips for Taking Pycnogenol

* Pycnogenol has excellent water solubility and is easily absorbed by the digestive tract. Be sure to take it with plenty of water to maximize effectiveness.
* Some people have sensitivity to OPCs that, from time to time, may result in mild digestive upset. Taking Pycnogenol with a small meal can help prevent this.
* Although safe for most healthy adults, there are currently no recommended dosages for pregnant and lactating women, those with liver challenges, and children.
* On its own Pycnogenol serves as a powerful weapon against oxidation. When combined with other free-radical fighters, such as vitamins C and E, alpha-lipoic acid, grape seed extract, green tea and carotenoids, its synergistic properties may offer complementary benefits.

Natural Companions for Pycnogenol ✦ Green tea extract, esterified vitamin C, antioxidants

CoFactors and Contraindications for Pycnogenol ✦ See Table 5 in the Appendix for more information.

GREEN TEA AND GREEN TEA EXTRACT (EGCg)

Major Application of Green Tea and EGCg ✦ Green tea (*Camellia sinensis*) contains impressive concentrations of polyphenols such as tannins and catechins. These cell-protecting plant extracts help safeguard cells from oxidation caused by environmental stress factors, poor diet, personal stress factors, and countless other issues and conditions. The plant's leaves also contain one of the most potent catechins (crystalline compounds with antioxidant properties) ever discovered, Epigallocatechin-gallate (EGCg).

An Overview of Green Tea and EGCg ✦ Second only to water, green tea continues to be one of the most widely consumed beverages in the world. This is *not* by chance. In nonclinical studies, EGCg has been shown to protect against chemical and environmental assault on the cells—encouraging news for cancer prevention.

Green tea.

How Green Tea and EGCg works • The polyphenols in green tea exhibit strong antioxidant activity that helps prevent DNA (the body's genetic material) from being damaged, which can help prevent cancer. Some studies show that green tea helps restrict liver enzymes from stimulating toxic carcinogens during certain stages of metabolism.

Its primary antioxidant component, EGCg, plays an interesting role. This ultra-powerful catechin jumpstarts a process called apoptosis, or programmed cell-death. During this process, dangerous cancer cells are sought out by antioxidants and eradicated. What's fascinating is that normal cells are not affected in the same way.

Therapeutic Uses for Green Tea and EGCg

- *Anti-aging.* Aging is not the result of passing time, but the result of what we're exposed to environmentally, physically, and chemically. It's the integrity of our *cells*, not our clocks, that determines how smoothly the process proceeds. As powerful antioxidants, the polyphenols in green tea can offer sound protection against oxidation and free radical assault.

- *Cancer prevention.* As mentioned earlier, the body produces cancerous cells every day. How we cope with this process biologically is clearly defined by how primed and fluid our cells are. Green tea has become highly celebrated in the prevention of certain cancers, especially breast, colon, liver, lung, ovarian, bladder, prostate, esophagus, and stomach cancers. Among the hundreds of studies that seem to support these claims, population studies are often the most persuasive. Take the Japanese, for example. For decades, they have been universally accepted as one of the world's leading consumers of green tea. Coincidentally, they also boast some of the lowest cancer rates anywhere on the planet.

- *Cardiovascular support.* The antioxidant polyphenols and catechins, especially EGCg, in green tea help prevent cholesterol from being used up during metabolism. Having less cholesterol in the blood is undoubtedly one of the best ways to prevent excess arterial plaque, but higher doses of green tea have also been shown to help prevent the oxidation of LDL cholesterol while raising HDL cholesterol levels.

• *Digestion.* There's more to green tea than just high-powered antioxidants. It's also rich in naturally occurring chemical compounds called tannins. When moderately consumed, tannins can help reduce diarrhea symptoms and soothe upset stomachs. Some researchers believe this is accomplished by green tea's ability to promote a gastrointestinal environment that welcomes good bacteria and discourages harmful bacteria.

Tips for Taking Green Tea and EGCg

• Many formulas don't list the actual extract content of their teas. It's therefore important to remember that 1 cup of strong tea is equivalent to roughly 100 mg of extract. Ten ounces of tea has been shown to fuel the body's antioxidant reserves for approximately 2 hours. For best results green tea should be sipped throughout the day.

• While many individuals may enjoy the light, grassy taste of green tea, it's primarily consumed for its wide-ranging health benefits, so it's important to find one that has a high concentration of polyphenols and catechins.

• If you're not much of a tea drinker or simply don't find that method convenient, consider taking a capsule formula. Not only will this allow you to control how much you take, but you can choose readily available caffeine-free green teas.

• Finding a quality brand is key. Your local grocery store may carry green tea, but don't expect to find the same selection there that you might find at your local health food retailer. It's important to be able to converse with staff members about which brands are not only popular, but also potent and pleasant-tasting.

- If you decide to take green tea in capsule form, be sure to do so with a meal and plenty of liquid to help increase absorption.
- Never boil green tea as you would other teas. Subjection to intense heat can render many of its active constituents ineffective.

NATURAL COMPANIONS FOR GREEN TEA EXTRACT ✦ Bioflavonoids, antioxidants, bitter orange and cayenne (for weight loss), CoQ$_{10}$, hawthorn, vitamin E, milk thistle, essential fatty acids.

COFACTORS AND CONTRAINDICATIONS FOR GREEN TEA AND EGCg ✦ See Table 8 in the Appendix for more information.

ESTER C®

Metaphorically, the human cardiovascular system is the lion in our biological jungle of existence and, as a result, it has many sworn enemies, one of which is free radical-induced oxidation.

Like regular vitamin C (ascorbic acid), Ester C® works wonders to protect the cells of the cardiovascular system from being corrupted by free radicals. *Esterifed* C takes things up a peg. It's more rapidly absorbed by the body, reaches higher intracellular levels, and is excreted in a much slower manner than regular vitamin C. This increased stability, rapid utilization, and longer half-life (see glossary) allows Ester C® to provide even greater cardiovascular and high-energy cellular protection than its vitamin C cousin.

Step Three: Homocysteine Regulators

TMG (TRIMETHYLGLYCINE)

MAJOR APPLICATION OF TMG ✦ Metabolic processes produce a number of interesting chemical byproducts. Most are extremely beneficial, but some are, well, not so beneficial. One of the most detrimental from the "not so beneficial" column is *homocysteine*. Under normal conditions this naturally occurring, toxic amino acid is converted into the amino acid methionine, a key factor in numerous metabolic pathways in a process known as methylation. Poor diet and unhealthy lifestyle activities can interfere with methylation and can often result in an unhealthy buildup of homocysteine. TMG is a *methyl donor* proven to help covert homocysteine into safe methionine that can be used by the body to serve other purposes.

AN OVERVIEW OF TMG ✦ TMG, or trimethylglycine, is also commonly referred to as betaine. An impressive number of clinical and nonclinical studies continue to illustrate what an important role it plays in keeping homocysteine levels under control. When the body is unable to find the TMG that it needs, the methylation process becomes severely roadblocked. This sparks a series of reactions that can interfere with DNA repair as well as the body's natural production of SAMe, the equally important methyl donor already discussed. Over time this ongoing sequence can result in poor circulation, stroke, atherosclerosis, blood clots, and weak joints.

HOW TMG WORKS ✦ You might call methyl donors such as TMG the biological the good Samaritans of the human body. They're always willing to lend themselves to other systems in need of a missing component. With regard to keeping homocysteine levels at a healthy level, TMG has an excellent working relationship with SAMe as well as with several members of the Vitamin B family. They work collectively to ensure that these dangerous metabolic bio-chemicals are reduced to harmless substances that the body can actually use for other purposes.

TIPS FOR TAKING TMG
+ Supplementing TMG won't completely correct a poor lifestyle, but it certainly does seem to complement a healthy lifestyle.
+ To help prevent even the most short-term homocysteine accumulations, it's wise to take TMG supplements throughout the day in divided doses.
+ Children should not take TMG or any homocysteine-regulating supplement.
+ Those with a family history of heart disease and anyone currently taking prescription medication are strongly advised to consult their physicians prior to taking any TMG supplements.

NATURAL COMPANIONS FOR TMG + Resveratrol, folic acid, vitamins B-6 and B-12, and SAMe

COFACTORS AND CONTRAINDICATIONS FOR TMG + See Table 6 in the Appendix for more information.

FOLIC ACID, VITAMINS B-6 AND B-12

Homocysteine increases risk of CVD through direct toxicity to artery walls, thus increasing blood clots, stroke, and coronary disease, as we have seen. It's also used as a diagnostic marker to indicate low levels of folic acid and vitamin B-6, which implies that these B vitamins may reduce levels of homocysteine.

A 14-year follow-up of 80,082 healthy women enrolled in a Boston nurses' health study revealed that those with a daily intake of 100 micrograms of folic acid lowered homocysteine levels by 6 percent. Each increase of 200 micrograms per day resulted in a 5.8 percent reduction in homocysteine. Intake of about 700 micrograms per day offered the best results.

Similarly, vitamin B-6 intake above 4.6 milligrams per day reduced homocysteine levels. However, the greatest benefit occurred when the women ingested higher amounts of both folic acid and vitamin B-6. No added benefit occurred with intake of riboflavin or vitamin B-2, or methionine. Additionally, although vitamin B-12 intake didn't seem to increase benefit, researchers concluded this was more a problem of absorption than of intake.

Step Four: Heart Energetics

COENZYME Q10 (COQ$_{10}$)

MAJOR APPLICATION OF CoQ10 ✦ CoQ$_{10}$ is currently used by millions and continues to be one of the most popular and effective natural heart-healthy supplements available. Its ability to produce energy at the cellular level, protect cardiovascular cells, eliminate harmful free-radicals, and potentially lower both blood pressure and LDL (bad) cholesterol has made CoQ$_{10}$ an absolute gem for anyone concerned with living a full, healthy life.

AN OVERVIEW OF CoQ10 ✦ CoQ$_{10}$ was discovered in 1957 by Frederick Crane, Ph.D., of the University of Wisconsin. Little did he know at the time that his research into this ubiquitous compound would eventually change the way many look at cardiovascular health. Word of his discovery piqued keen interest among Japanese scientists and, by the mid-60s, they had determined that CoQ$_{10}$ was a key component of the human heart with extraordinary antioxidant properties.

HOW CoQ10 WORKS ✦ This aggressive, multitasking, vitamin-like compound supports the activity of the body's enzymes, especially those responsible for many biochemical reactions. This makes it vital in the production of ATP (adenosine triphosphate), a phosphate molecule that provides the "spark" needed for energy production and storage. As one of the most versatile antioxidants in the body, CoQ_{10} moonlights as a free radical scavenger with a special fondness for high-energy organs such as the heart.

THERAPEUTIC USES FOR CoQ10

- *Cancer.* CoQ_{10} is a powerful antioxidant able to protect cells from abnormal activity, such as that caused by oxidation-prone free radicals. This ultimately encourages a more normalized immune system response. Research is ongoing, but some studies suggest that in light of its role as an antioxidant, CoQ_{10} may be able to stave off damage leading to certain types of cancers while hindering the spread of new abnormal growths. Some of the earliest studies determined that many cancer patients were deficient in CoQ_{10}, making this a keen area of interest for researchers.

> Many conventional cancer treatments kill cancer cells by allowing free radicals to form. Always consult your oncologist prior to using CoQ_{10} in conjunction with other cancer or radiation treatments.

- *Cardiovascular support.* On average, your heart beats approximately 100,000 times per day. Without adequate reserves of CoQ_{10}, this 24-hour-a-day task would be virtually impossible. Numerous studies have demonstrated CoQ_{10}'s ability to prevent the cholesterol oxidation that often leads to plaque buildup in the arteries. It has also been shown to improve the quality of heart cells and blood vessels, while producing the energy needed for more rhythmical contractions and healthy blood pressure.

    In short, without enough CoQ_{10}, the entire cardiovascular process suffers. Yes, it's *that* important.

- **Diabetes.** Diabetics have traditionally low levels of CoQ_{10} as well as other antioxidants. Supplementing with CoQ_{10} as part of a daily antioxidant program is a sound way to help support the body's ability to fight off infection caused by free radical damage.
- **Fatigue.** One of CoQ_{10}'s most basic duties is to promote the production of energy at the cellular level. Individuals with both chronic and acute fatigue stand to benefit from CoQ_{10} supplementation as it helps provide the spark needed to transport energy from enzyme to enzyme. This supports the production and storage of ATP, thus making it possible to run errands and chase kids for hours on end.
- **Healthy gums.** It has been estimated that well more than 30 million Americans suffer from some form of gum disease. CoQ_{10} has shown promise in treating this condition based on its ability to increase oxygenation within gum tissue and to boost the immune system to encourage healing. A select number of toothpaste manufacturers are now including small amounts of CoQ_{10} in their formulas to help combat bleeding caused by gingivitis.
- **Immune system support.** A compromised immune system needs every weapon it can get to fight infection. Supplementing with CoQ_{10} fuels the body with more free radical fighters, which in turn supports the immune system's ability to ward off bacteria and other foreign microbes.

A 1986 study (*Folkers and Per Langsjoen*) treated patients with moderate doses of CoQ_{10} and several subjects showed what researchers described as "striking improvement."

Tips for Taking CoQ10

- CoQ$_{10}$ is a fat-soluble compound and should be taken with food (especially those with some fat) to enhance absorption. To take the guesswork out you may want to choose a formula that combines CoQ$_{10}$ with a vegetable- or soy-oil based food.
- Antioxidants have natural synergy with one another. Taking CoQ$_{10}$ with partnering antioxidants such as vitamins A, E and C, alpha lipoic acid, and grape seed may be able to provide greater levels of cellular protection.
- To ensure freshness and potency always store CoQ$_{10}$ in a cool, dry place.
- Most users experience a slight energy boost right away. Depending on your unique situation, it may take weeks or even months to notice results.
- If you're taking CoQ$_{10}$ once daily, do so in the morning with a small meal that contains some fat. This is a good way to increase its effectiveness and assimilation.
- Despite its positive influence on general cardiovascular function, CoQ$_{10}$ is far from a cure-all. If you suffer from any type of heart disease such as angina, arrhythmia, atherocslerosis, cardiomyopathy, or congestive heart failure, do not substitute CoQ$_{10}$ to replace careful medical supervision, although it may be an important adjunct for certain cardio medications.

Natural Companions for CoQ10 ✦ Antioxidants, B-complex vitamins, hawthorn, lecithin, selenium, magnesium, L-carnitine, potassium, ginger, garlic, alpha lipoic acid.

Cofactors and Contraindications for CoQ10 ✦ See Table 5 in the Appendix for more information.

L-CARNITINE

MAJOR APPLICATION OF L-CARNITINE ✦ Contrary to myth, L-carnitine is not a *true* amino acid. It's an amino-like substance most abundantly found in red meat and dairy products and its primary function is to transfer fatty acids to cells, where it can be converted to energy. This makes it of great importance to the heart as well as to other high-energy-producing organs. Deficiencies are generally uncommon, although vegetarians are at the greatest risk.

AN OVERVIEW OF L-CARNITINE ✦ L-carnitine was discovered in 1905 by two Russian researchers and has since gained an immense popularity that continues to grow as word spreads. Based on the unique role it plays in producing mitochondrial energy, L-carnitine is now used by health-conscious people in just about every walk of life. Its solid reputation of safety and effectiveness has earned L-carnitine a loyal following, making it one of the most popular and widely used dietary supplements available today.

HOW L-CARNITINE WORKS ✦ L-carnitine goes into action by transporting the long-chain fatty acids from your diet (including those difficult to burn brown and saturated fats) into the mitochondria. From there these fats are converted into energy that can be put to immediate use. Your cells, in essence, are like an assembly line: Fat comes in, energy goes out. While this process sounds simple, it's important to keep in mind that we're not talking simply about the energy needed to go for a walk, but about the energy that's necessary to fuel your heart, lungs, metabolism, and a slew of other vital processes.

THERAPEUTIC USES OF L-CARNITINE

- *Athletic performance.* Like surf and turf, athletes and L-carnitine seem to complement each other. As one of the undisputed heavyweights of all dietary supplements, L-carnitine has a devout following that use it to help get the most out of training and workouts. When taken prior to an intense session, it can support the body's energy reserves, making it possible to train harder, longer, and with greater intensity.

Taken shortly after working out, many users report quicker recovery and reduced stiffness and soreness.

+ *Cardiovascular health.* Your heart is without question one of the hardest working organs in your body, beating more than 100,000 times per day. Needless to say, a feat of this magnitude requires an almost ridiculous amount of energy to perform successfully. Fortunately for the heart, carnitine appreciates this cardiovascular plight and appears to be unconditionally willing to lend a hand or, at the very least, some energy. Having an ample reserve of carnitine ensures that the body has all the tools needed to convert fat into energy. When the supply dwindles, the heart will use whatever is available as a source of metabolic fuel.

+ *Fatigue.* This hard-working amino-like compound has the power and know-how to give fat cells a metabolic makeover. By kindly escorting them into the mitochondria region of the cell, carnitine makes it possible for the body to use these stubborn fat deposits to produce energy. People who find themselves constantly tired, worn-down and motivationally challenged stand to benefit the most from its use, as they typically exhibit low levels of this essential substance. This should be of foremost concern to vegetarians, vegans, and anyone who doesn't eat meat and dairy— the two best sources of carnitine, despite also being generous in saturated fat.

+ *Memory and cognitive health.* Acetyl L-carnitine (ACL), a natural metabolite of carnitine produced by the brain, has become a subject of great interest to researchers in preventing age-related memory loss. Some studies have suggested that by donating its "acetyl" group, it can help increase the production of acetylcholine and dopamine, two vital neurotransmitters. These chemical messengers help increase the effectiveness of nerve transmissions and are believed to contribute greatly to many brain functions, among them learning, reasoning, memory, balance, emotion, and pleasure.

- *Weight loss and dieting.* Many people swear by carnitine as a sound way to maintain healthy body weight. Aside from its day-to-day task converting dietary fat into energy, carnitine also stimulates "brown fats" to produce more energy.

  Diets fail for many reasons and one of the most common is lack of cellular energy. This is why it's so important not to skip meals when dieting. When meals are skipped, the metabolism takes advantage of the light workload and essentially slacks off, hence the term, *slow metabolism.* Supplementing with carnitine keeps the process moving along by constantly looking for fat that can be used to keep you fueled.

TIPS FOR TAKING L-CARNITINE

- To maximize absorption take L-carnitine on an empty stomach. Nausea is very rare, but in the event that it does occur taking it with a small meal may help.
- Read labels carefully to make sure that you're purchasing the "L" form of carnitine, as it most closely resembles the form naturally produced by the body. The alternative is "D" carnitine, but we don't recommend this synthetic form.
- When using carnitine for athletic endurance and weight loss, choosing the right form is imperative. For quick, high-energy sessions, liquids are recommended because the body absorbs them quickly. Those using it for long, sustained workouts (such as distance rides and runs) may benefit more from high-potency tablets, which tend to release gradually.
- If you have a difficult time sleeping at night, avoid taking carnitine supplements close to bedtime. Taking it in the morning may be an excellent way to jumpstart your metabolism and energy reserves for greater efficacy throughout the day.

NATURAL COMPANIONS FOR L-CARNITINE ◆ Essential fatty acids (EFA), CoQ$_{10}$, chromium, magnesium, lysine, multi vitamins and minerals, antioxidants, B-complex, conjugated linoleic acid (CLA).

CO-FACTORS AND CONTRAINDICATIONS FOR L-CARNITINE ◆ See Table 6 in the Appendix for more information.

MAGNESIUM

It's almost mind-blowing to think that something as simple as magnesium can have such a profound influence on the quality of a person's heart, but it's true. Magnesium is undeniably one of the body's most talented multi-tasking compounds and its role in cardiovascular health is of vital importance. Keep something in mind: As we age our muscles, nerves, and the arteries that drive our cardiovascular systems age, too. While this is completely normal, a magnesium deficiency can put a tremendous strain on our hearts and severely complicate the process.

Sadly, more and more people are paving a way to cardiovascular disaster by neglecting their daily magnesium through poor diet, longer workdays, skipping breakfast, and a host of other factors. But make no mistake, without a proper magnesium level the the heart just can't use the constant supply of energy that it needs to function properly. Over time this can weaken the heart muscles and open the floodgates to many forms of heart disease including cardiomyopathy, angina, high blood pressure, and arrhythmia.

Supplementing with magnesium is unquestionably one of the safest, simplest, and most effective ways to encourage a healthy heart. Not only does it assist in the production of cellular energy, but it also helps strengthen, condition, and relax the complex components of the cardiovascular system as a whole. In the long scope of things, magnesium supplementation can be a priceless gift that your ticker will continue to thank you for.

HAWTHORN

This extract of *Crataegus oxyacantha* plants has been used for centuries by a number of civilizations and is extremely popular in many European regions. The plant itself has long, prickly branches and was originally planted to ward off trespassers and unwelcome drifters. It was eventually determined that hawthorn extracts could serve a much greater purpose, helping improve cardiovascular health and function.

Hawthorn contains a powerful class of antioxidants known as *vitexin*. Studies continue to show that these standardized extracts may be effective in promoting sound cardiovascular activity. Many researchers believe that the vitexin found in hawthorn can help increase blood flow to the heart by countering the arterial narrowing that restricts normal flow. This can result in more cardiovascular energy, a more stabilized heartbeat, stronger heart muscles, and greater circulation.

It's important to mention that hawthorn extracts are very potent and should be used wisely. If you're currently taking prescription heart medications, we strongly advise you to consult with your physician before taking hawthorn. Once you've made the decision to supplement with it, look for a formula that contains no less than 1.8 percent standardized vitexin.

Stage Five: Varicose Veins and Restless Legs

GRAPE SEED EXTRACT

MAJOR APPLICATION OF GRAPE SEED EXTRACT • Grape seed extract contains a class of powerful compounds known as flavanols. These OPCs exhibit what many researchers consider to be extraordinary antioxidant properties. As evidenced by a wealth of studies, these fearless free radical scavengers clearly have a positive impact on energy, aging, and the preservation of all-around wellness.

An Overview of Grape Seed Extract ◆ Nestled deep inside the red grapes that we all enjoy so much are tiny seeds that contain high concentrations of flavonoids. These powerful phytochemicals exhibit strong antioxidant properties, and are now commonly used to protect cells from the damage caused by unstable free radicals. Oligomeric proanthocyanidin complexes (OPCs) are among the most beneficial. Thanks to host of recent studies, many researchers and nutritionists agree that these potent flavonoids may offer great cellular protection than many other traditional antioxidants.

How Grape Seed Extract Works ◆ Once used by the body, flavonoids and other antioxidant compounds in grape seed extract go on a rampage, searching for anything that seems out of order. Along the way, these healthy scavengers encounter free radicals, inflammatory agents, enzymes, and histamines that can make life as we know it very uncomfortable if they're not discovered. Science has unveiled that the majority of these troublesome compounds are no match for the strong antioxidant properties inherent to grape seed extract.

Therapeutic Uses of Grape Seed Extract
- *Anti-aging.* We don't age simply because the days pass. The aging process is dependent on how nourished or malnourished our cells are. Grape seed's high concentrations of cell-protecting antioxidants serve as barriers against cell jeopardizing to reduce likelihood of abnormalities that catalyze premature-aging.
- *Cancer prevention.* This is another area where grape seed really likes to show its true colors. Its team of powerful antioxidant compounds scours the body to minimize the activity of abnormal cells, damaged DNA, and other tumor-prone structures. Grape seed's ability to safeguard these cells has led many researchers to believe that it can be an effective weapon in the prevention of certain types of cancer.
- *Clear skin.* Grape seed extract can be welcome news for people in their early 20s who experience skin blemishes that seem to appear out of nowhere. In just one week of supplementation some users note clearer

skin. Studies have also shown that grape seed extract can help treat psoriasis, eczema, and other skin conditions.

- *Healthy vision.* The blood vessels in the eyes are extremely small and often difficult to reach. Free radicals regard them as prime property. Once they make their mark there circulation becomes more and more difficult, resulting in blockages that often lead to eye disorders such as cataracts and macular degeneration. The antioxidants in grape seed can be helpful to prevent this damage and restore a healthier condition.
- *Varicose veins.* The OPCs in grape seed have been shown to lessen some of the more troubling conditions associated with varicose veins including swelling, leg pains, and a sensation of heaviness. This can be attributed to the natural anti-inflammatory properties common to OPCs, as well as their ability to help strengthen the body's blood vessels. Over time, use may be able to help reduce the unsightliness of varicose veins as circulation becomes normalized.

TIPS FOR TAKING GRAPE SEED EXTRACT

- Antioxidants are like a team. One alone may be able to perform a lot, but when the team comes together, more happens. Taking grape seed with other oxidation quenchers such as vitamin C, selenium, and alpha lipoic acid is a great way to form the team to keep your cells safe and healthy.
- Once you've decided to start supplementing with grape seed extract, do yourself a favor and make the commitment to take it everyday. It's powerful, but your body uses it quickly.
- Don't let a few dollars stand in the way of purchasing a high-quality, potent grape seed extract. Read labels carefully, and always choose a formula standardized to at least 90 percent polyphenols.
- Some antioxidants (vitamin E and others) work better when taken at the same time each day. To make things simple, take your antioxidants with breakfast as a part of your morning routine. It takes the guesswork

out of remembering what you took throughout the day, and can even give you a nice kick that will keep you running tip-top.

NATURAL COMPANIONS FOR GRAPE SEED EXTRACT ✦ Other antioxidants and bioflavonoids, quercetin, vitamins A, C and E, and essential fatty acids.

COFACTORS AND CONTRAINDICATIONS FOR GRAPE SEED EXTRACT ✦ See Table 5 in the Appendix for more information.

Step Six: Peripheral Circulation and Restless Legs

BUTCHER'S BROOM

MAJOR APPLICATION OF BUTCHER'S BROOM ✦ Some of the industry's most respected researchers and authorities regard taking butcher's broom (*Ruscus aculeatus*) as a safe and natural way to reduce the swelling associated with varicose veins and hemorrhoids. That's due to the high concentrations of *ruscogenins* that dwell within the shrub's roots and low-growing rhizomes. Europeans are now the number one users of butcher's broom, although interest in the U.S. continues to grow.

AN OVERVIEW OF BUTCHER'S BROOM ✦ Native to the Mediterranean, the thin, straw-like stalks of this evergreen were once gathered and used to construct brooms made especially for local butchers. It was also used to treat a wide range of ailments associated with the excretory and circulatory systems.

In the 1950s a group of European researchers discovered that the plant's extract was able to constrict blood vessels. This shed new light on its potential health benefits until it has gradually become one of the most popular natural ways to support healthy circulation throughout the body's lower extremities.

How Butcher's Broom Works ♦ The active extracts of butcher's brooms have venotonic properties. That means that they can help relieve the ache and tenderness of distended veins. This is of considerable importance to the body's lower extremities because, regardless of whether we're paying attention to it or not, this is an extremely high-demand region.

Standing, walking, working, driving, and even sitting are just a few of the routine activities that put tremendous strain on the legs, feet, ankles, knees, and hips. Over long periods of time, that stress can lead to inflammation and restricted blood flow. Butcher's Broom has been shown in several studies to help improve and restore blood flow throughout the lower regions of the body while strengthening and conditioning the inner walls of veins.

Therapeutic Uses for Butcher's Broom
- Varicose veins
- Hemorrhoids
- Leg cramps
- Poor circulation (lower extremities)

Tips for Taking Butcher's Broom
- Make sure that the formula you select contains standardized "root" extracts from *Ruscus aculeatus*, the most potent concentration of active components.
- To help encourage continuous lower extremity circulation, many nutritionists recommend taking butcher's broom throughout the day in divided doses.
- Those using prescription blood-thinning medications or being treated for prostate problems are advised to consult their physicians prior to using products that contain butcher's broom extracts.
- Use of MAO inhibitors can provide sharp increases in blood pressure when used in conjunction with butcher's broom.

- If you suspect that your circulation might be challenged, it's wise to seek immediate medical advice. Even the most minor circulatory problems can progress to more serious conditions.

NATURAL COMPANIONS FOR BUTCHER'S BROOM • Take in combination with vitamin C and flavonoids, pantethine, calcium, magnesium, potassium, and prickly ash bark to help increase effectiveness.

COFACTORS AND CONTRAINDICATIONS FOR BUTCHER'S BROOM • See Table 8 in the Appendix for more information.

PRICKLY ASH BARK

Native to the eastern United States and certain regions of low Canada, prickly ash (*Zanthoxylum americanum* and *Z. clava herculis*) is another safe and popular herbal supplement commonly used to help increase circulation to the body's biological southern hemisphere. Its medicinal use can be traced to Native American cultures where it was originally consumed in tonics to diminish the agony of toothaches, purify the blood, treat infections, and help cure a number of urinary and excretory issues. Today standardized extracts of this towering shrub have helped many people to improve leg circulation while reducing the pain, swelling, and unsightly appearance associated with varicose veins.

Prickly ash extracts are rich in a number of therapeutic alkaloid compounds such as *fagarine, magnoflorine, laurifoline, nitidine, and chelerythrine* as well as essential oils, tannins, phenols, and others. This, in the eyes of many researchers, is what allows prickly ash to have such a stimulating effect on the body's circulatory and lymphatic systems. Ironically, both play considerable roles in the development and onset of varicose veins.

To Sum It All Up

The progression of the 7 syndromes is now becoming clearer:

Chronic stress

$\longrightarrow$ Oxidative Stress

$\longrightarrow$ Metabolic Disturbances

$\longrightarrow$ Risk of Cardiovascular Problems

The *cardio syndrome* involves disturbances in fatty acid, protein, and carbohydrate metabolism. In addition, oxidative stress plays havoc with the heart and vascular apparatus from the largest arteries to the smallest capillaries.

There are five levels on which an individual may experience the *cardiovascular syndrome:*

• Disturbances in blood lipids
• Inflammation
• Homocysteine levels
• Heart energetics
• Peripheral circulation and restless legs

DISTURBANCES IN BLOOD LIPIDS • Examples of such disturbances include high levels of total cholesterol, LDL cholesterol, and triglycerides. Low levels of HDL cholesterol magnify the problem. These factors can be modified by exercise, change of diet, and supplements that help lower cholesterol. Most symptoms are also found in the *metabolic syndrome* and, along with obesity and altered glucose metabolism, contribute to cardiovascular risk factors.

INFLAMMATION • Inflammation is equally to blame for the faulty plumbing that occurs in *cardiovascular syndrome*. High levels of free radicals attack cells lining the blood vessels and they respond with scar tissue, a narrowed passageway for blood to flow, less elasticity, and an increased tendency for clots to form. Inflammation is the chief pathway to the *immune syndrome*, the topic of Chapter Five.

HOMOCYSTEINE LEVELS ✦ Homocysteine is a toxic byproduct of metabolism that's destructive to the cardiovascular system on several levels. One of its chief potential damaging qualities is that it alters DNA so that proteins encoded by this master molecule don't function properly, leading to most degenerative conditions including cancer. Consequently, homocysteine is destructive on a deeper level because it affects the cardiovascular system. Its presence is another high-risk factor for immune dysfunction, but levels appear to be reduced with the supplementation of three B vitamins that can be found in ideal levels in a good daily multiple.

HEART ENERGETICS ✦ This was the major topic we covered in this chapter, but mineral levels are critical to maintain a normal heart rhythm as well. Not only do electrolytes such as magnesium, calcium, potassium, and sodium maintain optimum heart and blood vessel function, they also maintain the life force in the trillions of cells in the human body, including those in the brain and nervous system. Electrolytes are also needed to maintain fluid balance and muscle contraction throughout the body. Certain semi-essential nutrients such as CoQ_{10} and L-carnitine are also important to maintain healthy hearts.

PERIPHERAL VEINS AND RESTLESS LEGS ✦ Minerals again play an extremely important role in peripheral circulation. Leg cramping and restless legs respond well to increased supplementation with minerals. When circulation is improved to the capillaries in legs, feet, and hands, fatigue and discomfort appear reduced.

CHAPTER FIVE

Immune Syndrome

ALLOUT FROM CHRONIC STRESS trickles down through other syndromes, as you have now seen in chapters three and four. You also saw how inflammation plays a key role in the *cardiovascular syndrome*. In this chapter we'll trace its effect on immunity.

During periods of high stress, infection-fighting cells called *macrophages* release signaling peptides known as *cytokines*, chemical messengers in the immune system. Cytokines recruit and activate immune warrior-cells in the *inflammatory response*.

The initial burst of activity starts several overlapping chain-reactions that include release of more cytokines and many other kinds of chemicals. Warrior cells congregate at the site of infection to detect and destroy bacteria, viruses and other pathogens, and to initiate repair.

The signal to fight is broadcast throughout the body and hormones, neuropeptides, and other chemicals join in battle. In one rather amusing tactic, macrophages grab and hold invading bacteria, carefully placing them so they are "presented" to white blood cells known as T-cells. T-cells recognize and mount a vigorous attack on the hapless bacteria—all the while transmitting cytokine messages for extra reinforcements. Additional immune cells respond to the signal, and antibodies arrive to expedite destruction by attaching microscopic tags to the foreigners.

All of this activity is normal, as long as the pro-inflammatory cytokines and their progeny are held in check by balancing anti-inflammatory cytokines. Chronic stress can continue the pro-inflammatory response for long periods of time and, as you can imagine, that can affect every other system in the body. It's not always immune depression that occurs, as you might think. Different kinds of stressors will elicit opposite responses. Nevertheless, the results are the same—altered immune response displayed as either lowered resistance (as seen in unremitting viral infections) or as the type of overzealous response that characterizes autoimmune conditions.

Examples of conditions that stem from chronic inflammation are inflammatory bowel disease, essential hypertension, coronary artery disease, rheumatoid arthritis, psoriasis, and asthma. Chronic inflammation can also accelerate aging and aging conditions such as diabetes, cardiovascular disease, cancer, hormone imbalance, digestive disturbances, and arthritis. Immune response naturally declines with age, which means one has to be extra vigilant to protect immune response with a good diet, exercise, positive mindset, and specific supplements.

Those who've had a string of health setbacks and are coping with chronic conditions such as heart disease are more vulnerable and should take extra precautions against inflammation. The lungs are the most common infection site and two of the conditions discussed in this chapter involve the lungs and upper respiratory tract. Other systems that will be affected are the digestive tract, which is the topic of Chapter Six and the urinary tract, discussed in Chapter Seven.

What You Will Find in This Chapter

- Chronic inflammation and autoimmunity
- Acute inflammation and infection
- Allergies
- Asthma

Chronic Inflammation and Autoimmunity

Rheumatoid arthritis, multiple sclerosis, Type 1 diabetes and at least 80 other conditions share one important aspect—autoimmunity—a situation in which the immune system mistakenly destroys the body's own cells. T-cells, mentioned above, are constantly on the prowl for invaders. The body has devised a system called "tolerance" that identifies what is "self" from what is foreign. T-cells must identify the foreign cell, either by having it presented to them or tagged for destruction, before they can take defensive action. Autoimmune disease develops when tolerance fails and T-cells misidentify self-cells as foreign. Another way autoimmunity develops is if antibodies mistakenly attach to self-cells and mark them for destruction.

Recent research by scientists at Duke University Medical School suggests that macrophage activity may be much more important in preventing and treating autoimmune conditions than previously thought. In a series of experiments, the Duke team found that macrophages ingest large amounts of dead tissue stemming either from injury or apoptosis. If the macrophages "fill up" with too many dead cells, they may burst and spew DNA from dead cells into the bloodstream. This would immediately elicit an immune response. If this happened on a continuing basis, an autoimmune condition might follow. Consequently, researchers suggest that bolstering macrophages can help the body maintain normal immunity levels.

Some autoimmune conditions affect only one organ, the pancreas in Type 1 diabetes, for example. An entire system may be affected in other autoimmune diseases including multiple sclerosis, which destroys the lining on the spinal cord and brain. In a few cases, the autoimmune process over-stimulates an organ. Such is the case with Graves' disease in which the thyroid gland produces too much thyroid hormone.

As we saw in Chapter Four, inflammation is a key factor in atherosclerosis. Now scientists think they know why. T-cells, macrophages, and a special class of antibodies that work against oxidized LDL cholesterol have all been found in atheromatous plaque. Scientists believe autoimmunity determines how fragile a plaque will become, and that these immune mediators and their cytokines increase the probably of plaque rupture.

More women than men are affected by autoimmune conditions, perhaps as a result of hormonal changes. A family tendency toward autoimmune conditions also places certain people at higher risk. Most research suggests that some trigger, such as a virus infection or extreme exposure to toxins, sets the autoimmune response in motion. The symptoms in autoimmune conditions tend to wax and wane, in some cases persisting for years and in others progressing quickly to disability. As in the other syndromes, a good daily multiple is recommended. In addition, certain other nutrients are important in dealing with autoimmune conditions.

ZINC

Major Application of Zinc ✦ Things we take for granted—working every day, running errands, chasing after hysterical children—put tremendous stress on the body and its trillions of cells. No surprise there. But did you know that each and every one of these cells needs zinc simply to make it through the day? It's true. This crucial trace mineral affects your vision, immune system, taste buds, toe nails, and even that soft patch of skin on the tip of your ear.

An Overview of Zinc ✦ It's not that difficult to get zinc from the diet, provided that you're consuming the right mix of foods and drinking plenty of water, but as *far* too many people have already figured out, wanting to eat right and actually doing it are often two very different things. Even more concerning, many popular medications can interfere with the body's ability to absorb zinc. This is a key contributor to mild deficiencies and even more reason to consider supplementation.

How Zinc Works ✦ Zinc wastes very little time getting right down to business once it's in the bloodstream. Its first duty is to stimulate the activity of white blood cells and then to cofactor more than 300 different enzymes that orchestrate everything from protein synthesis to cardiovascular activity. Along the way zinc lends help to other vital systems by reducing inflammation, healing minor wounds, regulating hormonal activity, protecting cells, repairing DNA, enhancing insulin levels, and metabolizing nutrients, especially vitamin A. Any way you choose to look at it, zinc is nothing short of a multi-tasking biological overachiever.

THERAPEUTIC USES OF ZINC

- *Acne.* Zinc is becoming more and popular among teens and adults who suffer from mild to moderate acne. This popularity can be attributed to the three-tiered attack it wages on breakouts. First, it helps regulate how much testosterone the body metabolizes. In doing so, it prevents testosterone from being converted into DHT, another hormone notorious for producing pore-clogging oil known as *sebum*. Zinc also helps reduce inflammation and boosts immune system activity.

- *Cold and flu symptom.* According to many studies, showering the throat with *zinc gluconate* lozenges is one of the best moves a person can make at the first sign of a common cold or bout with the flu. Researchers have determined that the presence of zinc seems to interfere with the bacteria responsible for these conditions, making it possible to recover at a much faster pace. The key word here is *lozenges*. While taking it orally can certainly help increase the body's immune system response, direct contact seems to be a much more effective way to go when struggling with a cold or flu.

- *Healing minor wounds.* Zinc provides an effective immune-boosting surge that's been shown to help expedite the healing of many epidermal challenges. It's simple, actually. When you cut yourself, the immune system responds by instructing your thymus gland to produce additional white blood cells to initiate the repair and healing process. Taking into consideration that zinc thrives on this activity, it's especially important to get the amount you need after suffering a non-life-threatening scuff.

- *Healthy vision.* A lifetime of exposure to sunlight and UVB rays can cause gradual eye damage that's essentially undetectable. Over time, however, this damage can steadily accumulate, leaving the macula subject to degeneration. Fortunately, zinc has what can best be described as a biological "fascination" with the eyes, as evidenced by the obvious role it plays in supporting and protecting their most vulnerable components.

- *Other therapeutic uses.* Benign prostate enlargement; blood sugar management; wound healing; healthy skin, hair, and scalp; immune system support; and sore throat.

Tips for Taking Zinc

- When taking zinc orally be sure to eat something. Many users report strong feelings of nausea after taking it on an empty stomach.

- For cold and flu symptoms, stick to using zinc gluconate lozenges. This is much more effective than taking it orally, as lozenges immediately coat the lining of the throat precisely where these bacteria like to stake their claim.

- If you're taking zinc to improve the quality of your skin, be consistent. It can take weeks before the effects begin to show, so don't get discouraged if you don't witness any "miracles" right away.

- Caffeine can reduce the amount of zinc that's absorbed by the body. If you spend your days swilling down lots of coffee or soda, leave yourself at least a 90-minute window before or after taking zinc supplements.

- Don't make the mistake of blowing out your copper reserves by taking too much zinc. Taking high doses can deplete the body's supply of copper. When taking added zinc, especially during cold and flu season, never exceed a dosage of more than 50 mg. daily and make sure that you're getting at least 2-5 extra mg. of copper to balance things.
- If you're taking a multi-formula, always factor its zinc content to your consumption of a zinc supplement to prevent any unwanted nausea or toxic reactions as a result of consuming more than your body needs.

NATURAL COMPANIONS FOR ZINC ✦ Vitamin A, Vitamin D, natural carotenoids including lutein for the eyes, selenium, alpha- lipoic acid, copper, trace minerals, quercetin, astragalus, B vitamins, organic mushrooms, omega-3 and -6 fatty acids.

COFACTORS AND CONTRAINDICATIONS FOR ZINC ✦ See Table 3 in the Appendix for more information.

SELENIUM

Selenium is one of the few, true immune system powerhouse supplements. A trace mineral (measured by micrograms), selenium is an elite antioxidant that's been shown in numerous studies to seek and conquer large amounts of free radicals. Based on this, it's currently a favorite among those with compromised immune system function and other autoimmune conditions.

Here's why. When an autoimmune-threatening virus enters the body, selenium activity levels become dramatically repressed, allowing the virus to replicate at an unheard of rate. Supplementing selenium has been shown to counter this process by shielding cells from free radical–induced oxidation. This is great news for the cardiovascular system, especially when you factor in how important it is to keep inflammation under control to protect it.

ALPHA LIPOIC ACID (ALA)

As one of the most versatile of all antioxidants, *alpha lipoic acid* is both fat- and water-soluble. This means it passes from one cellular compartment to another unhindered by lack of solubility. It can pass freely throughout every tissue and organ of the body and is used by every cell. Its uncanny ability to provide such a far-ranging level of effective immune system support has made it one of the most popular supplements available, even among the most supplement-savvy.

In fact, more and more physicians are suggesting that patients with auto-immune conditions supplement with ALA to support cellular strength and integrity. Supernutrient? We think so.

OMEGA 3 FATTY ACIDS

To this day the precious body oils of coldwater fish and other natural botanicals continue to astound even the most admired researchers. There's a reason why we refer to essential fatty acids as "essential." The body needs them for so many basic functions, but cannot manufacture its own supply. Somewhere buried in that list of biological responsibilities is immune system support.

Within the body omega-3 essential fatty acids can easily be converted into pain- and inflammation-fighting compounds called *prostaglandins*. This capability took center stage in 1998 when several clinical trials reported that scores of participants afflicted with rheumatoid arthritis showed remarkable improvements while supplementing with omega-3 fatty acids. Many were even able to curtail daily intake of prescription pain and inflammation medications.

MUSHROOMS

You might not realize this, but some of the earth's most delectable mushrooms are bursting with therapeutic and immune-supporting compounds. Shiitake mushroom is one striking example. In fact, of the more than 700 varieties of commonly consumed mushrooms, it's been estimated that as many as 30 percent may posses medicinal properties on some level. Maitake and Reishi are two that you won't find among culinary delights, but these mushrooms, along with a score of others, contain similar health-promoting benefits.

What researchers *have* learned is that medicinal mushrooms are teeming with immune-supporting compounds and contain strong concentrations of *1,3 beta-glucans*. Beta glucans are potent immune-boosting polysaccharides which play a huge role in the body's immune system response. Ironically, they're almost nonexistent in today's typical American diet, which is sad, especially when you consider how well they've been shown to support both innate and adaptive immunity.

In Asia, medicinal mushrooms are prized for their benefits and are commonly used to fight viruses and as a complementary treatment for cancer.

VITAMIN D

The evidence linking vitamin D with autoimmune diseases is mounting. Using data from the long-standing nurses' health study, Harvard scientists looked for links between vitamin D intake and development of multiple sclerosis among 185,000 women over a 19-year period. The nurses that took at least 400 IU of vitamin D daily had a 40 percent reduced risk of developing MS.

Acute Inflammation and Infection

ASTRAGALUS

MAJOR APPLICATION OF ASTRAGALUS • Astragalus root is one of the principal tonic herbs in Chinese medicine. It is considered adaptogenic in that it helps the body combat physical, environmental, and psychological stress. During periods of intense stress the body loses its ability to combat environmental forces such as cold, heat, humidity, and wind. It's also less able to mount a vigorous defense against viruses and other immune challenges.

AN OVERVIEW OF ASTRAGALUS • Astragalus (*Astragalus membranaceus*), also known as Huang Qi (or yellow energy), is a member of the pea family along with its famous cousin, licorice. Astragalus has strong antioxidant properties, attributable to its glycosides, polysaccharides, and saponins. This powerful adaptogenic herb is native to Northern China and has been used for centuries to stimulate the immune system, promote increased vigor, and protect cells. As the plant ages, its three main constituents concentrate in its roots, which have been shown in many studies to have a direct influence on the production and life span of the body's immune T- and natural killer-cells. This is important from a disease prevention perspective because those cells govern how effectively the body fights infection. They also help fight recurring viruses and other infectious agents and signal other immune cells to attack.

How Astragalus Works ♦ *Versatile* is the best word to describe astragalus. Its popularity can be attributed to the proven role it plays to promote all-around good health, fight infection, and help the body in post-illness recovery. Its roots are rich in several free radical–fighting phytochemicals and nutrients that work to prevent free radical damage. Otherwise, these unstable molecules wreak havoc among healthy cells.

Astragalus also promotes the activity of an active virus-fighting agent called interferon—an added bonus. This powerful chemical has a unique microbial memory and can prevent the reproduction of viruses it has previously encountered in the body.

Therapeutic Uses of Astragalus
- ♦ *Bronchitis and upper respiratory conditions.* Upper respiratory conditions often result from a compromised immune system. The highly active, immune-boosting components found in the roots of astragalus attack bacteria to help prevent respiratory infections from developing. In this application, astragalus is taken at the first sign of a cold and continued until there is no danger of infection. This can be an effective way to offset a tendency for repeated respiratory infections.

- *Chronic fatigue.* Astralagus was first used centuries ago to increase stamina and vigor while replenishing vital fluids. Today's lifestyle and poor diet overload the system with toxins, bacteria, and microbes. That causes the immune system to overwork in an effort to protect the body, leading to eventual energy depletion. Those with chronic fatigue have been unable to function normally for at least six months and many are bedridden. Astragalus helps restore vital energy, reduce pain and inflammation, and increase blood flow to tissues.
- *Cold and flu symptoms.* Astragalus is loaded with antioxidant compounds with the ability to ward off the free radicals that ultimately lead to infection. When taken at the first sign of symptoms, astragalus goes to work by stimulating an army of defense cells that seek and destroy unwelcome foreign invaders.
- *Cold sores and fever blisters.* These annoying, embarrassing, and ugly herpes simplex 1 lesions can be triggered by any number of factors. Cold, flu, fatigue, prolonged stress, menstruation, and a host of environmental changes can cause an outbreak with virtually no warning. A sluggish immune system response to stressful factors is the root cause of these outbreaks. Cycling two weeks with astragalus followed by two weeks of taking a mixture of organic medicinal mushrooms can increase the immune system's ability to prevent outbreaks and reduce recurrences.
- *HIV.* Astragalus stimulates the production, activity, and effectiveness of T-cells, B-cells, natural killer cells, interferon, and natural antibodies that make up the immune system's inflammatory response. Those living with HIV and AIDS stand to benefit from supplementing with astragalus as it has the unique ability to nonselectively increase the body's built-in defense mechanisms.
- *Other therapeutic benefits.* Improved stress adaptation.

TIPS FOR TAKING ASTRAGALUS

- If you take astragalus (as well as other immune-boosting herbs) over a long period of time, your body will come to depend upon them. To compensate, try cycling it with other adaptogenics such as cat's claw, ashwagandha, echinacea, and goldenseal.
- The most effective astragalus supplements are derived from its aged yellow roots. Look for a formula standardized to a minimum of at least 70 percent.

NATURAL COMPANIONS FOR ASTRAGALUS ✦ Astragalus seems to work wonderfully with various types of organic mushrooms. Some manufactures have taken note and are now combining it with organic mushroom blends that increase its synergistic potential.

CO-FACTORS AND CONTRAINDICATIONS FOR ASTRAGALUS ✦ See Table 8 in the Appendix for more information.

ECHINACEA

MAJOR APPLICATION OF ECHINACEA ✦ Of all the herbal supplements available today, very few can contend with the popularity that echinacea has seen over the years. It has been used by millions of health seekers and continues to serve as one of the most trusted of all naturally grown medicinal herbs.

To date, more than 400 studies have been conducted to better understand the extent of its clinical potential and many have arrived at the same conclusion: Echinacea seems to have a very positive effect on the immune system, inflammation, respiratory challenges, and an host of other health concerns. This action has made it a champion among supplements during the cold and flu season, as we'll explain later.

AN OVERVIEW OF ECHINACEA ✦ Also known as purple coneflower, there are a total of nine different species of echinacea growing today. Of them, only three are commonly used for medicinal purposes, and the two most popular are *angustifolia* and *purpurea*. Echinacea's immense popularity can be traced to the late 1800s when it was used by Native Americans to counter the venom of poisonous snake bites. It was also used to treat other infections, fatigue, and a number of respiratory conditions.

As time went on, use became more and more common among local physicians, especially those known for treating patients with herbs and other natural remedies. By the 1920s, echinacea "tonics" were a commercial smash among early consumers. Today echinacea supplements are at the peak of popularity and have been used by people from every walk of life to help bolster the immune system.

How Echinacea Works • When taken at the first sign of a cold, flu or other respiratory infection, echinacea has been shown to significantly lessen many of the common symptoms associated with this agonizing period, thus expediting the healing process. Researchers still don't seem to understand exactly why this is, so there's still no definitive explanation as to which specific compounds are responsible for echinacea's strong immune-boosting properties.

Science *has* determined, however, that echinacea plants are teeming with a number of active constituents. Among the most notable are polysaccharides, cichoric acids, and alkylamides. These compounds are believed to be responsible for the immune and antibody stimulation that's been shown to occur after consuming various parts of the plant.

Therapeutic Uses of Echinacea

- *Clear skin.* When taken internally or applied topically, echinacea has been shown to reduce symptoms associated with many common skin problems. Based on its strong antibiotic and virus-fighting properties, the plant's extracts have been used by many to treat conditions such as acne, cold sores, boils, eczema, shingles, and genital herpes.
- *Cold and flu.* Year after year it's estimated that close to half the nation's population suffers from either the common cold or any number of influenza strains. It should come as no surprise that most rush to the doctor

to obtain a high-powered prescription antibiotic capable of wiping out the responsible virus. But many don't realize that some of today's most popular antibiotics are ineffective. However, they will wipe out the body's "friendly" bacteria population.

Echinacea seems to work in a much more sophisticated manner. Instead of simply conquering everything in its path, it encourages the activity of immune system cells such as interferon and white blood cells. These cellular guardians only attack the microbes responsible for infection while preserving a safe environment for the body's friendly bacteria population. For more information about "friendly" bacteria, please refer to Chapter Six.

* *Yeast infections.* Echinacea is a sworn enemy of fungus. Based on its ability to help stimulate the production of white blood cells, it's believed that supplementation can be an effective way to help control yeast replication.

* *Other therapeutic benefits.* Immune system support, respiratory infections, urinary tract infections.

Tips for Taking Echinacea

* Echinacea is fueled by a combination of both alcohol- and water-soluble constituents. Be sure to choose a formula that uses pure root extract for maximum assimilation.

* Always take echinacea at the first sign of a cold or flu to help shorten its duration.

Echinacea.

- When taking echinacea for an extended period of time, it can be wise to take a week off after 6-8 weeks of supplementation to help prevent building a tolerance that could interfere with normal immune system function.
- Those with serious auto-immune conditions such as HIV, lupus, and rheumatoid arthritis should consult their physicians prior to supplementing with echinacea.
- Many users have found that "cycling" echinacea extracts with other known immune-supporting herbs, such as goldenseal and cat's claw, can possitively affect the immune system while preventing tolerance development.

NATURAL COMPANIONS FOR ECHINACEA ✦ Vitamin C, astragalus, olive leaf extract, bovine colostrum

COFACTORS AND CONTRAINDICATIONS OF ECHINACEA ✦ See purple cone flower in Table 8 in the Appendix for more information.

OLIVE LEAF EXTRACT

Since biblical times, the leaves of the olive tree (*Olea europaea*) have been providing health seekers with one of the most powerful and effective antimicrobial constituents ever to be discovered, *oleuropein*. But it's just in the past few decades that the olive leaf has started to receive the therapeutic respect it deserves.

Over the years a number of studies have been conducted to determine why these unique extracts seem to counter microbes so effectively. Many continue to suggest that the active compounds in olive leaf work at the cellular level and can help reduce free radical regeneration, eliminate harmful microbial attack, and increase the immune system's response to inflammation. Supplementing olive leaf won't necessarily cure a disease, but it can be very effective in destroying the pathogens that typically lead to infection. In our opinion, olive leaf is clearly one of the best all-around immune system boosters to keep on hand, especially during cold and flu season.

BOVINE COLOSTRUM

Ayurvedic physicians have used colostrum for thousands of years. Doctors in the U.S. used colostrum as an antibiotic prior to the introduction of sulfa drugs and penicillin. Colostrum has antioxidant and anti-inflammatory properties and was prescribed extensively for the treatment of rheumatoid arthritis in the 1950s. It has a long history of safety and efficacy.

Colostrum, the first secretion of the mammary glands after birth, contains numerous immune system and growth factors. Most notable are interferon, gamma globulin, lactoferrin, growth hormone, insulin-like growth factor (IgF-1), and protease inhibitors. Colostrum has been used clinically to treat viral illnesses, allergies and autoimmune conditions, heart disease, cancer, diabetes, leaky gut syndrome, and to speed wound healing.

Bovine colostrum is biologically transferable to all mammals, including humans. It contains a blocking hormone that prevents allergic reaction to bovine immune factors. It's important to use colostrum only from cows that have been certified as free of antibiotics, pesticides, and synthetic hormones.

Allergies

NAC (N-ACETYL CYSTEINE)

MAJOR APPLICATION OF NAC ✦ N-acetyl cysteine, or NAC, is a highly stabilized form of the amino acid L-cysteine. Its core function is to kick-start the activity of glutathione, one of the body's most beneficial antioxidant enzymes. In doing so it serves as a powerful antioxidant, capable of quickly quenching the ill-effects of free radicals and oxidation.

AN OVERVIEW OF NAC ✦ Studies continue to suggest that when the body's immune system decides to take a break, glutathione levels can decrease in alarming amounts. Without an adequate reserve of glutathione, cells are left vulnerable to unstable free radical attack. When you consider the millions of toxins and other airborne agents that we're all unsuspectingly exposed to every day, this is an invitation for disaster.

How NAC Works   •   In many ways NAC is like a 911 operator. When your body phones in a report of unwanted toxins and other foreign invaders, NAC dispatches glutathione to scour the scene. After a brief interaction, it escorts these cell-threatening free radicals to the liver, where they can be safely excreted.

Many people have found that supplementing with NAC can have a positive influence on the respiratory system. With its strong *mucolytic* (mucus-dissolving) properties, NAC is regularly recommended to smokers, those exposed to second-hand smoke, and those with chronic respiratory problems, such as pneumonia and bronchitis.

THERAPEUTIC USES OF NAC

- *Cancer prevention.* A growing number of researchers suggest that NAC has a promising role preventing of some forms of cancer. By reducing the amount of oxidation caused by free radicals, it appears able to reduce the potential for abnormal cell growth. Smokers and tobacco chewers stand to benefit the most, as it's been shown to stave off the early signs of leukoplakia.
- *Detoxification.* Based on its strong antioxidant properties and ability to rid the body of dangerous toxins, NAC appears to be safe and effective in treating acetaminophen and alcohol poisoning. A growing number of users swear by its ability to help control alcoholism and other chemicals addictions.
- *Healthy vision.* Oxidation from free radicals can be especially testing on the lens and macular regions of the eyes. Based on its ability to counter this activity, NAC may be able to help prevent the onset of macular degeneration and cataracts.

- *Immune system support.* By bolstering the activity of glutathione, NAC helps protect the body from cell-damaging free radicals. It also facilitates the production and activity of vital immune system components such as T-cells and other natural killer-cells.
- *Lung and respiratory health.* NAC helps thin mucus from the sinuses, lungs, and nasal canal. In fact, many physicians now suggest that those with chronic respiratory conditions supplement with NAC to help expedite recovery while also protecting these delicate tissues. A saline nasal wash may augment the activity of NAC.
- *Other therapeutic benefits.* Cardiovascular support, allergies, sinus, cold and flu symptoms.

Tips for taking NAC

- For better absorption NAC should be taken on an empty stomach prior to or between meals.
- Taking NAC on a frequent basis can force the body to excrete more copper in the urine. If you decide to make NAC part of your daily supplemental regime, make sure that you're getting enough copper from your diet or multiple to compensate.
- NAC is a feisty nutrient that completes for absorption with other proteins and amino acids. If you can discipline yourself enough to do so, try to avoid taking NAC at the same time that you take these other supplements.

Natural Companions for NAC ✦ Other antioxidants, especially vitamins A, E, C, and selenium.

Cofactors and Contraindications for NAC ✦ See Table 6 in the Appendix for more information.

QUERCETIN

Major Application of Quercetin ✦ To the delight of many allergy sufferers, this highly concentrated bioflavonoid can serve as the perfect natural solution. Quercetin is commonly found in fruits and onions, although supplementation makes it almost effortless to control how much (or how little) is being consumed. Better still, it's a natural food substance, reasonably priced, and free of many common side effects associated with OTC offerings.

An Overview of Quercetin ✦ This increasingly popular flavonoid is most commonly found in apples and may be the reason why teachers seldom play hooky. Either way, quercetin has become synonymous with good health and very popular among seasonal allergy sufferers. Like the thousands of other flavonoids, quercetin has been a subject of keen interest to researchers as more and more benefits are discovered.

How Quercetin works ✦ Quercetin is a powerful antioxidant that wastes no time attacking free radicals. This has made it especially useful to those interested in boosting the efficacy of their immune systems, protecting cells, and hindering the aging process. Finally, quercetin is a natural inflammation-fighter and has been used by many to ease gout, muscle aches, joint disorders, and a long list of other complaints.

Therapeutic Uses of Quercetin
- *Allergies.* Quercetin use has earned its reputation as a sound way to prevent inflammation and irritation in the bronchial airways and nasal passages. This can be attributed to its ability to hinder the release of histamine, the chemical trigger responsible for so many allergic reactions. Based on this, quercetin has become the supplement of choice for seasonal allergy sufferers as well as for those prone to upper respiratory and asthmatic challenges.
- *Cancer prevention.* Healthy cells are vulnerable to many types of biological attack. Quercetin works to prevent this by tapping into its

antioxidant properties to protect cells from the oxidation caused by free radicals. A recent study illustrated low cancer rates among people who regularly ate apples. If you do decide to go au naturel, be sure to eat the apple's skin, too.

+ *Cardiovascular support.* Anyone concerned with heart integrity should strongly consider making quercetin a part of everyday life. It limits how much LDL cholesterol the body is able to oxidize, thus preventing arterial wall damage. Quercetin also creates a friendly atmosphere for vitamin E, a primary safeguard to healthy heart cells. Finally, it promotes healthy circulation by naturally breaking up aggregated clots while they're still forming.

+ *Digestion.* Quercetin may be able to improve digestion in two very interesting ways. First, it's an anti-inflammatory. Based on this, many researchers believe that it can correct some conditions that prevent the small intestines from properly utilizing nutrients. This has made it a favorite among people who suffer from irritable bowel syndrome (IBS) and Crohn's disease. It also seems to be very good at preventing H. pylori (*Helicobacter pylori*), a nasty little ulcer-causing bacterium that embeds itself in the stomach lining.

+ *Healthy vision.* One of quercetin's best-kept secrets is its ability to prevent the formation of sugar-producing enzymes manufactured by the body. One of the most concerning of these is sorbitol, which has been linked to the formation of cataracts. This should be great news to anyone who smokes (please quit, by the way) or subjects him or herself to a lifetime of damaging UV rays caused by spending long hours in the sun.

+ *Respiratory health.* While it's a beautiful and hopeful time, the transition from winter to spring can be a nightmare for people with chronic respiratory conditions. Asthma, seasonal allergies, bronchitis, and others conditions seem to respond very well to quercetin. This can be attributed to the positive influence it has over histamine, the inflammatory chemical responsible for worldwide sneezing frenzies and record-breaking tissue sales. It also minimizes inflammation in the bronchial airways.

+ *Other therapeutic benefits.* Heartburn, inflammation.

Tips for Taking Quercetin

+ Quercetin and vitamin C work well together. If you're just taking it for general health purposes, look for a formula that contains at least 50 mg of vitamin C.
+ Bromelain is another natural synergist with quercetin and has become very popular to reduce season allergy symptoms.
+ Based on its rising popularity, many multi-antioxidant formulas now include quercetin as a primary ingredient. Getting a little extra certainly won't hurt, but if you're not taking it to treat a specific condition, you may be able to avoid the redundancy and expense of purchasing it separately.
+ There are mixed feeling on how to take it, although it seems to be gentle enough to take on an empty stomach. Of course, if taking it that way doesn't agree with you, taking it with a small meal won't hinder its ability.

NATURAL COMPANIONS FOR QUERCETIN + Other antioxidants, vitamin C, bromelain, vitamin A, calcium, pepZin, CoQ_{10}, and essential fatty acids.

COFACTORS AND CONTRAINDICATIONS FOR QUERCETIN + See Table 5 in the Appendix for more information.

VITAMIN C

Vitamin C plays many roles within the body, and is popular for its healing, cell-protecting, and immune-boosting properties. While natural C from citrus is still one of the best sources, vitamin C in supplemental form is available in a number of varieties including tablet, capsule, powder, liquid, and drink mix. A full description of vitamin C, its history, and its therapeutic uses is included in Chapter One.

NETTLE

The leaves and roots of nettle (*Urtica dioica*), or stinging nettle, as it's often referred to, are rich in a number of natural therapeutic compounds. Among the most important are polysaccharides, lignans, vitamin C, phytosterols, and malic acid. For centuries nettle has been consumed to treat a number of health conditions ranging from inflammation and PMS to urinary challenges and problem skin. One of the most fascinating facets of this flowering perennial, however, is the positive effect it seems to have on seasonal allergy sufferers. Based on a number of studies, standardized extracts from nettle's root and leaves contain natural compounds that have been shown to hinder the release of histamine, a vasoactive (blood vessel-affecting) substance that triggers the sneezing, runny nose, and watery eyes associated with allergies and hay fever. During allergy season the immune system is constantly on high alert due to the increased level of airborne allergens, such as pollen, dander, ragweed, and mold. When it detects their presence, the immune system sounds a biological alarm that ultimately results in the release of histamine. Many users report that nettle extracts seem to be very helpful to keep this under control.

PYCNOGENOL®

French maritime pine bark extracts such as Pycnogenol® and enzogenol have become revered as some of the most potent and versatile antioxidants in the world. Based on more than 100 clinical trials and published studies, we now know that Pycnogenol® extracts contain an impressive collection of biologically active compounds. They include bioflavonoids (catechins, epicatechins, taxifolins, monomers, and epicatechins); oligomeric procyanidnins (OPCs); and phenolic fruit acids, such as ferulic acid and caffeic acid. This strong profile is what ultimately makes Pycnogenol® useful in covering such a broad spectrum of health concerns.

As evidenced by a 2002 study published in the *Journal of Phytotherapy Research*, Pycnogenol® is more than just another high-powered cell safeguard. Aside from providing exceptional protection against free radical destruction, Pycnogenol® was also shown in this specific in vitro study to inhibit the release of mast cell histamines as effectively as a popular anti-asthmatic prescription drug. It also has strong anti-inflammatory properties that may be able to help soothe raw or irritated nasal and bronchial passages.

Asthma

FORSKOLIN

AN OVERVIEW OF FORSKOLIN ✦ Practitioners of India's traditional Ayurvedic medicine have relied on *Coleus forskohlii*, a not-so-distant member of the mint family, for hundreds of years to help treat a number of health concerns, especially those regulated by the body's circulatory and respiratory systems. Since its initial discovery in the 1970s, it's become very popular in treating hypothyroidism. Its abilities, however, are in no way limited to the production of thyroid hormones.

HOW FORSKOLIN WORKS ✦ Forskolin compounds have been shown to help stimulate activity of an enzyme known as adenylate cyclase while, at the same time, increasing the amount of cyclic AMP (cAMP) in cells. While this might sound tricky, it's really just a scientific way of saying that forskolin acts as sort of a "starting gun" for a long list of enzymatic and cellular reactions. Forskolin, by acting on cAMP, reduces inflammation, prevents platelet aggregation, reduces intraocular pressure (antiglaucomic), reduces blood pressure, stimulates release of fatty acids from storage sites (fat loss), and improves heart action.

Most important for asthmatics, forskolin has been shown to help prevent bronchial spasms while soothing and relaxing the muscles that allow them to occur. This has made it very popular with asthmatics as well as with those who suffer from both chronic and acute bronchitis.

Therapeutic Uses of Forskolin

* Asthma-related lung spasms
* Cardiovascular function
* Hypothyroidism (low thyroid hormone production)
* Neurotransmitter and cognitive support
* Vasoactive (blood vessel) conditioning

Tips for Taking Forskolin

* Forskolin supplementation is not meant to take the place of asthma medication and should be approved by a physician prior to use.
* Those who have been diagnosed with low blood pressure should avoid or use caution when taking forskolin because it has been shown to relax the arterial walls,
* Some studies have suggested that coleus extracts may increase the production of bile and other digestive fluids. With this in mind, anyone who struggles with digestive, gastrointestinal, or stomach lining issues may want to avoid supplements that contain forskolin.
* For optimal results we recommend taking forskolin in 2-3 divided doses with a small meal to increase absorption.
* When selecting a product be sure to look for those that contain extracts standardized to a minimum of at least 18 percent forskolin.

Natural Companions for Forskolin ✦ Quercetin, bromelain, vitamin C

Cofactors and Contraindications for Forskolin ✦ See Table 8 in the Appendix for more information.

QUERCETIN

If you're a red wine drinker, this one might ring a bell. Quercetin is a powerful water-soluble antioxidant that belongs to the bioflavonoid family. By nature bioflavonoids are plant pigments that help prevent and eliminate free radical damage throughout the body. This is one of the now famous cell-protecting compounds that has given red wine drinkers the idea that they're imbibing also to get "healthy." In fact, many researchers believe that quercetin is one of the reasons why the French seem to have such low occurrences of heart disease.

Among the long list of conditions for which quercetin is believed to be helpful is in treating asthma. As an antioxidant, it works by protecting the cells of the respiratory system, lessening the inflammation of the bronchial tubes and, perhaps most important, inhibiting the release of histamine. This three-tiered support makes quercetin one supplement that should rank high on the list for anyone suffering from asthma and allergies.

BROMELAIN

This pineapple-derived proteolytic enzyme could best be described as a natural enemy to asthma. For starters, bromelain possesses strong anti-inflammatory properties and may also be able to help lessen the severity of coughs and congestion, while preventing fluid from accumulating within the nasal passages. In addition, it has been shown to help reduce the volume and thickness of mucus. And, no, this might not paint the most appealing picture, but it's vital to anyone living with asthma or other bronchial inflammatory conditions.

One double-blind trial examined 48 people who suffered from sinusitis ranging from mild to chronic. After 6 days of supplementing with bromelain, researchers were amazed to discover that those who had been supplementing with bromelain experienced an 83 percent reduction in inflammation, while the placebo group averaged just a 53 percent reduction.

A growing number of nutritionists and users have reported greater success by supplementing quercetin and bromelain together for their synergistic effect.

Cofactors and Contraindications for Bromelain ◆ See Table 7 in the Appendix for more information.

To Sum It All Up

The immune system is the first line of defense against invading microbes. When such foreigners invade, the innate immune system triggers an inflammatory response, calling certain cells to flock to the infection site and wall it off to prevent the infection from spreading. These cells secrete an array of chemicals called cytokines that attract other immune cells and prime them for battle. Evidence of this activity can be seen on the surface of the body as swelling, redness, pain and, sometimes, fever. Inflammatory activity in one part of the body can have a debilitating effect on the rest of the body, resulting in fatigue, flu-like symptoms, and lack of appetite.

Inflammation and Autoimmunity

In some cases the inflammatory response is overly aggressive and continues for long periods of time. It may be triggered by a viral infection or extreme exposure to a toxins and is often found in those with a family history of auto-immune conditions. All told, more than 80 different autoimmune conditions have been identified. Women are more likely to have such diseases, perhaps the result of immune interplay with hormones. Cardiovascular disease, which involves long-standing inflammation, may stem in part from an autoimmune reaction in arterial walls.

Inflammation and infection is generally short-lived because of our innate immunity, but those with weakened resistance may have frequent infections. A primary site for repeated infections is the respiratory tract and lungs. In susceptible individuals, vaccination may be an option that can disrupt the process. That's because T-cells sport tiny tags that identify the invader to be destroyed. Other cells, known as B-cells, are coaxed into producing antibodies that detect the offending pathogen and quickly destroy it. This kind of immunity is called acquired or adaptive immunity. A key feature of adaptive immunity is the memory that trained T-cells and antibodies have for a particular pathogen. In many cases vaccination confers protection for years.

Allergies and asthma result from an exaggerated or inappropriate reaction to environmental factors. The rate of allergy and its complication, asthma, is on the rise due to the increasing presence of sensitizing factors. Hypersensitivity reactions can be classified as antibody-mediated or cell-mediated.

Antibody type hypersensitivity occurs immediately when a sensitizing antigen evokes a response such as skin rash, eczema, rhinitis, conjunctivitis, or asthma. In extreme cases, bronchioles in the lungs become constricted and blood pressure drops to dangerous levels. This is called anaphylaxis and can be life-threatening.

An allergic reaction can also be delayed, occurring several hours or days after contact with a sensitizing antigen. In this case, T-cells bearing tags for a specific antigen release cytokines in an inflammatory response. At the same time, they recruit macrophages which are transformed into huge mast cells that unleash a host of mediators, including histamine. Most allergy sufferers are acutely aware of the action of histamine—hay fever; itching, runny nose; sneezing; headache—from blood vessel dilation. In addition, pro-inflammatory progeny of fatty acids, called leukotrienes, prostaglandin, and thromboxanes, are released. Serotonin, a neurotransmitter that also dilates blood vessels and may induce sleepiness, is then released.

Use of the natural aids suggested in this chapter, in addition to avoiding foods and beverages that can worsen allergies, can go a long way to alleviate allergies. They may also be used along with conventional therapy, if that is required.

Our discussion of inflammation and the immune system flows right into the *malabsorption syndrome*, the topic of our next chapter.

CHAPTER SIX

Malabsorption Syndrome

"Death sits in the bowels . . . bad digestion is the root of all evil."

—*Hippocrates, 400 B.C.*

ARLIEST HISTORICAL RECORDS reveal that Chinese, Tibetan, Indian, Greek and Roman healers all recognized that a toxic bowel leads to ill health. Today the condition is known as *intestinal dysbiosis* and its relief continues to be a vital part in maintaining optimum health and good digestion.

As Sherry Rogers, M.D., states in her book *Detoxify or Die*, "If the gut isn't healthy, then nothing else can heal, for it houses half the detoxification system and half the infection-fighting immune system."

The entire digestive tract is an ecosystem of the highest complexity, containing more than 500 different species of probiotic ("for life") microflora. Surprisingly, the human gut contains 10 times more viable microorganisms than the total number of functioning cells within the body. So complex is this system that some researchers have termed it the *microbe organ*, and it is now recognized as rivaling the liver in the number of biochemical transformations and reactions that it orchestrates.

What You Will Find in This Chapter

+ The digestive process and malabsorption
+ Poor digestion and "leaky gut"
+ Ulcers, celiac and irritable bowel
+ Constipation and detoxification
+ Skin allergies and eczema

The Digestive Process and Malabsorption

Most of us give little thought to how food is transformed within us. Yet approximately 60 tons of food will be processed through the digestive system during a normal lifetime. The gastrointestinal tract forms an enormous interface between the human internal environment and the outside world. It's really a long tube, stretching nearly 9 meters (30 feet) from mouth to anus. Various sections of the digestive tube are specialized to perform specific functions and, in a nutshell, here is what they do.

The mouth, like the rest of the gastrointestinal tract, contains a sticky protective secretion called mucin and an acidic mucopolysaccharide, a kind of complex carbohydrate. These secretions aid swallowing and help move nutrients through the digestive system. The acid mantle provided by mucopolysaccharides prevents pathogens from adhering to mucosal cells and passing through them into circulation.

Chewing is important because it not only makes it easier to swallow food, it exposes more surface area in foods so that digestive enzymes can break them down. Enzymes secreted by the salivary gland located under the tongue begin this breakdown process on carbohydrates. Salivary enzymes also contain antibacterial agents which protect the mouth and gums from infection. A sticky "bolus" is created with food before it's swallowed and the act of swallowing prevents food from sliding down the wrong way. Wave-like contractions push food along the esophagus.

Enzyme	What it Acts Upon	Units of Activity
Amylase	Carbohydrates (starches and other polysaccharides)	DU or SKB
Protease	Protein (large amino acid chains)	PC or HUT
Peptidase	Peptides (smaller amino acid chains)	SPU
Lipase	Fats (triglycerides and other lipids)	LU or FIP
Lactase	Lactose (milk sugar)	LacU
Cellulase	Cellulose (plant fiber)	CU
Maltase	Maltose (malt sugar)	DP
Invertase	Sucrose (table sugar)	IAU or INVU
Phytase	Phytic acid in wheat and whole grains	
Bromelain	Anti-inflammatory, necrotic tissue (injury, burns)	GDU
Papain	Same	FCC PU
Pancreatin	Protease, lipase, amylase, anti-inflammatory	USP
Nattokinase	Proteolytic, anti-arthritic, anti-inflammatory	FU

Adapted from Brad Rachman, *Clinical Nutrition Insights*, 1997; Karen DeFelice, *Enzymes*, 2003.

FIGURE 6-1 **Enzymes, Their Functions and Measure of Activity**

The stomach is a pouch about the size of your fist that absorbs some substances such as alcohol and short- and medium-chain fatty acids. The stomach can expand to accommodate the contents of a large meal and sometimes we overuse this expansion capability—and live to regret it—and experience trouble sleeping or weight gain. Muscles (sphincters) at the top and bottom of the stomach prevent its contents from washing back up the esophagus or entering the intestine too soon. Considerable physical and chemical transformation of food occurs in the stomach. The enzyme pepsin initiates protein digestion, while gastric lipase breaks fats into smaller units for later digestion. As digestion proceeds, contractions push processed stomach contents through the sphincter and into the duodenum, the first section of the small intestine. Accessory organs such as the pancreas, liver, and gall bladder secrete digestive juices into the duodenum to continue the breakdown of carbohydrates, proteins, and fats.

Glands in the stomach lining secrete hydrochloric acid, or HCl. It is the only acid produced by the human body and is of greatest importance for nutrient absorption. The eight essential amino acids isoleucine, leucine, lysine, methionine, phenylalanine, threonine, tryptophan, and valine rely on HCL for absorption. So do 15 minerals and two B-vitamins, folic acid, and B-12. Minerals are the buffering agents the body uses to maintain a healthy, neutral pH and they cannot be liberated from food or absorbed without HCl. We think of HCL as necessary to activate pepsin for protein digestion, and it is. But HCL also destroys most of the bacteria that arrive in the stomach in food and beverages. Ironically, weak stomach acid secretion (not too much acid) is responsible for most digestive complaints and the *malabsorption syndrome*.

The pancreas has dual functions in digestion. First is the secretion of pancreatic juice, which contains enzymes that breakdown carbohydrates, proteins, and fats. Pancreatic enzymes require a higher pH to function, and so the pancreas also secretes bicarbonates that neutralize the acid contents of the stomach that have been discharged into the duodenum. Second, the pancreas secretes the hormones insulin and glucagon that control blood sugar metabolism.

Liver and Gall Bladder

The liver produces bile and the gall bladder, in turn, concentrates it. Bile is one of the most important digestive juices because it emulsifies fats so that they can be digested by lipases. It also helps eliminate wastes and contains bicarbonates to neutralize digestive stomach contents (chyme), a necessary step for lipases to break them down in the duodenum.

Sometimes called gall, bile salts contain cholesterol and, in some instances, become concentrated and insoluble. Small deposits known as gallstones can lodge in the gall bladder or bile duct leading to the duodenum, causing great pain. Gall bladder removal disrupts fat digestion, although the liver continues to produce it. Usually some modification in fat intake, at least for a time, is required after gall bladder surgery. The liver produces bile, but with more than 2,000 different enzyme reactions to keep track of, the liver can become overburdened. A toxic liver is a recipe for disaster, because its ability to detoxify the body and process nutrients and medicines is compromised. We'll talk more about what to do about this a little later on.

The small intestine consists of three sections; a short section called the duodenum, a long section called the jejunum, and a little, shorter section known as the ileum. The duodenal wall is lined with small glands that secrete digestive enzymes and the hormone secretin. Secretin stimulates bicarbonate and water secretion by the pancreas and *cholecystekinin* (CCK), a hormone that stimulates the gall bladder to release bile. The duodenum receives chyme from the stomach and is the entry point for secretions from accessory glands. Hooked onto the duodenum is the jejunum, which is followed by the ileum.

The surface of the jejunum, where most absorption of food and nutrients occurs, consists of tiny protrusions called villi, which give it a furry appearance. Each villus contains thousands of microscopic, absorptive units called microvilli or brush border cells. With its thousands of microvilli, the surface of the small intestine covers approximately 250-400 square meters (300-478 square yards).

Small units of digestive nutrients are then absorbed through the villi in the next section of intestine (jejunum), and enter the bloodstream or lymphatic vessels in the villi. The absorbed nutrients begin their journey to the liver for further processing and distribution to various parts of the body. Most vitamins, minerals, and other nutrients are absorbed in these first sections of the small intestine. As intestinal contents reach the ileum, most nutrients except vitamin B-12 have been absorbed.

The bowel, or colon, continues to process digestive liquids and some important processes occur here. Probiotics increase in concentration from the jejunum downward to the colon. Most benefits accrue here from the beneficial microflora, which produce important metabolites, such as short-chain fatty acids, B-vitamins, and vitamin K. The SCFAs stimulate the immune system and the probiotics absorb cholesterol so that it doesn't circulate back into the system. This helps keep cholesterol levels in normal range.

The colon, of a larger diameter and a fairly rigid organ, is shaped somewhat like an upside-down "U" with an ascending section on the right side of the abdomen, followed by a transverse section crossing under the umbilicus. The last section descends on the left side of the abdomen toward the rectum. Fermentation occurs in the ascending colon, while electrolytes and water are absorbed from the descending colon. Stools start to form in the transverse colon. Ideally, it takes 18-24 hours for food to pass from the mouth through the entire system. This is referred to as bowel transit time and is used as one measure of digestive efficiency. It would be nice if digestion occurred just as it's supposed to, but unfortunately this isn't the case for many people. We will now discuss the various kinds of *malabsorption syndrome*.

Malabsorption

Malabsorption is a general term for poor digestion, microbial contamination, and abnormalities in gut mucosa.

Poor digestion can result from lack of digestive enzymes, accessory organ dysfunction, illness or stress. Stress has profound effects on digestion and nutrient absorption.

The enteric nervous system (ENS) guides all the play action of the digestive system. The ENS, or "gut brain," contains many of the same hormones, peptides, and neurotransmitters that the central nervous system does. These hormones, peptides, and neurotransmitters signal how much of a particular kind of enzyme will be needed based on what's in the meal.

The sensory organs of smell, sight and taste pick up much of this information—another reason to chew your food carefully and enjoy every bite. You will find this advice repeated in *7-Color Cuisine*. Enjoying your food is also an excellent way to combat stress. Once food arrives in the stomach and intestines, sensory receptors pick up additional information which is relayed to accessory glands, triggering release of appropriate enzymes and other substances that make up the digestive milieu. These sensory receptors are also charged with making sure that protective mucus secreted by stomach glands is sufficient to protect it against attack by digestive acids.

Normally there is a balance between sympathetic (fight or flight) and parasympathetic (relaxed) nervous response. During times of stress, sympathetic response dominates, and its effects on the gastrointestinal tract include slowing movement of food through the system and reduction of digestive secretions. Sphincters that separate the individual compartments of the digestive system tighten, further impeding the flow of food through the digestive system.

People perceive stress signals differently. One may be compelled to eat more, while another will not want to eat at all. Obviously, if either goes on for extended periods, serious illness will result.

Microbial Contamination

Hydrochloric acid is extremely strong and kills most bacteria that enter the stomach. Hypochloridria refers to low levels of stomach acid and has been implicated in gastric ulcers, particularly those occurring in the higher fundic region of the stomach. Autopsy of gastric mucosa in hypochloridria patients has shown that many species of bacteria, including *Helicobacter pylori*, cover the gastric lining and can also infiltrate to deeper layers of tissue, causing mechanical and biochemical damage. It's thought some of these bacteria may contribute to stomach cancer by producing harmful nitrosamines.

Yeast (*Candida albicans*) organisms are normally found in the colon along with several special of pathogenic bacteria, such as *Escherichia coli*. These organisms are kept in check by probiotics. However, when the microflora environment is upset, often by extended antibiotic use, candida takes over, causing gas, bloating, and discomfort that can also colonize other parts of the body because Candida mycelia can be transported in the bloodstream. The biggest problem with candida overgrowth occurs when it grows into the mucosa and leaves holes or large pores through which undigested particles, toxins, and bacteria can enter the bloodstream. Pathogenic bacteria putrefy colonic contents and produce deadly by-products, noxious gases, and toxins.

These produce local irritation and may be involved in colon cancer and other diseases.

ABNORMALITIES IN GUT MUCOSA

These include "leaky gut," which describes the condition of having large pores in the intestinal mucosa. Conditions attributable to leaky gut are many and include neurological symptoms (mood swings, anxiety, nervousness, nail biting, finger or cheek chewing, brain fogginess), chronic joint and muscle pain, GI disturbances (diarrhea, constipation, indigestion), bladder infections, migraines, poor immunity, and skin rashes. Let's delve a little deeper into the implications of leaky gut.

Poor Digestion and "Leaky Gut"

Probiotic microflora maintain a delicate balance between the immune system and the gastrointestinal tract. When this balance is upset, disease and inflammation result. Immune receptors line the entire gastrointestinal tract (GIT) to form a protective shield against pathogens, toxins, and other potentially harmful substances. The mouth, throat, stomach, and intestines are constantly exposed to a wide variety of microbes and their toxic metabolites that come from what you eat, drink, and breathe. If you didn't have an active immunity in your digestive tract, you wouldn't survive.

A gastrointestinal tract with adequate mucus production, secretion of hydrochloric acid (HCl), digestive enzymes, bicarbonate secretion, efficient gut motility, and a balance in microfloral species is the basis of good health.

Many chronic and degenerative diseases have been linked to alterations in intestinal microflora. Included are irritable bowel syndrome and inflammatory bowel disease, which encompasses celiac, Crohn's, and ulcerative colitis. Autoimmune conditions, such as rheumatoid arthritis and ankylosing spondylitis, have also been linked to disturbances in intestinal microflora. Fortunately it's fairly easy to restore a healthy balance in intestinal microflora.

ACIDOPHILUS

Major Application of Acidophilus ✦ Acidophilus is a single-celled member of the *probiotic* family, which, as we have seen, is essential for sound health. This "good" bacteria helps the body maintain a positive, friendly digestive environment by eliminating the presence of harmful bacteria and engaging in nutrient uptake and production of helpful metabolites.

An Overview of Acidophilus ✦ Mere mention of the word "bacteria" can conjure some rather nasty images, but the body *needs* good bacteria to maintain a healthy intestinal environment.

The digestive tract is home to hundreds of different bacterial and yeast strains. Some are good and, as it turns out, some are not good at all. *Lactobacillus acidophilus* belongs to a family of microbes more commonly known as probiotics. As one of many friendly bacteria, probiotics such as acidophilus encourage a healthy gastrointestinal (GI) tract by maintaining a balance with pathogenic bacteria.

How Acidophilus Works ✦ It doesn't take much for harmful bacteria to increase in the GIT. Poor diet, environmental factors, exposure to chemicals, and a wealth of other situational conditions can all contribute to high levels of bad GI bacteria. One of the most common causes of harmful bacteria build-up, ironically, is use of antibiotics. When prescribed for ailments like the flu, upper respiratory, and other infections, antibiotics are commonly used to knock out the infection.

What very few people realize is that these medications also wipe out good bacteria in the process. Probiotics, such as acidophilus, not only help protect the digestive tract, but can also restore the good bacteria that have been swept away after a bout of infection. Consequently, it is advisable to take acidophilus supplements during and following a course of antibiotic therapy.

- *Cold sores.* These embarrassing and painful lesions, also known as fever blisters, can be triggered by just about anything. Among the most detrimental causes are stress, sun, minor trauma to the lips, poor diet, dental treatment, allergy to certain foods, and any immune system challenge that produces an increased metabolic rate or fever. Susceptibility to these lesions that often occur at the vermilion border of the lips is much greater than was once thought, because of widespread infection by the herpes virus. Some have found that taking acidophilus at the initial "tingle" can help shorten the duration of cold sores and, in some cases, prevent onset altogether.

  In cases of repeated herpes occurrence, taking the amino acid lysine along with vitamin C, zinc, and acidophilus may be an effective method to thwart appearance of lesions. This happens because lysine suppresses viral growth while its antagonistic amino acid arginine increases it. The American diet is generally higher in arginine than lysine.

- *Healthy digestion.* When we refer to the community of bacteria that resides within the human digestive tract, we're essentially referring to its *flora.* Supplementing with acidophilus and related species is unquestionably one of the smartest (and easiest) ways to ensure that your digestive tract has a healthy flora. Recently, the yogurt industry has been touting use of its products as a hip, tasty way to accomplish this. And, yes, yogurt does contain probiotics. However, most containers don't list how much or if they contain "live" cultures, and this can leave you guessing about whether you're getting enough or the correct strain. Supplementation eliminates the guesswork, as supplements clearly state how many billions of organisms are contained in each serving.

- *Immune system support.* Allowing your GI tract to become infested with harmful bacteria is the biological equivalent of asking your immune system and liver to work overtime, without pay. Supplementing with acidophilus encourages a healthy floral population capable of fighting infection within the GI tract. Ultimately, this gives the immune system one less thing to worry about, leaving it free to keep tabs on other vital systems in need of protection.

- *Yeast infections* (**Candida**). One of the most grossly misconceived notions about yeast is that it is something that affects only women. This is absolutely false, as yeast (*Candida albicans*) lives inside each and every one of us. For the most part, it enjoys a quiet, humble existence and generally keeps to itself. But it can turn on you without warning, especially after treatment of an infection with antibiotics. Antibiotics do not affect candida, but do destroy healthy microflora along with pathogenic bacteria when they are used. Thus candida, now left unchecked, responds with overgrowth. In addition to vaginal infection, excess yeast can lead to flatulence, diarrhea, constipation, fatigue, and urinary tract infections.

- *Other therapeutic benefits of acidophilus.* Skin disorders, ulcers.

TIPS FOR TAKING ACIDOPHILUS

- It's extremely important to read labels long before taking your first dose of acidophilus. Select a formula that contains at least 1-2 billion "live" organisms per tablet or capsule.

- Properly storing your acidophilus supplements will make the difference on how well they flourish within your GI tract. Remember, they're alive and should never be subjected to excessive cold or heat. To be absolutely safe, we recommend keeping all probiotics refrigerated.

- If you're using acidophilus for the first time, you may want to take it with meals. This will allow your body to adjust to the increased presence of "good" bacteria, while preventing the possibility of flatulence or diarrhea.

- Staying consistent with your probiotic regime is strongly recommended. Get in the habit of taking acidophilus with meals in order to promote a flora that's saturated with helpful, friendly bacteria. Over time, many users report increased energy, less stomach discomfort, and better metabolism.

Natural Companions for Acidophilus ◆ Prebiotics such as arabinogalactans (discussed in chapter 5), milk thistle, digestive enzymes, ground flax seed, psyllium seed powder.

Cofactors and Contraindications for Acidophilus ◆ See Table 7 in the Appendix for more information.

DIGESTIVE ENZYMES

Enzymes are the workhorses of the body. All are protein catalysts for more than 3,000 biochemical transformations. Enzymes can be grouped into three categories; metabolic enzymes that carry out cellular functions, digestive enzymes that transform food into nutrients available for absorption, and enzymes that are contained in raw foods. It's the latter two categories of enzymes that we will discuss in this section.

Cooking anything at a temperature of greater than 120 degrees Fahrenheit—about the temperature you can comfortably eat—destroys food enzymes. Raw foods are teeming with active enzymes. This is evidenced by the growth of new leaves or sprouts on vegetables left in the refrigerator for more than a week. Cooked foods will merely sit there and ferment or decay from bacterial action. Eating most foods raw is one way to be sure that what you eat comes prepackaged with sufficient enzymes to digest it, but warm, cooked foods are more desirable during cold weather. In addition, carotenoids that are so ubiquitous in golden, orange and red winter vegetables are more bioavailable when cooked.

That leaves us needing another option, and that's an oral digestive enzyme. These can be animal, plant, or microbial enzymes. Animal enzymes (pancreatin) have a narrow pH range within which they are active. Plant and microbial enzymes are active over a much wider pH range, giving them a distinct advantage. Plus, they go to work as soon as they come in contact with food, even in the mouth.

For instance, plant enzymes begin breaking down food as it's chewed and microbial enzymes go to work as soon as they're moistened. Animal enzyme activity will be delayed until the proper pH is reached, usually in the duodenum. This can be as long as one-and-a-half hours later, depending on the composition of the meal. Figure 6-1 lists the major enzymes and what they digest. Enzyme formulas group different types of microbial enzymes according to the specific function they're designed to perform. Some formulas are designed for fat digestion, others for protein or carbohydrate digestion.

Proteolytic Enzymes are an interesting group of enzymes in that they're used systemically to digest foreign or dead material. The primary application for proteolytic enzymes is to reduce inflammation, scavenge necrotic matter, and help repair injuries. Proteolytic enzymes are also applied topically to burns to help clean the area of dead tissues (debridement) and stimulate new, healthy tissue growth.

TIPS FOR TAKING DIGESTIVE ENZYMES
+ Don't take digestive enzymes at the same time as acidophilus.
+ Choose your enzyme formulas carefully, using the guide listed above.
+ Take enzymes at the beginning of the meal
+ When using proteolytic enzymes, take them between meals.

NATURAL COMPANIONS FOR ENZYMES + Acidophilus, BioPerine®, milk thistle, L-glutamine, deglycyrrhized licorice.
+ *BioPerine®*. Black pepper is one of the most widely used spices in the world. Historically used as a preservative, pepper contains phytonutrients that aid digestion. According to one report, during medieval times court physicians observed that when guests were served highly peppered dishes they experienced considerably fewer digestive problems. Unfortunately, most Americans are not even aware of the medicinal

properties of pepper and, like most herbs and spices, pepper loses most of its potency when stored for prolonged periods of time. That's why peppercorn-grinding mills have become popular. The aromatic oils in peppercorns are retained when they're freshly ground.

While adding black pepper (*Piper nigrum L.*) aids digestion, it's a particular active component called piperine in pepper that's important. A special extract known as BioPerine® contains 95 percent piperine and is used to enhance the absorption of dietary supplements.

Derived from the fruit of black pepper plants, BioPerine® is a patented standardized extract which helps the body to absorb nutrients. Based on its safety and growing popularity, many supplement manufacturers are now including it in digestive support supplements. The primary function of this thermonutrient is to stimulate the body's own thermogenic (creating heat) process. Clinical studies have shown that this is critical to facilitate the predigestion process and to increase gastrointestinal absorption.

In one study of several nutrients, among them beta carotene, vitamin B-6, and the mineral selenium in the form of selenomethionine, 30 men and women took supplements either fortified or nonfortified with BioPerine®. Results showed that blood levels of beta carotene increased by 60 percent, selenium levels by 30 percent, and vitamin B-6 levels were 2.5 times higher when the supplements were fortified with BioPerine®.

COFACTORS AND CONTRAINDICATIONS FOR DIGESTIVE ENZYMES ◆ See "plant enzymes" in Table 7 in the Appendix for more information.

Detoxifying the Liver

MILK THISTLE (SILYBUM MARIANUM)

Milk thistle (*Silybum marianum*), discussed in Chapter Three, is the undisputed champion of all liver supplements and celebrates a history of side effect-free use that dates back thousands of years. Among the seemingly never-ending list of digestive functions that milk thistle influences, three *really* stand out.

Milk thistle stimulates the production and flow of bile. Bile is the body's number one digestive juice and, without enough of it, the liver can have a very difficult time filtering everything that enters our bodies. This includes foods, beverages, smoke, heavy metals, exhaust, and billions of other unwelcome airborne agents.

Milk thistle fights free radicals within the digestive system. Any abnormal interference in the digestive process can throw things completely off-kilter. One common challenge occurs when the body's reserve of glutathione runs low. This tripeptide (composed of three) amino acid is a powerful free radical fighter, notorious for scouring the digestive tract in search of toxins to eliminate.

Milk thistle helps protect and repair liver cells. One of the most fascinating traits of milk thistle rests in its ability to protect and repair damaged liver cells. Unlike other organs, the liver is capable of regenerating itself under optimal conditions and, from your liver's perspective, nothing creates a more favorable environment than milk thistle. It establishes a protective barrier around the membrane of questionable liver cells, thus preventing the liver from being biologically corrupted by toxins. It also assists to facilitate the regeneration process by encouraging the replacement of compromised cells with healthy, new cells.

Soothing Minor Irritation in the Stomach and Duodenum

L-GLUTAMINE

If we all ate perfect diets, there would be no reason to talk about glutamine (discussed as a companion for protein powder in Chapter Three). Not because it lacks importance, but because it is a nonessential amino acid, and the body is quite capable of manufacturing its own supply, provided we regularly consume foods that contain the basic amino acids needed to produce it. But, as we all know, perfectly balanced diets are rarely seen these days and,consequently,a glutamine deficiency can be bad news for the digestive process.

Under normal circumstances, glutamine works by protecting and conditioning the delicate walls of the digestive tract and stomach. These are both very vulnerable tissues of the body and must replace themselves every five days or so. Mucosal cells, as we have seen, are targets for an unthinkable assortment of microbes and parasites. Over time, this unfavorable environment can open the doors to infection, ulcers, and other more serious diseases, such as Crohn's, irritable bowel syndrome, leaky gut, and colitis.

If you're one of the few who still prepares every meal using only fresh ingredients, good for you. And if your life is relatively free of stress, you're probably in the clear. If you're not, it might be time to consider changing your diet or making glutamine part of your daily supplementation regime.

COFACTORS AND CONTRAINDICATIONS FOR GLUTAMINE ✦ See Table 6 in the Appendix for more information.

Ulcers, Celiac, and Irritable Bowel

Inflammatory bowel diseases are extremely serious and require medical help. Nevertheless, the supplement suggestions in this section can serve as adjunctive therapy.

Celiac disease, sometimes known as gluten intolerance, is quite common and responds well to elimination of foods containing gluten, such as wheat, barley, and rye. Distant relatives of these grains include oats, rice, corn, sorghum, and millet. Although they contain small amounts of gluten, they may be better tolerated than wheat, rye, and barley products.

A surprising number of disorders can be traced to celiac disease, including anemia, anxiety, depression, arthritis, ADHD, autism, chronic fatigue syndrome, fibromyalgia, irritable bowel syndrome, osteoporosis, schleroderma, thyroiditis, and vitamin K deficiency.

Other inflammatory bowel diseases that involve nutrient deficiencies are ulcerative colitis and Crohn's disease. These conditions are marked by gut permeability and extensive nutrient malabsorption. Surprisingly, non-steroidal inflammatory drugs are believed to cause colitis and to exacerbate existing conditions by increasing gut permeability to sensitizing foods, bacteria, and toxins. Refined sugars and fast food top the list of offending foods. Specific foods to which an individual is allergic should be determined, as adopting a hypoallergenic diet may reduce symptoms substantially. A high-dose vitamin

Alkaline-Forming Foods	Neutral Foods	Acid-Forming Foods (Ideal = 20% or less of the diet)
• Fruits, except some berries some citrus, • Vegetables • Grains (amaranth, millet, quinoa only) • Beans (green, lima, peas, snap, soybeans, soy products) • Nuts (almonds, chestnuts, coconut, pine nuts) • Sprouted seeds (alfalfa, chia, radish, sesame) • Sweeteners (brown rice, barley malt, honey, Sucanat) • Beverages (fruit juices, vegetable juices, herbal teas)	• Natural dairy products • Eggs • Probiotics • Yogurt, unsweetened • Oils	• Meat, animal fats • All processed foods (including processed dairy products, i.e. margarine, cheeses) • Beverages (coffee, tea, sodas, sweetened juices, wine, beer, spirits) • Tomato products • Fruit (grapefruit, oranges, blueberries, cranberries, plums, prunes) • Grains • Rice • Legumes • Cereals • Flour products • Nuts (brazil, cashews, filberts, macadamia, peanuts, pecans, pistachios, walnuts) • Seeds (pumpkin, sunflower, wheat germ) • Sweeteners (artificial, sugar, maple syrup, molasses)

FIGURE 6-2 **Acid, Neutral and Alkaline Foods**

Malabsorption Syndrome

formula taken throughout the day in addition to the suggested supplements detailed below can also help reduce inflammation and replace lost nutrients.

The body tends to become more acidic as we grow older. The pH of body fluids is normally about 7.4. A slight shift downward into the acidic range is a major factor in many aging conditions, such as arthritis, inflammation, respiratory disorders, cancer, and bone loss. A good diet that allows the balance of foods eaten to be alkaline when they're metabolized is the best way to insure optimum pH. Yet the typical American diet contains 90 percent acid-forming foods. Figure 6-2 lists alkaline and acid foods. At first glance it may seem that some foods, such as lemons, should be acidic, but it's the post-digestive pH that matters. Lemons, like most other fruits, are alkaline when metabolized.

ACID REDUX™

MAJOR APPLICATION OF ACID REDUX™ ✦ Digestion begins the moment a bite of food is taken—not in the stomach, liver or intestines, but in the mouth. This is emphasized in *7-Color Cuisine*. The enzymes *amylase* and *lipase* are released from the salivary glands under the tongue to begin the digestive process. Simultaneously, nerves in the mouth trigger the release of hydrochloric acid and digestive enzymes in the stomach, duodenum, pancreas, and gall bladder. The activity in the mouth is what ultimately allows the solid foods to be broken down into nutrient-rich liquids ready to be absorbed and to nourish the body.

Unfortunately, many people produce more stomach acid than they actually need. This can be a result of stress, eating the wrong foods, or not relaxing during meals. This overproduction accounts for the mild heartburn that we experience after eating meals, especially those containing mostly animal foods, which are highly acidic. Acid Redux™ has been shown to help support normal stomach acid levels, thus protecting the stomach lining.

AN OVERVIEW OF ACID REDUX™ ✦ Acid Redux™ is a patented digestive support supplement driven by two highly alkaline (capable of neutralizing acids) compounds, potassium hydroxide and magnesium hydroxide. It also contains supporting nutrients, such as calcium carbonate, and vitamins D and C. Its primary function is to prevent the body from overproducing hydrochloric (stomach) acid, although it also helps to raise the stomach's pH level and to nourish sore, damaged stomach mucosa cells. Together, these actions create a very favorable environment for the stomach.

How Acid Redux™ Works ◆ Though it can be helpful to just about anyone who suffers from frequent bouts of mild heartburn, Acid Redux™ seems to be most beneficial for people who suffer from a digestive condition known as GERD, or gastroesophageal reflux disease. This is a much more serious condition that's caused by a dysfunctional esophageal sphincter. The side effects of GERD are similar to those of heartburn, however they can be much more painful and far more damaging in the long run.

Here's why. When the esophageal sphincter becomes damaged, or unable to seal in stomach acids, these acids begin to travel upward, into the esophagus. This results in a painful burning sensation that can cause serious damage as it gradually erodes the cells of the esophagus. Acid Redux™ has been shown to help prevent this from happening by controlling the production and release of hydrochloric stomach acids while buffering them in the process. Even more encouraging, studies have shown that it works very quickly. A comparison study between Acid Redux™ and leading brands of antiacids has shown that Redux™ goes to work faster and has greater buffering capability over extended periods of time. This is due to the buffering strength of the alkaline-earth (calcium, magnesium) and alkali (potassium) minerals that make up Acid Redux.™ These are key minerals is maintaining optimal health, making Acid Redux™ an ideal mineral supplement.

Therapeutic Applications of Acid Redux™
- *Heartburn*
- *Poor digestion*
- *Peptic ulcers*

- *GERD (Acid reflux)*
- *Stomach lining support*

TIPS FOR TAKING ACID REDUX™

- First and foremost, GERD, peptic ulcers, and frequent heartburn are all very serious conditions and should not be taken lightly. They can incite massive amounts of damage if left untreated, and should be addressed immediately if symptoms persist.

- For optimal results, the manufacturer of Acid Redux™ suggests taking it on an empty stomach prior to meals.

- When taking supplements that inhibit the release of stomach acids, it's important to ensure that there are no underlying enzyme deficiencies at play. This could seriously interfere with the digestive system's ability to break down solid foods prior to entering the intestinal tract. Supplementing a gentle, plant-based enzyme, such as papain or bromelain, can be very helpful.

- At all cost, try to avoid or limit the excessive consumption of highly acidic beverages, such as coffee and carbonated sodas, as well as tomato, grapefruit, and orange juices.

- Acid Redux™ is not intended to replace any current ulcer or reflux medications that you might be taking. Consult your physician prior to making it part of your nutritional program.

NATURAL COMPANIONS FOR ACID REDUX

- *Deglycerrized Licorice (DGL).* Licorice (*Glycyrrhiza* spp.) is one of the most widely used herbs in the world and a centerpiece of Chinese medicine. According to the *ABC Clinical Guide for Herbs*, licorice is now being investigated for its effects on oral, gastric, and duodenal ulcers. DGL is a mild licorice extract that promotes healing of ulcers and dyspepsia (upset stomach). Chewable tablets of DGL are particularly suited to healing oral ulcers, especially in children. DGL chewed between meals is also effective for peptic and duodenal ulcers.

One of the most interesting therapeutic qualities of DGL takes place within the digestive system. Studies have shown that DGL extracts are capable of manufacturing a protective coating that encompasses the delicate lining of the stomach and other digestive organs, such as the duodenum and esophagus. In the eyes of researchers, this unique ability to safeguard these delicate tissues against the damaging effects of gastric acid may hold the key to preventing many common and serious digestive disorders. Any person can safely use DGL licorice, but pregnant women should not use glycyrrhizin-containing licorice.

- *Branched-Chain-Amino Acids (BCAA).* Legendary among bodybuilders and strength-training athletes, the three branched-chain amino acids (leucine, isoleucine and valine) account for nearly one-third of those found in muscle tissue protein. Their function, however, is in no way limited to muscle tissue repair. Amino acids, including branched-chain amino acids, are the primary building blocks of the human body and play an important role to protect and repair damaged tissues throughout it.

  Recent scientific findings suggest that BCAAs may be helpful in safeguarding the mucous membrane of the stomach against damage caused by peptic and duodenal ulcers. Aside from facilitating the process of repairing these delicate tissues, some studies indicate that supplementing BCAAs may help shield the cells of the stomach mucosa from *H. pylori,* a common bacteria linked to ulcer development.

- *Whey Protein.* While it's most commonly associated with athletes and post-workout recovery, taking whey protein is by far one of the best ways to help support a healthy stomach lining. Protein is a macronutrient and one of the most vital to repair and heal tissues. The delicate mucosal lining of the stomach is no exception to this rule, and many researchers believe that malnutrition (especially in the protein department) is a key reason why so many adult American are walking around with painful holes in their stomachs. When consumed in adequate amounts, whey protein can encourage an environment unfavorable to bacteria growth which can typically lead to peptic ulcer formation.

Constipation and Detoxification

PSYLLIUM

Major Application of Psyllium ✦ The husks and seeds of pysllium plants (*Plantago psyllium* and *P. ovata*) have been used throughout the ages to help alleviate a number of digestive troubles, including some of today's most common—constipation, bloating, gas, and obesity. Completely safe to use regularly, pysllium is loaded with soluble fiber and possesses remarkable bulking abilities. Trials have shown that certain parts of the plant can actually swell to nearly 100 times their original density, making psyllium an excellent natural supplement for keeping regular—a crucial factor in wellness.

An Overview of Psyllium ✦ The integrity of the American diet has taken a complete nosedive. Despite how much we continue to learn about the dangers of fast, processed, and genetically modified foods, it seems as if we just can't consume them quickly enough. Without pointing any fingers, this could very well be one of the main reasons why close to 100 million Americans continue to live with some type of digestive disorder. When you consider how low in soluble fiber most fast and processed foods are, and how much of them we consume, it doesn't seem an impossible conclusion.

Simply put, the body needs fiber. Not only does it need fiber, it needs lots of it! In fact, if you're not consuming at least 20 grams of fiber on a daily basis, there's a very good chance that, at some point in your life, you will more than likely develop a digestive disorder. Still, it's amazing how many of these challenges can be avoided by simply drinking more water and consuming plenty of fiber throughout the day.

How Psyllium Works • If you're like most people, you're probably operating under the dangerously false assumption that the digestive tract can "take care" of itself. This couldn't be *more* incorrect. Keep in mind that the average digestive tract stretches about 30 feet in length. That's more than enough distance for things to go terribly wrong. This is especially true for anyone who deprives his or her digestive tract of the essentials; most notably, water and soluble fiber.

Here's why. When the digestive system isn't continually supplied with ample amounts of soluble fiber and water, it becomes extremely difficult for the body to properly "flush" digestive waste out of the small intestine and colon. This inevitably results in a build-up of feces that can best be described as a toxic disaster waiting to happen. Instead of leaving the body, waste is left to collect and rot inside the colon. Toxins that remain are then absorbed into the bloodstream and, over time, this creates an environment of bacteria that the body simply can't keep up with. And that situation opens the floodgates to infection, disease, and a plethora of digestive disorders.

Supplementing psyllium with generous amounts of water is clearly one of the easiest ways to ensure that the digestive process goes off without a hitch. Its high concentrations of soluble fiber and powerful bulking properties make its use a simple way to naturally soften stools, making them much easier to pass.

Therapeutic Uses for Psyllium
- Constipation
- High cholesterol
- Weight loss
- Hemorrhoids
- Diarrhea

- Always take psyllium supplements with lots of water, at least 8-10 ounces. This is very important because the last thing anyone wants is an esophagus full of bulked-up fiber.
- If you use other supplements or medications, allow at least a three-hour window between taking them and using pysllium. Not doing so has been known to prevent absorption.
- First-time users can expect to experience some initial bloating and gas. This is very common and can be prevented by starting with a small amount and gradually increasing the amount over time.
- For even better digestive cleansing, add a few drops of black or green walnut or wormwort to the water used to consume psyllium. It can help eliminate many of the parasitic deposits that call the intestines home.

COFACTORS AND CONTRAINDICATIONS OF PSYLLIUM ✦ See Table 7 in the Appendix for more information.

FLAXSEED

MAJOR APPLICATION OF FLAXSEED ✦ Flaxseed (*Linum usitatissimum*) is an excellent and increasingly popular source of omega-3 essential fatty acids or EFA. These "good fats" are vital to many biological functions, although often absent from today's typical diet. The lack, according to many researchers, is one of the primary reasons why nearly one-third of the U.S. population is overweight.

AN OVERVIEW OF FLAXSEED ✦ The use of flax for food dates back to ancient Babylon (3,000 BC), where an elaborate irrigation system was developed at the convergence of the Tigris and Euphrates rivers to insure a rich harvest of flax. Later, it was used as medicine to treat burns, wounds, and skin irritations. Early users discovered that these seeds could also be used as digestive aids and to promote bowel regularity.

Today flax is used to promote healthy skin, fight pain, reduce inflammation, support normal digestion, combat fatigue and depression, improve circulation and cardiovascular function, promote fertility, reduce the symptoms of menopause, and support prostate health. And flaxseed oil is an important source of omega-3 fatty acids. Mountains of clinical research, not to mention scores of loyal users, support many of these claims.

How Flaxseed Works • There are many nutritional components in flax-seeds, but the most beneficial are essential fatty acids (EFA). The human body needs EFA to carry out many of its most basic biological functions, yet cannot manufacture its own supply. One of the primary functions of EFA is to act as a gatekeeper for cellular membranes. It does this by allowing healthy substances into the cells, while preventing harmful substances from being utilized.

One of the most powerful, naturally occurring EFA in flaxseed is alpha-linoleic acid. This potent omega-3 fatty acid (a precursor to those found in fish oil) has been shown to reduce the risk of heart disease and other cardiovascular ailments. In addition, flax is teeming with lignans. These phytonutrients account for many of the health benefits associated with flax, and play a part in everything from hormone regulation to heart health.

Therapeutic Uses of Flaxseed

- *Cancer prevention.* The lignans in flax are believed to have a positive influence on certain types of cancer, especially cervical, breast, colon, skin, and prostate cancers.
- *Cardiovascular support and high blood pressure.* Omega-3 fatty acids have been shown to limit the amount of LDL cholesterol the body uses. This can ultimately result in reduced risk for coronary disease. It's also been determined that flaxseed oil may be beneficial in preventing chest pain, high blood pressure, and other cardiovascular challenges.

- *Fertility.* The combination of a swollen prostate and unhealthy sperm doesn't offer much hope for anyone trying to conceive. Fortunately, the EFA and lignans in flax have been shown to help with both.
- *Pain and inflammation.* Inflammation can trigger a number of health concerns ranging from very mild to disturbingly severe. The omega-3 EFA in flaxseed oil helps prevent inflammation by improving the body's response to it in skin, joints, and other vulnerable tissues.
- *Skin disorders.* The anti-inflammatory properties of flaxseed seem to be highly useful in reducing the redness, swelling and itching associated with skin disorders, such as eczema, psoriasis, and rosacea. Many acne sufferers have found relief from blemishes by thinning out the oily sebum notorious for clogging pores. Over time, this can help keep the skin clear and zit-free.
- *Sunburn.* Okay, so it won't stop your friends and co-workers from making annoying little clichéd jokes about how red you are if you stay too long in the sun. But on the plus side, flax may be able to help expedite the healing process for bad sunburns.
- *Other therapeutic benefits of flaxseed.* Cholesterol management; digestion; PMS and menopause; and dry, flaky skin (flaxseed oil).

TIPS FOR TAKING FLAXSEED
- Oil is clearly one of the most popular ways to obtain flaxseed. It's convenient, completely versatile, and ultra-potent. Always keep it refrigerated to avoid a sour, bitter taste. This is delicate oil and not to be used for cooking.
- Capsules can be very convenient, but you'll need quite a few of them to match the potency of just one tablespoon of oil. Most oils deliver anywhere from 10-15 grams of flax. Capsules, on the other hand, typically include 1,000 mg (1 gram) each. When you do the math, it can get very expensive.
- Flaxseed oil has a soft, nutty flavor that has an unexplainable way of growing on you. If you're a regular protein user, try adding a tablespoon

of oil to one of your shakes. Not only does it complement the taste of most flavors, it also supercharges nutritional value.

• Debate is ongoing about which flaxseed color is more beneficial, brown or golden. The truth? It makes no difference which way the coin lands on this one. They both contain generous amounts of EFA and lignans. Take your pick and enjoy the perks.

• Not many things in this life are as frustrating and uncomfortable as a bout with constipation. When the time comes, a tablespoon or two of ground flaxseed once or twice a day with a big glass of water can work wonders. Flaxmeal can easily be added to cereals or baked goods.

NATURAL COMPANIONS FOR FLAXSEED

• *Triphala.* This potent digestive tonic has been at the core of India's practice of Ayurvedic medicine for centuries. As the name might imply, it's made up of a combination of three powerful fruit extracts, *Harada, Amla, and Behada.*

In addition to protecting the cells of digestive tract, triphala is also a very effective (and nonlaxative) bowl tonic. By this we mean that it has a way of normalizing the waste removal process in a manner which doesn't over-stimulate the colon or cause diarrhea. Unlike some of today's most popular chemical laxatives, triphala is completely natural and nonhabit-forming.

In just the past few years, impressive studies have suggested that this combination of highly versatile fruit extracts is able to purify the blood, cleanse and fortify the liver, increase the body's flow of bile, and improve the quality of blood lipids. We couldn't agree more. Triphala is very effective, offers a wealth of health benefits, is completely safe to take, and doesn't interfere with most prescription medications. Based on this, we strongly recommend triphala for anyone interested in taking charge of his or her digestive and metabolic health.

• *Fructooligosaccharides (FOS).* Understandably, the concept of prebiotics and probiotics can be confusing. But it's actually quite simple.

Prebiotics are nondigestible food compounds that help stimulate the growth and activity of friendly, beneficial bacteria within the digestive tract. Probiotics, on the other hand, consist of the friendly bacteria that help maintain healthy flora levels within the gastrointestinal tract. These "beneficial" microorganisms are essential to sound digestion and, without them, our systems would potentially become riddled with harmful bacteria and other foreign microbes capable of wreaking havoc on healthy cells.

FOS is a *prebiotic* that spends all of its time making sure that the body's population of friendly bacteria has everything it needs to function at its best. By supporting an environment that especially caters to probiotics, FOS can help bolster the activity and effectiveness of the friendly bacteria we need for digestion, absorption, and a long list of other digestive and biological functions.

- *Citrus pectin.* The peels of oranges, lemons, limes, grapefruits, and other citrus fruits are rich in natural fibers that contain D-galacturonic acid, a monosaccharide (basic 6-carbon sugar) that helps support healthy digestion and regularity. Using pectin is one of the most mild and natural ways to overcome an occasional bout with constipation, and is commonly used for weight loss, too. When consumed, it can deliver a feeling of fullness that has helped many individuals to curb their appetites while also helping to restore digestive regularity.

   Some researchers believe that pectin may also be able to help prevent certain types of cancer. It's important to note that this is a very presupposed theory and clearly needs more scientific exploration. With regard to digestion, however, pectin is safe, effective, and very popular among those who wish to avoid taking harsh, chemically inspired laxatives.

- *Other essential fatty acids, especially fish oil, borage, and evening primrose.*

NATURAL COMPANIONS FOR FOS

- *Essential fatty acids, especially fish oil (omega-3s)*
- *Borage*
- *Evening primrose oils (omega-6s)*

Healthy Glowing Skin

GLA (GAMMA LINOLENIC ACID)

MAJOR APPLICATION OF GLA ♦ This popular omega-6 essential fatty acid has gained a loyal following based not only on positive word of mouth, but on supporting research as well. As it does with all essential fatty acids (EFA), the body relies on omega-6 to carry out many biological functions. Sadly, the typical American diet is dangerously high in saturated fats, and therefore in a near-constant state of imbalance. Incorporating GLA into the diet is a smart step in the right direction.

AN OVERVIEW OF GLA ♦ Nutritional oils, including borage, evening primrose, black currant, and a host of others, are saturated with one of the best natural substances on earth—gamma linolenic acid, or GLA.

This polyunsaturated (good) omega-6 essential fatty acid has been used for centuries to help fight depression and other emotional imbalances, and has steadily gained popularity thanks to increased research.

Like the omega-3s found in fish oil and flax, the body relies on omega-6 essential fatty acids, especially because it can't manufacture its own supply. Users who suffer from conditions such as arthritis, PMS, and skin disorders, swear by it.

HOW GLA WORKS ♦ GLA is among the most biologically influential omega-6 fatty acids available, although it does have a very specific primary role. Shortly after entering the body, it's converted into prostaglandins and leukotrienes, two hormone-like substances which have been shown to both prevent and cause inflammation. This alone has given it rock-star status to people who suffer from stiff, painful joints, including those caused by osteo- and rheumatoid-arthritis, as well as to those who live with a number of skin disorders. In addition, GLA has shown great promise in making PMS much more manageable by playing a role in hormone regulation.

Therapeutic Uses of GLA

* *Acne.* As anyone who suffers from acne will tell you, breakouts are no fun. Aside from the obvious embarrassment, acne can cause scars and redness that last for months and even years. GLA has been shown to help control the secretion of sebum, a greasy, pore-clogging substance that just loves causing blemishes. Cystic acne can be even more troubling, as it forms deep under the skin, thus taking longer to heal naturally. GLA's anti-inflammatory properties help reduce the swelling associated with these painful, frustrating pimples.

* *Arthritis and inflammation.* This is definitely one area where GLA seems to shine. Once used by the body, it stimulates production of the hormone-like substances that make it possible for the body to naturally counter inflammation. One of the most famous, university-led studies was able to determine that GLA can be effective in reducing arthritis pain and swelling. Other studies suggest that GLA may also reduce the amount of damage in articular cartilage.

* *Eczema and psoriasis.* These two embarrassing skin conditions are typically the result of high saturated-fat levels and very low levels of omega-3 and -6 essential fatty acids. Over time, the body runs out of good fat to safely convert to linolenic acid. Supplementing with GLA in the form of borage and evening primrose oil provides ample amounts of healthy EFA that can be used to normalize the conversion process.

* *Fertility.* Couples trying to conceive should definitely consider making GLA a part of everyday life. Many conception hold-ups are often caused by high blood pressure, high cholesterol, and poor circulation. In males, GLA has been shown to help increase blood flow to the penis.

Women stand to benefit, too, because the GLA in evening primrose and borage oils seems to create a more welcoming and supportive uterine environment.

- *Premenstrual syndrome (PMS).* It's been well documented that PMS sufferers generally have low or reduced levels of GLA in their systems. Supplementing with evening primrose oil has been shown to reduce the effect of the inflammation-causing prostaglandins responsible for cramps and breast tenderness. Moreover, it helps increase the body's ability to better use iodine, an important precursor to the production of thyroid and metabolic hormones.
- *Sore throat.* One of the earliest known uses for borage oil was to treat dry, scratchy throats. Borage oil is naturally rich in a sticky, yet soothing substance called *mucilage.* Not only does it help coat the lining of the throat, but it's also a natural expectorant which can help bring up excess mucous. Don't forget your handkerchief.
- *Other therapeutic uses for GLA.* Eczema and psoriaisis; healthy neural activity, including age-related memory; and PMS .

TIPS FOR TAKING GLA

- Always look for a formula that delivers a minimum of 240 mg of GLA per serving.
- Mega-dosing GLA won't provide any extra benefits. Taking more than necessary will only serve to send you running to the nearest restroom.
- GLA products should always be taken with food to help the body absorb it and to reduce the chance of flatulence and upset stomach.
- As with all essential fatty acids, balanced use is of great importance. If you decide to incorporate omega-6 EFA into your dietary regime, don't make the mistake of neglecting your omega-3s.
- Omega-3 and omega-6 fatty acids, although both very important, tend to compete for absorption within the body. To be sure that you're using both to the fullest extent, try to take them at separate times.

- If you're taking a blood thinner, talk to your physician before using GLA supplements.
- Although it may help increase the likelihood of conception, more research is clearly needed before recommending GLA products to pregnant and nursing women.

NATURAL COMPANIONS FOR GLA ✦ Spirulina, hyaluronic acid, vitamins A, C and E, omega-3 fatty acids (fish oil and flax), milk thistle, antioxidants, CoQ$_{10}$, B-complex vitamins.

COFACTORS AND CONTRAINDICATIONS FOR GLA ✦ See Table 7 in the Appendix for more information.

SPIRULINA (BLUE-GREEN ALGAE)

MAJOR APPLICATION OF SPIRIULINA ✦ Spirulina (or blue-green algae, as it's very commonly referred to) is a type of seaweed that grows abundantly in many lakes and ponds.

Legend has it that Chinese medicinal healers were among the first to use it, although it was also used throughout Mexico and Africa. Based on its high concentration of nutrients, many users believe that it can help promote wellness on a number of levels, the most significant being improvements to immune system function, allergy relief, infection mitigation, and liver health support.

AN OVERVIEW OF SPIRULINA ✦ It would be impossible to talk about this superfood without talking about a number of other nutrients and pro-health compounds as well.

Blue-green algae is loaded with protein and most varieties are made up of well over 60-70 percent amino acids, making it a favorite among vegetarians and others who might not consume adequate amounts of protein on a daily basis. Spirulina's nutritional profile is not limited to protein, however. It's also naturally rich in chlorophyll, a pigment that accounts for the greenish-blue tone of most lakes and ponds.

From a supplemental perspective, chlorophyll is commonly used to boost the immune system, heal wounds, and fight infection. Additionally, spirulina is teeming with nutrients, such carotenoids, gamma linolenic acid, vitamins B and E; a mineral profile that includes selenium, zinc, copper, and manganese, and very high amounts of iron. It's an especially good source of vitamin B-12.

How Spirulina Works • Despite being touted as a "cure all" for a number of diseases, this common sea algae still puzzles researchers. We do, however, know that there is simply no arguing that it offers an impressive and complete nutritional profile. Most notably, spirulina is an outstanding source of protein and has become a staple in the vegetarian community. Deficiencies in protein can lead to a host of health concerns, including obesity, loss of energy and concentration, and muscle loss.

Not only does spirulina contain a wide variety of nutrients, but many are natural synergists with one another, capable of boosting each other's effectiveness. One of the best examples of these naturally occurring partnerships is that between vitamin E and selenium. This combination has become one of the most trusted to support healthy immune system response, a core prerequisite to good health.

Therapeutic Uses for Spirulina
- Immune system support
- Healthy digestion
- Energy
- Alkalizing agent
- Muscular atrophy
- Allergies
- Cancer prevention

Tips for taking Spirulina

- Algae supplements seem to offer the most beneficial effects when taken throughout the day in divided doses.
- While most formulas tend to be safe, it may be wise to use only those formulas from well established, GMP-certified manufacturers.
- Look for formulas that list complete nutritional profiles. This is a good indicator that the formula you select has been properly assayed and screened for microbes, contaminants such as microcystins. Oregon, for example, is very strict in governing the amount of toxins in the algae and spirulina products the state produces.

Natural Companions for Spirulina

- *Hyaluronic Acid.* Hyaluronic acid is a mucopolysaccharide that roams abundantly throughout the body. Inherent to virtually every cell in the body, greatest concentrations of hyaluronic acid can be found in the skin and in the synovial fluid that lubricates joint structures. As a key component in the extra-cellular matrix that surrounds and supports human cells, HA is remarkable in its ability to bind and retain water. This makes it vitally important to the formation of the gel-like substance that holds the cells of the body together. As we age, our pool of HA gradually diminishes. Many researchers believe that this decline is one of the main reasons why so many of us have become conditioned to measuring the aging process by skin and articular joint structure quality.

  From a cosmetic perspective, HA is like a cellular sponge that's capable of retaining unimaginable amounts of moisture. In fact, a single molecule of HA can hold up to 1000 times its own weight in water. This trait is just one of the reasons why HA is commonly referred to as "nature's moisturizer" and should serve as wonderful news for anyone concerned with improving the skin's quality and appearance. When applied topically, HA works by trapping moisture in both the dermal (lower) and epidermal (upper) layers of skin. When these cells lack an adequate supply of HA, they'll inevitably lack moisture and elasticity. Over time, these deficiencies are what typically lead to the formation of wrinkles, lines, sagging, and roughness.

* *Vitamins A and C; Zinc.* Discovered in 1930, vitamin A is a fat-soluble vitamin growth factor and antioxidant which has been used by millions to help support healthy vision and healthy immune system function, promote healthy growth and development, support wound healing, and to aid in healing digestive disorders. In addition to these uses, it's also considered by many to be one of the best ways to promote healthy skin. This has been evidenced by hundreds of studies that have evaluated the role it plays in treating skin conditions, such as acne, psoriasis, eczema, and dry scalp.

   While it can definitely be effective, it's important to use caution and moderation when taking vitamin A in supplement form. Vitamin A is stored in the liver and used as needed by various systems of the body. This makes it very difficult to get more than you need when it's obtained from the beta-carotene content of food.

   Vitamin A supplements, however, are presynthesized and can be toxic when taken in large amounts, especially over long periods of time. One of the best ways to prevent this is to make sure that you're not consuming more vitamin A than your body realistically needs. Nausea, dry scalp, brittle skin, and reddening of the skin are all signs that your body can't keep up with the amount of retinol that you're taking in.

Zinc is needed for the enzymatic reactions that vitamin A catalyzes, and supplementing with this important mineral as well helps ensure its optimum function.

Vitamin C is required for the synthesis of collagen, the protein that makes up skin and articular joints. In fact, collagen is the most plentiful protein in the body. In addition to providing the necessary cofactor for collagen production, vitamin C is the primary free- radical scavenger in body fluids, including those within and surrounding cells.

To Sum It All Up

Commercials for digestive aids to alleviate everything from intestinal gas to acid reflux flood evening news broadcasts. Former Denver quarterback John Elway tells viewers how a little purple pill has relieved his battle with acid reflux. In another commercial, three ladies seated in a movie blow up to four times normal size, but only one is able to "deflate" after chewing a popular remedy.

Why do you suppose these commercials are so popular? Is it because people are watching the evening news while eating dinner? Anyone doing so is a perfect candidate for digestive upset, given how world disasters dominate news reports. The practice of frequently eating on the run, while driving, or late at night are all recipes for digestive disaster. No wonder 59 percent of Americans report some kind of digestive disorder.

Yet digestive complaints indicate a much more important aspect of one's overall health. As we've seen, a toxic bowel is a breeding ground for immune dysfunction, inflammation, nervous disorders, and malnutrition. Intestinal dysbiosis plays a key role in the *metabolic* and *cardiovascular syndromes* as well as in liver toxicity, hormone imbalances, and bone loss. Digestive complaints deserve more serious recognition for the pivotal role the digestive system plays in optimum health. Merely masking digestive discomforts doesn't resolve the issues associated with the underlying problems.

Obviously, diet plays the most important role in how good digestion will be. You can follow the guidelines in *7-Color Cuisine* for an easy, step-by-step way to improve nutrition and enjoy meals.

Consider leaky gut as the basis for symptoms which you've probably never associated with digestion, such as allergies, runny nose, itching, fingernail biting, nail ridges, rough skin, and sore and swollen joints. Common complaints such as gas, bloating, diarrhea, and heartburn all respond well to the addition of digestive enzymes with meals.

Finally, if you have not had the best diet and have been taking antibiotics, you may need to improve intestinal flora with prebiotics and probiotics. More serious and long-lasting GI conditions will require medical help, but the suggestions in this chapter serve as a good adjunct therapy.

CHAPTER SEVEN

Hormone Syndrome

T HE WORDS *hormone* and *steroid* have a malefic association for many people, yet these remarkable chemicals make up an exquisite design for controlling living processes. Their chief function is to enable communication between cells—neighboring cells sharing the same function as well as those performing completely different functions some distance from one another.

One of the best examples of this unique activity is that of thyroid hormones, which are released from two small glands at the base of the neck. It takes a signal from the pituitary gland, located in the base of the brain, to prompt the thyroid to relinquish its hormones. They then travel via the bloodstream to all parts of the body, affecting the metabolic rate of every cell. Eventually they journey to the pituitary, which turns off its own thyroid-stimulating hormone (TSH). This amazing regulatory process is known as the *feedback mechanism*.

The hypothalamus sits on top of the pituitary and these two glands initiate the release of signaling proteins and hormones. The glands also act as a rheostat, constantly registering circulating hormone levels, monitoring their effects, and initiating signals to keep them in balance. This is also the center of emotional, neurological, and physical functions, so it isn't surprising that hormonal fluctuations disrupt these functions, making them intimately involved in the *hormone syndrome*.

What You Will Find in This Chapter

+ General discussion of hormones
+ Premenstrual syndrome
+ Menopause
+ Andropause and virility

Endocrine Gland	Signaling Molecule or Hormone	Steroid, Amino Acid
Hypothalamus	+ Thyrotropin releasing hormone (TRH) + Gonadotropin releasing hormone (GnRH) + Corticotropin releasing hormone (CRH) + Growth hormone (GH) + Prolactin releasing factor (PRF) + Melanocyte-stimulating factor (MRF)	
Posterior Pituitary	+ Oxytocin Corticotropin, ACTH + Vasopressin	
Anterior Pituitary	+ Adrenocorticotropic hormone + Follicle-stimulation hormone (FSH) + Growth Hormone (GH) + Prolactin (PRL) + Thyroid-stimulating hormone (TSH) + Luteinizing hormone (LH) + Melanocyte-stimulating hormone (MSH) + Lipotropin	
Thyroid		+ Thyroxine (T4) + Triiodothyronine (T3)
Pancreas	+ Insulin + Glucagon + Insulin-like growth factors (IGFs) + Somatostatin + Pancreatic polypeptide	

FIGURE 7-1 **Hormones and their actions**

- Urinary
- Energy and sleep

Hormone research is extremely dynamic as new information is constantly being uncovered. Surprisingly, new findings often emerge from research in other areas of medicine. For example, scientists studying cancer have identified new hormones associated with that disease. Additionally, some classes of

Endocrine Gland	Signaling Molecule or Hormone	Steroid, Amino Acid
Gastrointestinal	• Gastrin • Secretin • Cholecystokinin	
Parathyroid	• Parathyroid • Calcitonin • Parathyroid hormone-related peptide (PTHrP)	1,25-dihydroxy D3
Adrenal cortex	• Corticotropin-releasing factor (ACTH) • Angiotensin	• Cortisol • Aldosterone
Adrenal medulla		• Epinephrine • Norepinephrine
Testes	• Luteinizing hormone (LH) • Follicle-stimulating hormone (FSH)	• Testosterone • Dehydroepiandrosterone (DHEA)
Ovaries	• Follicle-stimulating hormone (FSH) • Luteinizing hormone (LH) • Prolactin • Human chorionic Gonadotropin (HCG) • Relaxin • Oxytocin • Inhibin • Human placental lactogen (hPL)	• Estradiol • Progesterone
Kidneys	• Atrial natriuretic factor (ANF) • Erythropoietin • Kallikreins • Kinins • Rennin	Aldosterone
Thymus	• Thymosin alpha-1 • Thymosin alpha-4	
Cells		Prostaglandins

Adapted from Norman and Litwack, *Hormones* (second edition).

chemicals, such as prostaglandins and neurotransmitters, are now considered part of the hormone family because they have hormone-like effects. Let's begin with some important general topics related to hormones.

Classes of Hormones

Simply stated, various glands located throughout the body secrete hormones. What distinguishes hormone-secreting glands from other glands (such as those discussed in the digestive tract) is that hormones can act on sites far removed from the glands that release them. Endocrine, which literally means "internal secreting," denotes these glands. By this we mean that the gland discharges its secretions (hormones) directly into the bloodstream, lymphatic system, and tissue fluids. By contrast, nonendocrine glands discharge their secretions into tubes or ducts for delivery to nearby sites.

There are several subgroups of hormones; systemic, paracrine, autocrine, neurotransmitter, and steroids. Without getting technical, the following is what distinguishes those subgroups.

Systemic hormones are stored in the glands that secrete them, waiting for a signal from another gland, usually the hypothalamus, before being released into general circulation. The hormone then travels throughout the body searching for target cells bearing specific receptors for it.

Paracrine hormones are released close to their adjacent target organs and thus travel a very short distance. *Autocrine hormones* don't travel at all, but instead act on the same cell that released them.

Neurotransmitter hormones are similar to paracrine hormones in that they await a signal before being released and travel long distances along the axon of nerve cells. But they differ from paracrine hormones in that they're released within the brain and central nervous system.

Steroid Hormones are unique in that they belong to a chemical family of compounds known as isoprenoids. Other members of this family include the carotenoids, vitamin E, Co-Q10, and vitamin K. Steroid hormones differ from other isoprenoids in that they are derived from cholesterol and share the core ring structure of cholesterol. There are seven classes of steroid

Steroid class	Steroid hormone	Action
Estrogens	Estradiol	Female characteristics
Androgens	Testosterone	Male characteristics
Progestins	Progesterone	Maintains Endometrium
Glucocorticoids	Cortisol	Stress Response
Mineralocorticoids	Aldosterone	Electrolyte balance
Vitamin D steroids	1,24-Dihydroxyvitamin D3	Growth factor
Bile acids	Cholic acid	Digestive stimulant

FIGURE 7-2 **Classes of Steroids**

hormones; estrogens (female sex steroids), androgens (male sex steroids), progestins, mineralocorticoids, glucocorticoids, vitamin D with its daughter metabolites, and cholesterol-containing bile acids. Table 7-2 lists classes of steroids and the principal active steroid for each.

Regulation of Hormone Secretion

Hormone production is regulated by the need for a specific biological response that can be orchestrated only by the hormone in question. In other words, the hormone is retained in its endocrine gland until circulating levels fall below normal. For example, during menopause levels of estrogen and progesterone begin to decline. This is picked up by the hypothalamus and it secretes follicle-stimulating hormone, or FSH, in an effort to goad the ovaries into producing estrogen and progesterone. As the ovaries become increasingly unresponsive to the signal from FSH, its levels continue to rise. High serum levels of FSH are, in fact, used to determine if menopause is in progress.

Hormone Receptors

As we've mentioned throughout the book, cell membranes are fluid envelopes that allow certain chemicals to pass into the cell and block others. Embedded between the fatty double-layer of the membrane are receptors and channels. These are constantly on the hunt for specific molecules needed by the cell. Among these receptors are those looking for a particular hormone. Georgetown University's Candice Pert, M.D., has rather humorously described how these receptors with glycoprotein "arms" attach, extending into the fluid-filled intercellular space where target molecules pass by. Like hailing a taxi in New York, the receptors flag down the molecules they wish to attract. In healthy fluid membranes, receptors have considerable latitude to wiggle and shimmy about, changing shape and position as needed to successfully grab their desired hormone.

Once contact has been established, the hormone is then able to exert its action. Steroidal hormones are insoluble in body fluids and, because of this, they travel around piggybacked onto carriers (in other words, conjugated). When they approach a target cell, the carrier docks onto its specific receptor and the steroid is uploaded into the cell. The steroids are now free to move to their appointed locations within the cell.

Receptors for all the free-steroid hormones, including estradiol, cortisol, androgens, progesterone, and aldosterone, are located in the nucleus of the cell or in a partition between the nucleus and cytoplasm. In addition, the non-steroidal thyroid hormone, dihyroxy vitamin D, and retinoic acid (vitamin A) also have receptors in the nucleus. The proximity of these hormones to DNA-binding sites means that they influence how DNA controls cellular growth and differentiation.

Hormone Action

Hormones belong to a unique class of molecules known as *biological response modifiers*. This means that they have a tremendous influence over thousands of metabolic reactions within the body. A hormone deficiency, even in the most modest sense, has a profound effect on the way the rest of the body functions. One of the most influential is thyroid hormone. This peptide, composed of the amino acid tyrosine and iodine, controls the speed at which metabolism proceeds. Steroidal hormones, because of their cellular location near the nucleus, have direct access to directions for protein synthesis as encoded by DNA onto messenger RNA. This is one reason why some are implicated in cancer initiation and progression.

Now let's discuss the specific conditions that make up the hormone syndrome.

Premenstrual Syndrome

Surveys suggest that 50-80 percent of women experience premenstrual symptoms (PMS) at some time during their reproductive years. Between 2-5 percent of these women experience symptoms that are severe enough to be disabling. The most commonly reported PMS symptoms are bloating, tenderness in the breasts, sleep abnormalities, mood swings, and poor concentration. In most cases, the symptoms abate once menstruation begins. It's important for women to keep track of exactly which symptoms they experience and when they occur during their cycles. This will be necessary in seeking treatment for PMS.

Foods and Beverages	Reason to Avoid
Sugar, alcohol, caffeine, tea and cigarettes	PMS women are often hypoglycemic, so a consistent blood-sugar level is important
Red meats	• High in fat, which decreases the liver's efficiency in metabolizing hormones. • High in phosphorus which compete with calcium for uptake and utilization
Salt and high-sodium foods	• Increase water retention • Cause breast tenderness
Dairy products	• Interfere with magnesium absorption • High in sodium and fat
Cold foods and beverages	Can contribute to cramping by reducing abdominal circulation
Sweet foods	• Are non-nutritive foods • Deplete vitamin and mineral stores, especially vitamins B and C, magnesium, chromium • Create hormone fluctuations, aggravating menstrual problems • Cause extremes in blood-sugar levels • Create stress for adrenals, pancreas • Trigger hot flashes • Inhibit calcium absorption, heightening risk of osteoporosis • Are addictive (they activate neurotransmitters)

FIGURE 7-3 **Red Light Foods for PMS Sufferers**

Diet plays a big role in PMS and the worst cases occur among women with the poorest diets. A 1980s landmark study by Guy Abraham, M.D., revealed that low dietary intake of zinc, manganese, and iron, accompanied by high consumption of refined sugar and carbohydrates, was common among PMS sufferers. Changing diet and avoiding foods that promote PMS symptoms continue to be the basis of programs to overcome the syndrome. Figure 7-3 lists red-light foods for PMS suffers.

Mainstream medicine has offered little relief for women with PMS and the tendency for many years was to think the symptoms were all "in the woman's head." Consequently, women have taken matters into their own hands, trying various remedies until they find one that works. Among the most helpful are vitamin B6, calcium, and magnesium. Additionally, chaste tree berry and progesterone have been effective remedies for PMS. Let's take a closer look.

CHASTE TREE *(VITEX AGNUS CASTUS)*

MAJOR APPLICATION OF CHASTE TREE ✦ According to well known naturopathic physician Tori Hudson, N.D., author of *Women's Encyclopedia of Natural Medicine*, chaste tree (*Vitex agnus castus*) is the single most important plant for the treatment of premenstrual syndrome. Both chaste tree berries, which contain flavonoids, and leaves have been used for PMS.

OVERVIEW OF CHASTE TREE ✦ PMS has eluded clear description. There doesn't seem to be a single model that describes the syndrome, although many theories have been put forth. These include elevated estrogen levels, reduced progesterone levels, elevated prolactin, the hormone that stimulates lactation, and increased aldosterone. PMS has even been subdivided into four categories depending upon which symptoms dominate; anxiety, carbohydrate craving, depression, or water retention. A toxic liver has also been blamed for PMS and, while the liver plays an important role in steroid metabolism, its involvement in PMS has not been proven.

How Chaste Tree Works ✦ Chaste tree berries stimulate the hypothalamus to increase lutenizing hormone, which acts on the ovaries to increase progesterone during the second phase (luteal) of the menstrual cycle. Progesterone is responsible for preparing the uterine lining for a possibly pregnancy. Since low progesterone and high estrogen levels mark PMS in many women, the ability of vitex to increase the ratio of progesterone to estradiol is important to PMS management.

Vitex also reduces high levels of prolactin during the luteal phase. Prolactin's function is to stimulate lactation in nursing mothers, and it sometimes gets overzealous in stimulating the breast tissue of women who aren't pregnant. Seventy percent of women with breast tenderness respond favorably when prolactin levels are kept in check. Limiting caffeine intake also helps reduce breast tenderness and pain.

Scientists have found that linoleic acid found in vitex can bind to estrogen receptors and induce certain estrogen-active genes. Other scientists have found the vitex reduces both somatic (pain) and psychic (neurological) symptoms in PMS. The beneficial effects of vitex are not due to estrogenic activity, and it doesn't contain hormones.

Therapeutic Uses of Chaste Tree

- *Premenstrual syndrome.* Vitex is very effective in reducing symptoms of PMS, including mood swings, depression, anxiety, craving, and water retention. In a large German study involving 1,634 women, after treatment with Vitex for three cycles, 93 percent reported a decrease in symptoms and many reported that their complaints were resolved. This is apparently the result of balancing neurotransmitters, including serotonin, dopamine, and norepinephrine.
- *Breast tenderness.* Cyclic breast tenderness often increases as women approach perimenopause and may decrease after menopause. Exactly what causes breast tenderness is unclear although some scientists believe it may be related more to fatty acid imbalances than to hormones. Vitex contains linoleic acid, an essential fatty

acid, and this component may be responsible for reducing breast tenderness. However vitex alone doesn't eliminate symptoms. Adding evening primrose oil containing a derivative of linoleic acid called gamma linolenic acid, or GLA, may be needed to eliminate discomfort.

* *Menstrual cycle abnormalities. Dysmenorrhea* is the term applied to menstrual cramps. This is a condition that plagues about half of menstruating women—most often between the ages of 20 and 24—but it can begin within a few months of the first menstrual period. A smaller percentage of these women have pain severe enough to incapacitate them for up to three days each month. Dysmenorrhea can result from some physical abnormality, such as endometriosis or fibroids, or it can be associated with lifestyle. The cause of the discomfort needs to be determined by a health care practitioner.

As with other syndromes, stress plays a major role in dysmenorrhea and symptoms worsen around exam time or when deadlines approach. Christiane Northrup, M.D., writes in her book, *Women's Bodies, Women's Wisdom;* "... when my life is in balance, I don't have cramps. When I become too busy or stressed out, I'll have a few hours of cramps..." Dr. Northrup's experience sums it up very nicely: Women in conflict about their roles in life, or trying to juggle too many things, are likely candidates for dysmenorrhea.

A diet high in meat and dairy products also contributes to the disorder because that diet produces too much prostaglandin PGF2. Adopting a diet high in complex carbohydrates, fruits, vegetables and fish and low in saturated fats and meat may significantly relieve symptoms. Adding vitex can help, because its linoleic acid helps reduce PGF2 by producing an opposing prostaglandin, PGE1, that has anti-spasmodic and anti-inflammatory effect.

* *Polymenorrhea (**too-frequent periods**), amenorrhea (**no periods**), and menorrhagia (**heavy or prolonged periods**).* These conditions respond well to

supplementation with vitex. Its use may also assist women who are infertile due to luteal phase defect and high prolactin levels.

+ *Other therapeutic benefits.* Hot flashes, infertility.

Tips for Taking Chaste Tree

- Chaste tree doesn't act quickly, and therefore it should be taken for at least three months before benefits may be noticeable.
- Chaste tree is best taken in the morning, just one capsule of standardized extract or 40 drops of a fluidextract.
- Since chaste tree doesn't have estrogenic effects, it may be safer to use for PMS symptoms if estrogen levels need to be kept under control.

Natural Companions for Chaste Tree

- *Calcium and magnesium.* Prior to menstruation, a woman's calcium and magnesium levels have a tendency to sharply decline. This common mineral imbalance can affect the production of other hormones that intensify common PMS-related symptoms. It can also open the door to many other health challenges, including osteoporosis and others associated with low levels of these two very key minerals. Regular supplementation of calcium and magnesium has been shown in several placebo-controlled studies to help reduce the severity of these symptoms by encouraging specific hormone activity.

  It's very important, however, to be sure that proper ratios are consumed when taking calcium and magnesium for support of PMS and other female-specific concerns. While these two minerals work closely together, they also compete for absorption and, as we've learned, calcium can be difficult to absorb. For this reason we recommend a 2:1 ratio of calcium to magnesium in order to increase absorption and overall effectiveness. If dairy products are consumed, it may be necessary to increase magnesium supplementation to the same level as calcium.

- *Pyridoxine, vitamin B-6.* Vitamin B-6 is a vital coenzyme involved in hundreds of chemical reactions throughout the body. Among the most important, B-6 is heavily involved in the regulation of hormones and neurotransmitters that account for many of the most common symptoms of PMS, including mood swings, headaches, breast tenderness, and fatigue.

A 1999 review of nine randomized, placebo-controlled studies suggested that women who took 100 mg. of B-6 experienced fewer PMS-related symptoms than those who were given placebo pills. This has led a growing number of researchers to believe that B-6 supplementation may be quite helpful in treating premenstrual symptoms and depression.

Birth control pills reduce vitamin B-6 and women using them should make sure to get at least 50 mg of the vitamin each day. Vitamin B-6 can be toxic in doses greater than 500 mg a day, particularly if continued over a prolonged period of time. Symptoms of neurological toxicity, such as tingling in the extremities, resolve once high dose vitamin B-6 is discontinued.

- *Iron.* Iron is clearly one of the most important trace minerals in the body. Aside from making sure that every cell in the body has a generous supply of oxygen-rich, energy-producing hemoglobin, iron is also responsible for supporting a healthy immune system, muscle contractions, neurological health and red blood cell formation. A number of controlled clinical studies have been conducted over the years to determine what specific role iron plays in preventing the many symptoms of PMS.

What we do know is that heavy menstrual cycles (menorrhagia) can quickly deplete the body's iron reserve. Ironically, many researchers also question whether or not long-term iron deficiencies can lead to heavy menstrual cycles. It's the question of which came first, the chicken or the egg? One double-blind, placebo-controlled study examined the effect of iron supplementation on the "heaviness" of menstrual flow. Seventy-five percent of the women in this study who took iron (in comparison with the placebo group) reported a decrease in menstrual blood flow. This suggests that iron may be helpful to reduce the volume of blood flow during menstruation. A simple blood test can accurately indicate any underlying iron deficiencies. Most multiple vitamin formulas include iron and should be taken into account before purchasing one separately. Vitamin C enhances the uptake of iron and bioflavonoids, including rutin, and strengthens uterine capillaries to reduce bleeding.

NATURAL COMPANIONS FOR CHASTE TREE
+ *Evening primrose oil*
+ *Vitamin E*
+ *Vitamin C*
+ *Bioflavonoids*

COFACTORS AND CONTRAINDICATIONS FOR CHASTE TREE + See Table 8 in the Appendix for more information.

5-HTP (5-HYDROXYTRYPTOPHAN)

PMS can have a very negative impact on many of the chemical compounds produced naturally by the body. Serotonin, a chemical messenger that affects mood, reason, and emotion, is one of the hardest hit. When a woman's hormone balance is upset—as in PMS—neurotransmitter balance is also upset, making it difficult for her body to produce enough serotonin. As a result mood swings, crying, sleeping difficulties, and emotionally explosive behavior can result.

5-HTP, previously discussed in Chapter Two, is a mood-supporting compound which the body produces naturally from the amino acid tryptophan, the now-famous amino acid that's found in turkey and other protein-rich foods. The molecules of 5-HTP readily pass the discriminating "blood-brain" barrier that block most substances from entering the brain. Once 5-HTP has arrived in neurons, it can be converted into serotonin.

Menopause

At birth, a girl has about half a million ova, but by age 40, she has about 50 remaining. Of these, many will not mature or be released. During this preclimacteric phase, anovulatory (no ova are released) periods are common. At the same time, estrogen and progesterone levels begin to decline as the corpus luteum become less responsive to FSH.

In addition to stimulating female hormones, the hypothalamus has many other jobs, including controlling body temperature and metabolic rate; maintaining water balance; and regulating appetite, sleep patterns, and toleration for stress. It's not surprising that the symptoms of menopause involve these other hypothalamic factors. Table 9 in Appendix A lists 35 symptoms associated with menopause.

There are currently about 60 million baby boomers in the United States and women in this age group will either enter the climacteric (change of life) soon, or have already begun experiencing menopausal symptoms. Unlike previous generations of women who dreaded their postmenopausal years, today's women often view the passage as a period of increased freedom from family obligations and the opportunity for new options and adventures.

The average age of menopause is 51.3 years, as calculated from the long-standing Brigham and Women's Nurses' Health Study. Women whose menarche (first period) occurred later in their teens may go through menopause later, some closer to age 60.

Once a woman has entered the climacteric, menopausal symptoms can be severe. Research has shown that women who had PMS are more likely to have problems with menopause symptoms. The most common symptoms include hot flashes, mood changes, depression, cognitive changes, vaginal dryness, a decreased libido, painful intercourse, decreased energy, sleep disturbances, and weight gain.

Hot flashes or *power surges*, a term which appeals more to today's woman, are the hallmark symptom that the climacteric is in progress. A hot flash is characterized by a sudden feeling of intense heat in the head and upper torso that's usually accompanied by sweating in the face, neck and chest. They often occur at night and can result in significant loss of sleep. Heart palpitations, irritability, anxiety, and panic are sometimes associated with hot flashes.

Hormone replacement therapy (HRT), using either estrogen alone or a combination of estrogen and progestogens for women with intact uteruses, has been standard medical treatment for most menopausal women. HRT significantly reduces hot flashes, helps prevent bone loss, and was thought to protect a woman from cardiovascular disease. However, estrogen increases the incidence of uterine and breast cancers among women who are at high risk. In 2002, the Women's Health Initiative found that women receiving HRT (Prempro®), a combination of equine derived estrogens and synthetic progestins, are at increased risk for stroke and at moderatedly increased risk for breast cancer.

Uncertainty about benefits versus risks of HRT has driven many women to seek alternative sources of estrogen, primarily from herbal therapies. The most common herbs used for menopause include red clover, dong quai, black cohosh, soy, licorice, and vitex. A recent analysis of some herbs used for menopause has shown that while some contain estrogen-like activity, others do not. The information from this study is presented in Figure 7-4. This information is useful when choosing which supplement may be right. If estrogen levels are low, herbs with estrogen-like activity may be a good choice; on the other hand, if estrogen levels are normal, nonestrogenic herbs would be best.

Vitex is extremely helpful for women going through the climacteric because of its somatic and psychic symptom-relieving attributes. Once menopause has occurred, vitex is no longer needed. As mentioned above, vitex does not have estrogenic effects.

Menopause Remedies

RED CLOVER

Red clover, or *Trifolium pratense* as it's botanically known, belongs to the pea family, whose members contain biologically active compounds called *phytoestrogens*. These are plant-based compounds that are functionally similar to estrogen. Based on strong supporting science, supplementing with phytoestrogens has become increasingly popular in alleviating hot flashes, vaginal dryness, and other symptoms commonly associated with menopause.

Red clover extracts also contain all four isoflavones (*genistein* and *daidzein*, *formononetin* and *biochanin*) in addition to unique flavonoid compounds of extremely potent estrogenic activity. Based on this unique profile, many of today's most popular female and menopausal support formulas now include red clover as a core ingredient. Although it's relatively new to the natural marketplace, red clover appears to be both safe and effective when taken as directed. Red clover may be combined with other herbs with estrogenic effects, such as soy isoflavones, Fo-ti, licorice, or hops.

COFACTORS AND CONTRAINDICATIONS FOR RED CLOVER ✦ See Table 8 in the Appendix for more information.

BLACK COHOSH

Black cohosh (*Cimicifuga racemosa L.*) has been a popular menopause remedy for many years. Native to North America and a premier botanical remedy among American Indians, it was used for general malaise, malaria, rheumatism, sore throat, menstrual irregularities, and to ease childbirth. The herb was used in Europe for gynecological purposes long before settlement of the New World.

Among its modern uses, the ABC monograph lists premenstrual discomforts. Black cohosh improves circulation and dilates blood vessels and traditional herbalists use it to help initiate menstrual flow because of its vasodilating effects. However, this use would not be a good idea when menstrual flow is already heavy.

One study of menopausal women examined the effect of two doses of black cohosh, 39 milligrams and 127 milligrams, each taken for 12 weeks. Both doses were effective in reducing hot flashes, anxiety, profuse sweating, insomnia, and vaginal dryness. Another study duplicated these doses, but found the herb to be effective in just two weeks. No hormone level changes were observed in either study.

The primary uses of black cohosh are for menopausal symptoms, including hot flashes, heart palpitations, nervousness, irritability, sleep disturbances, ringing in the ears, dizziness, perspiration, and depression. Black cohosh is anti-inflammatory, analgesic, and antipyretic. Its specific effects are characterized as selective estrogen-receptor modulators and it's been found to enhance the anti-estrogenic effects of tamoxifen. Research suggests it can be used for the treatment of menopausal symptoms in women with histories of breast cancer.

COFACTORS AND CONTRAINDICATIONS FOR BLACK COHOSH ✦ See Table 8 in the Appendix for more information.

DONG QUAI

Dong quai (*Angelica sinensis*) has been an important herb in Chinese medicine for centuries, described as functioning to "nourish blood" and invigorate circulation. It has been used clinically in the west to treat anemia, abdominal pain, and menstrual disorders. Additionally, dong quai has been used for conditions that commonly arise in later years, such as arthritis, coronary heart disease, and angina pectoris. In China, dong quai roots are used for both men and women, although it's especially revered as a blood tonic for women.

Dong quai helps to prevent blood clots and platelet adhesiveness as well as is useful in blood building, immune support, and uterine toning. It has both antispasmodic and uterine stimulating properties and is an excellent tonic herb to restore energy and balance after menstruation or menopause. Dong quai is an extremely nutritive herb with significant levels of vitamin A, carotenoids, vitamin B-12, vitamin E, ascorbic acid, folic acid, biotin, various phytosterols, calcium, magnesium, and other essential micro-minerals.

COFACTORS AND CONTRAINDICATIONS FOR DONG QUAI ◆ See Table 8 in the Appendix for more information.

SOY ISOFLAVONES

Asian women have experienced considerably fewer hot flashes and other menopausal symptoms than have women living in the west. Researchers have long attributed this to the high intake of soy foods in the Asian diet. In a recent study published in the *American Journal of Epidemiology*, Chisato Nagata, M.D., and colleagues from Gifu University School of Medicine in Japan, report that consumption of soy products is an effective strategy to prevent hot flashes.

The study involved 1,106 women between the ages of 35 and 54 at the beginning of the trial. None of the women were menopausal initially but, six years later, 101 women reported menopausal symptoms. The scientists adjusted the study data for age, total energy intake, and menopausal status, and found that hot flashes were significantly reduced among the women with the greatest soy product consumption and isoflavone intake.

Isoflavones are related to flavonoids and are able to modify estrogen concentrations. Isoflavones inhibit key enzymes involved in estrogen production and its conjugation in the liver. It's also thought that the estrogen-like activity of isoflavones reduces estrogen synthesis by altering the hypothalamic-pituitary-gonadal axis. In one Japanese study, consumption of 400 milliliters (14 ounces) of soymilk daily for two months reduced serum estradiol concentrations by 33.2 percent.

While consumption of soy products by all women has many benefits, use of isoflavone supplements among premenopausal women has raised some questions of safety within the scientific community, particularly among women at risk for breast cancer. However, these supplements appear to be safe for short periods of time to treat menopausal symptoms in women not at risk for breast cancer.

CofACTORS AND CONTRAINDICATIONS FOR SOY ISOFLAVONES ◆ See Table 7 in Appendix A for more information.

5-HTP

5-HTP, discussed in detail in Chapter Two and highlighed earlier for its effectiveness in treating symptoms of PMS, is another safe and effective therapy for hot flashes, anxiety, mood swings, and depression in menopausal women. The proposed mechanism of action is related to an increase in serotonin production, which adjusts the set point for the brain's thermoregulator. These actions are similar to those seen with serotonin selective reuptake inhibitors or SSRIs—without the side effects of the drugs commonly prescribed for menopause.

I3C (INDOLE-3 CARBINOL)

Indole-3 carbinol (I3C) is a phytochemical found in many plant foods, including cruciferous vegetables, such as broccoli, cauliflower, Brussels sprouts, and cabbage. I3C helps regulate the rate at which cells develop and replicate. Oral I3C is converted in the intestines into several metabolites that have anti-estrogenic activity. One of these, *diindolylmethane* (DIM), has been shown to selectively bind to estrogen receptors, thus preventing estrogen from activating abnormal cellular growth.

I3C metabolites induce certain liver enzymes to alter estrogen metabolism in both women and men, in turn decreasing incidence of certain tumors. Estrogen metabolism in the liver can follow three pathways, two of them cancer-promoting (16-hydroxyestrone, 4-hydroxyestrone) and the third (2-hydroxyestrone) offering anti-estrogenic and anti-proliferative activity. By influencing the body to use the 2-hydroxyestrone metabolic pathway, I3C makes it possible for the body to convert estrogen into a form it can use while also controlling abnormal growth and development in neighboring cells.

The regulation of estrogen-related cell growth is a reasonable factor for determining the likelihood of developing cancers, including those of the breasts and cervix in women and the prostate in men. Additionally I3C may block replication of the herpes simplex virus. Human trials have demonstrated that I3C is well tolerated at doses of 200-400 milligrams daily and that is has a sustained estrogen-modifying effect.

I3C helps incite normal cell death among those that show signs of abnormality—a process better known as *apoptosis*. This is the primary mechanism of action in prevention of prostate cancer, as we shall see a little later on.

COFACTORS AND CONTRAINDICATIONS ◆ See Table 7 in the Appendix for more information.

Herb	Uses
black cohosh (Cimicifuga racemosa)	low levels of phytoestrogens, menopause, dysmenorrhea, blood tonic
*chaste tree berry (Vitex agnus-castus)	PMS, menopause
dong quai (Angelica sinensis)	menstrual and menopausal disorders, antispasmodic, decreases hot flashes
*fo-ti or he-shou-wu (Polygonum multiflorum)	menopause, blood and innume tonic
*hops (Humulus lupulus L.)	sedative, relieves tension, anxiety, promotes sleep
*licorice (Glycyrrhiza glabra)	
*phytoestrogens, isoflavones, genistein, lignans, coumestans	menopause, hot flashes, binds to estrogen receptors, weak estrogenic effect
*red clover (Trifolium pratense)	anti-inflammatory, blood cleanser
Wild yam (Dioscorea villosa) *progesterone precursor*	ferulic acid converted to progesterone in the lab, not in the body

* Herbs with measurable estrogen-equivalent compounds.

FIGURE 7-4 **Herbs with Estrogen-Like Activity**

Andropause and Virility

Young men typically have robust energy and assertiveness because levels of testosterone, the primary male hormone, are high. Men also have estrogens, but the ratio of testosterone to estrogen is very high in youth. As men reach middle age, the ratio between these hormones is about half what it was when they were younger, and this is accompanied by lower energy levels and fat accumulation around the waistline. Most middle-aged men mellow out, which is helpful at a time in life when they are likely to be dealing with teen-aged offspring. Many become more supportive of wives who are working, trying to juggle too many activities, and perhaps entering perimenopause.

As men reach their older years, their girths may expand even more, and many men experience breast enlargement or gynecomastia. Some men become very lethargic and can even become depressed. Muscle tone decreases, as does bone mass. Yes, older men get osteoporosis, too, and may suffer hip fractures. These changes are all due to an even lower ratio of testosterone to estrogen. Surprisingly, the source of both testosterone and estrogen is progesterone. Normally thought of as a female hormone, progesterone therapy has been helpful for many men. Thinning skin is a normal part of aging and some men find that progesterone helps maintain skin integrity. Topical forms of progesterone are most popular and progesterone therapy doesn't carry the risks of testosterone therapy.

Andropause, which marks the decline of testosterone levels, has been likened to the male equivalent of menopause. Although the process of declining male hormones, primarily testosterone, begins in the mid-30s, the drop occurs very slowly. But, by age 65, levels are about one-quarter what they were in younger men. High alcohol intake, which raises estrogen levels, can accelerate these processes.

DHEA (7-KETO)

MAJOR APPLICATION OF DHEA ✦ As the most abundant steroid hormone in the body, DHEA (Dehydroepiandrosterone) rarely finds itself bored and looking for something to do. It has a powerful influence on many of the body's other hormones, and is imperative in the production of both testosterone and estrogen. After age 30, the body's natural production of DHEA gradually begins its slow decline. As a result, the hormones that rely on DHEA follow suit and become less active as we age.

AN OVERVIEW OF DHEA ✦ "Fountain of youth," "miracle fat-burner," "anti-aging wonder pill," and "the mother of all hormones," DHEA certainly has its fair share of nicknames, many of which have been assigned in the past decade.

Since its discovery in 1934, DHEA has been the subject of more than 5,000 studies. Some of the most reputable have suggested that this influential steroid hormone can improve metabolism, fertility, immune function, cardiovascular health, DNA repair, digestion, and a long list of ailments. Needless to say, these are some *very* bold claims. How can one little supplement accomplish so many tasks? Let's investigate.

How DHEA works ✦ DHEA doesn't have one specific, clear-cut responsibility. Instead it serves as a catalyst to nearly 20 of the body's hormonal systems. As the body ages, many biological process begin to slow down. This happens for two primary reasons.

First, the billions of cells within your body become compromised by free radicals and gradually fall victim to oxidative stress. This is a completely unavoidable process that takes place every time you're exposed to a chemical, toxin or other noxious airborne agent. Next, hormone production declines, and DHEA is no exception. But, unlike less-governing hormones, when your DHEA level begins its inevitable decline, a number of other systems are affected as a result.

It has been estimated that by age 50, the average adult produces just half of the DHEA he or she did in his or her 20s and early 30s. By age 70, most adults will be fortunate to produce even 20 percent of what they once did. This has led many researchers to believe that by supplementing DHEA, it may be possible to rekindle youthful metabolism, memory, mental clarity, energy, and a long list of other sought-after qualities.

THERAPEUTIC APPLICATIONS OF DHEA

- *Anti-Aging.* A lifetime of oxidative stress is what ultimately causes the body to age. Over the course of our lives, this process becomes more and more biologically influential. Based on the consistent rate at which DHEA declines with age, many researchers believe that there is an unmistakable correlation between how much DHEA we produce and how fast (or slowly) we age. This, coupled with the influence that DHEA has on other hormones including sex hormones, such as testosterone, estrogen, pregnenolone, and androstenedione, makes DHEA a supplement well worth considering.

- *Impotence.* Considering that DHEA is a direct precursor to testosterone, the primary male sex hormone, it probably didn't take researchers too long to piece this puzzle together. One of the most famous studies involved 40 men age 41-69 who suffered from impotence. At the conclusion of this 24-week, placebo-controlled study, it was determined that the group taking DHEA had improved feelings of arousal and satisfaction as well as longer-lasting erections.

- *Memory.* It's well documented that the human brain contains very high levels of DHEA. Accordingly, many researchers continue to believe that DHEA may play a major role in our ability to learn, think clearly, and recall memories. Additional studies are now being conducted to determine whether or not DHEA can help subdue the symptoms of depression, dementia, manic/bipolar diseases, and other neurological conditions.

- *Menopause.* Okay, so this is the men's section, but we need to include just a word about the role of DHEA in menopause. As we have seen, many women experience sharp declines in a number of different hormones, including estrogen and progesterone, as well as in DHEA. As these chemical changes take place, the body responds with hot flashes, bone calcium loss, vaginal dryness, and a number of psychological symptoms. Most of these symptoms are caused by the rapid decline in estrogen. One of DHEA's primary actions is to support the natural production of sex hormones, including estrogen. However, women should have their hormone levels tested before using DHEA, since it may cause some masculine characteristics in women who already have sufficient amounts.

- *Weight loss.* Metabolism rate is one of the many systems affected by declining DHEA levels and users continue to swear by DHEA as a way to help achieve and maintain a healthy body weight. But, make no mistake—DHEA is not a fat burner. Instead, it works by supporting the production of two crucial thyroid hormones (T3 and T4) needed to properly regulate metabolism.

- *Other therapeutic benefits of DHEA.* Cardiovascular support, fatigue, Immune system support.

Tips for Taking DHEA

- Anyone considering using DHEA should first have DHEA levels tested by a physician. Simple blood or saliva tests can accurately determine whether or not supplementation is appropriate and beneficial.

- *7-Keto* is a natural metabolite of DHEA that's becoming more and more popular among users. It has no influence on the body's sex hormones, but still functions in much the same manner as regular DHEA.

- DHEA can be very effective when used properly, however misuse can have some rather undesirable side effects. Always use DHEA as recommended to avoid hormonal complications.

- Avoid taking DHEA if you are being treated for any hormone-related cancer, such as prostate, breast, testicular, ovarian, or thyroid.
- For best results, DHEA should be taken in the morning with a balanced meal.

NATURAL COMPANIONS FOR DHEA ✦ Melatonin, antioxidants, selenium, CoQ_{10}, omega-3 and -6 essential fatty acids, phosphatidylserine, lecithin, progesterone.

COFACTORS AND CONTRAINDICATIONS FOR DHEA ✦ See Table 6 in the Appendix for more information.

Other Important "Male" Supporting Compounds

It's very common for men in their 40s and 50s to experience some type of urinary, prostate, or libido-related challenges. Most are generally harmless in nature and can be attributed to the inflammation and circulation changes associated with the normal aging process. Fortunately, many of these common biological hurdles can be easily addressed through dietary supplementation. Many of today's most popular male-support formulas now include natural compounds, such as tribulus, pygeum, nettles, pumpkin, cayenne, maca, and damiana. These natural compounds are frequently used to help reduce inflammation, promote hormone balance, encourage healthy blood flow, and increase stamina.

TRIBULUS TERRESTRIS

Tribulus was unleashed in the mid-1990s and has remained one of the most popular and effective of all male-supporting supplements. What makes this supplement so intriguing is its complex nutritional profile. Tribulus terrestris is bursting with active compounds that help support male reproductive health and sexual function. Among those compounds are steroidal saponins, flavonoids, glycosides, essential oils, plant sterols, and, one of particular interest, *protodioscin*. This potent and effective saponin has been the subject of intense clinical research for decades, and is believed to hold the secrets behind tribulus's ability to increase virility, testosterone production, and physical performance.

This was evidenced in an 8-week, university-led, placebo-controlled human study that put protodioscin to the test. Researchers were able to determine that protodioscin extracts (standardized to 20 percent) inherent to products containing tribulus terrestris had a positive effect on the production of testosterone in male subjects.

Based on its history of safety and very positive feedback, we're confident recommending tribulus as a way to help encourage male reproductive health, libido, and virility.

Cofactors and Contraindications for *Tribulus Terrestris* ✦ See Table 8 in the Appendix for more information.

ZINC

Without question, zinc, discussed in detail in Chapter Five, is the one nutrient that no man should deprive himself of. An essential trace mineral, zinc works at the cellular level to help facilitate hundreds of different biological activities throughout the body. For openers, it's one of the most fundamental nutrients needed for prostate health and has helped many members of the aging male population prevent and reduce the effects of BPH (benign prostate hyperplasia), a common, noncancerous enlargement of the prostate gland. It also helps support healthy testosterone levels and sperm counts, and is vital to healthy hair growth.

MUIRA PUAMA

Native to Brazil, muira puama has become one of the most popular natural remedies to encourage healthy libido and improve overall sexual function in healthy males. Muira puama roots are teeming with a number of active compounds, including fatty acids, plant sterols, essential oils, and a unique collection of esters. But, despite this impressive profile, researchers are still puzzled as to why muira puama appears to work as well as it does. Some have suggested that it has a lot to do with the extract's diverse combination of esters, fatty acids, and naturally occurring chemical agents, such as *muirapuamine*, *pholbaphene*, *alpha-resinic acid*, *beta-resinic acid*, and alkaloids.

Regardless, there is certainly no shortage of men who swear by it. Some of the most popular male virility supplements now contain muira puama, and it's not uncommon to hear it referred to as nature's answer to Viagra®. Aside from presupposed sexual benefits, some users say that it may also help prevent hair loss, help with neurological disorders, improve circulation, reduce fatigue, and promote general well being.

COFACTORS AND CONTRAINDICATIONS FOR *MUIRA PUAMA* ✦ See Table 8 in the Appendix for more information.

L-ARGININE

L-arginine is a semi-essential amino acid, meaning that for many people, it's one that their bodies can't supply in sufficient quantities. One of the primary roles of arginine is the production of nitric oxide (NO), a potent vasodilator. In men with erectile disorder (ED) due to abnormal NO deficiency, arginine may be useful therapy. In a large, controlled study, men with ED treated with 1600 milligrams of arginine for 6 weeks showed significant improvement as compared to the men in the study who were not given arginine.

Arginine is required for normal sperm production and low levels may be responsible for infertility. A study conducted more than 50 years ago found that men who were fed an arginine deficient diet for just nine days saw their sperm counts decreased by 90 percent. More recently it was found that supplementation with 500 milligrams for 6-8 weeks markedly increased sperm count and motility and resulted in successful pregnancies.

Arginine is a potent immunomodulator and supplementation has been shown to be useful in postoperative stress, reducing infection, and speeding wound healing. These results have been observed in older patients as well as younger ones. As noted, arginine may be out of balance with lysine in patients who have herpes simplex. As a precaution, they should take lysine along with arginine.

CoFactors and Contraindications for L-Arginine • See Table 6 in the Appendix for more information.

Prostate Health

Prostate enlargement affects approximately half of men over age 40. It's referred to as benign prostatic hypertrophy, or BPH, and, while symptoms can be extremely annoying, it may never progress to a more serious condition. While the cause has defied attempts to explain it, changes in hormone levels in middle-aged and elderly men are thought to be factors.

Urination problems are the most common symptom, because the enlarged prostate presses on the urinary bladder. Resulting difficulties include the urgency to urinate frequently (even at night), pain upon urinating, decreased flow, and urine volume. In addition, bladder infections, urine leaking, and irritation to the urethra are common. It's important to maintain prostate health and to work to prevent more serious prostate conditions.

About one-fourth of middle-aged and older men complain about impotence or inability to attain or sustain an erection sufficient for sexual intercourse. Psychological issues are commonly involved with impotence, but declining testosterone levels can also affect libido.

SAW PALMETTO

Major Application of Saw Palmetto • This supernutrient for men is derived from the berries of the low-growing saw palmetto plants (*Serenoa repens*) plentiful in Florida and other tropical areas. Loaded with sterols, fatty acids, and a number of other biologically active compounds, the extracts are now commonly used to prevent and reduce enlargement of the prostate caused by benign prostatic hyperplasia, or BHP. Relatively harmless in nature, BHP is unusually common and affects an estimated 4 out of every 5 men over age 60.

Contrary to what the name might suggest, researchers have determined that BHP does not appear to be cancerous. Its symptoms, however, are *not* unlike those that often accompany prostate cancer. Pain and difficulty during urination are among the most common symptoms, and saw palmetto seems to work very well to minimize these side effects.

Researchers are still scratching their heads over what specifically causes BHP. What they *do* know, is that it doesn't appear to be cancerous. Widespread trials have indicated that its prevalence could very well be linked to a number of lifestyle-related variables, including age, poor diet, high cholesterol, lack of exercise, and excessive alcohol consumption. Still, it's important to point out that none of these have been labeled "official" as of this writing.

AN OVERVIEW OF SAW PALMETTO ✦ The timeline that underscores saw palmetto use is an interesting one. Native Americans are believed to have been the first to use it for medicinal purposes and, according to historical record, its berries were consumed whole or made into tinctures. This was apparently a common remedy among men who suffered from urinary difficulties and among women who frequently experienced breast pain and other problems.

Today it's use is immensely popular in many parts of Europe. Here in the United States, its popularity continues to increase among the aging male population. This should come as a shock to no one, especially when you consider that many clinical and placebo-controlled studies have concluded that saw palmetto can be just as effective as some of today's most popular BHP prescription medications.

HOW SAW PALMETTO WORKS ✦ While it's unclear as to *why* saw palmetto seems to help with prostate problems, it does appear to help. In fact, it's been estimated that as many as 70 percent of the men who use saw palmetto report marked improvements in urinary function. The common, recommended dose is a standard one, and consists of 320 mg/day of extract standardized for fatty acid content. Some users respond very quickly, although it generally takes several weeks to see real results.

There are many noble theories about why why these unique extracts are able to support prostate health. One of the most universally accepted suggests that the extract's diverse concentration of active compounds reduces prostate levels of *dihydrotestosterone*, or DHT (an active form of the male sex hormone testosterone). Another suggests that it prevents the activity of IGF-1. IGF-1, or insulin growth factor, is commonly associated with prostate development.

TIPS FOR TAKING SAW PALMETTO

- When using saw palmetto, standardized extracts containing 25 percent fatty acids are the ideal way to go. Always look for formulas that contain a minimum of 160 mg per capsule, from *Serenoa repens*.
- The ABC Herbal monograph suggests a dosage of 400 mg twice daily of standardized extracts. This is the most universally accepted dose and has been shown to work very well.
- Although very rare, some men may experience nausea or upset stomach when taking saw palmetto on an empty stomach. A small meal can help prevent this.
- Saw palmetto is not a "cure all" for BHP, and should not be the green light to abandon other BHP medications. It's best used for mild to moderate symptoms, not for a serious condition. A brief chat with your physician can determine whether or not supplementation is appropriate.
- Saw palmetto is now commonly included in many men's formulas. However, it's important to verify that the male formula you select delivers a daily minimum of 800 mg from standardized extract.
- Saw palmetto is not an overnight solution and users should be patient, as it takes 4-6 weeks to reap the benefits. Healthy men in their mid-to-late 30s can get a jump on the process by starting young as a means of prostate support.

- If conditions worsen or do not improve within a few weeks, discontinue use and seek the advice of a medical practitioner.

Natural Companions for Saw Palmetto
- *Lycopene.* Lycopene is the red pigment in tomatoes, pink grapefruit, papaya, and pink guava and its benefits were briefly discussed, along with its other carotenoid family members, in Chapter One. High blood and tissue lycopene levels have been found to reduce risk of prostate and lung cancers. According to a statement published by the Department of Epidemiology at the Harvard School of Public Health, "The strongest known dietary risk factor for prostate cancer is a lycopene deficit."

   Furthermore, lycopene in cooked tomato products is two times more bioavailable than that found in fresh tomatoes. This news was greeted by thousands of happy male pizza lovers who figured that they now had a medical reason to bolt down their favorite food—and lycopene may even help prevent oxidation of all those fats that come with pizza! Moreover, olive oil and beta carotene may enhance the absorption of lycopene.

   The Food and Drug Administration has just announced that it will allow limited food claims for lycopene and cardiovascular disease. The claim doesn't apply to synthetic supplements, but natural lycopene supplements contain oil pressed from tomato seeds, the major repository for lycopene in tomatoes. A number of studies support the role of lycopene supplements in prostate health—without the problems that might come of eating too much mozzarella cheese.

   The promise of lycopene as a cancer preventive is significant enough that the National Cancer Institute is sponsoring Phases I, II, and III chemoprevention trials for prostate, breast, and colon cancers.
- *Other natural companions for lycopene.* Pygeum, nettles.

COFACTORS AND CONTRAINDICATIONS FOR SAW PALMETTO: ✦ See Table 8 in the Appendix for more information.

Urinary

CRANBERRY EXTRACT (VACCIUM MACROCARPON)

MAJOR APPLICATION OF CRANBERRY EXTRACT ✦ For more than a century now, the bitter extracts of cranberries have helped scores of women prevent and lessen many of the symptoms commonly associated with bladder infections. This is believed possible due to the plant's high concentration of OPCs (proanthocyanidins). By increasing urine acidity, cranberry extracts have been shown in several studies to help discourage bacteria from clinging to the lining of the bladder and the urinary tract.

AN OVERVIEW OF CRANBERRY EXTRACT ✦ Native Americans were the first to use the berries of cranberry plants (*Vaccium macrocarpon*) to ease the pain, burning, and frequency of urination. As word spread, its use quickly became popular with many early physicians who also used it to prevent the formation of small stones in the bladder, known as "bladder gravel." Shortly after the turn of the 19th century, cranberry was partially accepted as an effective remedy for scurvy. This makes sense when you understand that the bitter juices house a respectable amount of vitamin C.

Fast-forwarding to more modern times, cranberry supplementation is extremely popular and strongly revered as one of the safest and simplest ways for women to encourage healthy bladders and urinary tracts. It's available in a wide variety of forms, although juices and extracts seem to be the most sought-after.

HOW CRANBERRY EXTRACT WORKS ✦ The bladder and urinary tract are lined with mucous membranes that seem to have a natural attraction to bacteria, including *E. coli*. Many of these urinary culprits are easily flushed away during urination. On a more discouraging note, an equal number of these bacterial invaders are true survivors. They grab on to the mushy walls of the bladder and urinary tract and simply refuse to let go. But the OPCs and other active compounds in cranberry are rich in vitamin C and increase acidity of urine. This creates an environment that makes it very difficult for bacteria to "keep their grip," making it almost effortless to flush them from the body during normal urination.

Most recent research suggests that cranberry may also be able to prevent and possibly reverse the damaging effects of ulcers. *Helicobacter pylori* is another "clingy" bacteria commonly associated with the formation of peptic ulcers. Unlike the previously mentioned bacteria, H. pylori prefers to make its home in the stomach lining. Once embedded, it can cause a gradual erosion, allowing digestive juices to seep through unsuspected. While cranberry has shown some promise in this regard, research is ongoing.

OTHER THERAPEUTIC BENEFITS OF CRANBERRY EXTRACT
- Urinary tract infections
- Kidney stones
- Ulcers

TIPS FOR TAKING CRANBERRY EXTRACT
- There are many options available when it comes to using cranberry. Supplements are by the far the most cost-effective.
- When using cranberry, it's important to remember that "prevention" is the key word. Use has been shown to help ease many symptoms, however it seems to serve a much greater purpose when taken as a means of prevention.
- Bacteria that commonly collects in the urinary tract is not fond of acidic environments. Taking cranberry supplements with additional vitamin C can increase the acidity of the urine, making it much easier to flush them from the system.
- Individuals using blood thinners should consult their physicians prior to using cranberry to avoid the possibility of internal bleeding.

- If you decide to consume cranberry in juice form, look for those that contain no less than 30 percent juice. Many commercially available cranberry drinks are loaded with sugar that can interfere with its activity and cause more problems in the long run.
- Be sure to consume plenty of water while using cranberry supplements. This is essentially what provides the "flushing out" of urinary bacteria.

NATURAL COMPANIONS OF CRANBERRY EXTRACT

- *D-mannose.* Cranberries and blueberries contain a simple sugar known as D-Mannose. The body is capable of metabolizing small amounts of it, but most is rapidly excreted in the urine. Within the bladder, D-Mannose can adhere to bacterial lectins, preventing them from sticking to the bladder lining. Once this process occurs, they can be flushed away during urination. This helps prevent the formation of bacterial colonies within the urinary tract. And, because the body can use just minimal amounts of D-Mannose, it won't interfere with normal blood-sugar regulation.
- *Vitamin C.* Unhealthy LDL cholesterol deposits and free radical damage are two of the most common culprits associated with urinary problems. Vitamin C is a powerful and highly versatile antioxidant that helps inhibit the body from oxidizing LDL cholesterol, while also preventing the oxidative damage that can be caused by high levels of free radicals. Look for formulas that contain supporting compounds, such as vitamin E and flavonoids. In addition, vitamin C increases the acidity of urine, making it more difficult for the bacteria that cause urinary tract infections to survive.
- *Pygeum africanum (Prunus africana).* Pygeum is an old-world remedy that was "discovered" by European explorers visiting Africa in the 1700s. African healers used it to treat problems that often plague older men,

including bladder discomfort and associated urinary problems. European herbalists revived interest in the herb in the mid-1960s when they began using it to treat benign prostatic hypertrophy (BPH). Today pygeum is the most commonly used herb to treat BPH in France.

Pygeum has anti-inflammatory and anti-congestive properties and appears to reduce bladder sensitivity to excessive electrical stimulation. The result is an increase in urinary flow and a reduction in urgency, strain, and hesitancy to urinate. Pygeum also reduces prolactin and blocks the accumulation of cholesterol by the prostate. Instead, pygeum enhances the action of cholesterol by making available more binding sites for harmful dihydrotestosterone (DHT) in the prostate. Pygeum is a natural partner of saw palmetto in the treatment of BPH because saw palmetto inhibits the production of DHT, while pygeum clears it from circulation. These are the primary herbs used to treat male urinary disorders.

COFACTORS AND CONTRAINDICATIONS FOR CRANBERRY EXTRACT ✦ See Table 7 in the Appendix for more information.

Herb	Uses
B-sitosterol and other sterols	mild testosterone-like effect
muira puama (Ptychopetalum olacoides)	anabolic, libido
saw palmetto berries (Serenoa repens)	anabolic, prostate health
smilax (Smilax officinalis)	mildly anabolic
suma (Pfaffia paniculata)	anabolic, adaptogenic
Tribulus terrestris	anabolic effects, antiaging
wild oats (Avena sativa) (combined with nettle root)	anabolic, libido
Wild yam, Mexican yam (Dioscorea villosa)	anabolic, anti-inflammatory

Adapted from Bucci, L.R.: "Selected herbals and human exercise performance." Am J Clin Nutr 2000;72(suppl): 624S-36S.

FIGURE 7-5 **Herbs with Testosterone-Like (anabolic) Activity**

Energy and Sleep

MELATONIN

Major Application of Melatonin ✦ Have you ever wondered why your body just naturally seems to shut down at night? Sure, it might have a lot to do with how busy you were that day, but there's much more to the "shutting down" process than that. The ability to fall asleep, stay asleep, and awake refreshed doesn't happen by chance. In fact, it's almost completely dictated by the body's internal alarm clock, the pineal gland. One of the key chemicals produced by this glandular CEO is melatonin, an antioxidant hormone that helps regulate the body's sleep cycles.

An Overview of Melatonin ✦ Melatonin was discovered in the late 1950s, but wasn't made commercially available until a few decades later. Initially used to help travelers cope with jet lag as well as mild bouts of insomnia, as the quality of scientific research progressed, we've been able to learn more and more about the potential health, sleep, and anti-aging benefits of this highly versatile hormone. For example, melatonin is responsible for overseeing one of the most important roles in the human body, the regulation of our 24-hour cycle of biological processes, or *circadian*, rhythms. This is our internal day-at-a-glance calendar, and essentially reminds our biological selves of what we should be doing at certain times throughout the day.

How it works ✦ At birth, each of us is equipped with an internal clock that tells us when to sleep, when to wake, when to eat, when to digest food, and so on. Melatonin is a component of this mechanism, although its primarily responsibility lies in monitoring the "sleep cycle" side of things. As children and throughout our childhood years, our natural production of melatonin is at its highest level. As we age, however, the amount that we're able to self-manufacture begins to wane. This is a key reason why children and teenagers typically have no problem sleeping until late in the day. Many adults, on the other hand, have a tendency to wake easily, experience more difficulty staying asleep, and become accustomed to waking at hours that are consistently earlier.

How then, you may be wondering, does the body know when to begin (and stop) producing melatonin? There are several factors at play here. The most influential rests in the amount of retinal exposure to light. Here's how it works.

The pineal gland begins the process of secreting melatonin in response to darkness, peaks during the early hours of the morning, and begins to cut back at about the same time the sun decides to rise. Once melatonin production has ceased for the day, the pineal gland switches gears and begins to produce serotonin, a mood and emotion-supporting neurotransmitter used to send chemical messages—including thoughts—throughout the body.

THERAPEUTIC APPLICATIONS OF MELATONIN

- *Anti-aging.* An explosion of studies during the past decade suggests that melatonin has very strong antioxidant properties and is capable of protecting cells against free radicals and oxidative damage. This is of great importance, especially when you consider that our bodies age from the inside out. Poor sleep quality, unceasing patterns of exhaustion, high stress levels, and long-term exposure to free radical oxidation can expedite the aging process faster than you might imagine. Melatonin has shown exceptional promise in each of these four key areas, which should come as great news for anyone looking to rewind a few years.

- *Depression and stress-related anxiety.* To date there's no definitive proof that melatonin can actually cheer a person up. But it may certainly be able to help that same person get the sleep he or she so desperately needs. Stress—whether physical or emotional—can take a ruinous toll on a person's ability to fall asleep and, more important, stay asleep. Some researchers believe that this may be caused by an imbalance in the pineal gland that regulates the production of serotonin and melatonin. Aside from that, stress can make it even more challenging to remain in a deep sleep. Melatonin seems to have an effect not only on the ability to doze off, but the ability to stay in dreamland for extended periods of time.

* *Insomnia.* Many who experience difficulty sleeping have found melatonin to be one the most effective, nonaddictive natural substances at their disposal. While there are really no clear-cut guideline for dosage, many adults respond positively when taking anywhere from 0.5 mg or 500 mcg shortly before bedtime. This can be especially beneficial for older adults, who naturally produce very low levels of this critical hormone.

Today, most manufacturers offer melatonin products in 500 mcg to 3 mg potencies. Some even offer sustained-release formulas, designed especially to help you sleep deeply throughout the night. See our product recommendations for more information about choosing the right formula.

Over the years, we've learned that there's much more to melatonin than just a good night's sleep. It's also a powerful antioxidant that, in the eyes of many researchers, is capable of quenching many of the damaging free radicals that expedite the aging process. In addition, melatonin is currently being looked at as a natural way to alleviate symptoms of depression and anxiety, headaches, high blood pressure, menopause, PMS, chronic pain, and long list of other conditions that interfere with normal sleep patterns.

* *Jet lag.* As evidenced by years of successful use among world travelers and airline employees, melatonin is one of the most effective and simple ways to adjust to time zone changes and reestablish normal sleeping patterns after a long flight. Begin taking it a day or two before traveling to enable a quicker adjustment to new time zones. Shift workers have found melatonin to be very useful in establishing normal sleep patterns, particularly if their jobs require shift rotation. That kind of schedule imposes a similar condition to traveling between time zones.

- It's not a good idea to take melatonin if you have any immediate plans to drive a vehicle or operate heavy machinery, especially in the evening hours.

- For best results, melatonin should be taken prior to bed at roughly the same time each day. This is especially important if you're trying to reestablish normal sleep patterns.

- If you're currently under the care of a physician for depression, anxiety, or other neurological conditions, consult him or her prior to using melatonin supplements.

- Children, pregnant women, and expecting mothers should not take melatonin.

- The deep sleep that can result from taking melatonin has been known to encourage some rather interesting dreams. If they become a problem, it would be wise to cut your dose a bit. This occurence is most common in doses greater than 3 mg.

- When using melatonin, start small and gradually increase your dose over time. Skipping a night on occasion can be wise, and may encourage your pineal gland to continue producing its own natural supply.

Natural Companions for Melatonin • Ribose, GABA, L-Theanine

- *Ribose.* Ribose is an important supplement for the production of cellular energy, but, before we explain why, it's important to have a basic understanding of ATP, or adenosine triphosphate. ATP makes it possible for cells to produce, store, and exchange chemical energy. Taking that one step further, ATP is what essentially allows us to synthesize proteins, contract muscles, lift a suitcase, and so on. In fact, many biochemists refer to ATP as *molecular currency*. It's the fuel that drives every move we make, every thought we think, and countless activities we aren't even aware of. Without it, we would be physically and mentally helpless.

Ribose is a simple 5-carbon sugar that provides the metabolic "spark" needed for the body to produce ATP and other molecules called nucleotides. In addition to ATP, this group includes RNA, DNA, and the nucleotides produced from niacin, riboflavin, and pantothenic acid. Nucleotides are some of the body's most important molecules and they all have a ribose core. Here we are focusing on the role of ribose in ATP production and function, although it should be recognized that ribose aids in repair and recovery as well.

Not surprisingly, ribose was popularized as a dietary supplement by bodybuilders and strength-training athletes who wanted to preserve their cellular energy reserves. But you don't need to be a bodybuilder to benefit from it. Taking ribose is an excellent way to accelerate your body's own natural energy stores. It has been particularly useful for middle-aged men and women engaged in exercise regimens, because it allows them to work more efficiently with less resulting pain.

• *GABA.* Often referred to as the "brain's natural calming agent," GABA, or *gamma amino butyric acid,* is an amino acid derivative and the body's most active inhibitory neurotransmitter. It works by preventing neurons from "over-firing" chemical messages from the brain to other regions of the body. GABA also plays an important role in glands controlled by the sympathetic nervous system, including the pancreas (insulin resistance), the duodenum (digestion and assimilation), and the thymus (immunity). GABA may be useful in reducing nervous eating and anxiety attacks following alcohol withdrawal.

GABA is produced in the body from the nonessential amino acid glutamic acid. However, as one grows older, the enzyme needed to make the conversion decreases and low levels of manganese, which cofactors the conversion, can make the problem worse. At a time when disturbances in brain metabolism, digestion and immunity increase, GABA levels are likely low, making supplementation a viable option. The brain produces small amounts of gamma-hydroxybutyrate (GHB), a sleep-inducing amino acid from GABA.

In light of its unique calming and sleep-inducing ability, GABA is becoming more and more popular among people who suffer from mood swings, depression, anxiety, and a number of other neurological conditions. Loss of sleep is a major health problem because it reduces work efficiency, leads to more accidents, increases sick days, and reduces cognitive function. By maintaining a calming balance with stimulating neurotransmitters, including glutamine, GABA can help encourage a natural state of relaxation, ease nervous tensions, and allow the body to doze off peacefully.

* *L- Theanine.* L-theanine is the principal amino acid in green tea and is responsible for many of the health benefits of drinking tea. In the brain, L-theanine induces alpha-brain wave activity, which produces a relaxed, yet alert, state of mind. This happens totally without sedation and occurs approximately one half-hour after drinking tea or taking 200 milligrams of the supplement. Drinking green tea has traditionally been a good way to increase brain energy—in a nice, focused way.

L-theanine is also credited with offsetting the stimulating effects of caffeine in green tea, which can contain more caffeine than coffee. In animal studies L-theanine has been shown to increase both serotonin and dopamine levels in the brain. It may also have a place in regimens to reduce blood pressure. Theanine also protects normal cells from damage during chemotherapy, no doubt due to its ability to increase glutathione levels.

COFACTORS AND CONTRAINDICATIONS FOR MELATONIN • See Table 6 in the Appendix for more information.

To Sum It All Up

Hormones and the system that produces them equal the neurological system in complexity and whole-body effects. In fact, the two are so closely linked that it's difficult to describe one without the other.

This chapter on hormones could easily have been placed right after Chapter Two, describing the *stress syndrome*. However, we decided on the order *7-Syndrome Healing* follows because the actions of hormones are so subtle and so far reaching, that they aren't as recognizable to most people as are the syndromes we have chosen to discuss in the preceding chapters. Syndrome order was also established following the natural progression of conditions, each hinging on health issues arising from the previous syndrome.

The endocrine system includes hormones, peptides, prostaglandins, and neurotransmitters that operate with a feedback mechanism. This means that one gland signals another to release its products directly into circulation or to another part of the tissue. As circulating levels of the product normalize, release of additional product is subdued.

In an ideal situation, perfect balance is achieved and other body systems are regulated properly. Cortisol is the one hormone that doesn't obey the feedback mechanism by shutting down as circulating levels rise. The set point for circulating cortisol rises as stress levels increase and the body equips itself for defense. The orderly balance that other hormones adhere to is disordered, and the mechanics for 7-syndrome conditions are set in motion.

One of the most important regulating hormones we need to explore further now is 1,25-dihydroxy cholecalciferol or vitamin D-3 hormone. In Chapter Eight, The *Osteo Syndrome*, we'll discuss the role of this important hormone in the skeleton and jaw and highlight emerging information about the regulating role of this important hormone on other parts of the body.

Osteo Syndrome

I N MANY WAYS, the skeletal system is the most elegant and beautiful system of the body, despite being one of the most neglected and drastically misunderstood, so the *osteo syndrome* is a fitting final salute in our exploration of the 7 healing syndromes. Most of us regard our skeletons as things that hold up bones and bend in strategic places for locomotion. A number of people view their teeth as annoyances that collect food particles, cause periodic discomfort, and invite the spine-bending hiss of high-powered dental drills.

Putting those images aside, we'd like to introduce you to the more intricate and fascinating side of the osteo system. It will forever change your perception of the bones that support you, earning your admiration and gratitude for the remarkable series of tasks they perform.

What You Will Find in This Chapter

- Osteo power
- Muscle, tendon, and ligament power
- Bone health
- Joint pain and osteoarthritis
- Injury and recovery
- Bone loss
- Oral health

Osteo Power

It's been estimated that a person weighing about 155 pounds (70 kilograms) has approximately 100 acres of bone crystals bathed in just a few liters of bone fluid. While we're confident that this should get your attention, there's more: Bone is actually considered "connective" in nature, which makes it related it to blood and a number of other tissues. This may seem like an odd comparison, but it highlights the dynamic nature of human bone. The major difference between the two tissues is that bone has solids between its cells, while blood has fluids. Still, the two are intimately interconnected, providing nourishment, new cells, and other important bio-molecules for one another. Let's examine them.

Bones are constructed of collagen protein, which constitutes one-third of the body's total protein. Fifty-seven percent of the body's collagen reserve can be found in bone. Collagen is extremely strong and contains three intertwined protein strands with cross-links for stability. Surrounding bone collagen is a web of agents that consists of fibers, nutrients, and a gel-like substance known as *proteoglycans*. These compounds are encased by minerals known as *hydroxyapatite*, which consists primarily of calcium and phosphorus, as well as a few other minerals.

Hydroxyapatite is a *living* crystal that can change chemical composition by simply shifting electrons and attracting different types of minerals to its surface. Don't be fooled by the seemingly unstable nature of bone, however. In total, the bony structures of the body are incredibly strong. This strength comes from two key sources, the collagen matrix and its corresponding crystalline structure. It's been said that the strength of bones compares favorably to that of reinforced concrete, which uses steel to provide tensile strength and a cement mixture to offer compressional strength. Fortunately, bones are much lighter.

The crystal lattice of bone consists of three layers; the interior, the surface, and the hydrating shell. Mineral ions move among all three layers of bone, with the greatest activity accounting for the maintenance of equilibrium between the surface and the hydrating shell. If minerals are drawn from the shell, others from the surface quickly replace them. Similarly, if the concentration of minerals exceeds that of the surface, they move to the interior. Bones in young people have a generous reserve of moisture. With age, however, bones gradually dry out, and this can take a serious toll on the rate of mineral exchange.

You'd never know it, but the body actually uses bones as storage units for minerals. It draws on the rich supply of minerals in bone whenever blood levels are low or when they're required for buffering an acidic body. In addition, long bones are filled with marrow and used by the body to produce healthy blood cells. Bones have a rich blood supply capable of delivering vital nutrients, transporting blood cells produced in the marrow, and removing dead cells or waste products.

Mineral exchange in the bone matrix continues throughout life and is orchestrated by two kinds of cells: Osteoblasts build new cells and deposit minerals and osteoclasts break them down and reabsorb deposited minerals. During our more youthful years, mineral deposits are more frequent than is mineral resorption. Osteoclasts remove old bone cells and replace them with new, healthy cells. This is accomplished by first solubilizing the minerals, then digesting the collagen matrix with enzymes. The body's long bones, such as those in the legs and arms, have a more dense structure (cortical) than those in joints and the vertebrae (trabecular).

Bone modeling accelerates during puberty at about 8 percent per year, and is influenced by an increase in hormone production. By the age of 20, the body's skeletal framework typically reaches maturity. In the years that follow, bone growth continues at a pace of approximately 1 percent per year, finally leveling off around the age of 35. Thereafter, bone density begins its slow and inevitable decline. In women, bone loss accelerates during the 10-15 years that encompass menopause, and has been linked to the sharp drop in estrogen levels. Men lose bone mass, too, most commonly around the age that their testosterone levels begin to decline. For men, this process occurs at a slower rate.

Like bone structures, teeth are also composed of hydroxyapatite crystals, but they're much more dense. Just like bone structures, the crystals are arranged in a lattice around collagen but, unlike bones, teeth are nourished by a blood and lymph supply that's located in the pulpy interior and do not contain osteoblasts or osteoclasts. The hydroxyapatite crystals in teeth have carbonate, as well as several other minerals, adhering to the surface. This allows for a dynamic flow of minerals in and out of the lattice network.

Enamel is composed of an even denser grade of hydroxyapatite than that of the tooth interior and, as a result, little to no mineral exchange occurs at the enamel's surface. Hydroxyapatite is wrapped around a network of tough proteins (similar to keratin in hair) and is capable of resisting acids, enzymes and other corrosive agents. Once the teeth have erupted through the gums, enamel is no longer formed. This is why irritants on the surface of the teeth can attack and damage their once pearly, white finish. Advancements in modern dentistry have made it relatively easy to repair the translucent surface without the unattractive and toxic filling materials once used.

Teeth are anchored in the periodontal membrane by a bony substance appropriately called *cementum*. Collagen fibers from the periodontal membrane pass into the cementum to firmly anchor the tooth into its socket. Periodontal tissues are some of the most dynamic and metabolically active in the body. Constant exposure to food, water, airborne substances, and bacteria pose a significant threat to healthy periodontal tissues. Additionally, crystals can form under the gum line, creating pockets that resemble free beachfront property to oral bacteria.

Make no mistake, good dental hygiene is not just about obtaining a pretty smile. In fact, it is one of the most important measures you can take to improve your health. As you read in Chapter Four, periodontal disease is a contributing factor in cardiovascular disease. Additionally, chronic inflammation of gum tissue can lead to serious immune problems, as you'll recall from Chapter Five. In a nutshell, the same nutritional factors that govern bone health also apply to healthy teeth.

Muscle, Ligament, and Tendon Power

Movement diversity is one of the most remarkable functions of the human body, especially when you consider that we manage to do it on just two legs while most animals rely on four. This vertical human blessing imposes special adaptations for balance and locomotion unique to our species. Sadly, it also leaves us far more vulnerable to imbalance and injury. Nervous and electrical stimulation is needed to get us moving, and we'll explain how this works later in this chapter. For now, we'd like to heighten your appreciation for what the joints and muscles are put through day in and day out.

Approximately one half of the body's weight comes from muscle. The majority is skeletal, while roughly 10 percent consists of specialized tissues for heart and intestinal function. Muscle contractions occur in a novel slip-slide motion initiated by nerve signals and then immediately activated by electrical stimulus. During a muscle contraction, the fibers slide closely together and the muscle shortens. A bulging bicep is one of the best examples. When contracted (flexed), the fibers of the bicep closest to the muscles of the forearm (brachialis) slide in an "upward" fashion toward the anterior deltoid. This is what essentially causes the bicep to bulge. As the muscle relaxes, the fibers slip back into their initial position and the muscle lengthens.

Let's take the process one step further. Once the muscle has been stimulated, calcium ions move from storage compartments in muscle cells. This inevitably changes the electrical potential of the cell in a process that takes less than a split second. Shortly after, the calcium ions dash back home to restore the cell's resting electrical potential. During the calcium outflow, the muscle fibers slide together as the calcium ions flow back into their storage vesicles. This reverses polarity and causes the muscle fibers to slide apart. Biologically, this sounds simple but, as we'll point out, there are some pitfalls.

Due to their constant and unceasing role in movement, range of motion and structural support, muscles are some of the most energy-demanding parts of the body. In order to do their respective tasks efficiently, they rely on four sources for their energy needs:

- ATP from the mitochondria,
- Creatine phosphate to supply the phosphorus (P) that creates ATP,
- ADP form myokinase (a muscle enzyme), and
- Glycogen to combat lactic acid.

The latter (glycogen) should be familiar to you from our earlier discussion of the *metabolic syndrome*. Anyone who has ever experienced that dreaded post-workout soreness is already *well* familiar with lactic acid.

Energy production is accomplished by exploiting certain cellular capabilities and potentials. It's an elegant system that integrates structure and function and can be used to "train" muscles for a particular response.

Endurance athletes, strength coaches, and those who are well versed in training stand to benefit the most by understanding the versatility of muscle fibers, as well as their varying energy demands. Let's take a look at some of the most important elements in understanding muscle fibers and the energy that drives them.

Slow Twitch Muscle Fibers (Type I)
Unless you fall under the category of professional athlete, lumberjack, or furniture mover, most of what you do on a daily basis is dictated by your supply of "slow twitch" muscle fibers. These low-resistance fibers are used to carry out aerobic activities, such as jogging, walking, standing, and running light errands. They are highly resistant to fatigue, contract slowly, and contain high amounts of mitochondria, myoglobin, and blood capillaries.

Fast Twitch Muscle Fibers (Type II)
Unlike slow twitch fibers that contract slowly, "fast twitch" fibers are used for strength, power and other explosive (anaerobic) bursts of energy. There are two types of fast twitch fibers; type II-A and type II-B.

Type II-A fast twitch fibers have a moderately low resistance to fatigue, a high concentration of mitochondria, myoglobin, and blood capillaries, and a high capacity for oxygen. Similarly, type II-B fast twitch fibers have a very low resistance for fatigue, contract at an extremely fast rate, and are primarily used for short-burst, high intensity movements. Both types of fast twitch fibers rely on creatine phosphate and glycogen to meet their energy demands.

ATP (adenosine triphosphate) – ATP molecules serve as the primary source of energy for all living plants and animals and are stored—in limited amounts—within the cells of muscle and other tissues. Every voluntary and involuntary move we make uses ATP in some capacity, although high-intensity training and exercise can deplete the body's reserve very rapidly.

ADP (adenosine diphosphate) – ADP is an equally important element in energy production, and is created when ATP is broken down to initiate the muscle contraction in question. Once it has been used to fuel a contraction, is converted back into ATP; a process better known as the phosphorous cycle, or phosphorylation.

Enlargement of muscle fibers requires that the muscle in question contract at least 75 percent of its maximum tension. As this takes place, enlarged muscles require more nutrients, a greater blood supply, and more ATP. Amino acids can be utilized for energy, most notably the three branched chain amino acids – leucine, isoleucine, and valine. The nutrient requirements of the heart muscle, on the other hand, are far more comprehensive and rely heavily on fatty acids, magnesium and CoQ_{10} for energy. This is one of the body's most frustrating catch-22s. If one of your goals is to build and strengthen your heart muscle, you had better be prepared to supply it with the fatty acids and other nutrients that it needs to meet the increase in demand.

In order for movement and flexibility to work, skeletal bones need to be attached to one another as well as to the muscles that move them.

Tendons

These are tough, flexible fibrous bands that attach muscles to bones. When the muscle contracts, it exerts force on the tendon, which in turn moves the bone that it's attached to.

Tendons can be very small, such as those that move your fingers or the lens of the eye. They may also be quite large, such as the Achilles tendon that attaches the calf muscle to the heel. Normally, tendons slide smoothly back and forth. However, tendonitis is quite common, because tendons can become inflamed, not to mention very painful. Most athletes and exercise enthusiasts will be the first to attest to this. The most common cause of tendonitis is overuse, and that generally occurs when additional demands are put upon the tendon. A relatively poor blood supply and narrow passage for movement under the top of the shoulder blade (acromion bone) make the rotator cuff tendons particularly vulnerable to overuse.

Starting an exercise regimen or achieving a new level of exercise may be rewarding, but that doesn't eliminate the need to stretch, increase exercise gradually, and always respect your physical boundaries. In addition, tendons can be affected by both age and lifestyle changes. Poor circulation, as well as a lack of sufficient nutrients and water, can have significant impact on normal tendon function.

In any event, training properly and avoiding uncomfortable, painful movements is always the best strategy. Alternating your specific training routine can also be helpful. If deep squats or leg extensions become too painful to tolerate, perhaps an elliptical workout is more your speed. If your years of playing tennis eventually make it too difficult to do three sets of bicep curls, try isometrics or another form of low-resistance training. Either way, subjecting your tendons to massive amounts of physical stress that they simply can't handle is something that your body won't forget. You may not feel it immediately, but as the years pass, so will your body's ability to recover as it once did.

Dietary supplements have come a long way in the past few decades and have helped millions of people counter the inflammation and pain they may live with. We will review some of the most popular and effective later in this chapter. For now, let's run down the "do and don't" list essential to exercise, cardiovascular conditioning, and weight training.

DO

- Seek the advice of a personal trainer if you're new to exercising.
- Always stretch before and after any type of exercise activity.
- Drink plenty of fluids before, during, and after exercise.
- Respect your body's physical restrictions.
- Increase your training (duration and weights) gradually.
- Take a break if you feel dizzy, nauseous, or faint.
- Dedicate your final few minutes of cardiovascular training to a light cool down.
- Make sure that your diet is well balanced, consisting of fresh fruits and vegetables, as well as low glycemic carbohydrates and essential fatty acids.
- Ditch the "I'll be just fine" attitude. Injuries happen to even the strongest people when they least expect it.
- At all cost, try to avoid training alone. If something beyond your control were to go wrong, you're on your own.

DON'T

- Ever push yourself beyond what your body can handle physically.
- Starve yourself in order to lose fat. Your body needs the nutrients from balanced meals to fuel itself for growth and recovery.
- Justify your high saturated fat intake by promising to go the gym later that day. Your body won't know the difference, and will store what it needs to.
- Ever begin a workout without first stretching. And when you do stretch, don't bounce—this is a connective nightmare just waiting to happen.
- Ever train when injured or ill. Your immune will already be focused on getting you back to good health, and may not be able to respond to the increase in inflammation and lactic acid.
- If you need to wake early, don't train too close to bedtime. It takes time for your heart to return to its true resting rhythm. You could potentially override the natural release of melatonin that would otherwise be lulling you into sleep.

Ligaments

These are white, fibrous bands of connective tissue that link two or more bones (or cartilaginous structures) together. They provide stability to bones and prevent them from hyper-extending and hyper-flexing. They also prevent bone movement in certain directions, a key feature of joints that reduces the risk of dislocation and excessive movement that might cause breakage.

Certain ligaments have become quite famous. Unfortunately, this fame often comes at the expense of some very painful dislocations, strains and tears. Among the most popular are the cruciate ligaments; anterior (ACL) and posterior (PCL) in the knees, and shoulder ligaments. Injuries to these ligaments are nonjudgmental, and can plague weekend warriors with the same swift blow that they use on the most finely tuned professional athletes. Ligament tears are extremely common among football and basketball players. Television instant replay is unquestionably one of the best ways to appreciate the horribly odd twists and turns that often cause these tears, as well as the thousands of broken bones in professional athletes. Anyone who has not made it his or her life's work to perfect the physical self can do damage to ligaments with much less effort!

Ligaments also support many internal organs including the uterus, bladder, liver, and diaphragm. They also help support and shape the breasts. Finally, ligaments are an integral part of the vertebral column, especially in keeping it stabilized and protected.

Bursae

These sacs are filled with viscous fluid and covers bony prominences in the body, such as those in the shoulder. They also cushion joints in knees and elbows, facilitating movement and reducing friction. Constant irritation to joint structures can inflame the bursa and eventually lead to bursitis, a common injury among those who exercise regularly.

Bone Health

Nutrition is an important component of bone health, and the structural values of minerals such as calcium are now very well established. Both women and men who have higher calcium intake have been shown to exhibit stronger bones, particularly in the hips, than do those who consume less calcium. As we'll discuss, it *is* possible to maintain positive bone balance with a good osteo program.

Protein intake is extremely important, because it increases lean body mass. Lean body mass and bone density decrease with age, but a diet that includes plenty of protein can help offset these decreases. A dietary plan that balances animal and vegetable proteins appears to be optimum. There has been a vigorous debate among scientists regarding the benefits of animal versus vegetable protein. Animal protein produces acid residues that make the body more acidic and may draw calcium out of bones. In contrast, vegetable proteins have a buffering capacity that favors calcium uptake in bones.

If you enjoy red meat, try to eat it less frequently and introduce more fish and poultry. Fish contains healthy omega-3 fatty acids that are important for building strong, healthy bones. Range-fed meat and game are also good options. Just remember to include plenty of fresh fruits and vegetables along the way. For more information on acid/base balance and an ideal eating plan, consult the companion to this book, *7-Color Cuisine*.

A lean body doesn't just look good, it can also stimulate osteoblasts by exerting mechanical stress on bones. Using those muscles is part of the deal if you want the best scenario for your skeleton. Resistance exercise is particularly important for older women and, yes, low-to-moderate intensity exercise such as climbing stairs, housework, and gardening all add up. If you fancy an occasional walk, consider this: Walking at a brisk pace increases bone density in your hips and forearms, while walking at a more leisurely pace (for a longer period of time) benefits the spine and neck bones.

A life that includes exercise can be extremely beneficial to your health, emotion, and overall survival rate. Better still, it's *never* too late to start. Getting off the sofa is the first and most important step.

CALCIUM

MAJOR APPLICATION OF CALCIUM ✦ Nothing says strong, healthy bones better than a daily dose of calcium. This essential mineral is available in a number of varieties, including carbonate, citrate, malate, bone calcium, and coral calcium. When making your selection, it's important to keep in mind that some can be more difficult to absorb than others. To eliminate the guesswork, we recommend supplementing calcium complexes from citrate, malate, aspartate, or coral sources. Each one is readily absorbed by the body, safe to take, and comes in a wide variety of potencies and forms.

An Overview of Calcium • It took the dairy industry just a few years to revolutionize the phrase "got milk?" Not only is this one of the most brilliant marketing campaigns ever devised, it's also *great* advice to "get milk." That's because milk is loaded with one of the most beneficial nutrients in the world—calcium. Milk contains notable amounts of this bone-supporting mineral, and more than half the calcium intake in the United States comes from consuming dairy products. Easy enough, right? Wrong. Most of us get only about half of the calcium we need on a daily basis.

Milk, cheese, ice cream, and yogurt all contain calcium. Unfortunately, many people avoid these foods for fear of sending their bathroom scales into a spinning frenzy. Fortified orange juice is a good option, as many of these juices now contain as much calcium as a glass of milk. Other foods that serve as a good source of calcium are tofu, canned sockeye salmon, sardines, clams, oysters, turnip and mustard greens, collards, sea vegetables, broccoli, kale, legumes, brewer's yeast, and dried fruits. What? These foods aren't on your list of favorites? If not, supplementation is probably your best alternative.

Another thing to consider when looking for calcium-rich foods is the bio-availability of the calcium they contain. Spinach, beet greens, rhubarb, and peanuts are all excellent sources, but they contain oxalic acid, an agent that binds calcium in a manner that prevents it from being absorbed. Wheat and other cereal grains contain phytate, which can also inhibit calcium absorption. When applicable, cooking can partially offset this problem.

The calcium in most supplements is absorbed just as effectively as the calcium found in milk. Consequently, supplementing calcium is one of the easiest ways to be sure that you're getting enough without the terror that often accompanies stepping on a scale or shopping for a new pair of jeans.

The Myth of Testing Your Calcium Supplement

It's been suggested that you can test your calcium supplement at home using the vinegar test. This theory presupposes that if you drop your calcium tablet or capsule in a glass of vinegar, it should dissolve within 30 minutes. This test is based on the fact that eggshells will dissolve if left in vinegar. However, this advice is flawed for several reasons:

- Calcium tablets are coated to be acid resistant. They will dissolve faster in tap water.
- Vinegar is a weak acid and nowhere near as powerful as the brutal acids of the human stomach.
- Body heat and churning are needed to completely breakdown supplements. If you drop your tablet into a ¼ cup of body temperature-identical water, swirling it occasionally, your tablet should begin to disintegrate almost immediately. It will fall apart when shaken at the end of 30 minutes.

How Calcium Works • The most abundant mineral in the body, calcium is largely responsible for keeping bones strong and teeth and gums healthy and has recently been shown to play a number of other significant roles in human health. Ninety-nine percent of the body's calcium reserve is stored in the bones and teeth. At any given time, it's been estimated that about 10 percent of the calcium in bones is on the move, either building and repairing bone cells, or exiting to maintain blood calcium levels.

One percent of the body's calcium supply can be found in the blood, where it's involved in the transmission of nerve impulses, hormone regulation, muscle contractions, and blood clotting. It also helps activate several enzyme systems, including those that allow you to produce energy and digest meals. Additionally, calcium has been found to help regulate blood pressure and glucose levels, and to help prevent colon and rectum cancers.

THERAPEUTIC USES OF CALCIUM

- *Colon health.* As the second most prevalent form of cancer among adults in the U.S., many common colon disorders are offset by high concentrations of bile and fatty acids. Calcium has shown great promise in its ability to reduce the influence of these two substances, which in turn creates a more positive environment. Ultimately, this makes it easier for the colon to go about its business peacefully.

- *Healthy bones.* Having a well-established reserve of calcium is like a winning lottery ticket to your bones. It burrows deep inside bone structures to reduce the risk of thinning, fractures, poor posture, and height loss. Yes, we *shrink.* Calcium supplementation is of considerable value to anyone over the age of 60. During the early golden years, the body has a much more difficult time absorbing it and, as a result, the aging body becomes susceptible to osteoporosis and other degenerative conditions.

- *Heartburn.* Many popular antacids contain a type of calcium known as carbonate. On a temporary basis, it can help neutralize the stomach acids responsible for painful post-meal burning sensations. It's important to note that while such over-the-counter remedies may offer temporary relief, they won't undo any serious medical conditions. Plus, taking them over a long period of time may cause even more serious problems. If you experience heartburn on a regular basis and find yourself at the mercy of antacids, we strongly suggest that you seek the advice of a physician.

- *High blood pressure.* Researchers continue to notice a trend in those who suffer from high blood pressure; many have unusually low blood-calcium levels. The theory is that calcium helps stabilize the cellular membranes in blood vessels, thus preventing them from hardening and restricting blood flow. For this reason, it's important to get calcium from supplementation, as opposed to milk, which is traditionally high in saturated fat.

- *PMS.* Mood swings, cramping, fatigue, soreness, and other conditions associated with PMS can make life so much more difficult than it needs to be. Recent studies suggest that calcium can help balance and regulate the production and activity of hormones, thus alleviating many of the most common PMS symptoms.
- *Other therapeutic benefits for calcium.* Healthy gums and teeth, high cholesterol and/or blood pressure, leg cramping, especially at nighttime.

Tips for Taking Calcium
- The body can only absorb so much calcium at one sitting. Taking 500 mg in divided doses or at bedtime can be a wise move.
- Once in the body, calcium competes with other minerals for absorption. To keep things fair, try to get adequate amounts of others as well.
- Listen to your nutritionist and don't be afraid to buy the best calcium supplement available. They're not terribly expensive and will serve you well in the long run. Always look for formulas that list their true calcium content. (See our recommendations at the back of this book).
- Not only does the body better use calcium citrate than in some other forms, but supplementing it in this particular form may also help prevent the flatulence associated with those.
- Having a tough time dozing off? Try taking your calcium supplements at night, as it's been shown to induce natural slumber.
- Despite some urban legends, taking high doses of calcium will not cause bone spurs or painful deposits. The body uses what it needs and eliminates what's not needed.
- Always take calcium with food to help increase absorption.
- Avoid taking calcium supplements with antibiotics, as calcium may reduce the functionality of these prescription medications.

+ *Magnesium.* Magnesium is a specific cofactor to more than 300 different enzymes, although it's most recognized for its role in energy production. Among its other duties, magnesium activates B vitamins, regulates calcium balance, helps hydroxyapatite formation, contracts muscles, promotes relaxation, transmits nerve signals and synthesizes protein.

Oddly, magnesium doesn't get anywhere near the respect it deserves. But it's just as important as calcium is in maintaining strong bones, as high calcium/low magnesium intake can have a number of adverse affects, including compromised blood coagulation. Some researchers have even credited magnesium with statin-like activity. Data from two national surveys indicates that 70 percent of Americans do not get their daily requirement of magnesium. The body contains four major cations (minerals) that are positively charged; calcium, magnesium, potassium, and sodium. Together these four help maintain proper electrolyte balance and membrane transport systems throughout the body.

On average, the human body contains 20-28 grams of magnesium, and 65 percent of it is found in bone structures. The majority of what remains is found is soft tissues, such as muscle. Calcium and magnesium are partners in many functions, but they're also very competitive when it comes to intestinal uptake. That's why it's so important to supplement both with minerals from aspartate, creatinate, malate, or citrate. In addition to being more easily absorbed, these forms have also been shown to survive the acid attack that takes place in the stomach.

Magnesium also gets along well with potassium, another equally helpful mineral. Together, these two natural partners cooperate by pumping nutrients into cells. In fact, many cardiovascular-supporting dietary supplement formulas contain both, as well as the amino acid taurine. Vitamin B6 is another important biological colleague of magnesium, particularly in the support of the brain and nervous system. Additionally, the combination of magnesium and B6 has been shown helpful in the prevention of kidney stones.

- *Zinc, copper, and manganese.* These three minerals serve as a power-house trio who love to form complexes with enzymes. If one of them cofactors an enzyme, it's highly likely that one of the others will activate another enzyme downstream. Collectively they stabilize enzymes by fitting into cozy little niches within their structural folds. When the time is right, they put enzymes to work by providing just the right spark, at just the right time. Repair and maintenance of bones and joints cannot occur unless these minerals are present. Based on this, it's super important to make sure that the bone and/or joint repair supplement that you choose includes all three. Each of these minerals has a very specific role in bone health.

  Zinc activates alkaline phosphatase, an enzyme that assists in bone formation. It does the same for collagenase, the enzyme that breaks down collagen in osteoclasts. These are the primary bone-specific duties of zinc, although it activates a number of additional enzymes, many of which are involved in other reactions that contribute to overall bone health. Zinc even maintains tiny "fingers" in DNA repair enzymes that control bone growth.

  Copper is required for activating an enzyme to build collagen in the bone matrix and in tendons, ligaments, cartilage, and other connective tissues. It's also essential for healthy skin. Copper is also needed for the production of elastin, another structural protein that helps the aorta and arteries maintain flexibility.

  Manganese activates two enzymes that regulate the formation of cartilage and is required for the synthesis of the gel-like cushioning agent found in joints. It is considered the most important enzyme cofactor in the maintenance of healthy joint function.

- *Potassium.* Sodium (and potassium) regulates tiny cellular pumps needed to provide the cells with nutrients, to remove cellular products and secretions, and to eliminate wasted materials. When the pump is at rest, sodium ions hang out near the cell, while potassium ions wait inside. As the pump kicks into gear, potassium rushes outside through a little gate, appropriately called a "leak channel," and sodium takes its place inside the cell. This switch-a-roo only takes a millisecond, but it's more than enough time to actively transport the needed compound into the cell membrane. Once the task is accomplished, the ions change places and move to their original positions. It's a neat device that requires some energy, while allowing room for rejection or accumulation.

Because of potassium's great importance in priming the cell, the National Research Council has recommended that adults consume 3.5 grams per day. Sodium intake, however, should be limited, as it's commonly found in many of today's most popular foods. Experts contend that there is little danger of potassium overload from diet due to the efficiency of the kidneys in maintaining potassium balance. Still, many supplements contain just 99 mg. This amount was set to prevent individuals from taking too much at one time.

- **Vitamin C and flavonoids.** Prior to the 19th century, sailors were often the unfortunate victims of Vitamin C deficiency. Months at sea without fresh fruit or vegetables led to the scurvy epidemic. Those suffering from this fatal disease experienced dislocated joints, rotting teeth and soft, brittle bones. Soldiers literally fell apart and thousands were buried at sea. Those fortunate enough to reach land before dying recovered quickly when they were given a tea containing citrus extracts. Although they didn't realize it at the time, these teas and tonics were rich in vitamin C and flavonoids. It was later discovered that limes could stave off scurvy and would stay fresh on ships for many months.

Vitamin C activates three enzymes that participate in collagen synthesis. Without C, the collagen structures of the body, skin, joints, bones, and internal organs eventually break down. Three interlocking bands of collagen proteins twist around one another and are secured in place by flavonoid links. Flavonoids also protect collagen from being broken down by enzymes.

• *Vitamin D.* Fifteen minutes in the summer sun can fuel the human system with everything it needs to manufacture the "sunlight" vitamin. Thanks to ongoing research, we've learned that vitamin D deficiencies aren't as rare as they were once thought to be. In fact, many of these studies suggest that American adults may actually need additional vitamin D in order to help prevent bone thinning and other osteo-related conditions. More and more adults are taking drastic measures to avoid exposure to the sun's UV rays, but those who work long hours in offices, live in seasonally cold or northern regions, post-menopausal women, adults older than 50, dairy-intolerant individuals and anyone who doesn't spend time in the sun, need to be concerned to get enough vitamin D.

Without a sufficient reserve of it, the body can have an extremely difficult time absorbing calcium. To compensate, it takes what it needs from healthy bone structures to supply the rest of the body. This can be devastating over extended periods of time, and is one of the primary reasons why bone thinning occurs later in life. Supplementing vitamin D with calcium on a regular basis is one of the easiest ways to prevent a deficiency of this vital nutrient.

• *Vitamin K.* This highly overshadowed micronutrient is most commonly found in green, leafy vegetables, especially kale and spinach. Aside from its involvement in normal blood clotting, vitamin K is also actively involved in bone structure formation and development by increasing the body's ability to synthesize osteocalcin, a highly abundant, calcium-binding compound that serves as one of the most essential elements in the formation of human bone matrix. Based on this, it may also be helpful in preventing bone fractures and osteoporosis, especially in women older than 50. (See our section on multiple vitamins for formulas that contain vitamin K).

- *Boron.* Boron is familiar to most people as boric acid or borax. Although these are not forms that are used in supplements, their virtual lack of toxicity is welcome news to scientists looking for the specific role of boron in human nutrition. A specific enzyme action for boron has not been identified, although numerous studies have shown that boron is clearly involved in bone metabolism. Boron deprivation impairs calcium and energy metabolism, and these effects can be accentuated when the body falls short of vitamin D. Boron also helps facilitate the absorption and balance of calcium, magnesium, and phosphorus.
- *Other natural companions of calcium.* Multi-mineral formulas, antioxidants.

Joint Pain and Osteoarthritis

In the United States alone, an estimated 1 million people develop arthritis each year. The National Arthritis Foundation estimates that by the year 2020, 60 million people will have the condition. Nearly half of adults older than 65 have some kind of arthritic pain, and younger people have various other kinds of joint pain, usually the result of injury or trauma. Injury to joints will be discussed in the following section; for now, we'll focus on osteo and rheumatoid arthritis, and their related autoimmune conditions.

Osteoarthritis, or OA, is the most common form of arthritis, characterized by degenerative loss of joint cartilage, hardening of the material that covers bones, and enlargement of the joints. An imbalance between inflammatory and noninflammatory processes and collagen breakdown is also involved. The primary symptoms of OA are pain, stiffness, and decreased mobility.

Natural treatments for OA include shedding pounds if overweight, reducing inflammation and pain, and initiating joint tissue repair. Nutraceuticals that reduce inflammation and pain include proteolytic enzymes, fatty acids, and methylsulfonyl methane, or MSM. Antioxidants help protect against further damage due to overuse or injury. Glucosamine sulfate, glucosamine hydrochloride, chondroitin sulfate, hyaluronic acid, and minerals are all popular support and healing agents. MSM shoulders two key tasks, as it has been shown to help reduce pain as well as to repair compromised joint structures.

Rheumatoid Arthritis, or RA, is a chronic autoimmune condition that mainly affects the joints in the hands, feet, knees, and elbows. In the most serious conditions, RA can progress to the hips, making the simple act of walking terribly painful. Research has taught us that RA onset can be the result of an individual's immune system gone awry. Over time this can lead to the progressive destruction of once healthy joints. Symptoms include inflammation, stiffness, swelling, overgrowth of cartilage, and pain. RA patients tend to have disfigured joints due to swelling. About 20 percent of patients form nodules of fibrous tissue around affected joints, further compromising normal joint function. Muscles adjacent to inflamed joints can become the victims of atrophy (tissue wasting) and become less functional in the process. This can significantly compromise the body's most basic movements and range of motion.

The cause of RA is unknown, however a person's genetic susceptibility, lifestyle choices, nutritional factors, food allergies, and toxins from microorganisms seem to be strong indicators. Women are affected three times more often than men, with onset generally occurring age 40-60. Estrogen plays a central role in the condition, as low estrogen activity has been known to coincide with flare-ups. Smoking can also increase a woman's risk of developing RA.

It has been noted that many RA patients suffer from chronic constipation and this has led researchers to suspect a link involving altered bowel function. As mentioned during our discussion of the *malabsorption syndrome* in Chapter Six, intestinal permeability and toxic bowel conditions can heighten immune response. Other conditions that appear to be related to RA include fibromyalgia, lupus erythematosus, and schleroderma.

Many Ayurvedic physicians have treated RA with a combination of 450 mg Ashwagandha (*Withania somnifera*), 100 mg Guggul (*Boswellia serrata*), 50 mg turmeric (*Curcuma longa*), and 50 mg zinc. A study published in the *Indian Journal of Pharmacology* that used a combination of these ingredients for three months showed that patients experienced less pain, decreased morning stiffness, improved range of motion, and a drop in red blood cell sedimentation, a clinical marker for RA. In addition, *Celadrin®* is a novel fatty acid formula that has been shown to significantly reduce pain and swelling. It appears to be very helpful in RA, as we'll discuss later in this chapter.

GLUCOSAMINE AND CHONDROITIN SULFATE

MAJOR APPLICATION OF GLUCOSAMINE AND CHONDROITIN ✦ This extremely popular duo has given hope to millions of those who live with sore, stiff, achy joint structures. By encouraging the production of vital fluids needed to support and restore cartilage, glucosamine and chondroitin supplements remain one of the most popular ways to help alleviate joint pain and restore a more normal range of motion. This should serve as wonderful news to the nearly 70 million Americans who regard this type of pain a part of daily life.

AN OVERVIEW OF GLUCOSAMINE AND CHONDROITIN ✦ To better appreciate why so many people are now unconditionally loyal to this combination of joint-supporting compounds, it's important to have an understanding of joint structures and cartilage in general. Essentially, cartilage is nothing more than a rubbery matrix wedged between bones. Its primary purpose is to prevent bones from grinding during motion, allowing joint structures to move in smooth, fluid motion. As we age, these structures gradually harden. Overuse, high-impact exercise, poor diet, and a number of other factors can lead to deterioration that results in pain, stiffness, inflammation, and a host of other motion-centric conditions.

When taken orally, glucosamine and chondroitin supplements have been shown to help provide many of the essential compounds needed to restore and support healthy joint structures. Individually each plays a major role in the structural integrity of healthy joints and articular cartilage. Let's take a closer look at each.

- ✦ *Glucosamine.* Glucosamine, as the name might suggest, is a natural amino sugar that the body uses to build, maintain, and restore cartilage. Once ingested, glucosamine is easily absorbed through the digestive tract, but, unfortunately, these compounds are not available from food—unless you feast regularly on a diet of shells from crabs, oysters, shrimp and other crustaceans—and can only be obtained from supplementation.

* *Chondroitin sulfate.* One of the most impressive qualities of glycos-aminoglycans, a product produced in the body from chondroitin sulfate, is its ability to neutralize several of the enzymes responsible for cartilage deterioration. For many years it was assumed that the body lacked the ability to absorb chondroitin, but a surge of studies in the early 1990s proved otherwise. Not only was it discovered that chondroitin sulfate could be readily absorbed, but also that it could be absorbed in remarkable fashion.

How Glucosamine and Chondroitin work * Rarely do we think of joints as structures that require nutrition. This couldn't be more incorrect. In fact, joint structures (including cartilage) are constantly on the lookout for the compounds they need in order to remain healthy. Without them they can become brittle and damaged and eventually begin to "flake" off. Over time, this unnoticeable process can snowball, making it more difficult to enjoy the youthful range of motion that so many of us take for granted.

Glucosamine and chondroitin supplements have been shown in numerous studies to help deliver the vital compounds and fluids that help cushion bones. This, coupled with the natural synergism they share, has made the combination of glucosamine and chondroitin a staple in the field of alternative medicine and joint health.

Therapeutic Uses of Glucosamine and Chondroitin
* Arthritis
* Muscle strains
* Carpal tunnel syndrome
* Back pain

- Glucosamine and chondroitin supplements are available in both oral and topical forms. Some of the best success stories have come from those who used the two in combination.
- People with shellfish allergies should not use products that contain glucosamine sulfate. (See our sections on Celadrin and MSM for suitable alternatives).
- Glucosamine and chondroitin supplements should be taken throughout the day as recommended, with a meal or on an empty stomach.
- Consult your physician if you're currently taking prescription medications for osteoarthritis or other degenerative disorders before taking these supplements.
- One of the biggest mistakes people make when supplementing with glucosamine and chondroitin is giving up too soon. Keep in mind that it may take up to two months before the effects are genuinely felt. Be patient, and don't lose hope too soon!
- If you're one of the very lucky few who doesn't live with any type of joint disorder, count your blessings. Supplementing with even the most modest amounts of glucosamine and chondroitin is a great way to keep joints and cartilage strong and fully functional.

CALCIUM AND MAGNESIUM

The combination of calcium and magnesium is *vital* for healthy bones and teeth. This much we know. But it often comes as a surprise to most that this duo of essential minerals can also offer relief to sore, aching, and over-worked joints. Calcium is the most abundant mineral in the body, and more than 99 percent of the body's reserves of it are stored in the bones. Magnesium, on the other hand, is needed to help relax muscle contractions, prevent cramping, and synthesize the vitamin D that helps calcium find its way into the bloodstream. Developing a deficiency in either of these minerals, especially at a young age, can weaken the integrity of bone structures and force the joints to take on more of the shock and impact that we encounter every day.

Still, they can be difficult to utilize and actually compete for absorption. We recommend taking them together, in a 2:1 calcium-to-magnesium ratio.

MANGANESE

This essential mineral was discussed earlier for the role it plays in enzyme activation. It deserves another look here to emphasize its role in joint repair. In addition to the hundreds of enzymatic and biological functions that manganese performs throughout the body, one of the most interesting involves bone and joint health, primarily in proteoglycans synthesis. These key components in the matrix are used to create and support collagen and cartilage tissues at the ends of our bones. Many who live with osteoporosis and other types of degenerative joint disorders have been shown to exhibit very low levels of manganese.

While deficiencies have always been considered rare in healthy adults, a growing body of evidence suggests that, in light of the poor diets that more and more adults are adopting as normal, many may not be getting enough manganese for optimal health. Daily supplementation of 2-5 mg can ensure that you're getting the amount you need to support healthy cartilage and joint structures.

HYALURONIC ACID (HA)

By now we've touched on the vast importance of mucopolysaccharides in regard to joint health. They are key components of the synovial fluid in joints and are abundant in the cartilage tissues that cushion joints from the bone-on-bone grinding responsible for many types of joint disorders. Hyaluronic acid is one of the most fascinating of all mucopolysaccharides, as it is capable of binding enormous amounts of water at the cellular level. This is what essentially allows cartilage and collagen cells to "gel" together.

As we grow older, the amount of HA in our systems gradually declines, as does its ability to bind water within the synovial fluids and cartilage. This has led many researchers to believe that supplementing HA can serve as an effective method to promote healthy cartilage and joint structures. As an added bonus, HA may also have a positive effect on the skin and eyes, two regions where it can be found in abundance.

Joint Injury and Recovery

Once a tissue is injured, the healing process begins immediately. Cells that are injured alter their metabolisms to produce materials that initiate the inflammatory process, characterized by redness, tenderness, and an increase in body temperature. As mentioned in Chapter Five, injury elicits the acute stress response by dispatching white blood cells, phagocytes, and inflammatory mediators, such as cytokines, to the site in question. Fluid accumulates in order to barricade the injured area. This is a defense/repair mechanism that the body relies on to restrict the activity of potentially infectious materials from entering it. It also immobilizes the area to prevent further damage to tissues and blood vessels. If the injury breaks the skin, a blood clot will form to stem the flow of blood and seal the opening. Mast cells release histamine which makes capillary walls more permeable to passage of immune mediators.

The second stage of healing occurs when fibroblasts form scar tissue. This begins immediately after injury and lasts approximately 4 weeks. Rehabilitation therapy during this period most often limits use of the injured body part. Fibroblastic cells form the proteoglycans and glycoproteins that make up the ground substance around which new connective tissue will form. As collagen is formed, the strength of the tissue increases and more aggressive physical therapy can then be initiated. Gradually, healthy connective tissue replaces weaker scar tissue.

Immune cells launch a full-blown attack on free radicals, and are fired off like bullets at bacteria in order to eliminate them. In the process, many white blood cells die, thus adding to a growing pile of cellular rubble that must be cleared before healing can proceed. Proteolytic enzymes take care of this. Some free radicals miss their targets and end up injuring healthy tissues. If the area is repeatedly injured, the damage can become painful and movement may be impaired. This often happens with small joints, such as those in the fingers, toes, and feet. One of the most important strategies to counter this damage is to supply the body with plenty of antioxidants to neutralize excess free radicals before damage begins.

Supplement strategies for injury and recovery involve several important steps. When used properly, many supplements can reduce pain and swelling, tame inflammation, fight infection, quench free radicals, and supply repair materials to help restore normal functionality.

CELADRIN®

"Forty-three million Americans report that a doctor told them they have arthritis or other rheumatic conditions. Another 23 million people have chronic joint symptoms, but have not been diagnosed with arthritis. Arthritis is the leading cause of disability in the United States, limiting the activities of more than 16 million adults." —U.S. Center for Disease Control, 2005

MAJOR APPLICATION OF CELADRIN® ✦ Celadrin® is a patented blend of acetylated fatty acids, esters, and other synergistic agents that enhance the quality of cell membranes throughout the body. Despite being relatively new to the consumer market, it is quickly becoming a staple among scores of individuals who live with chronic joint pain and other inflammatory conditions. This was evidenced in August of 2004 when the highly distinguished *Journal of Rheumatology* published the results of a double-blind, placebo-controlled study that opened the eyes of millions. It states:

Topical treatment with cetylated fatty acids significantly increased physical performance (e.g., balance, stair climbing ability, ability to rise from a chair, and walking) in patients with knee OA. A unique finding was an immediate effect of this treatment 30 minutes after initial cream application. The results of this study provide support for the use of cetylated fatty acids as part of a pain relief treatment in patients with knee OA.

AN OVERVIEW OF CELADRIN® ✦ It would be easy to dedicate hundreds of pages to Celadrin®. But let's focus our attention on a few of the qualities that truly set it apart. First and foremost, it has been proven to work, and work very well. As simple as this may sound, it is unconditionally one of the most important qualities of *any* supplement. Celadrin® research continues to yield extremely high success rates among users, most notably in the areas of pain, inflammation, mobility, and functional performance.

Next, Celadrin® has been shown to work in as little as 30 minutes, according to a 2005 study published in the *Journal of Strength and Conditioning*. This particular trial used topical application, although it can also be taken orally. Celadrin® is also very reasonably priced, far less expensive than many of the most popular anti-inflammatory and arthritis prescription medications.

Because it does not contain shellfish extracts, Celadrin® is completely suitable for those who are unable to take glucosamine and chondroitin sulfate. Perhaps most impressive, Celadrin® has been shown to offer cumulative results, meaning that joint structures can actually be repaired and restored over time. Researchers believe that this is possible due to the unique action of the cetylated fatty acids inherent to Celadrin®.

How Celadrin® Works ✦ Unlike popular non-steroidal anti-inflammatory drugs (NSAIDS) that simply mask joint discomfort, Celadrin® targets the *root* source of pain and inflammation by restoring vital fluids and conditioning the cell membranes that cushion bones and joints. Ultimately, this is what makes it possible to enjoy a free range of motion without the bone-on-bone grinding that can limit daily activity.

By working in much the same manner that other fatty acids do, Celadrin's® patented blend of esterified fatty acids sparks positive changes at the cellular level. Over time, cell membranes may regain their responsiveness and become less prone to articular cartilage deterioration.

Tips for Taking Celadrin®
* Many users report better results when using topical creams and oral supplements together.

- For topical use, Celadrin® seems to work best when applied to the troubled area shortly after a warm bath or shower. This opens the pores and allows the active compounds to penetrate deeply.

- Despite a spotless history of safety, anyone concerned with supplementing Celadrin® in combination with other prescription medications should first consult with his or her physician.

- If you prefer to supplement Celadrin® orally, try to divide doses throughout the day. It can be taken with or without meals, although most manufacturers suggest taking it prior to a morning and/or evening meal.

- Many topical products also contain menthol. To avoid a potentially uncomfortable episode, do not apply Celadrin® topically to open or exposed skin, too close to the eyes, to open sores, or near the genitals.

NATURAL COMPANIONS OF CELADRIN®

- *Holy basil.* Practitioners of India's Ayurvedic medicine regard holy basil (*Ocimum sanctum*) as one of the most sacred compounds on the planet and have been using it for thousands of years to help address a wide range of health challenges. Accordingly, the historical popularity of this powerful adaptogenic herb has inspired a number of studies. Findings continue to suggest that holy basil can help the body recover from injuries, adjust to various forms of stress, reduce inflammation, and alleviate minor aches and pains. In fact, some researchers believe that holy basil might even be able to reduce inflammation as effectively as many of today's most popular over-the-counter painkillers without potentially damaging the delicate stomach lining.

- *Turmeric.* If you regularly consume curry powder or yellow mustard, you may already be reaping the health benefits of turmeric. Like holy basil, turmeric (*Curcuma longa L.*) is classified as an adaptogenic herb and has remained a cherished element of India's Ayurvedic medicine for thousands of years. A swarm of research over the past three decades has helped us understand more about what seems to make this member of the ginger family so beneficial in pain management and injury recovery.

Aside from being naturally rich in a number of free radical-fighting antioxidants, turmeric also contains a number of biologically active derivatives called *curcuminoids*. One of the most promising is curcumin, a powerful antioxidant compound that exhibits remarkable anti-inflammatory properties. Countering the effects of inflammation is essential in recovery, and turmeric has been shown to work quite well to do just that.

• *Glisodin® (SOD, superoxide dismutase)*. As mentioned earlier, superoxide free radicals are widely accepted as one of the body's greatest health threats. In addition to inciting massive amounts of oxidative stress throughout various tissues of the body, the cellular damage caused by superoxide free radicals can dramatically decrease the body's response to inflammation and a number of other stress factors. Glisodin is a patented compound that helps increase production of our three "built-in" antioxidant enzymes, superoxide dismutase, glutathione peroxidase, and catalase. Clinical studies have shown that action may help the body to become more effective to defend against the damage caused by superoxide molecules.

Until very recently, scientists had a difficult time developing an orally effective form of SOD. This was due largely to the denaturing that occurs when SOD is exposed to hydrochloric (stomach) acids. The issue was finally put to rest when a team of researchers determined that by using a wheat protein matrix, glisodin (a specialized nongenetically-modified melon extract) could bypass stomach acid degradation, thus making it readily available for the body to use. This discovery represents one of the most significant breakthroughs in the fight against free radical damage and inflammation.

• *Fish oil (omega-3 fatty acids)*. Essential oils from coldwater fish are teeming with EPA (eicosapentaenoic acid) and DHA (docosahexanoic acid). Within the body, these essential polyunsaturated fatty acids are converted into biologically active, hormone-like chemicals called *prostaglandins*. Aside from assisting the body in regulating blood pressure, muscle contractions, and reproduction, prostaglandins have very strong anti-inflammatory properties. Over the years, many studies have closely examined the roles of EPA and DHA on inflammation and have found that a substantial number of those who suffer from inflammatory conditions have had success when consuming 3 grams of EPA and DHA from fish oil daily.

+ *Other natural companions of Celadrin®.* Daily multiple, bromelain, calcium with magnesium, glucosamine and chondroitin, MSM.

Bone Thinning

Bone strength depends upon two factors; bone mass and the quality of its components. It follows, then, that bone fragility is due to loss of bone mass and deterioration of its architecture. According to the National Institutes of Health Consensus Panel on Osteoporosis Prevention, several factors heighten the risk of bone fragility:

+ Bone mass attained early in life may be the most important determinant of skeletal health later in life.
+ Genetic factors exert a strong influence on peak bone mass.
+ Physiological, environmental, and modifiable risk factors can play a significant role.
+ Bone loss increases with age.
+ Race and gender are factors in bone loss. Both men and women experience bone loss, but women experience greater loss in the early postmenopausal years.
+ Small stature increases the risk of bone thinning.
+ Bone thickness varies by race/ethnicity: Greatest in African Americans > Mexican Americans > white non-Hispanics > Native Americans.

An estimated 40 percent of postmenopausal Caucasian women in the United States are expected to sustain an osteoporotic fracture during their lifetimes. The estimated costs of treating such fractures in both men and women are between $10 and $15 billion annually. These figures do not take into account lost wages or productivity of the patient, not to mention caregiver expenses. Creighton University's Robert Heaney, M.D., a leader in osteoporosis research, has this to say:

"Despite substantial advances in the past 10 years, most patients with osteoporotic fractures are still not being treated for the underlying bone cause of the fracture, and most people at risk for fracture are not being offered known protective regimens. The foundation of any therapeutic program is adequate nutrition—specifically protein, calcium, phosphorus and vitamin D."

With regard to phosphorus, too much intake appears to be more of a problem than too little. Frequent consumption of sodas containing phosphoric acid can deplete bone calcium by competing with it. High animal protein intake coupled with a low intake of fruits and vegetables rich in magnesium and trace minerals can also facilitate calcium loss.

Over-supplementation of vitamin A may also be a factor in bone loss in older people. If they eat several foods fortified with the vitamin, and then take supplements high in vitamin A over an extended period of time, they may be getting too much. It's a good idea for older people to assess how much of the vitamin they are getting on a daily basis. Hypertension also appears to decrease bone mineral density, particularly among middle-aged women.

Maintaining healthy bones is multi-factorial. Nutrition, exercise, and supplements are vital to maintaining bone health. Of special interest in bone loss is the status of the minerals zinc and copper. Calcium *alone* does not build strong bones, and excessive intake may impair copper and zinc absorption. Fortunately, both can be found in quality multiple formulas.

In addition to the suggestions provided, *ipriflavone* helps increase the uptake of calcium in bones. It is equally beneficial during times of greater decline in

BMD in the latter half of life, particularly during the years that immediately follow menopause.

IPRIFLAVONE

This synthetic derivative of the isoflavones found in soy beans mimics the activity of estrogen, and is believed to help offset the process of bone thinning, a common condition among menopausal and postmenopausal women. The first ipriflavones were developed in the late 1960s as a way to specifically help prevent osteo-related conditions in a manner that did not raise estrogen levels or lead to other hormone-related effects typically associated with estrogen treatment.

Over the years, a handful of studies have been conducted to determine whether or not this could actually be accomplished. For the most part, findings have been positive and promising, especially when ipriflavones have been taken in conjunction with a quality calcium supplement that contains vitamin D. Accordingly, the popularity and use of ipriflavone supplements has grown steadily, especially among menopausal and postmenopausal women. It is worth noting, however, that ipriflavones are very specific in what they can and cannot do within the body, meaning that they were carefully engineered to prevent bone thinning and have not been shown to have any positive impact on other menopausal symptoms.

Oral Health

It's almost ironic that oral health just happens to be our last topic of discussion. Not only is it one of the most important avenues of human health, it is also one of the most commonly neglected and misunderstood. As mentioned earlier, there's much more to a healthy mouth than a bright, lustrous smile. Your teeth may be one of your most visibly cosmetic features, but it's important to understand that they, as well as your gums and jaw, are extremely complex structures—among the most complex in the body. And whether you're aware of it or not, that smile you flash says more about your health than you might imagine.

It's been estimated that as many as 90 percent of all diseases can be traced back to poor oral health on some level. This borders the terrifying, especially when you consider how many otherwise healthy people neglect visiting the dentist twice a year—not to mention those who allow years and decades go by. Aside from the fear of root canals and the squealing of high-pitched drills, there are many reasons why we fail to take oral health as seriously as we should. If you're like most people, you're probably under the assumption that daily brushing and flossing are enough to help support a bright, healthy smile. While these measures are clearly important, there's more to it than just that. Your mouth, like every other system of the body, needs the right mix of nutrients in order to function at its highest level.

In light of its complexity and system-wide importance, we could easily dedicate an entire book to oral health. Many writers have. So let's just address some of the most important elements behind this final piece of the 7-syndrome puzzle.

Tooth decay is one of the most common and disheartening after effects of poor oral health, and it occurs over time when untreated dental caries (cavities) erode the tooth's enamel surface. The warm, moist environment of the mouth, coupled with thousands of undetectable, plaque-harboring cracks and crevasses, serves as the perfect environment for bacterial build-up. Regular brushing and flossing may be able to loosen and sweep these bacteria away, but they are in no way total solutions. Teeth are composed of highly dense, hydroxyapatite calcium crystals, and are therefore vulnerable to acidic attack. Keeping in mind that acid is what eventually leads to cavity formation, one of the best things we can do to prevent cavities is to reduce the amount of acid in our mouths. This can easily be accomplished by adhering to three simple guidelines.

Reduce your intake of sugary snacks and beverages

Regardless of how often or how thoroughly you brush, keep in mind that sodas, candies, and many other goodies are loaded with sugars that become embedded in the sticky plaque deposits of the teeth and gums. This is bad news any way you look at it, because oral bacteria have the nasty habit of converting sugars and starches into acid, and, as stated earlier, plaque and excess acid formation can erode the hard mineral surface of the teeth. If left un-addressed, this erosion can progress to gum disease, nerve damage, and tooth loss. Replacing heavily refined table sugars with natural sugar alcohols such as xylitol or erythritol is one of the easiest and most effective measures a person can take when it comes to safeguarding a spectacular set of teeth.

Nourish your mouth

In addition to brushing, flossing, and pulling the plug on conventional table sugar, it's equally important to be sure that your total oral system is well nourished. This can be easily accomplished by paying close attention to what your mouth needs in order to remain healthy. Since teeth are made up primarily of calcium, you should make sure that your daily nutritional regime includes at least 1,000 mg of an easily absorbed calcium supplement, along with vitamin D and magnesium. Not only will this provide the basic building blocks essential to keep teeth strong and dense, it will also facilitate the mineral exchange so vital to their longevity and day-to-day function.

And let's not forget about the gums. If you've made it to your mid-30s, there's about a 75 percent chance that you don't know that you're living with some type of gum disease. What often starts out as tenderness or swelling can rapidly advance to more serious conditions, such as gingivitis and periodontitis, two common and advanced forms of gum (periodontal) disease. Not surprisingly, gingivitis shares the same origin as cavities—plaque. In the case of gum disease, however, the embedded layers of plaque harden to produce a substance known as tartar, a rock-hard compound that can't be removed with normal brushing. Over time, tartar buildup can cause the gum lines to recede, leaving the exposed tissues wide open to bacteria and infection.

In addition to daily care, regular cleanings and a healthy diet, antioxidants, such as vitamins A, E and C, as well as CoQ_{10}, NAC, and folic acid can help ward off many of the free radical attacks that lead to the formation of plaque and tarter.

Use sugar alcohols, not sugar

As we'll discuss later in this chapter, sugar alcohols (polyols), such as xylitol, mannitol, and sorbitol, are ideal and highly recommended for anyone trying to take charge of his or her oral and total system health. These natural compounds have a unique chemical structure that prevents them from being used by the millions of bacteria that like to call your mouth home. Due to their resilience to acid and plaque formation, they are becoming more common in toothpastes, oral rinses, and chewing gums.

Xylitol remains one of the most popular sugar alcohols and a number of international studies continue to suggest that it may be able to reduce and prevent the formation of plaque, while also contributing to the remineralization of the tooth's surface. Unlike an artificial sweetener, a jar of sugar alcohol is difficult to distinguish from a jar of table sugar. Both are white, crystalline, and share similarities in both texture and appearance. Perhaps their most appealing quality is their taste. Sugar alcohols are sweet, but not nearly as overpoweringly or dominatingly sweet as traditional sugar. This has made them a favorite in healthy kitchens all over the world, including those of both authors of this book.

Ten things you can do for a truly healthy smile.
1. Brush and floss daily, after each meal or snack, if possible.
2. Rinse with a xylitol-based mouthwash everyday.
3. Reduce your intake of table sugar and sweets.
4. Nourish your mouth by supplementing calcium, magnesium, and antioxidants.
5. Brush at a 45° angle for optimal results.
6. Massage your gums (gently) on a regular basis.
7. See your dentist every six months for check-ups and cleanings.

8. Eliminate use of tobacco products.

9. Chew your food thoroughly to stimulate enzymes and loosen bacteria.

10. If you do not own a professional-grade electric toothbrush, invest in one.

XYLITOL

AN OVERVIEW OF XYLITOL • Though the word *xylitol* might be new to your health vocabulary, your body has been using it since the day you were born. In short, xylitol is a 5-carbon compound which is naturally produced by the human body, as well as by many plants, fruits, and vegetables. In fact, humans produce as much as 15 grams of xylitol everyday during normal metabolism. First synthesized by French and German chemists in the late 1800s, xylitol's potential wasn't commercially realized until the 1970s, when it began showing up in chewing gums throughout various regions of France, Switzerland, and Finland.

During that nearly 80-year stint, xylitol was considered by many to be nothing more than another carbohydrate sweetener. As a result, it enjoyed a relatively modest European popularity. But as time went on, advancements in research allowed scientists to determine that this sugar alcohol was much more than some run-of-the-mill sweetener. Aside from containing approximately 40 percent fewer calories than conventional sugar, xylitol's unique 5-carbon atom structure makes it virtually useless to many of the bacteria that reside in the mouth. And, unlike traditional sugar, xylitol won't cause pH levels of the mouth to plummet to levels consistent with an acidic attack.

HOW XYLITOL WORKS • Making the switch to xylitol is one of the most effortless first steps a person can take when trying to control sugar intake. Hundreds of health challenges can be traced back to excess sugar consumption and, sadly, our culture has become fixated on it. The reality of the matter is that sugar is rotting more than our teeth. This is evidenced by skyrocketing increases in obesity, chronic infectious diseases, diabetes, and a number of digestive disorders. In light of this and other factors, more and more researchers are suggesting that many problems could easily be prevented by swapping one crystalline power for another that's much more beneficial.

Many people can't tell the two apart, and those who can report only the slightest of noticeable differences. Xylitol has a taste and texture that closely resembles the conventional sugar that we've all grown accustomed to. It's sweet, but not overpowering. And, most important, xylitol offers a number of important health benefits. Let's review the most substantial.

- *Xylitol inhibits oral bacteria.* Because it is a 5-carbon compound, xylitol molecules are not useful to the bacteria of the mouth. Not only does this help reduce a person's likelihood of developing plaque-forming cavities, but it also makes it difficult for other bacteria to bind and flourish. This property has led researchers to conclude that daily use of xylitol-based products can reduce the potential for bacteria within the mouth, nose, and throat.

- *Xylitol helps prevent plaque and cavities.* Science has taught us that if bacteria can't successfully attach itself to the most vulnerable plaque deposits of the mouth, they simply can't survive. This notion presupposes the idea that by limiting the presence of oral bacteria, we can reduce the number of acidic attacks and, therefore, maintain a more favorable pH level in the mouth. Xylitol makes it very difficult for these bacteria to bind to the mouth's cellular walls and, as a result, most can be easily brushed or rinsed away.

- **Xylitol is safe.** During the past four decades, xylitol has been the subject of *intense* international research. Aside from studies to evaluate its primary methods of action and system-wide benefits, xylitol's unblemished safety and effectiveness record ultimately makes it a wise choice. As a compound that the body naturally produces, xylitol has been shown to exhibit absolute safety for users of all ages, including infants. At present, xylitol is officially endorsed by six international dental associations and its popularity continues to surge in the U.S.

- Xylitol is available in a number of product offerings that include tooth-pastes, mouthwashes, chewing gums, lozenges, and pure crystalline powders. Find the one that works best for you and get in the habit of using it on a daily basis.
- Try to consume at least 3 grams (3/4 teaspoon, 7 calories) of xylitol per day, while not exceeding more than 12-15 grams. Too much can lead to mild diarrhea or an upset stomach.
- Xylitol-based products seem to be the most effective when used after and between meals.
- When using xylitol in its crystalline form (desserts, coffee, tea, et cetera), keep in mind that you may have to use a bigger spoon to dish it out. It has a very similar taste and texture, but is noticeably less sweet than the sugar you probably grew up with. Don't be afraid to experiment. You'll eventually be able to gauge how much is perfect for your unique palate.
- Xylitol can have a very mild laxative effect when taken in high amounts. If you have discomfort, reduce your intake to a level that's more intestine friendly.
- Children of all ages can benefit from xylitol. Accordingly, many companies now offer candies, chewing gums, and other xylitol-based treats. (Trust us, they'll *never* know it isn't sugar).

ANTIOXIDANTS

Throughout this book, hundreds of references have been made to the pro-health benefits of supplementing with antioxidants. Oral health is no exception, and there are years of clinical studies that support the role antioxidants play in the mouth. As we've discussed, antioxidants seek out and eliminate free radicals that cause oxidation. This is of great benefit to both the teeth and gums, especially when you consider how totally vulnerable they are to free radical damage *and* bacterial attack. Aside from being on the frontline of everything we consume, the mouth is also one of the last regions of the body to receive a "cut" of the nutrients that we ingest. Organs belonging to larger, high-energy/high-demand systems, including the metabolic, cardiovascular, and central nervous systems, are among the first to stake their claims to the nutrients and antioxidants that we take in. As ironic as it may seem, the mouth is left to sift through the little that remains.

This double-edged dental sword makes it extremely important to ensure that we are well armed with the right antioxidant mix, because without an adequate reserve of these free radical quenching compounds in our systems, it becomes much easier for bacteria to thrive in the oral cavity. Take our word on this: The combination of too much sugar and being last on the list to receive the needed nutrients can make life miserable for oral tissues and cells trying to stay strong and regenerate themselves with some level of biological dignity.

CoQ_{10}, folic acid, vitamins A, E and C, and alpha lipoic acid are some of the very best when it comes to protecting the delicate cells of the mouth and expediting the healing process. Recent research suggests that polyphenols, another group of naturally occurring antioxidant compounds, can be equally beneficial.

POLYPHENOLS

Those occasional and slightly silly looking episodes of "berry tongue" that we get after eating dark berries may be more blessing than embarrassment. That's because a purple tongue is one of the best indicators that polyphenols are binding to the cells of the teeth, the gums, the tongue, and the roof of the mouth, as they should. There's only so much vacant space on these tiny microscopic cells to be occupied, so when beneficial compounds, such as polyphenols, bind to them, the bacterium that leads to cavities, plaque, and disease loses the ability to do so.

A 2004 study conducted by the University of Rochester's Dr. Hyun Koo was carried out to determine whether or not cranberry, a high-ORAC compound that's rich in polyphenols, could prevent the growth of bacteria on the enamel surface of teeth. ORAC is an acronym for oxygen radical absorbance capacity, a measure of free radical savaging ability. For two days artificial teeth were exposed to a liquid containing 25 percent cranberry juice. At the conclusion of the study it was determined that bacterial attachment and growth had been reduced by as much as 85 percent under normal conditions.

This is among the strongest evidence to date to suggest that the high-ORAC antioxidant polyphenols in dark berries may offer an entirely new way to prevent cavity formation, plaque accumulation, and, quite possibly, periodontal disease in general. If you decide to incorporate cranberry (from juice), do yourself a favor and take a trip to your local health food store, because many commercial brands are made from concentrate and contain very little actual juice. They also contain considerable sugar, which offsets the berry benefits.

ALOE VERA (TOPICAL APPLICATION)

Topically applying pure aloe vera is a natural and seemingly effective way to soothe some of the most common mouth problems. According to a number of recently published studies, it may also be one of the most helpful in preventing and healing them. In one such study a subject suffering from *lichen planus*, a condition of the skin and oral mucous membrane, drank 2 ounces of aloe vera juice daily and used a topical application of an aloe vera lip balm with cumulative positive results at the end of 4 weeks.

Today, research is ongoing. Aloe continues to show great promise as treatment for conditions from blister and cold sores to canker sores and more severe lesions.

To Sum It All Up

The bony structures of the body have fascinated artists and physicians for centuries as illustrated in the 16th century drawings on the next two pages (Figure 8-1). Many risked imprisonment and even death to obtain human remains so they could study the skeleton. If you have not found such images particularly appealing before, take a moment to study the prints and focus on appreciating this remarkable structure.

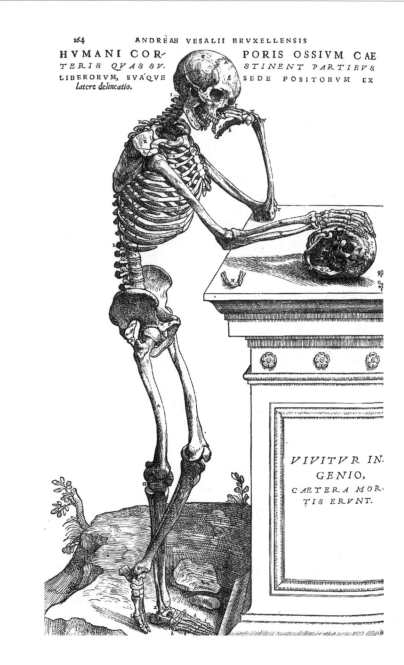

FIGURE 8-1 **The Human Skeleton.** *Two images from Andreas Vesalius's* **De humani corporis fabrica** *(1543).*

7-SYNDROME HEALING

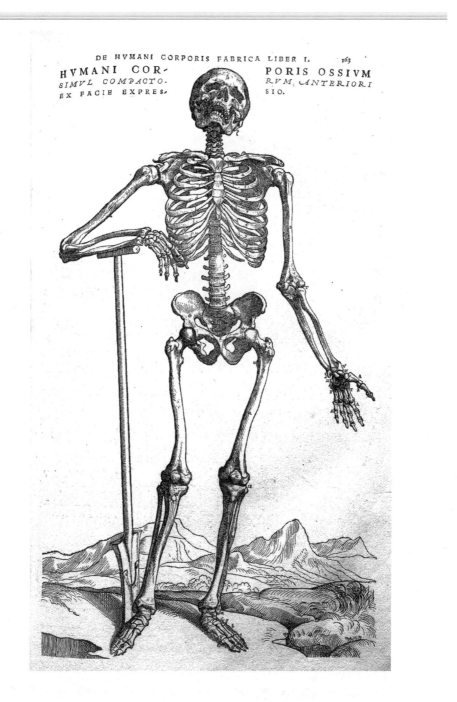

DE HVMANI CORPORIS FABRICA LIBER I. 163

HVMANI COR-   PORIS OSSIVM
SIMVL COMPACTO-   RVM ANTERIORI
EX FACIE EXPRES.   SIO.

EPILOGUE

꿏

As science continues to validate the healing power of aloe and the other natural remedies presented in *7-Syndrome Healing*, we are reminded of Thoreau's words:

From the forest and wilderness come the tonics and barks which brace mankind . . .

We can benefit from supplements and all-natural compounds only if we understand how they work and are willing to accept them as nature's therapy. They are gifts of immeasurable worth that can help us live healthier lives.

We hope that we have helped shed light on your healing journey and that you have enjoyed reading *7-Syndrome Healing* as much as we have enjoyed creating it for you.

Tables

T HE DRUG/NUTRIENT/VITAMIN INTERACTIONS given in the following tables have been reviewed T.C. Theoharides, H.D., M.D., Director, Laboratory for Molecular Immunopharmacology and Drug Discovery, Tufts University School of Medicine; Clinical Pharmacologist, Massachusetts Drug Formulary Commission (1986-2004).

TABLE 1 *The Basics: Choosing a Good Multiple Vitamin and Mineral Formulation*

Vitamin or Mineral	RDA	Range of Potency	Special Considerations
Vitamin A	5,000 IU	5,000 IU to 10,000 IU	listed as retinyl palmitate or vitamin A palmitate
Carotenes	No upper limit	5,000 IU to 10,000 IU vitamin A potential	mixed natural carotenoids, including alpha, beta carotenes, cryptoxanthin, lutein, lycopene, zeaxanthin. Avoid synthetic beta carotene
Vitamin C	60 mg	100 to 1,200 mg	ascorbic acid or mixed mineral ascorbates
Vitamin D$_3$	400 IU	400 to 800 IU	cholecalciferol is the natural form. Avoid synthetic ergocalciferol
Vitamin E	30 IU	100 to 400 IU	natural d-alpha tocopheryl succinate and mixed tocopheryls and tocotrienols are desirable
Vitamin K$_1$	80 mcg	30 to 100 mcg	phytonadione
Thiamin	1.5 mg	25 to 100 mg	vitamin B$_1$

Vitamin or Mineral	RDA	Range of Potency	Special Considerations
Riboflavin	1.7 mg	25 to 50 mg	vitamin B_2
Niacin	20 mg	25 to 200 mg	vitamin B_3 usually included as niacinamide
Pyridoxine	2 mg	10 to 50 mg	vitamin B_6 may be in Pyridoxal phosphate (P-5-P)
Folic Acid	400 mcg 800 mcg for pregnancy	200 to 800 mcg	may be listed as tetrahyrofolate
Cobalamin	6 mcg	100 to 200 mcg	vitamin B_{12} may be listed as methylcobalamin
Biotin	300 mcg	50 to 300 mcg	may be listed as USP
Pantothenic Acid	10 mg	50 to 200 mg	listed as d-calcium pantothenate
Calcium	1,000 mg	100 to 1,000 mg	citrate, malate, carbonate, ascorbate, chelate are all acceptable forms
Iron	18 mg	10 to 30 mg	amino acid chelated iron is the best form
Iodine	150 mcg	50 to 225 mcg	from kelp
Magnesium	400 mg	100 to 500 mg	amino acid chelate, aspartate, citrate or oxide (least desirable)
Zinc	15 mg	10 to 30 mg.	Monomethionine, aspartate, picolinate, amino acid chelate
Selenium	70 mcg	25 to 200 mcg	L-selenomethionine, amino acid complex
Copper	2 mg	0.5 to 2 mg	may be listed as mcg (1,000 mcg = 1 mg)
Manganese	2 mg	2 to 10 mg	amino acid chelate
Chromium	120 mcg	50 to 200 mcg	GTF, polynicotinate, picolinate
Molybdenum	75 mcg	25 to 150 mcg	amino acid chelate
Other Nutrients that are desirable but not required			
Boron	none	1 to 3 mg	amino acid chelate, aspartate, citrate
Vanadium	none		amino acid chelate, bis-glycinato oxovanadium, citrate
Choline	445 to 550 mg	50 to 150 mg	from choline bitartrate
Inositol	none	50 to 100 mg	may be from inositol hexanicotinate

Vitamin or Mineral	RDA	Range of Potency	Special Considerations
PABA	none	15 to 50 mg	para-aminobenzoic acid
Bioflavonoids	none	50 to 250 mg (500 to 1000 mg for non–fava bean sources)	look for percentage of bioflavonoids. May list rutin, hesperidin
Enzymes	none	25 to 100 mg	bromelain, papain, lipase, amylase, betaine HCL, glutamic acid
Base of fruits and vegetables	none	200 to 1,000 mg	chlorophyll, spirulina, broccoli, barley grass, green tea
Herbal Extracts*	none	20 to 200 mg	green tea, grape seed extract, bilberry, ginkgo, milk thistle

Additional information	
Brands to look for	Eco-Green by NOW, Daily Complete by Ultimate Nutrition, Super Twin by Twinlab
Possible depletion or interactions with medication	ACE inhibitors, accutane, accupril, aspirin, phenylpropanolamine, ramipril, nizatidine, chemotherapy, captopril, cephalosporins, warfarin, penicillamine, erythromycin, famotidine, ofloxacin, isoniazid, mineral oil, sulfasalazine, tetracycline

* Herbal Extracts are generally required in dosages of at least 100 mg to be effective. We reserve the use of herbs for specific syndromes and suggest they are not an important addition to a multiple vitamin and mineral formula. On the other hand, the addition of some fruit and vegetable powders imparts a pleasant aroma to multiples and may improve utilization.

† For greater detail on individual vitamins, minerals, herbs and other supplements, see below tables.

TABLE 2 *The Vitamins*

Vitamin	Medications that interfere with it and contraindications	Recommended for Syndrome	Brands to look for
A	corticosteroids, bile acid sequestrants, statin drugs, medrox yprogesterone, oralcontraceptives. **CONTRAINDICATION:** Retin-A or other prescription forms of vitamin A. Perhaps chemotherapy	Basics	vitamin A 25,000 IU Emulsified, from Carlson A and D, from Source Naturals
C	acetaminophen, tetracycline, ephedrine, doxorubicin, corticosteroids, ephedrine, pseudoephedrine, antibiotics, phenylpropanolamine, oral contraceptives, chemotherapy	Basics, Cardio, Immune, Osteo	products containing Ester-C¨, from Zila Nutraceuticals, Ester-C¨ Complex with Bioflavonoids, from NOW, Emer'gen-C¨, Alacer
Carotenoids	none known	Basics, Stress, Metabolic, Hormone	Veggie Carotenoids, from NOWCarotene, from Solaray
D	corticosteroids, thiazide diuretics, estradiol, heparin, anticonvulsants, bile acid sequestrants, sterols, verapamil, cimetidine, isoniazid, medroxy-progesterone, neomycin, cimetidine (Tagamet)	Basics, Osteo	D-1000 IU, from NOW, Allergy-D 400 IU, from Twinlab
E	Insulin (animal source), adriamycin, AZT, bile acid sequestrants, colestipol, cyclosporine, valproic acid, glyburide, haloperidol, isoniazid, Zocor. **CONTRAINDICATIONS:** Vitamin E increases the effect of blood-thinning agents including aspirin, Alka-Seltzer¨, anticoagulants and coumadin	Basics, Cardio, Hormone	400 IU Natural E (d-alpha tocopherols) w/ Selenium, from NOW E-Gems, 200 IU, from Carlson

Vitamin	Medications that interfere with it and contraindications	Recommended for Syndrome	Brands to look for
K	reduced by tetracycline, cortico-steroids, antibiotics, anti-convulsants, bile acid sequestrants, doxycycline, isoniazid, mineral oil, cephalosporins. CONTRA-INDICATIONS: High dose vitamin K, not necessarily amounts found in multiples, oppose the action of anti-coagulants, check with your doctor. High dose vitamin E may interfere with uptake of vitamin K	Basics, Osteo, Malabasorption	Vitamin K 100 mcg, from Solgar,K-1 Vegetarian 100 mcg, from Country Life Super K with K2, from Life Extension, K-100, from Thompson

TABLE 3 *The Minerals*

Mineral	Medications that interfere with it and contraindications	Recommended for Syndrome	Brands to look for
Calcium	Reduced absorption by tetracycline, corticosteroids, albuterol, thiazide diuretics, aluminum hydroxide, caffeine, thyroid hormones, antacids, bile acid sequestrants, verapamil, oral contraceptives, conjugated estrogens, Medroxyprogesterone, lactase, doxycycline, erythromycin, isoniazid. Alendronate (Fosamax) calcium taken at the same time interferes with uptake of Fosamax. Must take calcium at another time.	Basics, Malabsorption, Osteo	Calcium Citrate Plus by NOW, Calcium Citrate plus Magnesium by Twin Lab, Calcium Citrate by Source Naturals
Magnesium	reduced by tetracycline, corticosteroids, tobramycin, albuterol, thiazide diuretics, theophylline, warfarin, atorvastatin, mizatidine, azithromycin, epinephrine, loop diuretics, cimetidine, oral contraceptives, conjugated estrogens, Medroxyprogesterone, digoxin, erythromycin, ofloxacin, gentamicin, isoniazid, metformin, famotidine (Pepcid), cimetidine (Tagamet), ranitidine (Zantac)	Basics, Cardio, Osteo	Albion amino acid chelated products

Mineral	Medications that interfere with it and contraindications	Recommended for Syndrome	Brands to look for
Potassium	reduced by ACE inhibitors, ibuprofen, corticosteroids, albuterol, thiazide diuretics, naproxen, theophylline, heparin, senna, epinephrine, magnesium hydroxide, captopril, cisplatin, heparin, mineral oil	Basics	Complexed Potassium by Carlson, Target Mins Potassium by Country Life
Sulfur	none	Osteo	Joint Support, MSM by NOW
Iron	reduced by aspirin, tetracycline, ibuprofen, carbidopa, methyldopa, naproxen, sodium bicarbonate, AZT, oral contraceptives, magnesium hydroxide, warfarin, penicillamine, thyroid hormones, vitamin C (enhances uptake), haloperidol	Basics, Hormone	Ferrochel‴ Iron by Carlson and NOW
Zinc	reduced by ACE inhibitors, aspirin, tetracycline, corticosteroids, warfarin, bile acid sequestrants, captopril, thiazide diuretics, valproic acid, oral contraceptives, Medroxyprogesterone, conjugated estrogens	Basics, Immune,	Opti-Zinc and Cold-Ease lozenges by NOW, Chelated Zinc by Country LifeZinc carnosine
Manganese	depleted by oral contraceptives, ciprofloxacin,	Basics, Osteo	Chelated Manganese by Carlson
Copper	reduced by ACE inhibitors, ibuprofen, naproxen, ramipril, naproxen, antacids, nizatidine, AZT, oral contraceptives, penicillamine, oxaprozin, valproic acid, vitamin C enhances uptake	Basics	Chelated Copper by Carlson
Selenium	reduced by cisplatin, valproic acid	Basics, Immune	Products containing Selenomax‴, by Nutrition 21

Mineral	Medications that interfere with it and contraindications	Recommended for Syndrome	Brands to look for
Molybdenum	none	Basics, Metabolic	Reduced Glutathione Sublingual + Molybdenum by NOW, Alive by Nature's Way
Iodine	none		
Chromium	enhances effects of insulin, glyburide	Basics, Metabolic	ChromeMate™ 200 mcg, from NOW yeast-free Chromium from Source Naturals, Chromium Picolinate by NOW, GTF Chromium by Albion
Boron	none	Basics, Osteo, Malabsorption	Bone Density Factors by Country Life, Tri-Boron by Twin Lab, Osteo Boron by NOW
Vanadium	none	Basics, Metabolic	Vanadyl complex from Kal, Super Vanadyl Fuel by Twin Lab, Vanadyl Sulfate by Ultimate Nutrition
Silicon	reduced by thyroid hormones	Basics	In the base of most multiples
Acid Redux (antacid)	same as calcium and magnesium	Malabsorption	Products containing Acid Redux[a] from Scientific Food Solutions
ZMA zinc and magnesium aspartate	same as magnesium and zinc	Metabolic	ZMA Fuel, from Twinlab ZMA, from NOW ZMA, from Ultimate Nutrition

TABLE 4 *The B Vitamins*

B- Vitamin	Medications that interfere with it and contraindications	Recommended for Syndrome	Brands to look for
Thiamin, Cocarboxy-lase and Thiamin Pyrophos-phate (B-1)	reduced by tricyclic antidepressants (amitriptyline, desipramine, Tofranil), oral contraceptives (Enovid, Genora, Ovcon), loop diuretics (Bumex, Demadex, Edecrin)	Stress	single B-vitamins can be found in store private label, and by Carlson, Country Life, Nature's Plus, Nature's Way, Source Naturals, Solaray, Solgar, Twinlab— Pantethine 300 mg (Pantesin¨), from NOWCholestoril¨ 300 mg Pantethine from Enzymatic Therapy — Instant Energy B-12, from NOW B-12 Dots, from TwinlabB-12 Methylcobalamin, from Source Naturals —Folic Acid Caps, from Twinlab100% Vegetarian Folic Acid, from Bluebonnet
Riboflavin and Riboflavin 5- Phosphatae(B-2)	reduced by tetracycline, doxorubicin, tricyclic antidepressants, oral contraceptives	Stress, Malabsorption	
Niacin, niacinamide and hexanicotin-ate(B-3)	reduced by statin drugs (Lovastatin, Mevacor), tricyclic antidepressants, oral contraceptives, Isoniazid	Stress, Cardio, Hormone	
Pantothenic Acid and Pantetheine(B-5)	reduced by tricyclic antidepressants	Cardio, Immune	
Pyridoxine (B-6) and pyridoxal phosphate (P-5-P)	reduced by tetracycline, fluorouracil, corticosteroids, anticonvulsants, penicillin class of antibiotics, levodopa, Isoniazid, phenelzine, theophylline	All, Hormone	
Cobalamin and methylcobal-amin (B-12)	reduced by neomycin, tetracycline, nitrous oxide, oral contraceptives, tricyclic antidepressants, antacids, Pepcid AC, Prilosec, Tagamet, Zantac	All, Cardio, Stress	
Folic Acid and Tetrahydro-folate	reduced by medroxyprogesterone, oral contraceptives, aspirin, antacids, bile acid sequestrants, chemotherapy, methotrexate, Isoniazid, lithium, metformin, neomycin, tetracycline, erythromycin, Indomethacin, nitrous oxide	All, Cardio, Stress	
Biotin	reduced by insulin, anticonvulsants, glyburide		

B- Vitamin	Medications that interfere with it and contraindications	Recommended for Syndrome	Brands to look for
B-Complex	all above indications	All	Coenzyme B-Complex by NOW, Daily Complete by Ultimate Nutrition, SuperTwin by Twinlab

TABLE 5 *The Semi-Vitamins and Antioxidants*

Semi-Vitamin or antioxidant	Medications that interfere with it and contraindications	Recommended for Syndrome	Brands to look for
Astaxanthin	none reported	Basics, Stress (vision)	products containing BioAstin¨ Astaxanthin
Alpha lipoic acid	none reported	Stress, Metabolic, Cardio, Immune	ALA 600 mg w/grape seed extract by NOW, ALA 300 mg by Life Time, ALA 200 mg by Bluebonnet
CoQ10	tricyclic antidepressants, statin drugs, warfarin, doxorubicin, propranolol	Stress, Cardio	400 mg softgels and powder from NOW, 300 mg by Carlson, 100 mg by Enzymatic Therapy
Grape seed extract	none reported	Immune, Osteo	Masquelier's OPC by Nature's Way, Grape Seed Antioxidant by NOW
Lycopene	none reported	Hormone (prostate health)	Look for products containing LycoMato[a]
phosphatidyl serinePS	none reported	Stress (memory)	100 mg Phosphatidyl Serine w/ Choline and Inositol, from NOW; Neuro-PS from Country Life
Pycnogenol	none reported	Stress, Cardio	Look for products containing Pycnogenol[a] by Horphag, Pycnogenol 30 mg. + Bioflavonoids, from NOW
Quercetin	none reported	Immune, Osteo (inflammation)	Quercetin with Glucasamine and Chondroitin, ArthroSoft®, Arthro Supreme® by Algonot Quercetin with Bromelain by NOW
SOD	none reported	Stress, Osteo	GliSODin[a] from NOW, SODzyme with GliSODin[a] from Life Extension, GliSODom powder from Source Naturals
Antioxidant complex	chemotherapy depletes, but antioxidants may be contraindicated; check with your doctor.	Stress, Osteo	VitaBerry[a]& Super Antioxidants by NOW, ACES by Carlson Antioxidant Factors, by Solgar, Super Antioxidant Caps, by NOW
SAMe (S-adenosyl methionine)	none reported	Cardio, Stress (depression)	
SAMe with luteolin, rutin, bitter willow		Cardio	CardioProtek® by Algonot

TABLE 6 *Amino Acids, Peptides, Hormones*

Amino acid, peptide or hormone	Medications That Interfere with it and contraindications	Recommended for Syndrome	Brands to look for
L-arginine	**CONTRAINDICATION:** Do not take if you have had a heart attack	Hormone	Carlson, Country Life, NOW
Branched chain amino acids (BCAA)	none reported	Malabsorption	1000 mg BCAA, from Ultimate Nutrition BCAA Caps from, NOW Sports BCAA Gelcaps, from IDS
L-carnosine, zinc carnosine	none reported	Malabsorption	Products containing PepZinGI[a], from Lonza Ulcetrol, from NOW
L-carnitine, Acetyl-L-carnitine	doxorubicin, AZT, anticonvulsants, valproic acid,	Cardio (muscle weakness)	Products containing Carnipure" from Lonza Acetyl L-Carnitine 500 mg., from NOWAcetyl L-Carnitine with ALA 500 mg., from Source Naturals Acetyl L-Carnitine 500 mg., from Twinlab
GABA (gamma amino butyric acid)	**CONTRAINDICATION:** antidepressants, antiseizure meds; check with doctor	Stress	GABA 750, from Ultimate Nutrition750 mg. GABA Vcaps" from NOW GABA 250 mg., from Enzymatic Therapy
Glutamine	**CONTRAINDICATION:** chemotherapy, taxol, antiseizure meds; check with doctor	Malabsorption	Glutamine Fuel, Twinlab1500 mg L-Glutamine tablets, from NOW 750 mg L-Glutamine, from Life Extension
5-HTP	**CONTRAINDICATION:** antidepressants, carbidopa and sumatriptan	Stress, Hormone	5-HTP 200mg. Caps, from NOW 5-HTP 100mg., from Source Naturals

Amino acid, peptide or hormone	Medications That Interfere with it and contraindications	Recommended for Syndrome	Brands to look for
Melatonin	CONTRAINDICATION: don't use with corticosteroids, benzodiazepines, anticonvulsants, chemotherapy, all antidepressants, tamoxifen,	Stress, Hormone	My Favorite Melatonin, from Natrol 1 mg Two-stage Release Melatonin, from NOW 3 mg. Melatonin, from Life Extensionm
NAC (N-acetyl cysteine)	CONTRAINDICATION: may reduce effect (detoxify) acetaminophen, interferon, Doxorubicin, corticosteroids, chemo-therapy, nitroglycerine, isosorbide mononitrate, check with doctor	Immune	600 mg. NAC, from TwinlabBioChem NAC, from Country Life NAC 500, from AST
7-keto DHEA	CONTRAINDICATION: have hormone levels tested to prevent altering hormone balance	Hormone	7-Keto DHEA, from KAL, DHEA 25 mg., from LifeTime, 7-Keto, from NOW
SAMe (S-adenosyl-L-methionine)	CONTRAINDICATION: possible with some antidepressants, check with doctor	Stress, Osteo (pain)	400 mg Enteric-coated SAMe, from NOW 400 mg Enteric-coated SAMe, from Source Naturals 200 mg. SAMe, from Natrol
SAMe wi thluteolin, rutin, bitter willow		Cardio	CardioProtek® by Algonot
TMG (trimethyl glycine)	CONTRAINDICATION: haloperidol	Stress, Cardio	1,000 mg Extra Strength TMG, from NOWTMG 500 mg, from Life Extension 750 mg TMG, from Source Naturals
Soy powder (whey or soy protein isolate)	none; except in cases of milk or soy allergies	Metabolic, Malabasorption	Designer Protein, from Next NutritionUltraMyosyn, from Met-Rx; 100% Whey Isolate, from NOW Sports SPIRU-TEIN, from Nature's Plus EcoTein, from NOW Ultra XT, from Genisoy

TABLE 7 *Food Factors and Nutraceuticals*

Food factor or nutraceutical	Medications That Interfere with it and contraindications	Recommended for Syndrome	Brands to Look For
Acidophilus	none	Malabsorption	PB8, from Nutrition Now, Acidophilus Pearls, from Enzymatic Therapy, Gr-8 Dophilus, from NOW
Bromelain	**CONTRAINDICATION:** may reduce effectiveness of amoxicillin, erythromycin, penicillin V, and enhance effect of warfarin	Immune, Malabsorption, Osteo	500 mg Bromelain 2000 GDU, from NOWMega Bromelain Caps, from TwinlabBromelain Plus, from Enzymatic Therapy
Cetylated fatty acids	none reported	Osteo	Look for products containing Celadrin¨Celadrin Liposome Lotion, from NOW, 500 mg. Celadrin® Caps, from Doctor's Best.
CLA (conjugated linoleic acid)	none reported	Metabolic	CLA Extremeª, from NOW SportsCLA Fuel, from Twinlab
Colostrum	none reported	Immune	Colostrum Powder, from Source Naturals Colostrum 500 mg. (min. 0.6% Lactoferin), from NOW
Cranberry	**CONTRAINDICATION:** lansoprazole, omeprazole, check with doctor	Hormone	400 mg. Standardized Cranberry, from Nature's WayCranberry (Vaccinium spp.), from Nature's ApothecaryCranActin, from Solaray
DHA (docosahaenoic acid)	none reported	Stress	450 mg DHA w/ EPA, from Nordic Naturals DHA-250, from NOW Super-DHA, from Carlson
DHA + luteolin, rutin, bitter willow	none reported	Cardio	CardioProtek® by Algonot

Food factor or nutraceutical	Medications That Interfere with it and contraindications	Recommended for Syndrome	Brands to Look For
Flaxseeds and flaxseed oil	none reported	Malabsorption, Hormone	Omega Twin, from Barlean's Flax-O-Mega, from Nutra Golden Flax Meal, from NOW, High Lignan Flaxseed Oil from Spectrum Organic
FOS	none reported	Malabsorption	Nutra Flora FOS, from NOW 1000 mg FOS, from Source Naturals
GLA, evening Primrose oil (EPO)	none reported	Malabsorption	EPO 500 mg from NOW, EPO 1300 mg. Nature's Way
Glucosamine (chondroitin sulfatae)	none reported	Osteo	ArthroSoft® by Algonot, Glucosamine, Chondroitin Sulfate by NOW
	Combined with hyaluronic acid and quercetin: none reported	Interstitial cystitis	CystoProtek® by Algonot
Hyaluronic acid	none reported	Hormone, Osteo	Products containing Injuve¨ Skin Eternal Plus, from Source Naturals HA Firming Serum, from NOW HydraPlenish Hyaluronic Acid Plus MSM, from Nature's Way
Indole-3-carbinol	CONTRAINDICATION: hormone therapy especially thyroid, chemotherapy, enhances effect of eating cruciferous vegetables	Hormone	Indole-3-Carbinol (200 mg. with Flax Lignans), from NOW Dual Action Cruciferous Vegetable Extract, from Life Extension
Isoflavones	CONTRAINDICATION: chemotherapy	Hormone	Extra Strength Soy Isoflavones, from NOW The Essential Woman Liquid, from Barleans

Food factor or nutraceutical	Medications That Interfere with it and contraindications	Recommended for Syndrome	Brands to Look For
Ipriflavone	none reported	Osteo	Ostevone, from Enzymatic Therapy Bone Support with Ostevone, from Twinlab
Kelp	CONTRAINDICATION: thyroid hormone therapy	Hormone	Kelp granules, capsules and powder from NOW, Kelp tablets from Country Life
D-mannose	none reported	Hormone	500 mg. D-Mannose Caps, from NOW U.T. Vibrance, (Urinary Tract), from Vibrant Health
Octacosanol	none reported		
Omega 3 fatty acids, fish oil	none reported	Cardio, Malabsorption, Osteo	Omega Twin, from Barleans, Ultimate Omega, from Nordic Naturals, Molecularly Distilled Omega-3, from NOW. Super Omega-3 from Carlson Labs
Pectin	none reported	Malabsorption	Grapefruit Pectin, from CarlsonCitrus Pectin from, NOW
Plant enzymes	none reported	Malabsorption, Osteo (proteolytic enzymes)	Acid Soothe Plant-Based Enzymes, from Enzymedica Mega-Zyme Acid Ease, from Enzymatic Therapy, Dairy Digest Complete, Optimum Digestive System from NOW, Dairy-Zyme Caps, from Country Life Serrazymes, from NOW, Natto-K from Enzymedica
Policosanol	none reported	Cardio	20 mg. Policosanol Caps, from Source NaturalsPolicosanol, from Natural Life10 mg. Policosanol Vcaps¨, from NOW

Food factor or nutraceutical	Medications That Interfere with it and contraindications	Recommended for Syndrome	Brands to Look For
Pomegranate	none reported	Hormone	Pomeratrol[a] (with trans-Resveratrol), from NOWPomegranate (standardized 40% Ellagic Acid), from Nature's Way Wonderful Pomegranate Juice, from POM
Psyllium (Plantago ovata)	**CONTRAINDICATION:** may reduce blood levels of lithium, verapamil, lovastatin, propoxyphene; increases activity of Metamucil and other bulking agents, check with doctor	Malabsorption	Orange Psyllium Fiber, from NOW 100% Psyllium Husk, from Health Plus, Inc.
Quercetin, rutin	none reported	Inflammation, Hormone (prostate), Osteo	Prostatek® by Algonot
Red rice yeast	**CONTRAINDICATION:** don't use with lovastatin	Cardio	Red Yeast Rice with CoQ10, from NOWOnce Daily Red Yeast Rice, from KAL
Ribose	none reported	Hormone	D-Ribose Pure Powder, from NOW Sports Ribose 3000, from Sci-Fit, Ribose Fuel, from Twinlab
Spirulina or blue green algae	none reported	Hormone	Look for products that contain Klamath Lake Blue Green Algae
Trans resveratrol	none reported	Hormone	Pomeratrol[a] (with trans-Resveratrol), from NOW
Zylitol	none reported	Osteo (oral health)	XyliWhite, from NOW (toothpaste and rinse)Spry Xylitol Gum, from XlearXylitol Pure Powder, from NOW

TABLE 8 *Herbs*

Herb	Medications That Interfere with it and contraindications	Recommended for Syndrome	Brands to Look For
Aloe (Aloe vera)	none reported	Osteo (oral health)	Lily of the Desert, from New ChapterAloe Farms; Softskin® from Algonot
Ashwagandha (Withania somnifera)	**CONTRAINDICATION:** not for use during pregnancy or lactation	Stress	Ashwagandha 4.5 mg. Withanolides, from Nature's Herbs Ashwagandha (Standardized 2.5% Withanolides), from Nature's Herbs
Astragalus (Astragalus membranaceous)	none reported	Immune	Herbal defense Extract, from Nature's ApothecaryAstragalus Power, from Nature's Herbs Astragalus, from Paradise Herbs
Bitter melon (Mormordica charantia)	none reported	Metabolic	Look for Mormordica charantria 2.5% standardized extract from Sabinsa.Pure Noni 100, from All Noni, LLC
Black cohosh (Cimicifuga racemosa)	none reported	Hormone	Vegetarian Black Cohosh, from Enzymatic Therapy Black Cohosh Root, from Nature's Way Black Cohosh Extract, from Nature's Apothecary
Butcher's broom (Ruscus aculeatus)	none reported	Cardio	470 mg Butcher's Broom, from Nature's Way500 mg Butcher's Broom, from Source Naturals Butcher's Broom Extract, from Nature's Apothecary
Chaste tree berry (Vitex agnus-castus)	none reported	Hormone	Chaste Berry (Vitex agnus-castus), from Nature's ApothecaryVitex Fruit, from Nature's Way Vitex with Dong Quai, from NOW
Chinese club moss (Huperzine A) (Huperzia serrata)	none reported	Stress	Memory Complex, from Natrol,Brain Elevate, from NOW

Herb	Medications That Interfere with it and contraindications	Recommended for Syndrome	Brands to Look For
Cinnamon (Cinnamomun zeylanicum)	none reported	Metabolic	600 mg Ceylon Cinnamon Bark, from NOW200 mg Cinnamon Extract, from Planetary Formulas
DGL deglycyrrized licorice (Glycyrrhiza glabra)	CONTRAINDICATION: aspirin, naproxin, ibuprofen, interferon, loop and thiazide diuretics, digoxin, corticosteroids, isoniazid, check with doctor	Malabsorption	DGL Chewables, from Enzymatic Therapy 400 mg DGL with Glycine, from NOWDGL Licorice Gumlet, from Solaray
Dong quai (Angelica sinensis)	CONTRAINDICATION: blood thinners: heparin, warfarin, ticlopidine	Hormone	Dong Quai, (Angelica sinensis), from Nature's ApothecaryDong Quai, from Solgar
Fenugreek (Trigonella foenum-graecum)	CONTRAINDICATION: don't use with insulin, heparin, warfarin, ticlopidine, glipizide, check with doctor	Metabolic	626 mg Fenugreek Seed, from Nature's Herbs 610 mg Fenugreek Seed, from Nature's Way
Forskolin (Coleus forskolii)	none reported	Immune	10 mg Forskolin, from Life ExtensionColeus Forskohlii Extract, from Enzymatic Therapy
Fo-ti (Polygonum multiflorum)	none reported	Hormone	Fo-Ti 610 mg capsules from Nature's Way
Garlic (Allium sativum)	CONTRAINDICATION: may enhance blood thinning effects of aspirin and anticoagulants: warfarin, ticlopidine, check with doctor	Cardio	Kyolic Reserve Aged Garlic 600 mg, from KyolicPure-Gar" 600 mg, from NOWGarlicin Cholesterol Control 350 mg, from Nature's Way

7-SYNDROME HEALING

Herb	Medications That Interfere with it and contraindications	Recommended for Syndrome	Brands to Look For
Ginger (Zingiber officinale)	**CONTRAINDICATION:** anesthetics, heparin, warfarin, chemotherapy, thiazide diuretics, ticlopidine, check with doctor	Malabsorption	Ginger Root 550 mg capsules from Solaray or Nature's Way
Ginkgo (Ginkgo biloba)	**CONTRAINDICATION:** don't use with thiazide diuretics, heparin, warfarin, cyclosporine, fluvoxamine, paroxetine, sertraline	Stress, memory	Ginkgold[a], from Nature's WayGinkgo Biloba 24% Standardized Extract, from NOW
Ginseng (Panax ginseng)	**CONTRAINDICATION:** hypertension, use with stimulants, warfarin, influenza vaccine, ticlopidine	Hormone	Red Panax 10cc vials, from Superior Trading
Green tea (Camelia sinensis)	**CONTRAINDICATION:** ephedrine, theophylline, atropine, codeine	Cardio	EGCg Green Tea Extract, from NOWGenaSlim with EGCg, from Country Life Green Tea Extract (EGCg), from Source Naturals
Gymnema (Gymnema sylvestre)	**CONTRAINDICATION:** may enhance effects of insulin, glyburide, glipizide, check with doctor	Metabolic	Nature's Herbs400 mg Gymnema Sylvestre Standardized Extract, from NOWGymnema 260 mg Standardized Extract, from Nature's Way
Hawthorn (Cratagus oxyacanths)	**CONTRAINDICATION:** may enhance effect of digoxin, check with doctor	Cardio	Standardized Hawthorn Extract, from NOW Hawthorn Standardized Extract, from Nature's WayStandardized Hawthorn, from Nature's Apothecary
Holy basil (Ocimum sanctum)	none reported	Osteo	Holy Basil Standardized, from New Chapter Standardized Holy Basil, from Nature's Way

Herb	Medications That Interfere with it and contraindications	Recommended for Syndrome	Brands to Look For
Medicinal mushrooms and beta glucans	none reported	Immune	Immune Renew, from NOW Full Spectrum 650 mg. Maitake, from Planetary FormulasMushroom Defense, from Source Naturals
Milk thistle or silymarin (Silybum marianum)	**CONTRAINDICATION:** reduces effectiveness of (detoxifies) acetaminophen, anesthetic, clofibrate, chemotherapy, clofibrate, haloperidol, metronidazole, lovastatin, pravastatin	Metabolic	300 mg Standardized Extract, by NOW175 mg Standardized Extract, by Nature's Way, 175 mg Standardized Extract, from Solaray
Muira puama (Ptychopetalum olacoides Benth).	none reported	Hormone	Muira Puama Root, from Gaia HerbsMuira Puama Bark, from Nature's Answer
Nettles (Urtica dioica)	none reported	Hormone	Nettle (COG) 435 mg from Nature's Way
Olive leaf extract (Olea europaea)	none reported	Immune	Extra Strength Standardized Olive Leaf, from NOW Olive Leaf Extract, from Nature's Way BioChem Olive Leaf, from Country Life
Prickly ash bark (Zanthoxylum americanum mill)	none reported	Cardio	Vein Supreme[a], from NOW
Purple cone flower (Echanacea purpurea, angustifolia)	**CONTRAINDICATION:** chemotherapy, econazole, check with doctor	Immune	Echinacea, Astragalus and Reishi, from Nature's Way Echinacea Defense Force, from Planetary Formulas Echinacea/Goldenseal, from Nature's Apothecary
Pygeum (Prunus africanum)	none reported	Hormone	Pygeum and Saw Palmetto, from NOWStandardized Pygeum Extract, from Nature's Way

7-SYNDROME HEALING

Herb	Medications That Interfere with it and contraindications	Recommended for Syndrome	Brands to Look For
Red clover (Trifolium pratense)	**CONTRAINDICATION:** conjugated estrogens, heparin, warfarin, ticlopidene	Hormone	Red Clover Power, from Nature's Herbs Red Clover/ Black Cohosh, from NOW
Relora¨ (Magnolia officinalis, Phellodendron amurense)	**CONTRAINDICATION:** may enhance effects of MAO inhibitors, antidepressants, blood pressure meds. Check with doctor.	Metabolic	Look for products containing Relora¨ Super Cortisol Support, from NOW
Rhodiola, arctic root or golden root (Rhodiola rosea)	none reported, effect of use during pregnancy and lactation is unknown	Stress, Hormone	500 mg. Rhodiola Rosea, from NOW327 mg. Rhodiola Rosea, from Planetary Formulas
St. John's wort (Hypericum perforatum)	**CONTRAINDICATION:** don't use with tricyclic antidepressants, trazodone, venla-faxine, fluvoxamine, fluoxetine, phen-elzine, nefazodone, paroxetine, sertraline	Stress (depression)	St. John's Wort 450 mg. Extended Release, by Nature's PlusSt. John's Wort 300 mg. standardized extract, from NOWSt. John's Wort 300 mg. standardized extract or Perika¨ from Nature's Way
Saw palmetto (Serenoa repens, Sabal serrulata)	none reported, clinical trials excluded men taking anticoagulants, diuretics and beta blockers, check with doctor	Hormone (benign prostate hyperplasia)	Prost-ease for Men, from Nature's Apothecary Standardized Saw Palmetto extract, from NOWProstActive Plus, from Nature's Way
Siberian ginseng (Eleutherococcus senticosus)	none reported	Stress, Hormone	Eleuthero Root Extract, from Nature's Apothecary Siberian Eleuthero Root Caps, from Nature's Way

Herb	Medications That Interfere with it and contraindications	Recommended for Syndrome	Brands to Look For
Smilax or sarsparilla (Smilax officinalis, ornata or medica)	**CONTRAINDICATION:** don't use with digitalis, hypnotics	Hormone	Look for liquid herbal extracts
Stevia (Stevia rebaudiana)	none reported	Metabolic	Stevia Balance Packets, from NOW Stevia Liquid Extract, from NOW
Suma (Pfaffia paniculata)	none reported	Hormone	Suma 500 mg from Nature's Way, or Rainbow Light

TABLE 9 *The 35 Symptoms of Menopause*

1.	Hot flashes, flushes, night sweats and/or cold flashes, clammy feeling.
2.	Irregular heart beat
3.	Irritability
4.	Mood swings, sudden tears
5.	Trouble sleeping through the night (with or without night sweats)
6.	Irregular periods; shorter, lighter periods; heavier periods, flooding; phantom periods, shorter cycles, longer cycles
7.	Loss of libido
8.	Dry vagina
9.	Crashing fatigue
10.	Anxiety, feeling ill at ease
11.	Feelings of dread, apprehension, doom
12.	Difficulty concentrating, disorientation, mental confusion
13.	Disturbing memory lapses
14.	Incontinence, especially upon sneezing, laughing; urge incontinence
15.	Itchy, crawly skin
16.	Aching, sore joints, muscles and tendons
17.	Increased tension in muscles
18.	Breast tenderness
19.	Headache change: increase or decrease
20.	Gastrointestinal distress, indigestion, flatulence, gas pain, nausea
21.	Sudden bouts of bloat
22.	Depression
23.	Exacerbation of existing conditions
24.	Increase in allergies
25.	Weight gain
26.	Hair loss or thinning, head, pubic, or whole body; increase in facial hair
27.	Dizziness, light-headedness, episodes of loss of balance
28.	Changes in body odor
29.	Electric shock sensation under the skin and in the head
30.	Tingling in the extremities
31.	Gum problems, increased bleeding
32.	Burning tongue, burning roof of mouth, bad taste in mouth, change in breath odor
33.	Osteoporosis (after several years)
34.	Changes in fingernails: softer, crack or break easier
35.	Tinnitus: ringing in ears, bells, 'whooshing,' buzzing etc.

Association of Women for the Advancement of Research and Education (project-AWARE.org); reproduced with permission

References

References for Chapter One

1. Armas, LAG; et al; "Vitamin D2 is Much Less Effective than Vitamin D3 in Humans" *J Clin Endocrinol Metab* 2004;89:5387-5391.

2. Ascherio, A; et al; "Relation of Consumption of Vitamin E, Vitamin C, and Carotenoids to Risk for Stroke Among Men in the United States" *Ann Intern Med* 1999;130:963-070.

3. Barclay, L; "High Dietary Antioxidant Intake May Reduce Risk for Age-Related Macular Degeneration" *Medscape* Jan 4, 2006.

4. Booth, SL; et al; "Associations between Vitamin K Biochemical Measures and Bone Mineral Density in Men and Women" *J Clin Endocrinol Metabl* 2004;89:4904-4909.

5. Booth, SL; et al; "Effect of Vitamin E Supplementation on Vitamin K Status in Adults with Normal Coagulation Status" *Am J Clin Nutr* 2004;80:143-8.

6. Booth, SL; et al; "Vitamin K Intake and Bone Mineral Density in Women and Men" *Am J Clin Nutr* 2003;77:512-6.

7. Britton, G; "Structure and Properties of Carotenoids in Relation to Function" *FASEB J* 1995;1551-1558.

8. Broekmans, WMR; et al; "Macular Pigment Density in Relation to Serum and Adipose Tissue Concentrations of Lutein and Serum Concentrations of Zeaxanthin" *Am J Clin Nutr* 2002;595-603.

9. Brown, L; et al; "A Prospective Study of Carotenoid Intake and Risk of Cataract Extraction in US Men" *Am J Clin Nutr* 1999;70:517-24.

10. Cass, H; English, J; *User's Guide to Vitamin C* North Bergen NJ 2003 Basic Health Publications.

11. Chamberlain, L; *What the Labels Won't Tell You* Loveland, CO 1998 Interweave Press.

12. Chan, JM; et al; "Supplemental Vitamin E Intake and Prostate Cancer Risk in a Large Cohort of Men in the United States" *Can Epidemiol Biomarkers Prev* 1999;8:893-899.

13. Chasan-Taber, L; et al; "A Prospective Study of Carotenoid and Vitamin A Intakes and Risk of Cataract Extraction in US Women" *Am J Clin Nutr* 1999;70:509-16.

14. Cherubini, A; et al; "Role of Antioxidants in Atherosclerosis: Epidemiological and Clinical Update" *Curr Pharm Des* 2005;11:2017-32.

15. Duffield-Lillico, AJ; et al; "Selenium supplementation, baseline plasma selenium status and incidence of prostate cancer: an analysis of the complete treatment period of the Nutritional Prevention of Cancer Trial" *BJU Int.* 2003 May;91(7):608-12.

16. Feher, J; et al; "Improvement of Visual Functions and Fundus Alterations in Early Age-Related Macular Degeneration Treated with a Combination of Acetyl-L-Carnitine, N-3 Fatty Acids, and Coenzyme Q10" *Ophthalmol* 2005;219:154-66.

17. Fuchs, CS; et al; "The Influence of Folate and Multivitamin Use on the Familial Risk of Colon Cancer in Women" *Can Epidemiol Biomarkers Prev* 2002;11:227-234.

18. "Genetic Factors in Age-Related Macular Degeneration National Eye Institute" www.clinicaltrials.gov. 2003.

19. Gorin, MB; "The Genetics of Age-Related Macular Degeneration" *Mol Vision* 1999;5:29-34.

20. Hathcock, JN; et al; "Vitamins E and C Are Safe Across a Broad Range of Intakes" *Am J Clin Nutr* 2005;81:736-45.

21. Hathcock, JN; "Vitamins and Minerals: Efficacy and Safety" *Am J Clin Nutr* 1998;67:351-3.

22. Herraiz, LA; et al; "Effect of UV Exposure and B-Carotene Supplementation on Delayed-Type Hypersensitivity Response in Healthy Older Men" *J Am Coll Nutr* 1998;17:617-624.

23. Holmquist, C; et al; "Multivitamin Supplements Are Inversely Associated with Risk of Myocardial Infarction in Men and Women – Stockholm Heart Epidemiology Program" (SHEEP) *J Nutr* 2003;133:2650-2654.

24. Huang, HY; Appel, LJ; "Supplementation of Diets with Alpha-Tocopherol Reduces Serum Concentrations of Gamma-and Delta-Tocopherol in Humans" *J Nutr* 2003;133:3137-40.

25. Jacobs, ET; et al; "Selenium And Colorectal Adenoma: Results Of A Pooled Analysis" *J Natl Cancer Inst.* 2004 Nov 17;96(22):1645-7.

26. Jianrong L; et al; "Novel Role of Vitamin K in Preventing Oxidative Injury to Developing Oligodendrocytes and Neurons" *J Neurosci* 2003;23:5816-5826.

27. Kado, M; et al; "Homocysteine versus the Vitamins Folate, B6, and B12 as Predictors of Cognitive Function and Decline in Older High-Functioning Adults: MacArthur Studies of Successful Aging" *Am J Med* 2005;118:161-7.

28. Khachik, F; "Distribution of Lutein, Zeaxanthin, and Related Geometrical Isomers in Fruit, Vegetables, Wheat, and Pasta Products" The *Journal of Agricultural Food Chemistry* 2003;

29. Khanna, S; et al; "Molecular Basis of Vitamin E Action" *J Biol Chem* 2003;278:43508-43415.

30. Krinsky, N; "Biologic Mechanisms of the Protective Role of Lutein and Zeaxanthin in the Eye" *Annual Reviews of Nutrition* 2003;23:171-201.

31. Krinsky, NI; et al; *Dietary Reference Intakes for Vitamin C, Vitamin E, Selenium and Carotenoids* Washington DC 2000, National Academy Press.

32. Lamson, DW; Plaza, SM; "The Anticancer Effects of Vitamin K" *Alt Med Rev* 2003;8:303-318.

33. Lininger, SW; et al; *Healthnotes A-Z Guide to Drug-Herb-Vitamin Interactions* Roseville, CA 1999, Prima Publishing pp 272-317.

34. "Lutein and Zeaxanthin: A Monograph" *Alternative Medicine Review* 2005;10:128-135. (author not listed)

35. Martin KR; et al; "The Effect of Carotenoids on the Expression of Cell Surface Adhesion Molecules and Binding of Monocytes to Human Aortic Endothelial Cells" *Atherosclerosis* 2000;150:265-74.

36. Mayne, ST; "Antioxidant Nutrients and Chronic Disease: Use of Biomarkers of Exposure and Oxidative Stress Status in Epidemiological Research" *J Nutr* 2003;133:933S-940S.

37. McCall, MR; Frei, B; "Can Antioxidant Vitamins Materially Reduce Oxidative Damage in Humans?" *Free Radic Biol Med* 1999;26(7-8):34-53.

38. McDaniel, MA; et al; "Brain Specific Nutrients: A Memory Cure?" *Nutrition* 2003;(11-12):957-75.

39. McKay, DL; et al; "The Effects of a Multivitamin/Mineral supplement on Micronutrient Status, Antioxidant Capacity and Cytokine Production in Healthy Older Adults Consuming a Fortified Diet" *J Am Coll Nutr* 2000;19:613-621.

40. Meyer, F; at al; "Antioxidant Vitamin and Mineral Supplementation and Prostate Cancer Prevention in the SU.VI.MAX Trial" *Int J Cancer* 2005; 116:182-6.

41. Miyazawa, T; et al; "Anti-Angiogenic Potential of Tocotrienol *in vitro*" Biochem (Moscow) 2004;69:67-69.

42. Murray, F; Tarr, J; *More Than One Slingshot: How the Health Food Industry is Changing America* Richmond, VA Marlborough Publishing Company 1984.

43. Navarro, M; Wood, RJ; "Plasma Changes in Micronutrients Following a Multivitamin and Mineral supplement in Healthy Adults" *J Amer Coll Nutr* 2003;22:124-132.

44. Nishino H; et al; "Cancer Prevention by Natural Carotenoids" *Biofactors* 200;13:89-94.

45. Nkondjock, A; Ghadirian, P; "Dietary Carotenoids and Risk of Colon Cancer: Case-Control Study" *Int J Cancer* 2004;110:110-6.

46. Pattison DJ; et al; "Dietary Beta-Cryptoxanthin and Inflammatory Polyarthritis: Results from a Population-Based Prospective Study" *Am J Clin Nutr* 2005;82:451-5.

47. Pitkin RM; et al; *Dietary Reference Intakes for B-Vitamins*. Washington DC 1998, National Academy Press.

48. Purev, E; et al; "Effect of All-trans Retinoic Acid on Telomerase Activity in Ovarian Cancer" *J Exp Clin Cancer Res* 2004;23:309-16.

49. Quadri, P; et al; "Homocysteine, Folate, and Vitamin B-12 in Mild Cognitive Impairment, Alzheimer Disease, and Vascular Dementia" *Am J Clin Nutr* 2004;80:114-22.

50. Reimund, JM; et al; "Immune Activation and Nutritional Status in Adult Crohn's Disease Patients" *Dig Liver Dis* 2005;37:424-31.

51. Romieu, L; "Nutrition and Lung Health" *Int J Tuberc Lung Dis* 2005;9:362-74.

52. Russell, R; et al; *Dietary Reference Intakes for Vitamin A, Vitamin K, Arsenic, Boron, Chromium, Copper, Iodine, Iron, Manganese, Molybdenum, Nickel, Silicon, Vanadium, and Zinc* Washington, DC, 2001 National Academy Press

53. Satia-Abouta, J; et al; "Dietary Supplement Use and Medical Conditions: the VITAL Study" *Am J Prev Med* 2003;24:43-51.

54. Schaffer, S; et al; "Tocotrienols: Constitutional Effects in Aging and Disease" *J Nutr* 2005;135:151-4.

55. Seddon, J; et al; "Dietary Carotenoids, Vitamins A, C, and E, and Advanced Age-Related Macular Degeneration" *JAMA* 1994: 272(18):1413-20

56. Seddon, J; et al; "Progression of Age-Related Macular Degeneration: Association With Body Mass Index, Circumference, and Waist-Hip Ratio" *Archives of Ophthalmology* 2003; 121(6):785-92.

57. Seddon, JM; et al; "Dietary Carotenoids, Vitamins A, C, and E, and Advanced Age-Related Macular Degeneration" *JAMA* 1994;272:1413-1420.

58. Shils, M; et al; *Modern Nutrition in Health and Disease, 8th ed.* Philadelphia, 1994 Lea & Febiger pp 259-426.

59. Sies, H; et al; "Nutritional, Dietary and Postprandial Oxidative Stress" *J Nutr* 2005;135:969-72.

60. Stahl, H; Sies, H; "Bioactivity and Protective Effects of Natural Carotenoids" *Biochim Biophys Acta* 2005;1740:101-7.

61. Stipanuk, MH; *Biochemical and Physiological Aspects of Human Nutrition.* Philadelphia, 2000, WB Saunders pp 458-537; 642-840.

62. Stone, WL; et al; "Tocopherols and the Treatment of Colon Cancer" *Ann NY Acad Sci* 2004;1031:223-33.

63. "A Randomized, Placebo-Controlled, Clinical Trial of High-Dose Supplementation With Vitamins C and E, Beta Carotene, and Age-Related Macular Degeneration and Vision Loss" The Age-Related Eye Disease Study Research Group, National Eye Institute *Archives of Ophthalmology* 2001;119(10):1439-52.

64. Tsaioun, KI; "Vitamin K-Dependent Proteins in the Developing and Aging Nervous System" *Nutr Rev* 1999;57:231-40.

65. Villamor E; Fawzi, WW; "Effects of Vitamin Supplementation on Immune Responses and Correlation with Clinical Outcomes" *Clin Microbiol Rev* 2005;18:446-64.

66. Weinstein, SJ; et al; "Serum Alpha-Tocopherol and Gamma-Tocopherol in Relation to Prostate Cancer Risk in a Prospective Study" *J Natl Cancer Inst* 2005;97:396-9.

67. White, E; et al; "Vitamins and Lifestyle Cohort Study: Study Design and Characteristics of Supplement Users" *Am J Epidemiol* 2004;159:83-93.

68. Wildman, RE; *Handbook of Nutraceuticals and Functional Foods* Boca Raton, FL 2001 CRC Press pp 143-168.

69. Woodall, AA; et al; "Carotenoids and Protection of Phospholipids in Solution or in Liposomes Against Oxidation by Peroxyl Radicals: Relationship Between Carotenoid Structure and Protective Ability" *Biochimica Biophysica Acta* 1997;1336:575-586.

70. Wu, K; et al; "Plasma and Dietary Carotenoids, and the Risk of Prostate Cancer: A Nested Case-Control Study Cancer" *Epidem Biomarkers Prev* 204:13:260-269.

71. Young, VR; et al; *Dietary Reference Intakes for Calcium, Phosphorus, Magnesium, Vitamin D, and Fluoride* Washington DC 1997, National Academy Press

72. Zandi, PP et al; "Reduced risk of Alzheimer Disease in Users of Antioxidant Vitamin Supplements" *Arch Neurol* 2004;61(1):82-8.

References for Chapter Two

1. Alpert, JE; et al; "S-Adenosyl-L-Methionine (SAMe) as an Adjunct for Resistant Major Depressive Disorder: An Open Trial Following Partial or Nonresponse to Selective Serotonin Reuptake Inhibitors or Venlafaxine" *J Clin Psychopharmacol* 2004;24:661-4.

2. Arnold, O; et al; "Double-Blind, Placebo-Controlled Pharmacodynamic Studies with a Nutracutical and a Pharmaceutical Dose of S-Adenosyl-L-Methionine (SAMe) in Elderly Subjects, Utilizing EEG Mapping and Psychometry" *Eur Neuropsycholpharmacol* Jul 19, 2005 (in print)

3. Arushanian, EB; et al; "Effect of Eleutherococcus on Short-Term Memory and Visual Perception in Healthy Humans" *Ekap Klin Farmakol* 2003;66:10-3.

4. "Baby Boomer Sports Injuries" U.S. *Consumer Product Safety Commission,* April 2000. http://www.cpsc.gov/LIBRARY/boomer.pdf.

5. Barbiroli, B; et al; "Lipoic (thioctic acid) Increases Brain Energy Availability and Skeletal Muscle Performance as Shown by In Vivo 31P-MRS in a Patient with Mitochondrial Cytopathy" *J Neurol* 1995;472-477.

6. Birdsall, TC; "5-Hydroxytryptophan: A Clinically-Effective Serotonin Precursor" *Altern Med Rev* 1998;3:271-280.

7. Blumenthal, M ed.; *The ABC Clinical Guide to Herbs* American Botanical Council, Austin Texas, 2003. New York, Thieme

8. Bratman, S; Kroll, D; *St. John's Wort and Depression* Rocklin, CA Prima. 1998 pp. 71-85.

9. Bressa, GM; "S-Adenosyl-L-Methionine (SAMe) As Antidepressant: Meta-Analysis Of Clinical Studies" *Acta Neurol Scand Suppl* 1994;154:7–14.

10. Brown, DJ; *Herbal Prescriptions for Better Health* Rocklin, CA 1995, Prima Publishing pp 119-128, 159-165.

11. Brown, RP; Gerberg PL; "Herbs and Nutrients in the Treatment of Depression, Anxiety, Insomnia, Migraine, and Obesity" *J Psychiatr Pract* 2001;7:75-91.

12. Byerley, WF; Judd, LL; Reimherr, FW; et al; "5-Hydroxytryptophan: A Review Of Its Antidepressant Efficacy And Adverse Effects" *J Clin Psychopharmacol*. 1987;7:127–137.

13. Cass, H; *De-Stress Your Life* in 8 *Weeks to Vibrant Health* New York, NY 2005, McGraw Hill pp. 107-124.

14. Cass, H; *St. John's Wort Nature's Blues Buster* Garden City Park, NY 1998. Avery pp. 54-88.

15. Castillo-Richmond, A; et al; "Effects of Stress Reduction on Carotid Atherosclerosis in Hypertensive African Americans" *Stroke* 2000;31:568-73.

16. Ceda, GP; et al; "Alpha-Glycerylphosphorylcholine Administration Increases the GH Responses to GHRH of Young and Elderly Subjects" *Horm Metab Res* 1992;24:119-121.

17. Cenacchi, T; et al; "Cognitive Decline in the Elderly: A Double-Blind, Placebo-Controlled Multicenter Study on Efficacy of Phosphatidylserine Administration" *Aging Clin Exp Res* 1993;5:123-133.

18. Choudhary, MI; et al; "Cholinesterase Inhibiting Withanolides from Withania somnifera" *Chem Pharm Bull* 2004;52:1358-1361.

19. Choudhary, MI; et al; "Withanolides, a New Class of Natural Cholinesterase Inhibitors with Calcium Antagonistic Properties" *Biochem Biophys Res Commun* 2005;334:276-87.

20. Cicero AF; et al; "Effects of Siberian Ginseng (*Eleutherococcus senticosus* maxim.) on Elderly Quality of Life: A Randomized Clinical Trial" *Arch Gerontol Greiatr Suppl*. 2004;(9):69-73.

21. Conlay LA; et al; "Decreased Plasma Choline Concentrations in Marathon Runners" *NEJM* 1986;315:892.

22. Cousins, N *The Healing Heart* New York, NY 1983 W.W. Norton & Company

23. Crook, TH; et al; "Effects of Phosphatidylserine in Age-Associated Memory Impairment" *Neurol* 1991;41:644-649.

24. Darbinyan, V; et al; "*Rhodiola rosea* in Stress Induced Fatigue – A Double blind Cross-Over Study of a Standardized Extract SHR-5 with a Repeated Low-Dose Regimen on the Mental Performance of Healthy Physicians during Night Duty" *Phytomed* 2000;7:365-371.

25. Das, YT; et al; "Safety of 5-Hydroxy-L-Tryptophan" *Toxicol Lett* 2004; 150:111-12.

26. Davidson RJ; et al; "Alterations In Brain And Immune Function Produced By Mindfulness Meditation" *Psychosom Med* 2003;65:564-70.

27. Dugas, Bernard C.S.O., Ph.D; "Glisodin, the Superoxide Dismutase/Gliadin Product" From www.glisodin.com. 2003.

28. Epel, ES; et al; "Accelerated Telomere Shortening in Response to Life Stress" *Proc. Natl Acad Sci* 2004;101:17312-17315.

29. Epel, ES; et al; "Stress and Body Shape: Stress-Induced Cortisol Secretion Is Consistently Greater Among Women With Central Fat" *Psychosom Med* 2000;62:623-632.

30. Fredman, SL; Rosenbaum, JF; "The Application of Nutrition to Psychiatric Illness" *Am Psych Assoc Annual Meeting*, June 29, 2004.

31. Freeman, MP; et al; "Selected Integrative Medicine Treatments for Depression: Considerations for Women" *J Am Med Womens Assoc* 2004;59:216-24.

32. Furmanowa, M; et al; "Phytochemical and Pharmacological Properties of *Rhodiola rosea* L." *Herba Polonica*1999;45:108-113.

33. Gaffney, BT; et al; "Panax Ginseng and Eleutherococcus senticosus May Exaggerate an Already Existing Biphasic Response to Stress via Inhibition of Enzymes Which Limit the Binding of Stress Hormones to Their Receptors" *Med Hypotheses* 2001;56:567-72.

34. Gindin, J; et al; "The Effect Of Plant Phosphatidylserine On Age-Associated Memory Impairment And Mood In The Functioning Elderly" Rehovot, Israel. Geriatric Institute for Education and Research and Dept. of Geriatrics, Kaplan Hospital, 1995.

35. Glatthaar-Saalmuller, B; et al; "Antiviral Activity of an Extract Derived from Roots of Eleutherococcus senticosus" *Antiviral Res* 2001;50:223-8.

36. Halford, JC; et al; "Serotonin (5-HT) Drugs: Effects on Appetite Expression and Use for the Treatment of Obesity" *Curr Drug Targets* 2005;6:201-13.

37. Jacobs, GD; "The Physiology of Mind-Body Interactions: The Stress Response and the Relaxation Response" *J Altern Comp Med* 2001;7:S83-S92.

38. Jaret, P; "The Herb That Came in from the Cold" *Altern Med* 2005:70-74, 104-107.

39. Jayaprankasam, B; et al; "Growth Inhibition of Human Tumor Cell Lines by Withanolides from Withania somnifera leaves" *Life Sci* 2003;74:125-32.

40. Jeong, HJ; et al; "Inhibitory Effects of Mast Cell-Mediated Allergic Reactions by Cell Cultured Siberian Ginseng" *Immunopharmacol Immunotoxicol* 2001;23:107-17.

41. Landsbergis, PA; et al; "Life-Course Exposure to Job Strain and Ambulatory Blood Pressure in Men" *Am J Epidemiol* 2003;157:998-1006.

42. Le Bars, PL; Katz, MM; Berman, N; et al; "A Placebo-Controlled, Double-Blind, Randomized Trial Of An Extract Of *Ginkgo Biloba* For Dementia" North American EGb Study Group *JAMA*. 1997;278:1327–1332.

43. Ley, BM; *Vinpocetine: Boost Your Brain Power*. Detroit Lakes, MN BL Publications, 2000.

44. Lindner, S; "*Withania somnifera*" *Aust J Med Herbalism* 1996;8:78-82.

45. Lopez, CM; et al; "Effect of a New Cognition Enhancer, Alpha-Glycerylphosphorylcholine, on Scopolamine-Induced Amnesia and Brain Acetylcholine" *Pharmacol Biochem Behav* 1991;39:835-840.

46. Manjunath, NK; Telles, S; "Influence of Yoga & Ayurveda on Self-Rated Sleep in a Geriatric Population" *Ind J Med Res* 2005;121:683-690.

47. Markowitz, JS; et al; "Siberian Ginseng (Eleutherococcus senticosus) Effects on CYP2D6 and CYP3A4 Activity in Normal Volunteers" *Drug Metab and Disposition* 2003;31:1033-1056.

48. Mohan, R; et al; "Withanferin A is a Potent Inhibitor of Angiogenesis" *Angiogenesis* 2004;7:115-22.

49. Mohanty, I; et al; "Mechanisms of Cardioprotective Effect of Withania somnifera in Experimentally Induced Myocardial Infarction" *Basic Clin Pharmacol Toxicol* 2004;94:184-90.

50. Monteleone P; et al; "Effects of Phosphatidylserine on the Neuroendocrine Response to Physical Stress in Humans" *Neuro-endocrinology* 1990;52:243-248.

51. Muller, WE; Kasper, S; Volz, HP; et al; "Hypericum extract (LI160) as an herbal antidepressant" *Pharmacopsychiatry* 1997;30(suppl 2):71–134.

52. Muth, CM; et al; "Influence of an Orally Effective SOD on Hyperbaric, Oxygen-Related Cell Damage" *Free Rad Res* 2004;38:927-932.

53. Nagamatsu, M; Nickander, KK; Schmelzer, JD; et al; "Lipoic acid improves nerve blood flow, reduces oxidative stress, and improves distal nerve conduction in experimental diabetic neuropathy" *Diabetes Care* 1995;18:1160–1167.

54. Nilsson M; et al; "Lifestyle Related Risk Factors in the Aetiology of Gastro-Oesophageal Reflux" *Gut* 2004;53:1730-5.

55. Packer, L; et al; "Alpha-Lipoic Acid as a Biological Antioxidant" *Free Rad Biol Med* 1995;19:227-250.S\

56. Padmavathi, B; et al; "Roots of *Withania somnifera* Inhibit Forestomach and Skin Carcinogenesis in Mice" *Ad Access Publ* 2005;2:99-105.

57. Parihar, MS; et al; "Phenolic Antioxidants Attenuate Hippocampal Neuronal Cell Damage Against Kainic Acid Induced Excitotoxicity" *J Biosci* 2003;28:121-128.

58. Pert, Candace *Molecules of Emotion* New York 1997, Simon & Schuster pp. 250-278.

59. Pfeiffer, C; Braverman, E; *The Healing Nutrients Within* New Canaan, CN 1987 Keats Publishing, Inc pp. 191-210.

60. Sahelian, Ray, M.D.; *Mind Boosters, A Guide To Natural Supplements That Enhance Your Mind, Memory And Mood* New York St. Martin's Griffin Publishing, 2000

61. Samuels, Michael, *Creative Healing: How to Heal Yourself by Tapping Your Hidden Creativity* New Jersey, John Wiley & Sons 1998.

62. Scheufele, PM; "Effects Of Progressive Relaxation And Classical Music On Measurements Of Attention, Relaxation, And Stress Responses" *J Behav Med* 2000;23:207-28.

63. Schmiedeskamp, M; "Preventing Good Brains from Going Bad" *Scientific American Presents* Summer 2004;85-91.

64. Scott BC; et al; "Lipoic and Dihydrolipoic Acids as Antioxidants. A Critical Evaluation" *Free Rad Res* 1994;20:119-133.

65. Seidman, MD; Khan, MJ; Bai, U; et al; "Biologic Activity Of Mitochondrial Metabolites On Aging And Age-Related Hearing Loss" *Am J Otol* 2000;21.

66. Shils, M; et al; *Modern Nutrition in Health and Disease* 8th edition Philadelphia PA 1994 Lea & Febiger pp 502-509.

67. Simon H; ed. Stress *CBS Health Watch* 9/1999 *http://cbshealthwatch.medscape.com*

68. Skolnick, A; "Old Chinese Herbal Medicine Used for Fever Yields Possible New Alzheimer Disease Therapy" *JAMA* 1997;227:776.

69. Spasov, AA; et al; "A Double-Blind, Placebo-Controlled Pilot Study of the Stimulating and Adaptogenic Effect of *Rhodiola rosea* SHR-5 Extract on the Fatigue of Students Caused by Stress During an Examination Period with a Repeated Low-Dose Regimen" *Phytomed* 2000;7:85-89.

70. Speca, M; et al; "A Randomized, Wait-Listed Controlled Clinical Trial: The Effect of Mindfulness Meditation-Based Stress Reduction Program on Mood and Symptoms of Stress in Cancer Outpatients" *Psychosom Med* 2000;62:613-22.

71. Stipanuk, MH; *Biochemical and Physiological Aspects of Human Nutrition* Philadelphia PA 2000 W.B. Saunders Company pp. 754-756, 903.

72. Szolomicki, J; et al; "The Influence of Active Components of Eleuterococcus senticosus on Cellular Defence and Physical Fitness in Man" *Phytother Res* 2000;14:30-5.

73. Tchantchou, F; et al; "Dietary Supplementation with 3-Deaza Adenosine, N-Acetyl Cysteine, and S-Adenosyl Methionine Provide Neuroprotection Against Multiple Consequences of Vitamin Deficiency and Oxidative Challenge: Relevance to Age-Related Neurodegeneration" *Neuromolecular Med* 2004;6:93-103.

Appendix B: References   333

74. Todaro, JF; et al; "Effect Of Negative Emotions On Frequency Of Coronary Heart Disease (The Normative Aging Study)" *Am J Cardiol* 2003;92:901-6.

75. Tolle, E; *The Power of Now: A Guide to Spiritual Enlightenment*. Novato, CA 1997 New World Library pp 9-37.

76. Tolonen, A; et al; "Phenylpropanoid Glycosides from Rhodiola rosea" *Chem Pharm Bull* 2003;51:467-470.

77. Vouldoukis I; et al; "Supplementation With Gliadin-Combined Plant superoxide Dismutase Extract Promotes Antioxidant Defends and Protects Against Oxidative Stress" *Phytother Res* 2004;18:957-62.

78. *Withania somnifera* Monograph *Alt Med Rev* 2004;9:211-214. (author not listed)

79. Yoon, MS; et al; "Evidence Based Medicine in Migraine Prevention" *Expert Rev Neurother* 2005;5:333-41.

80. Zimmerman, M; *7-Color Cuisine: A Nutrition Guide and Cookbook*, Roseville, CA 2006, Penmarin Books.

81. Zimmerman, M; Nutrition and Your Brain: Protect Against Alzheimer's Disease *Taste for Life* Nov. 2004. Article can be downloaded from *www.thenutritionsolution.com*.

References for Chapter Three

1. Aldoori, W; Ryan-Harshman, M; "Preventing Diverticular Disease. Review of Recent Evidence On High-Fiber Diets" *Can Fam Physician* 2002;48:1632–1637.

2. Ali, L; et al; "Studies on Hypoglycemic Effects of Fruit Pulp, Seed, and Whole Plant of *Momordica charantia* on Normal and Diabetic Model Rats" *Planta Med* 1992;59:408-411.

3. Biessels, GJ; Kappelle, LJ; "Increased Risk of Alzheimer's Disease in Type II Diabetes: Insulin Resistance of the Brain or Insulin-Induced Amyloid Pathology" *Biochem Soc Trans* 2005;33:1041-4.

4. Blankson, H; Stakkestad, JA; Fagertun. H; et al; "Conjugated Linoleic Acid Reduces Body Fat Mass In Overweight And Obese Humans" *J Nutr*. 2000;130:2943–2948.

5. Bosy-Westphal, A; et al; "Value of Body Fat Mass vs Anthropometric Obesity Indices in the Assessment of Metabolic Risk Factors" *Int J Obes* (Lond) 2005.

6. Burnett, AL; "Metabolic Syndrome, Endothelial Dysfunction, and Erectile Dysfunction: Association and Management" *Curr Urol Rep* 2005;6:470-5.

7. Castell, LM, Newsholme EA. Glutamine And The Effects Of Exhaustive Exercise Upon The Immune Response. *Can J Physiol Pharmacol*. 1998;76:524–532.

8. Chertow, G; "Advances in Diabetes for the Millennium: Vitamins and Oxidant Stress in Diabetes and Its Complications" *Medscape General Medicine* 2004;6(3s).

9. Cook, SA; et al; "Therapy Insight: Heart Disease and the Insulin-Resistant Person" *Nat Clin Pract Cardiovasc Med* 2005;2:252-60.

10. Cunnick, J; Takemoto, D; "Bitter Melon (*Momordica charantia*)" *J Naturopathic Med* 1993;4:16-21.

11. Ehrmann, DA; et al; "Prevalence and Predictors of the Metabolic Syndrome in Women with Polycystic Ovary Syndrome (PCOS)" *J Clin Endocrin Metab* 2005-1329;[Epub ahead of date]

12. Erdogan, D; et al; "Relationship of Serum Uric Acid to Measures of Endothelial Function and Atherosclerosis in Healthy Adults" *Int J Clin Pract* 2005;59:1276-82.

13. Feher, J; Desk, G; Muzes, G; et al; "Liver Protective Action Of Silymarin Therapy In Chronic Alcoholic Liver Diseases" *Orv Heti* 1989;130:2723–2727.

14. Ford, ES; et al; "The Metabolic Syndrome and Antioxidant Concentrations Findings From the Third National Health and Nutrition Examination Study" *Diabetes* 2003;52:2346-2352.

15. Hammarsten, J; Hogstedt, B; "Hyperinsulinaemia: A Prospective Risk Factor for Lethal Clinical Prostate Cancer" *Eur J Cancer* 2005;19.

16. Holt, S; Combat *Syndrome X, Y and Z* . . . Patterson, NJ 2002, Wellness Publications

17. Khan A, Safdar M, Ali Khan MM, et al. Cinnamon Improves Glucose And Lipids Of People With Type 2 Diabetes. *Diabetes Care*. 2003;26:3215-3218.

18. Kahn, R; et al; "The Metabolic Syndrome: Time for a Critical Appraisal" *Diabetes Care* 2005;28:2289-2304.

19. Khan, A; Safdar, M; Ali Khan, MM; et al; "Cinnamon Improves Glucose And Lipids Of People With Type 2 Diabetes" *Diabetes Care* 2003;26:3215-3218.

20. Kawamota, R; et al; "Metabolic Syndrome as a Predictor of Ischemic Stroke in Elderly Persons" *Int Med* 2005;44:922-027.

21. Liberopoulos, EN; et al; "Diagnosis and Management of the Metabolic Syndrome in Obesity" *Obes Rev* 2005;6:283-96.

22. Lucena, MI; Andrade, RJ; de la Cruz, JP; et al; "Effects Of Silymarin MZ-80 On Oxidative Stress In Patients With Alcoholic Cirrhosis. Results Of A Randomized, Double-Blind, Placebo-Controlled Clinical Study" *Int J Clin Pharmacol Ther.* 2002;40:2–8.

23. Miller, WM; et al; "Obesity and Lipids" *Curr Cardiol Rep* 2005;7:465-70.

24. Morrison, JA; et al; "Development of the Metabolic Syndrome in Black and White Adolescent Girls: A Longitudinal Assessment" *Pediatrics* 2005;116:1178-82.

25. Mertz, W; "Chromium In Human Nutrition: A Review" *J Nutr* 1993;123:626–633

26. Pavlidis, AN; et al; "Postprandial Lipemia in Men With Metabolic Syndrome, Hypertensives and Healthy Subjects" *Lipids in Health and Disease* 2005;4:21(open access)

27. Raman, A; Lau, C; "Anti-diabetic Properties and Phytochemistry of *Momordica charantria* L. (Cucurbitaceae)" *Phytomedicine* 1996; 2:349-362.

28. Russel, R; Food and Nutrition Board; *Dietary Reference Intakes Chromium, Molybdenum, Vanadium.* Washington D.C. National Academy Press, 2001.

29. Rutter, MK; et al; "Insulin Resistance, the Metabolic Syndrome, and Incident Cardiovascular Events in the Framingham Offspring Study" *Diabetes* 2005;54:3252-7.

30. Samaha, FF; Iqbal, N; Seshadri, P; et al. "A Low-Carbohydrate As Compared With A Low-Fat Diet In Severe Obesity" *N Engl J Med* 2003;348:2074–2081.

31. Schaumberg, DA; et al; "Dietary Glycemic Load and Risk of Age-Related Cataract" *Am J Clin Nutr* 2004;80:489-95.

32. Shanmugasundaram, ER; Rajeswari, G; Baskaran, K; Rajesh Kumar, BR; Radha Shanmugasundaram, K; Kizar Ahmath, B; "Use Of *Gymnema sylvestre* Leaf Extract In The Control Of Blood Glucose In Insulin-Dependent Diabetes Mellitus" *Journal of Ethnopharmacology*1990;30(3):281-294.

33. Shekelle, PG; et al; "Are Ayurvedic Herbs for Diabetes Effective?" *J Fam Pract* 2005;54:876-86.

34. Shen, BJ; et al; "Is the Factor Structure of the Metabolic Syndrome Comparable Between Men and Woman and Across Three Ethnic Groups: The Miami Community Health Study" *Ann Epidemiol* 2005;[Epub ahead of print]

35. Shimizu, K; Iino, A; Nakajima, J; et al; "Suppression Of Glucose Absorption By Some Fractions Extracted From *Gymnema sylvestre* Leaves" *J Vet Med Sci* 1997;59:245-251.

36. Shils, ME; ed; *Modern Nutrition in Health and Disease* 8th ed. Philadelphia, PA, Lea and Febiger, 1994. (chromium, molybdenum, vanadium)

37. Stipanuk, MH; *Biochemical and Physiological Aspects of Human Nutrition* Philadelphia, PA, W.B. Saunders Company, 2000. (chromium, molybdenum, vanadium).

38. Trent, LK; Thieding-Cancel, D; "Effects Of Chromium Picolinate On Body Composition" *J Sports Med Phys Fitness* 1995;35:273–280.

39. Wang, D; et al; "Endophasmic Reticulum Stress Increases Glucose-6-Phosphatase and Glucose Cycling in Liver Cells" *Endocrinology* 2005-1014;[Epub ahead of release]

40. West, D; "Reduced Body Fat With Conjugated Linoleic Acid Feeding In The Mouse" *FASEB J* 1997;11:A599.

References for Chapter Four

1. Abdelmalek, MF; Angulo, P; Jorgensen, RA et al; "Betaine, A Promising New Agent For Patients With Nonalcoholic Steatohepatitis: Results Of A Pilot Study" *Am J Gastroenterol* 2001;96:2711-2717.

2. Aneiros, E; Mas, R; Calderon, B; et al; "Effect of policosanol in lowering cholesterol levels in patients with type II hypercholesterolemia" *Curr Ther Res* 1995;56:176–182.

3. Angerer, P; Stork, S; Kothny, W; et al; "Effect Of Marine Omega-3 Fatty Acids On Peripheral Atherosclerosis In Patients With Coronary Artery Disease—A Randomised 2 Year Intervention Trial" *Eur Heart J* 2001;22(suppl):162.

4. Angulo, P; Lindor, KD; "Treatment Of Nonalcoholic Fatty Liver: Present And Emerging Therapies" *Semin Liver Dis* 2001;21:81-188.

5. Arruzazabala, ML; Molina, V; Mas, R; et al; "Antiplatelet Effects Of Policosanol (20 And 40 Mg/Day) In Healthy Volunteers And Dyslipidaemic Patients" *Clin Exp Pharmacol Physiol* 2002;29:891-897.

6. Balch, J. *The Super Antioxidants*, M. Evans and Company, 2005

7. Barclay, L; "Vegetable Protein Intake May Be Inversely Related to Blood Pressure" *www.medscape.com.* Jan 10, 2006.

8. Bauman, WA; Shaw, S, Jayatilleke, E; et al; "Increased Intake Of Calcium Reverses Vitamin B12 Malabsorption Induced By Metformin" *Diabetes Care* 2000;23:1227–1231.

9. Berman, M; Erman, A; Ben-Gal, T, et al, "Coenzyme Q10 In Patients With End-Stage Heart Failure Awaiting Cardiac Transplantation: A Randomized, Placebo-Controlled Study" *Clin Cardiol* 2004;27:295-9.

10. "Betaine Monograph" *Alt Med Rev* 2003;8:193-196. (authors not listed)

11. Binkoski, AE; et al; Balance of Unsaturated Fatty Acids is important to a Cholesterol-Lowering Diet: Comparison of Mid-Oleic Sunflower Oil and Olive Oil on Cardiovascular Disease *J Am Diet Assoc* 2005;105:1080-6.

12. Blumenthal, M; ed. *The ABC Clinical Guide to Herbs.* New York 2003, Thieme Publishers pp. 153-172.

13. Breithaupt-Grogler, K; Ling, M; Boudoulas, H; et al; "Protective Effect Of Chronic Garlic Intake On Elastic Properties Of Aorta In The Elderly" *Circulation* 1997;96:2649–2655.

14. Burnham, TH; Sjwein, SL; Short, RM; (eds); "Monascus" In: *The Review of Natural Products.* St. Louis, MO: Facts and Comparisons, 1997.

15. Castano, G; Mas, R; Arruzazabala, ML; et al; "Effects Of Policosanol And Pravastatin On Lipid Profile, Platelet Aggregation And Endothelemia In Older Hypercholesterolemic Patients" *Int J Clin Pharmacol Res* 1999;19:105–116.

16. Castano, G; Mas, R; Fernandez, L; et al; "Effects of Policosanol And Lovastatin In Patients With Intermittent Claudication: A Double-Blind Comparative Pilot Study" *Angiology* 2004; 55:361-71.

17. Cherchi, A; Lai, C; Angelino, F; et al; "Effects Of L-Carnitine On Exercise Tolerance In Chronic Stable Angina: A Multicenter, Double-Blind, Randomized, Placebo Controlled Crossover Study" *Int J Clin Pharmacol Ther Toxicol* 1985;23:569–572.

18. Cutler, R; Wilson, P; "Antibacterial Activity of a New, Stable, Aqueous Extract of Allicin Against Methicillin-Resistant *Staphylococcus aureus*" *Br J Biomed Sci* 2004;61:71-4.

19. Donati, C; Barbi, G; Cairo, G; et al; "Pantethine Improves The Lipid Abnormalities Of Chronic Hemodialysis Patients: Results Of A Multicenter Clinical Trial" *Clin Nephrol* 1986;25:70–74.

20. Dreosti, I; "Bioactive Ingredients: "Antioxidants and Polyphenols in Tea" *Nutrition Reviews* 1996; 54(11): S51-S58.

21. Erkkila, AT; et al; "Cereal Fiber and Whole-Grain Intake Are Associated With Reduced Progression of Coronary-Artery Atherosclerosis in Postmenopausal Women with Coronary Artery Disease" *Am Heart J* 2005;149:94-101.

22. Etingin, OR; ed.; "Beyond Your Cholesterol Numbers" *Food and Fitness Advisor Weill Medical College of Cornell University* 2005;8:1,8.

23. Feng, WH; Wei, HL; Liu, GT; "Effect Of Pycnogenol On The Toxicity Of Heart, Bone Marrow And Immune Organs As Induced By Antitumor Drugs" *Phytomedicine* 2002;9(5):414-418.

24. Folkers, K; "Basic Chemical Research On Coenzyme Q10 And Integrated Clinical Research On Therapy Of Diseases" *Biomed Clin Aspects Coenzyme Q* 1985;5:457–478.

25. Fuhrman, B; et al; "Pomegranate Juice Inhibits Oxidized LDL Uptake and Cholesterol Biosynthesis in Macrophages" *J Nutr Biochem* 2005;16:570-6.

26. Gaddi, A; Descovich, GC; Noseda, G; et al; "Controlled Evaluation Of Pantethine, A Natural Hypolipidemic Compound, In Patients With Different Forms Of Hyperlipoproteinemia" *Atherosclerosis* 1984;50:73–83.

27. Harel, Z; Biro, FM; Kottenhahn, RK; et al; "Supplementation With Omega-3 Polyunsaturated Fatty Acids In The Management Of Dysmenorrhea In Adolescents" *Am J Obstet Gynecol* 1996;174:1335–1338.

28. Heber, D; Yip, I; Ashley, JM; et al; "Cholesterol-Lowering Effects Of A Proprietary Chinese Red-Yeast-Rice Dietary Supplement" *Am J Clin Nutr* 1999;69:231–6.

29. Hennekens, CH; et al; "Sex-Related Differences in Response to Aspirin in Cardiovascular Disease: An Untested Hypothesis" *Nat Clin Pract Cardiovasc Med* 2006;3:4-5.

30. Huang, HY; et al; "Effects of Vitamin C and Vitamin E on *in vivo* Lipid Peroxidation: Results of a Randomized Controlled Trial" *Am J Clin Nutr* 2002;76:549-55.

31. Kannar, D; Wattanapenpaiboon, N; Savige, GS; et al; "Hypocholesterolemic Effect Of An Enteric-Coated Garlic Supplement" *J Am Coll Nutr* 2001;20:225–231.

32. Keenan, JM; et al; "Oat Ingestion Reduces Systolic and Diastolic Blood Pressure in Patients with Mild or Borderline Hypertension: A Pilot Trial" *J Fam Prac* 2002;51:

33. Kempuri, D; et al; "Flavonols Inhibit Proinflammatory Mediator Release, Intracellular Calcium Ion Levels and Protein Kinase C Theta Phosphorylation in Humna Mast Cells" *Br J Pharmacol* 2005;145:934-944.

34. Khatta, M; Alexander, BS; Krichten, CM; et al; "The Effect Of Coenzyme Q10 In Patients With Congestive Heart Failure" *Ann Intern Med* 2000;132:636-640.

35. Koch, HP; Lawson, LD; *Garlic: The Science and Therapeutic Application of Allium sativum L. and Related Species* 2nd ed. Baltimore, MD, 1996 Williams & Wilkins pp 66, 86.

36. Lee, IM; et al; "Vitamin E in the Primary Prevention of Cardiovascular Disease and Cancer: The Women's Health Study: A Randomized Controlled Trial" *JAMA* 2005;294:56-65.

37. Libby, P; "Atherosclerosis: the New View" *Sci Am* 2002;286:47-55.

38. Liu, F; Lau, BHS; Peng, Q; Shah, V; "Pycnogenol Protects Vascular Endothelial Cells From Beta-Amyloid-Induced Injury" *Biology and Pharmacology Bulletin* 2000;23(6):735-737.

39. Liu, FJ; Zhang, YX; Lau, BH; "Pycnogenol Enhances Immune And Haemopoietic Functions In Senescence-Accelerated Mice" *Cellular and Molecular Life Sciences* 1998;54(10):1168-1172.

40. Liu, X; Wei, J; Tan, F; Zhou, S; Wurthwein, G; Rohdewald, P; "Pycnogenol, French Maritime Pine Bark Extract, Improves Endothelial Function Of Hypertensive Patients" *Life Sciences* 2004;74(7):855-862.

41. Liu, L; et al; "Xuezhikang Decreases Serum Lipoproteins (a) and C-Reactive Protein Concentrations in Patients with Coronary Heart Disease" *Clin Chem* 2003;49:1347-1352.

42. Liu, S; et al; "A Prospective Study of Dietary Glycemic Load, Carbohydrate Intake, and Risk of Coronary Heart Disease in US Women" *Am J Clin Nutr* 2000;71:1455-61.

43. McSweeney, JC; et al; "Women's Early Warning Symptoms of Acute Myocardial Infarction" *Circulation* 2003;108:2619-23.

44. Middleton, E; Kandaswami, C; Theoharides, TC; "The Effects of Plant Flavonoids on Mammalian Cells: Implications for Inflammation, Heart Disease, and Cancer" *Pharm Rev* 2000;52:673-751.

45. "*Monascus purpureus* (Red Yeast Rice) Monograph" *Alt Med Rev* 2004;9:208-210. (authors not listed)

46. Mukamal, KJ; et al; "Impact of Diabetes on Long-Term Survival After Acute Myocardial Infarction" *Diabetes Care* 2001;24:1422-1427.

47. Newby, PK; et al; "Risk of Overweight and Obesity Among Semivegetarian, Lactovegetarian, and Vegan Women" *Am J Clin Nutr* 2005;81:1267-74.

48. Nordstrom, CK; et al; "Leisure Time Physical Activity and Early Atherosclerosis: The Los Angeles Atherosclerosis Study" *Am J Med* 2003;115:19-25.

49. Nowson, CA; et al; "Blood Pressure Change with Weight Loss is Affected by Diet Type in Men" *Am J Clin Nutr* 2005;81:983-9.

50. Osiecki, H; "The Role of Chronic Inflammation in Cardiovascular Disease and its Regulation by Nutrients" *Alt Med Rev* 2004;9:32-53.

51. Osono, Y; et al; "The Effects of Pantethine on Fatty Liver and Fat Distribution" *J Atheroscler Thromb* 2000;7:55-8.

52. "Pantethine Monograph" *Alt Med Rev* 1998;3:379-381. (author not listed)

53. Patrick, L; Uzick, M; "Cardiovascular Disease: C-Reactive Protein and the Inflammatory Disease Paradigm: HMG-CoA Reductase Inhibitors, alpha-Tocopherol, Red Yeast Rice, and Olive Oil Polyphenols. A Review of the Literature" *Alt Med Rev* 2001;6:248-271.

54. "Policosanol Monograph" *Alt Med Rev* 2004;9:312-317. (author not listed)

55. Qureshi, AA; et al; "Synergistic Effect of Tocotrienol-Rich Fraction of Rice Bran and Lovastatin on Lipid Parameters in Hypercholesterolemic Humans" *J Nutr Biochem* 2001;12:318-319.

56. Richard, C; Siow, J; Richards, K; Pedley, D; Leake, G; "Vitamin C Protects Human Vascular Smooth Muscle Cells against Apoptosis Induced by Moderately Oxidized LDL Containing High Levels of Lipid Hydroperoxides" *Arterioscler Thromb Vasc Biol* 1999; 19:2387-2394

57. Rimm, EB; et al; "Folate and Vitamin B6 From Diet and Supplements in Relation to Risk of Coronary Heart Disease Among Women" *JAMA* 1998;279:359-364.

58. Rimm, EF; et al; "Relation Between Intake of Flavonoids and Risk for Coronary Heart Disease in Male Health Professionals" *Ann Intern Med* 1996;123:384-389.

59. Rosenfeldt, F; Marasco, S; Lyon, W; et al; "Coenzyme Q10 Therapy Before Cardiac Surgery Improves Mitochondrial Function And In Vitro Contractility Of Myocardial Tissue" *J Thorac Cardiovasc Surg* 2005;129:25-32.

60. Schrager, S; "Dietary Calcium Intake and Obesity" *Medscape* Sept. 2, 2005.

61. Schroecksnadel, K; et al; "Anti-Inflammatory Compound Resveratrol Suppresses Homocysteine Formation in Stimulated Human Peripheral Blood Mononuclear Cells" *In Vitro Clin Chem Lab Med* 2005;43:1084-8.

62. Silagy, CA; Neil, HA; "A Meta-Analysis Of The Effect Of Garlic On Blood Pressure" *J Hypertens* 1994;12:463–468.

63. Sima, AF; et al; "Acetyl-L-Carnitine Improves Pain, Nerve Regeneration, and Vibratory Perception in Patients With Chronic Diabetic Neuopathy" *Diabetes Care* 2005;28:89-101.

64. Sinatra, S; "Nutritional Supplements for the Cardiac Patient" *Internl J Integrative Med* 2001;3:31-43.

65. Singh, RB; Niaz, MA; Rastogi, SS; et al; "Effect Of Hydrosoluble Coenzyme Q10 On Blood Pressures And Insulin Resistance In Hypertensive Patients With Coronary Artery Disease" *J Human Hypertens* 1999;13:203–208.

66. Smith DJ, Olive KE. "Chinese Red Rice-Induced Myopathy" *South Med J* 2003;96:1265–7.

67. Smulders, YM; Stehouwer, CD; "Folate Metabolism and Cardiovascular Disease" *Semin Vasc Med* 2005;5:87-97.

68. Spence, JD; et al; "Vitamin Intervention for Stroke Prevention Trial: An Efficacy Analysis" *Stroke* 2005;36:2404-9.

69. Steiner, M; Khan, AH; Holbert, D; et al; "A Double-Blind Crossover Study In Moderately Hypercholesterolemic Men That Compared The Effect Of Aged Garlic Extract And Placebo Administration On Blood Lipids" *Am J Clin Nutr* 1996;64:866–870.

70. Stengler, M. *The Natural Physician's Healing Therapies.* Alive Books, 1998

Appendix B: References 337

71. Stoll, AL; Severus, WE; Freeman, MP; et al; "Omega 3 Fatty Acids In Bipolar Disorder: A Preliminary Double-Blind, Placebo-Controlled Trial" *Arch Gen Psychiatry* 1999;56:407–412.

72. Suleiman, MS; "New Concepts in the Cardioprotective Action of Magnesium and Taurine During the Calcium Paradox and Ischemia of the Heart" *Magnes Res* 1994;7:295-312.

73. Sung, H; et al; "The Effects of Green Tea Ingestion Over Four Weeks on Atherosclerotic Markers" *Ann Clin Biochem* 2005;42:292-7.

74. Swain, R; Kaplan-Miachlis, B; "Magnesium for the Next Millennium" *Medscape* Feb 28, 2000.

75. Taglialatela, G; Navarra, D; Olivi, A; et al; "Neurite Outgrowth In PC12 Cells Stimulated By Acetyl-L-Carnitine Arginine Amide" *Neurochem Res* 1995 Jan;20(1):1-9.

76. Ueland, PM; et al; "Betaine: A Key Modulator of One-Carbon Metabolism and Homocysteine Status" *Clin Chem Lab Med* 2005;43:1069-75.

77. Vojdani, A; "A Look at Infectious Agents as a Possible Causative Factor in Cardiovascular Disease: Parts I, II, III" *Lab Med* 2003;34(3):7-11; 34(4):5-9; 34(5):24-31.

78. Volker, D; Fitzgerald, P; Major, G; et al; "Efficacy Of Fish Oil Concentrate In The Treatment Of Rheumatoid Arthritis" *J Rheumatol* 2000;27:2343–2346.

79. Wallström, P; et al; "Serum Concentrations of ffl-Carotene and ffl-Tocopherol and Associated with Diet, Smoking, and General and Central Adiposity" *Am J Clin Nutr* 2001;73:777-85.

80. Wang, H; "Determination Of Flavonols In Green And Black Tea Leaves And Green Tea Infusions By High Performance Liquid Chromatography" *Food Research International* 34; 2-3:223-227. 2001

81. Wang, J; Lu, Z; Chi, J; et al; "Multicenter Clinical Trial Of The Serum Lipid-Lowering Effects Of A *Monascus Purpureus* (Red Yeast) Rice Preparation From Traditional Chinese Medicine" *Curr Ther Res* 1997;58:964–77.

82. Watson, RR; "Pycnogenol and Cardiovascular Health" *Evidence Based Integrative Med* 2003;1:27-32.

83. Whelton, PK; et al; "Primary Prevention of Hypertension: Clinical and Public Health Advisory from the National High Blood Pressure Education Program" *JAMA* 2002;288:1882-8.

84. Zhao, SP; et al; "Xuezhikang, an Extract of Cholestin, Protects Endothelial Function Through Anti-inflammatory and Lipid-Lowering Mechanisms in Patients With Coronary Heart Disease" *Circulation* 2004;110:915-920.

References for Chapter Five

1. Bagchi, D; Garg, A; Krohn, RL; Bagchi, M; Tran, MX; Stohs, SJ; :Oxygen Free Radical Scavenging Abilities Of Vitamins C And E, And A Grape Seed Proanthocyanidin Extract In Vitro" *Res Commun Mol Pathol Pharmacol* 1997 Feb;95(2):179-89. 5.

2. Balch, J. *The Super Antioxidants*. M. Evans and Company Publishing, 2000

3. Barrett, B; "Medicinal Properties of Echinacea: A Critical Review" *Phytomedicine* 2003;10:66-86.

4. Barringer, TA; et al; "Effect of a Multivitamin and Mineral Supplement on Infection and Quality of Life" *Ann Intern Med* 2003;138:365-371.

5. Beck, MA; "Antioxidants and Viral Infections: Host Immune Response and Viral Pathogenicity" *J Nutr* 2001;20:384S-388S.

6. Beck, MA; et al; "Nutritionally Induced Oxidative Stress: Effect on Viral Disease" *Am J Clin Nutr* 2000 71(suppl):1676S-9S.

7. Beck, MA; et al; "Selenium Deficiency and Viral Infection" *J Nutr* 2003;133:1463S-1467S.

8. Beck, MA; et al; "Selenium Deficiency Increases the Pathology of an Influenza Virus Infection" *FASEB J* 2001;15:1481-83.

9. Beller, D; "Current Study May Help Explain Relation Between Infection and Onset of Autoimmunity" *American Autoimmune Related Diseases Association Report* http://www.aarda.org/research/research_reports.php.

10. Barringer TA, Kirk JK, Santaniello AC, et al. Effect of a multivitamin and mineral supplement on infection and quality of life. A randomized, double-blind, placebo-controlled trial. *Ann Intern Med* 2003;138:365-71.

11. Beta-Glutans, *www.nnfa.org/services/science/bg_betaglucans.htm*

12. Bisignano, G; et al; "On the In-vitro Antimicrobial Activity of Oleuropein and Hydroxytyrosol" *J. Pharm. Pharmacol* 1999, 51: pp. 971-974

13. Black, PH; Berman, AS; "Stress and Inflammation Cytokines": *Stress and Immunity* Boca Raton, Fl CRC Press 1999 pp 115-132.

14. Bone, K; Morgan, M; "Professional Review: *Astragalus membranaceus* – Astragalus" *MediHerb* 1999;67:1-4.

15. Braunig, B; Dorn, M; Limburg, E et al; "*Echinacea purpurearadix* For Strengthening The Immune Response In Flu-Like Infections" *Z Phytother* 1992;13:7–13.

16. Bravo, L; "Polyphenols: Chemistry, Dietary Sources, Metabolism, and Nutritional Significance" *Nutr Rev* 1998;56:317-333.

17. Brinn. LS; "New Finding Sheds Light on Mechanism of Inflammation in Lupus, Other Disorders Duke University Medical Center Report" *American Autoimmune Related Diseases Association Report* http://www.aarda.org/research/research_reports. php

18. Busse, E; et al; "Influence of Alpha-Lipoic Acid on Intracellular Glutathione *in vitro* and *in vivo*" *Arzheimittelforschung* 1002;42:829-31.

19. Campa, A; Shor-Posner, G; Indacochea, F; et al; "Mortality Risk In Selenium-Deficient HIV-Positive Children" *J Acquir Immune Defic Syndr Hum Retrovirol* 1999;20:508–513.

20. Cantorna, MT; Mahon, BD; "Mounting Evidence for Vitamin D as an Environmental Factor Affecting Autoimmune Disease Prevalence" *Exp Biol Med* 2004;229:1136-1142.

21. Carturla, N; et al; "Differential Effects of Oleuropein, a Biophenol form *Olea europaea*, on Anionic and Zwitterionic Phospholipid Model Membranes" *Chem Phys Lipids* 2005;137:2-17.

22. Caruso, C; et al; "Cytokine Production Pathway in the Elderly" *Immunol Res* 1996;15:84-90.

23. Chandra, RK; "Effect of Vitamin and Trace-Element Supplementation on Immune Responses and Infection in Elderly Subjects" *Lancet* 2002;340:1124-7.

24. Cutolo, M; "Interesting Roles for Melatonin in Rheumatoid Arthritis" *American Autoimmune Related Diseases Association Reports* http://www.aarda.org/research/research_reports.php

25. DeSouza, NJ; "Industrial Development Of Traditional Drugs: The Forskolin Example. A Mini-Review" *J Ethnopharmacol* 1993;38:177–180.

26. Elmer, GW; "Probiotics: "Living Drugs" *Am J Health-Syst Pharm* 2001;58:1101-1109.

27. Faleiro, L; et al; "Antibacterial and Antioxidant Activities of Essential Oils Isolated from *Thymbra capitata* L. (Cav.) and *Orignaum vulgare* L." *J Agric Food Chem* 2005;53:8162-8.

28. Fitzpatrick, DF; Bing, B; Rohdewald, P; "Endothelium-dependent vascular effects of Pycnogenol" *J Cardiovasc Pharmacol* 1998 Oct;32(4):509-15. 13.

29. "Gamma-Linolenic Acid (GLA) Monograph" *Alt Med Rev* 2004;9:70-78. (author not listed)

30. George, J; et al; "Autoimmunity as an Additional Risk Factor for Atherosclerosis: A Report" *American Autoimmune Related Diseases Association Report* http://www.aarda.org/research/research_reports.php

31. Gershwin, ME; "Zinc Deficiency and Immune Function" *Ann Rev Nutr* 1990;10:415-31.

32. Giles, CK; et al; "Probiotics in Health Maintenance and Disease Prevention" *Alt Med Rev* 2003;8:143-155.

33. Gluck, U; Gebbers, JO; "Ingested Probiotics Reduce Nasal Colonization with Pathogenic Bacteria (Staphylococcus aureus, Streptococcus Pneumoniae, and Beta-Hemolytic Streptococci)" *Am J Clin Nutr* 2003;77:517-20.

34. Goulding, NJ; Hall, ND; "Rhythms in the Immune System" *Pharmac Ther* 1993;58:249-261.

35. Grandjean, EM; Berthet, P; Ruffmann, R; et al; "Efficacy Of Oral Long-Term N-Acetylcysteine In Chronic Bronchopulmonary Disease: A Meta-Analysis Of Published Double-Blind, Placebo-Controlled Clinical Trials" *Clin Ther* 2000;22:209–221.

36. Hansen, NCG; Skriver, A; Brorsen-Riis, L; et al; "Orally Administered N-Acetylcysteine May Improve General Well-Being In Patients With Mild Chronic Bronchitis" *Respir Med* 1994;88:531–535.

37. Hauer, J; Anderer, FA; "Mechanism of Stimulation of Human Natural Killer Cytotoxicity by Arabinogalactan from *Larix occidentalis*" *Cancer Immunol Immunother* 1993;36:237-244.

38. Hemila, H; "Does Vitamin C Alleviate Symptoms Of The Common Cold? A Review Of Current Evidence" *Scand J Infect Dis* 1994;26:1–6.

39. Hilliquin, P; "Biological Markers in Inflammatory Rheumatic Diseases" *Cell Mol Biol* 1996;41:993-1006.

40. Hoheisel, O; Sandberg, M; Bertram, S; et al; "Echinagard Treatment Shortens The Course Of The Common Cold: A Double-Blind, Placebo-Controlled Clinical Trial" *Eur J Clin Res*. 1997;9:261–268.

41. Holick, MF; "Sunlight and Vitamin D for Bone Health and Prevention of Autoimmune Diseases, Cancers, and Cardiovascular Disease" *Am J Clin Nutr* 2004;80(suppl):1678S-88S.

42. Holmes, RP; Kummerow, FA; "The Relationship Of Adequate And Excessive Intake Of Vitamin D To Health And Disease" *J Am Coll Nutr* 1983;2:173–199.

43. Holmes, RP; "Nutrition and the Immune System from Birth to Old Age" *Eur J Clin Nutr* 2002;56:Suppl 3:S73-6.

44. Jain. AL; "Influence of Vitamins And Trace-Elements On The Incidence Of Respiratory Infection In The Elderly" *Nutr Res* 2002;22:85–87.

45. Josling, P; "Preventing the Common Cold With a Garlic Supplement: A Double-Blind, Placebo-Controlled Survey" *Adv Ther* 2001;18:189-93.

46. Keen, CL; "Zinc Deficiency and Immune Function" *Ann Rev Nutr* 1990;10:415-31.

47. Kekessy, D; et al; "Transmembrane Signaling Changes with Aging" *Ann NY Acad Sci* 673:165-71.

Appendix B: References   339

48. Kelly, GS; "Larch Arabinogalactan: Clinical Relevance of a Novel Immune-Enhancing Polysaccharide" *Altern Med Rev* 1999;4:96-103.

49. Lamson, DW; Plaza, SM "The Anticancer Effects of Vitamin K" *Alt Med Rev* 2003;8:303-318.

50. Liang, R; "Clinical Study On Braincalming Tablets In Treating 450 Cases Of Atherosclerosis" *J North Chin Med* 1985;1:63–65.

51. Luettig, B; et al; "Macrophage Activation by the Polysaccharide Arabinogalactan Isolated From Plant Cell Cultures of *Echinacea purpurea*" *J Natl Cancer Inst* 1989;81:669-675.

52. Metzig, C; Grabowska, E; Eckert, K; et al; "Bromelain Proteases Reduce Human Platelet Aggregation In Vitro, Adhesion To Bovine Endothelial Cells And Thrombus Formation In Rat Vessels *in vivo*" *In Vivo* 1999;13:7–12.

53. Meydani, SN; et al; "Vitamin E Supplementation Enhances Cell-Mediated Immunity in Healthy Elderly Subjects" *Am J Clin Nutr* 1990;52:557-63.

54. Middleton, E Jr; "Effect Of Flavonoids On Basophil Histamine Release And Other Secretory Systems" *Prog Clin Biol Res* 1986;213:493–506.

55. Middleton, E; "Biological Properties of Plant Flavonoids: An Overview" *Intn J Pharmacog* 1996;34:344-348.

56. Munger, KL; et al; "Vitamin D Intake and Incidence of Multiple Sclerosis" *Neurology* 2004;62:60-5.

57. Pauling, L. *Vitamin C and the Common Cold*. W H Freeman & Co, 1976.

58. Plettenberg, A; Stoehr, A; Stellbrink, HJ; et al; "A Preparation From Bovine Colostrum In The Treatment Of HIV-Positive Patients With Chronic Diarrhea" *Clin Investig* 1993;71:42–45.

59. Rona, A; "Bovine Colostrum Emerges as Immune System Modulator" *Am J Nat Med* 1998;5:19-22.

60. Ross, J; *The Diet Cure*. New York, NY. Penguin Books, 1999

61. Schoneberger, D; "The Influence Of Immune-Stimulating Effects Of Pressed Juice From *Echinacea Purpurea* On The Course And Severity Of Colds. (Results Of A Double-Blind Study)" *Forum Immunol* 1992;8:2–12.

62. Stengler, M. *The Natural Physician's Guide to healing remedies*. Alive Books, 1998

63. Stewart, MS; Spalholz, JE; Neldner, KH; et al; "Selenium Compounds Have Disparate Abilities To Impose Oxidative Stress And Induce Apoptosis" *Free Radical Biol Med* 1999;26:42–48.

64. Swanson, CA; Longnecker, MP; Veillon, C; et al; "Selenium Intake, Age, Gender, And Smoking In Relation To Indices Of Selenium Status Of Adults Residing In A Seleniferous Area" *Am J Clin Nutr* 1990;52:858–862.

65. Theoharides, TC; Cochrane, DE; "Critical Role of Mast Cells in Inflammatory Diseases and the Effect of Acute Stress" *J Neuroimmunology* 2004;146:1-12.

66. Tolonen. M; "Finnish Studies On Antioxidants With Special Reference To Cancer, Cardiovascular Diseases And Aging" *Int Clin Nutr Rev* 1989;9:68–75.

67. Torkos, Sherry; "Clinical Implications of Antibiotic and Probiotic Therapies" *Int J Integr Med* 1999;1:14-17.

68. Utiger, RD; "The Need For More Vitamin D" *N Engl J Med*. 1998;338:828–829.

69. Walker, Morton; *Nature's Antibiotic: Olive Leaf Extract*; New York, Kensington Books, 1997

70. Walker, Morton; "Olive Leaf Extract: The New Oral Treatment To Counteract Most Types Of Pathological Organisms" *Explore!*, Vol. 7, No. 4, 1996 4)

71. Wassef, Farid; "Inflammatory Modulators" *Int J Integr Med* 1999;1:10-13.

72. Wehrwein, P; ed. "Reining in Runaway Inflammation"; "Eight Things You Should Know About Restless Legs Syndrome" *Harvard Health Letter* 2002;27:4-6.

73. Zhang, YD; Wang, YL; Shen, JP; et al; "Effects On Blood Pressure And Inflammation Of Astragalus Saponin 1, A Principle Isolated From *Astragalus membranaceus* BGE" *Acta PharmSin*. 1984;19:333–337.

74. Ziccardi, P; et al; "Reduction of Inflammatory Cytokine Concentrations and Improvement of Endothelial Functions in Obese Women After Weight Loss Over One Year" *Circulation* 2002; 105:804-9.

References for Chapter Six

1. Akobeng AK, Miller V, Stanton J, et al. "Double-Blind Randomized Controlled Trial Of Glutamine-Enriched Polymeric Diet In The Treatment Of Active Crohn's Disease". *J Pediatr Gastroenterol Nutr.* 2000;30:78–84.

2. Anderson JW, Davidson MH, Blonde L, et al. "Long-Term Cholesterol-Lowering Effects As An Adjunct To Diet Therapy In The Treatment Of Hypercholesterolemia". *Am J Clin Nutr* 2000;71:1433–8.

3. Arjmandi BH, Khan DA, Juma S, et al. "Whole Flaxseed Consumption Lowers Serum LDL-Cholesterol And Lipoprotein(A) Concentrations In Postmenopausal Women". *Nutr Res.* 1998;18:1203–1214.

4. Armuzzi A, Cremonini F, Ojetti V, et al. "Effect Of *Lactobacillus* GG Supplementation On Antibiotic-Associated Gastrointestinal Side Effects During *Helicobacter Pylori* Eradication Therapy: A Pilot Study". *Digestion*. 2001;63:1–7.

5. Balch, J. "The Super Antioxidants". M. Evans and Company Inc, 2000

6. Baroody, TA; "Alkalize or Die". Waynesville, NC Holographic Health Press, 2002 pp 43-72.

7. Bassey EJ, Littlewood JJ, Rothwell MC, et al. "Lack Of Effect Of Supplementation With Essential Fatty Acids On Bone Mineral Density In Healthy Pre- And Postmenopausal Women: Two Randomized Controlled Trials Of Efacalffl V. Calcium Alone". *Br J Nutr*. 2000;83:629–635.

8. Blumenthal, M ed. "The ABC Clinical Guide to Herbs". Austin Texas, American Botanical Council, 2003 pp 273-281.

9. Boirie Y, et al, 1997. "Slow And Fast Dietary Proteins Differently Modulate Postprandial Protein Accretion". *Proceedings of the National Academy of Sciences*, 94:14930-14935.

10. Bounous G, Gold P, 1991. "The Biological Activity Of Undenatured Dietary Whey Proteins: Role Of Glutathione". *Clinical Investigative Medicine*, 14(4):296-309

11. Brandi, G; et al; "Bacteria in Biopsies of Human Hypochlorhydric Stomach: A Scanning Electron Microscopy Study". *Ultrastruct Pathol* 1996;20:203-9.

12. Castell LM, Poortmans JR, Newsholme EA. "Does Glutamine Have A Role In Reducing Infections In Athletes?". *Eur J Appl Physiol Occup Physiol*. 1996;73:488–490.

13. Colombel JF, Cortot A, Neut C, et al. "Yogurt with *Bifidobacterium longum* Reduces Erythromycin-Induced Gastrointestinal Effects". *Lancet*. 1987;2:43.

14. Dangin M, Boirie Y, et al, 2001. "The Digestion Rate Of Protein Is An Independent Regulating Factor Of Postprandial Protein Retention". Am J Physiol Endocrinol Metab, 280: E340-E348.

15. Davidson MH, Dugan LD, Burns JH, et al. "A Psyllium-Enriched Cereal For The Treatment Of Hypercholesterolemia In Children: A Controlled, Double-Blind, Crossover Study". *Am J Clin Nutr* 1996;63:96–102.

16. DeFelice, K "Enzymes for Autism and Other Neurological Conditions". Johnston IA, Thundersnow Interactive, 2003

17. Drisko, JA; et al; "Probiotics in Health Maintenance and Disease Prevention". *Alt Med Rev* 2003;8:143-155

18. Gursche, S; "Fantastic Flax". Vancouver, Canada Alive Books, 1999.

19. Hawrelak J. "Probiotics: What Are They And How Safe?". *Journal of the Australian Tradtional Medicine Society*. 2002;8(4):151-155.

20. Hawrelak, JA; Myers, SP; "The Causes of Intestinal Dysbiosis: A Review". Alt Med Rev 2004;9:180-197.

21. Head, KA; Jurenka, JS; "Inflammatory Bowel Disease Part I:Ulcerative Colitis – Pathophysiology and Conventional and Alternative Treatment Options". *Alt Med Rev* 2003;8:247-283.

22. Head, KA; Jurenka, JS; "Inflammatory Bowel Disease Part II Crohn's Disease". *Alt Med Rev* 2004;9:360-401.

23. Helms, S; "Celiac Disease and Gluten-Associated Diseases". *Alt Med Rev* 2005;10:172-192.

24. Henz BM, Jablonska S, van de Kerkhof PC, et al. "Double-blind, Multicentre Analysis Of The Efficacy Of Borage Oil In Patients With Atopic Eczema". *Br J Dermatol*. 1999;140:685–688.

25. Heymen S, Wexner SD, Vickers D, et al. "Prospective, Randomized Trial Comparing Four Biofeedback Techniques For Patients With Constipation". *Dis Colon Rectum* 1999;42:1388–1393.

26. Horrobin DF. "Nutritional And Medical Importance Of Gamma-Linolenic Acid". *Prog Lipid Res*. 1992;31:163–194.

27. Juss, S.S. "Triphala - The Wonder Drug". Indian Med. Gazette. 1997, 131(6), 194-96.

28. Kruger MC, Coetzer H, de Winter R, et al. "Calcium, Gamma-Linolenic Acid And Eicosapentaenoic Acid Supplementation In Senile Osteoporosis". *Aging (Milano)*. 1998;10:385–394.

29. La Grange L, Wang M, Watkins R, et al. "Protective Effects Of The Flavonoid Mixture, Silymarin, On Fetal Rat Brain And Liver". *J Ethnopharmacol*. 1999;65:53–61.

30. Leventhal LJ, Boyce EG, Zurier RB. "Treatment Of Rheumatoid Arthritis With Gammalinolenic Acid". *Ann Intern Med*. 1993;119:867–873.

31. Lucena MI, Andrade RJ, de la Cruz JP, et al. "Effects Of Silymarin MZ-80 On Oxidative Stress In Patients With Alcoholic Cirrhosis. Results Of A Randomized, Double-Blind, Placebo-Controlled Clinical Study". *Int J Clin Pharmacol Ther*. 2002;40:2–8.

32. Merchant RE, Andre CA. "A Review Of Recent Clinical Trials Of The Nutritional Supplement *Chlorella pyrenoidosa* In The Treatment Of Fibromyalgia, Hypertension, And Ulcerative Colitis". *Altern Ther Health Med*. 2001;7:79–80, 82–91.

33. Meydani SN, Ha WK. "Immunological Effects Of Yogurt". *Am J Clin Nutr*. 2000;71:861–872.

34. Nakaya N, Homma Y, Goto Y. "Cholesterol Lowering Effect Of Spirulina". *Nutr Rep Int*. 1988;37:1329–1337.

35. Nobaek S, Johansson M-L, Molin G, et al. "Alteration Of Intestinal Microflora Is Associated With Reduction In Abdominal Bloating And Pain In Patients With Irritable Bowel Syndrome". *Am J Gastroenterol*. 2000;95:1231–1238.

36. Pedone CA, Bernabeu AO, Postaire ER, et al. "The Effect Of Supplementation With Milk Fermented By *Lactobacillus casei* (strain DN-114 001) On Acute Diarrhoea In Children Attending Day Care Centres". *Int J Clin Pract*. 1999;53:179–184.

Appendix B: References　　　　　　　　　　　　　　　　　　　　　　　　341

37. Quan ZF, Yang C, Li N, Li JS. "Effect Of Glutamine On Change In Early Postoperative Intestinal Permeability And Its Relation To Systemic Inflammatory Response". *World J Gastroenterol*. 2004;10:1992-4.

38. Rogers, SA; "Detoxify or Die". Sarasota, FL 2002, Sand Key Company p. 80.

39. Salmi HA, Sarna S. "Effect Of Silymarin On Chemical, Functional And Morphological Alterations Of The Liver. A double-blind controlled study". *Scand J Gastroenterol*. 1982;17:517–521.

40. Schoon, EJ; et al; "Low Serum and Bone Vitamin K Status in Patients with Longstanding Crohn's Disease: Another Pathogenetic Factor of Osteoporosis in Crohn's Disease?". *Gut* 2001;48:473-477.

41. Schulz V, Hansel R, Tyler VE. "Rational Phytotherapy: A Physicians' Guide to Herbal Medicine, 3rd ed". Berlin, Germany: Springer-Verlag; 1998:185.

42. Siguel EN. "Essential And *Trans* Fatty Acid Metabolism In Health And Disease". *Compr Ther*. 1994;20:500–510.

43. Singer P, Jaeger W, Berger I, et al. "Effects Of Dietary Oleic, Linoleic, And Alpha-Linolenic Acids On Blood Pressure, Serum Lipids, Lipoproteins And The Formation Of Eicosanoid Precursors In Patients With Mild Essential Hypertension". *J Hum Hypertens*. 1990;4:227–233.

44. Stengler, M. "The Natural Physician's guide to healing remedies". Alive Books, 1998

45. Stoll AL, Locke CA, Marangell LB, et al. "Omega-3 Fatty Acids And Bipolar Disorder: A Review". *Prostaglandins Leukot Essent Fatty Acids*. 1999;60:329–337.

46. Testino, G; et al; "Gastric Cyto-Secretory Correlations in Peptic Ulcer" *Hepatogastroenterology* 1999;46:2710-2.

47. Townsend D, et al; "The Importance Of Glutathione In Human Disease" *Biomedicine and Pharmacotherapy* 2003;57:145-155.

48. Tso, P; Crissinger, K; "Overview of Digestion and Absorption". Stipanuk, MH, ed; Biochemical and Physiological Aspects of Human Nutrition. Philadelphia WB Saunders Company 2000 pp. 75-90.

49. Van der Hulst RR, van Kreel BK, von Meyenfeldt MF, et al. "Glutamine And The Preservation Of Gut Integrity". *Lancet*. 1993;341:1363–1365.

50. Vani, T. et.al. "Antioxidant Properties Of The Ayurvedic Formulation Triphala And Its Constituents". *International J. Pharmacognosy*. 1997, 35(5), 313-17.

51. Webb, G. "Citrus Pectin May Inhibit Metastasis of Prostate Cancer". *HerbalGram*. 1997;40:17

52. Zimmerman, MR "Enzyme Power: Consider These Important Catalysts" *Taste for Life* 12/2004.

References for Chapter Seven

1. Anderton MJ; et al; "Pharmacokinetics and Tissue Disposition of Indole-3-Carbinol and its Acid Condensation Products After Oral Administration". *Clin Can Res* 2004; 10:5233-5241.

2. Adimoelja A. "Phytochemicals And The Breakthrough Of Traditional Herbs In The Management Of Sexual Dysfunctions". *Int J Androl*. 2000;23:82–84.

3. "*Angelica sinensis* (Dong quai) Monograph". *Altern Med Rev* 2004;9:429-433. (author not listed)

4. Baber RJ, Templeman C, Morton T, et al. "Randomized Placebo-Controlled Trial Of An Isoflavone Supplement And Menopausal Symptoms In Women". *Climacteric*. 1999;2:85–92.

5. Bell IR, Edman JS, Morrow FD, et al. "Brief communication. Vitamin B 1, B 2, and B 6 Augmentation Of Tricyclic Antidepressant Treatment In Geriatric Depression With Cognitive Dysfunction". *J Am Coll Nutr*. 1992;11:159–163.

6. Bendich, A; "The Potential for Dietary Supplements to Reduce Premenstrual Syndrome (PMS) Symptoms". *J Am Coll Nutr* 2000;19:3-12.

7. Bertone-Johnson ER; et al; "Calcium and Vitamin D Intake and Risk of Incident Premenstrual Syndrome". *Arch Intern Med* 2005;165:1246-52.

8. Brignall, MS; "Prevention and Treatment of Cancer with Indole-3-Carbinol". *Altern Med Rev* 2001;6:580-589.

9. Bradlow HL, Sepkovic DW, Telang NT, et al. "Multifunctional Aspects Of The Action Of Indole-3-Carbinol As An Antitumor Agent". *Ann N Y Acad Sci*. 1999;889:204–213.

10. Brown, DJ; "Herbal Prescriptions for Better Health". Rocklin, CA Prima Publishing 1995; pp 179-184, 167-172, 234-236,253-257.

11. Calabrese, G; "Nonalcoholic Compounds of Wine: The Phytoestrogen Resveratrol and Moderate Red Wine Consumption During Menopause Drugs". *Exptl Clin Res* 1999;25:111-114.

12. Cambell, J; et al; "Tomato Phytochemicals and Prostate Cancer Risk". *J Nutr* 2004;134:3486S-3492S.

13. Chase JE, Gidal BE. "Melatonin: Therapeutic Use In Sleep Disorders". *Ann Pharmacother*. 1997;31:1218–1226.

14. "*Cimicifuga racemosa* (Black cohosh) Monograph". *Altern Med Rev* 2003;8:186-189. (author not listed)

15. Curcio, JJ; et al; "The Potential Role of 5-Hydroxytryptophan for Hot Flash Reduction: A Hypothesis". *Altern Med Rev* 2005;10:216-221.

16. Dawson-Hughes B, Dallal GE, Krall EA, et al. "A Controlled Trial Of The Effect Of Calcium Supplementation On Bone Density In Postmenopausal Women". *N Engl J Med*. 1990;323:878–883.

17. Derman O; et al; "Premenstrual Syndrome and Associated Symptoms in Adolescent Girls". *Eur J Obstet Gynecol Reprod Biol* 2004;116:201-6.

18. Freeland-Graves JH. "Manganese: An Essential Nutrient For Humans". *Nutr Today*. 1988;23:13–19

19. Folkard S, Arendt J, Clark M. "Can Melatonin Improve Shift Workers' Tolerance Of The Night Shift? Some Preliminary Findings". *Chronobiol Int*. 1993;10:315–320.

20. Fraschini F, Cesarani A, Alpini D, et al. "Melatonin Influences Human Balance". *Biol Signals Recept*. 1999;8:111–119.

21. Fugh-Berman, A; Kronenberg, F; "Complementary and Alternative Medicine (CAM) in Reproductive-Age Women: A Review of Randomized Controlled Trials". *Reprod Toxicol* 2003;17:137-52.

22. "Gamma-Linolenic Acid (GLA) Monograph". *Alt Med Rev* 2004;9:70-78.

23. Giovannucci E, Ascherio A, Rimm EB, et al. "Intake Of Carotenoids And Retinol In Relation To Risk Of Prostate Cancer". *J Natl Cancer Inst*. 1995;87:1767–1776.

24. Hardy, ML; "Herbs of Special Interest to Women". *J Am Pharm Assoc* (Wash) 2000;40:234-42.

25. Hemila H. "Vitamin C and Common Cold Incidence: A Review Of Studies With Subjects Under Heavy Physical Stress". *Int J Sports Med*. 1996;17:379–383.

26. Hirata JD, Swiersz LM, Zell B, et al. "Does Dong Quai Have Estrogenic Effects In Postmenopausal Women? A double-blind, placebo-controlled trial". *Fertil Steril*. 1997;68:981–986.

27. Hudson, T; *Women's Encyclopedia of Natural Medicine* Los Angeles, CA Keats Publishing 1999; pp 245-255, 135-191.

28. Howes JB, Sullivan D, Lai N, et al. "The Effects Of Dietary Supplementation With Isoflavones From Red Clover On The Lipoprotein Profiles Of Post Menopausal Women With Mild To Moderate Hypercholesterolaemia". *Atherosclerosis*. 2000;152:143–147.

29. "Indole-3-Carbinol Monograph". *Altern Med Rev* 2005;10:337-342.

30. Klein, KO; et al; "Estrogen Bioactivity in Fo-Ti and Other Herbs Used for Their Estrogen-like Effects as Determined by a Recombinant Cell Bioassay", *J Clin Endocrinol Metab* 2003;88:4077-4079.

31. Kohno, H; et al; "Pomegranate Seed Oil Rich in Conjugated Linolenic Acid Suppresses Chemically Induced Colon Carcinogenesis in Rats". *Cancer Sci* 2004;95:481-486.

32. L-Arginine Monograph *Altern Med Rev* 2005;10:139-147. (author not listed)

33. Lindsey, LLM; et al; "Use of Dietary Supplements Containing Folic Acid Among Women of Childbearing Age – United States". 2005 *MMWR Weekly Centers for Disease Control* 10/05/2005;54:955-958.

34. Liu, J; et al; "Isolation of Linoleic Acid as an Estrogenic Compound form the Fruits of *Vitex agnus-castus* L. (chaste-berry)". *Phytomedicine* 2004;11:18-23.

35. Loch, G; et al; "Treatment of Premenstrual Syndrome with a Phytopharmaceutical Formulation Containing Vitex agnus castus". *J Womens Health Gend Based Med* 2000;9:315-20.

36. Longtin, R; "The Pomegranate: Nature's Power Fruit". *J Nat Can Inst* 2003;95:346-348.

37. "L-Theanine Monograph". *Alt Med Rev* 2005;10:136-138. (author not listed)

38. "Lycopene Monograph". *Altern Med Rev* 2003;8:336-342. (author not listed)

39. Marks LS, Partin AW, Epstein JI, et al. "Effects Of A Saw Palmetto Herbal Blend In Men With Symptomatic Benign Prostatic Hyperplasia". *J Urol*. 2000;163:1451–1456.

40. Morales AJ, Nolan JJ, Nelson JC, et al. " Effects Of Replacement Dose Of Dehydroepiandrosterone In Men And Women Of Advancing Age". *J Clin Endocrinol Metab*. 1994;78:1360–1367.

41. Mroueh A. "Effect of Arginine On Oligospermia. *Fertil Steril*". 1970;21:217–219.

42. Nagata, C; et al; "Effect of Soymilk Consumption on Serum Estrogen and Androgen Concentrations in Japanese Men". *Can Epidemiol Biomarkers Prev* 2001;10:179-184.

43. Nagata, C; et al; "Soy Product Intake and Hot Flashes in Japanese Women: Results From a Community-Based Prospective Study". *Am J Epidemiol* 2001;153:790-793.

44. Norman, AW; Litwack, G; "*Hormones* 2nd edition". San Diego, CA Academic Press 1997; 5-86, 341-386.

45. Osmers, R; et al; "Efficacy and Safety of Isopropanolic Black Cohosh Extract for Climacteric Symptoms". *Obstet Gynecol* 2005;105:1074-83.

46. Pert, CB; "Molecules of Emotion". New York, NY Touchstone 1997 p 23.

47. Philp, HA; Hot Flashes – "A Review of the Literature on Alternative and Complimentary Treatment Approaches". *Altern Med Rev* 2003;8:284-302.

48. Poldinger W, Calanchini B, Schwarz W. "A Functional-Dimensional Approach To Depression: Serotonin Deficiency As A Target Syndrome In A Comparison Of 5-Hydroxytryptophan And Fluvoxamine". *Psychopathology.* 1991;24:53–81.

49. "Pygeum africanum (*Prunus africana*)". Monograph *Altern Med Rev* 2002;7:71-74.

50. Regelson W, Loria R, Kalimi M. "Dehydroepiandrosterone (DHEA)—the "Mother Steroid." I". Immunologic Action. *Ann N Y Acad Sci.* 1994;719:553–563.

51. Sahelian, R. "Mind Boosters; A Guide To Natural Supplements That Enhance Your Mind, Memory And Mood". New York St. Martin's Griffin; 1st ed edition (July 7, 2000)

52. Schmidt DR, Sobota AE. "An Examination Of The Anti-Adherence Activity Of Cranberry Juice On Urinary And Nonurinary Bacterial Isolates". *Microbios.* 1988;55:173–181.

53. Strous RD, Maayan R, Lapidus R, et al. "Dehydroepiandrosterone Augmentation In The Management Of Negative, Depressive, And Anxiety Symptoms In Schizophrenia". *Arch Gen Psychiatry.* 2003;60:133–141.

54. Stewart A. "Clinical And Biochemical Effects Of Nutritional Supplementation On The Premenstrual Syndrome". *J Reprod Med.* 1987;32:435–441.

55. Suhner A, Schlagenhauf P, Johnson R, et al. "Comparative Study To Determine The Optimal Melatonin Dosage Form For The Alleviation Of Jet Lag". *Chronobiol Int.* 1998;15:655

56. Tullson PC, Terjung RL. "Adenine Nucleotide Synthesis In Exercising And Endurance-Trained Skeletal Muscle". *Am J Physiol.* 1991;261(2 pt 1):C342–C347.

57. Yuan, CS; Bieber, EJ "Textbook of Complimentary and Alternative Medicine". Boca Raton, FL Parthenon Publishing Group 2003; pp 319-341.

References for Chapter Eight

1. Abou-Seif, MA, Youssef AA. "Evaluation Of Some Biochemical Changes In Diabetic Patients". *Clin Chim Acta.* 2004 Aug 16;346(2):161-70.

2. Ammon HPT, Wahl MA. "Pharmacology of *Curcuma longa*". *Planta Med.* 1991;57:1–7.

3. Anderson, JJB; "Oversupplementation of Vitamin A and Osteoporotic Fractures in the Elderly: To Supplement or Not To Supplement With Vitamin A". *J Bone Min Res* 2002;17:1359-63.

4. Beiswanger, BB, Boneta AE, Mau MS, Katz BP, Proskin HM, Stookey GK. "The effect of chewing sugar-free gum after meals on clinical caries incidence". *J. Am. Dent. Assoc.* 1998;129:1623-6.

5. Benton D, Fordy J, Haller J. "The Impact Of Long-Term Vitamin Supplementation On Cognitive Functioning". *Psychopharmacology.* 1995;117:298-305.

6. Booth, SL; et al; "Vitamin K Intake and Bone Mineral Density in Women and Men". *Am J Clin Nutr* 2003;77:512-6.

7. Bostick RM, Fosdick L, Grandits GA, et al. "Effect Of Calcium Supplementation On Serum Cholesterol And Blood Pressure: A Randomized, Double-Blind, Placebo-Controlled, Clinical Trial". *Arch Fam Med.* 2000;9:31–39.

8. Chandra RK. "Effect Of Vitamin And Trace-Element Supplementation On Cognitive Function In Elderly Subjects". *Nutrition.* 2001;17:709-712.

9. Choi J, Rees HD, Weintraub ST, et al. "Oxidative Modifications And Aggregation Of Cu,Zn-Superoxide Dismutase Associated With Alzheimer And Parkinson Diseases". *J Biol Chem.* 2005 Mar 25;280(12):11648-55.

10. Cohen M, Wolfe R, Mai T, et al. "A Randomized, Double Blind, Placebo Controlled Trial Of A Topical Cream Containing Glucosamine Sulfate, Chondroitin Sulfate, And Camphor For Osteoarthritis Of The Knee". *J Rheumatol.* 2003;30:523–528.

11. Davies KM, Heaney RP, Recker RR, et al. "Calcium Intake And Body Weight". *J Clin Endocrinol Metab.* 2000;85:4635–4638.

12. Davies, KM; et al; "Determinants of Endogenous Calcium Entry into the Gut" *Am J Clin Nutr* 2004;80:919-23.

13. Dawson-Hughes B, Dallal GE, Krall EA, et al. "A Controlled Trial Of The Effect Of Calcium Supplementation On Bone Density In Postmenopausal Women". *N Engl J Med.* 1990;323:878–883.

14. Dawson-Hughes, B; et al; "Effect of Vitamin D Supplementation on Wintertime and Overall Bone Loss in Healthy Postmenopausal Women". *Ann Intern Med* 1991;115:505-512.

15. Ervin RB, Kennedy-Stephenson J. "Mineral Intakes Of Elderly Adult Supplement And Non-Supplement Users In The Third National Health And Nutrition Examination Survey". *J Nutr.* 2002;132:3422–3427.

16. Hamdy, RC; "Osteoporosis 2002: Headline News". *South Med J* 2002;95:567-568.

17. Hayes, Catherine, DMD; DMSc. "The Effect Of Non-Cariogenic Sweeteners On The Prevention Of Dental Caries: A Review Of Evidence". Harvard School Of Dental Medicine (from website)

18. Heaney, RP; et al; "Calcium Fortification Systems Differ in Bioavailability". *J Am Diet Assoc* 2005;105:807-9.

19. Heaney, RP; et al; "Advances in Therapy for Osteoporosis". *Clin Med Res* 2003;1:93-99.

20. Heaney, RP; "Functional Indices of Vitamin D Status and Ramifications of Vitamin D Deficiency". *Am J Clin Nutr* 2004;80(suppl):1706S-9S.

21. Heaney, RP; "The Vitamin D Requirement in Health and Disease". *J Steroid Biochem Mol Biol* 2005;97:13-19.

22. Heaney, RP; Weaver, CM; "Newer Perspectives on Calcium Nutrition and Bone Quality". *J Am Coll Nutr* 2005;24(6 Suppl):574S-81S.

23. Hungerford DS. "Treating Osteoarthritis With Chondroprotective Agents". *Orthopedic Special Edition*. 1998;4:39–42.

24. Ilich-Ernst, J; et al; "Critical Factors for Bone Health in Women Across the Age Span: How Important is Muscle Mass?". *Women's Health eJournal* 2002;7(3)

25. Jugdaohsingh, R; et al; "Dietary Silicon Intake and Absorption". *Am J Clin Nutr* 2002;75:887-93.

26. Kraemer WJ; et al; "The Effects Of Cetylated Fatty Acid Cream On Pain, Range Of Motion And Quality Of Life Of Patients With Osteoarthritis". *Jour of Rheu*. 2003

27. Kraemer WJ; et al.; "Effect of a Cetylated Fatty Acid Topical Cream on Functional Mobility and Quality of Life of Patients with Osteoarthritis". *Jour of Rheu* 2005;.

28. Krall, EA; et al; "Calcium and Vitamin D Supplements Reduce Tooth Loss in the Elderly". *Am J Med* 2001;111:452-6.

29. Kritz-Silverstein, D; et al; "Isoflavones and Cognitive Function in Older Women: The Soy and Postmenopausal health in Aging (SOPHIA) Study". *Menopause* 2003;10:196-202.

30. Kulkarni, RR; et al; "Efficacy of an Ayurvedic Formulation in Rheumatoid Arthritis: A Double-Blind, Placebo-Controlled, Cross Over Study". *Indian J Pharmacol* 1992;24:98-101.

31. Lanhan-New, SA; "Nutritional Influences on Bone Health: An Update on Current Research and Clinical Implications". *Medscape* 2006.

32. Lewis NM, Marcus MS, Behling AR, et al. "Calcium Supplements And Milk: Effects On Acid-Base Balance And On Retention Of Calcium, Magnesium, And Phosphorus". *Am J Clin Nutr*. 1989;49:527–533.

33. Lipkin, M; "Early Development of Cancer Chemoprevention Clinical Trials: Studies of Dietary Calcium as a Chemopreventive Agent for Human Subjects". *Eur J Cancer Prev* 2002;11 Suppl 2:S65-70.

34. Lowe, NM; et al; "Is There a Potential Therapeutic Value of Copper and Zinc for Osteoporosis?". *Proc Nutr Soc* 2002;61:181-5.

35. McCarty, MF; "The Neglect of Glucosamine as a Treatment for Osteoarthritis – A Personal Perspective". *Med Hypothesis* 1994;42:323-327.

36. Miller JZ, Smith DL, Flora L, et al. "Calcium Absorption From Calcium Carbonate And A New Form Of Calcium (CCM) In Healthy Male And Female Adolescents". *Am J Clin Nutr*. 1988;48:1291–1294.

37. Minihane AM, Fairweather-Tait SJ. "Effect Of Calcium Supplementation On Daily Nonheme-Iron Absorption And Long-Term Iron Status". *Am J Clin Nutr*. 1998;68:96–102.

38. Nakamura, Ryo, Gian Paolo Kittarru, et al; *Proc Nat Acad Sci* 1974;71:1456-1460

39. New, SA; "Calcium Supplementation in Postmenopausal Women Medscape". Ob/Gyn & Women's Health 2003; 8(2) *www.medscape.com*

40. New, SA; "Dietary Influences on Bone Mass and Bone Metabolism: Further Evidence of a Positive Link Between Fruit and Vegetable Consumption and Bone Health?". *Am J Clin Nutr* 2000;71:42-51.

41. NIH Consensus Development Panel on Osteoporosis Prevention, Diagnosis, and Therapy, March 7-29, 2000: Highlights of the Conference. *http://womenshealth.medscape.com*

42. Noack W, Fischer M, Forster KK, et al. "Glucosamine Sulfate In Osteoarthritis Of The Knee". *Osteoarthritis Cartilage*. 1994;2:51–59.

43. Norman, AW; "Intestinal Calcium Absorption: A Vitamin D-Hormone-Mediated Adaptive Response". *Am J Clin Nutr* 1990;51:290-300.

44. Persiani, S; et al; "Glucosamine Oral Bioavailability and Plasma Pharmacokinetics After Increasing Doses of Crystalline Glucosamine Sulfate in Man". *Osteoarthritis Cartilage* 2005;12:1041-9.

45. Promislow, JH; "Protein Consumption and Bone Mineral Density in the Elderly: The Rancho Bernardo Study". *Am J Epidemiol* 2002;155:636-44.

46. Qiu, GX; et al; "A Multi-Central, Randomized, Controlled Clinical Trial of Glucosamine Hydrochloride/Sulfate in the Treatment of Knee Osteoarthritis". *Zhonghua Yi Xue Za Zhi* 2005;85:3067-70.

47. Rafferty, K; et al; "Potassium Intake and the Calcium Economy". *J Am Coll Nutr* 2005;24:99-106.

48. Reginster JY, Deroisy R, Rovati L, et al. "Long-term Effects Of Glucosamine Sulphate On Osteoarthritis Progression: A Randomised, Placebo-Controlled Clinical Trial". *Lancet*. 2001;357:251–256.

49. Russell, R; ed; et al; "Dietary Reference Intakes of Boron, Copper, Manganese and Zinc". Institute of Medicine 2001 *National Academy Press*.

50. Ryder, KM; et al; "Magnesium Intake from Food and Supplements is Associated with Bone Mineral Density in Healthy Older White Subjects". *J Am Geriatr Soc* 2005; 53:1875-80.

Appendix B: References

51. Sellmeyer, DE; et al; "A High Ratio of Dietary Animal to Vegetable Protein Increases the Rate of Bone Loss and the Risk of Fracture in Postmenopausal Women". *Am J Clin Nutr* 2001;73:118-22.

52. Shield MJ. "Anti-inflammatory Drugs And Their Effects On Cartilage Synthesis And Renal Function". *Eur J Rheumatol Inflamm.* 1993;13:7–16.

53. Simanek, V; et al; "The Efficacy of Glucosamine and Chondroitin Sulfate in the Treatment of Osteoarthritis: Are These Saccharides Drugs or Nutraceuticals?". *Biomed Pap Med Fac Univ Palacky* Olomouc, Czech Repub 2005;1-6.

54. Siris, ES; et al; "The Effect of Age and Bone Mineral Density on the Absolute, Excess, and Relative Risk of Fracture in Postmenopausal Women Aged 50-99: ". Results from the National Osteoporosis Risk Assessment (NORA) *Osteoporosis Int.* 2006; Jan 4:1-10.

55. Sreejayan N, Rao MNA. "Free Radical Scavenging Activity Of Curcuminoids." *Arzneimittelforschung.* 1996;46:169–171.

56. Stang J, Story MT, Harnack L, et al. "Relationships Between Vitamin And Mineral Supplement Use, Dietary Intake, And Dietary Adequacy Among Adolescents". *J Am Diet Assoc.* 2000;100:905-910.

57. Stendig-Lindberg, G; et al; "Trabecular Bone Density in a Two Year Controlled Trial of Peroral Magnesium in Osteoporosis". *Magnes Res* 1993;6:155-63.

58. Stipanuk, MH "Biochemical and Physiological Aspects of Human Nutrition". Philadelphia PA WB Saunders Company 2000 pp 741 – 759, 827

59. Suleiman, MS; "New Concepts in the Cardioprotective Action of Magnesium and Taurine During the Calcium Paradox and Ischaemia of the Heart". *Magnes Res* 1994;7:295-312.

60. Tamir, E; Brenner, S; "Gender Differences in Collagen Diseases". *SKINmed* 2003;2:113-117.

61. Towheed, TE; et al; "Glucosamine Therapy for Treating Osteoarthritis". *Cochrane Database Syst Rev* 2005;2:CD002946.

62. Tucker, K; "Regular Cola Consumption Linked to Lower Bone Density in Women". American Society for Bone and Mineral Research 25th Meeting *Abstract SU259* 9/21/2003.

63. Vanderhaeghe, L. "Get a grip on Arthritis". Bearing Marketing Communications, 2004

64. Vouldoukis I, Conti M, Krauss P et al. "Supplementation With Gliadin-Combined Plant Superoxide Dismutase Extract Promotes Antioxidant Defences And Protects Against Oxidative Stress". *Phytother Res.* 2004 Dec;18(12):957-62.

65. Weiss, LA; et al; "Ratio of n-6 to n-3 Fatty Acids and Bone Mineral Density in Older Adults: The Rancho Bernardo Study". *Am J Clin Nutr* 2005;81:934-8.

66. Wozinicki, K; AAOMS: "Periodontal Disease Starts Young, Increases Pregnancy Risks". *www.medpagetoday.com.* 2006.

67. Wu, K; et al; "Calcium Intake and Risk of Colon Cancer in Women and Men". *J Natl Cancer Inst* 2002;94:437-46.

Index

A

Abdominal pain, 324. *See also* Digestion; Malabsorption syndrome

Abraham, Guy, M. D., 224

Acetylcholine, breakdown of, 48, 70

Acetyl L-carnitine (ACL), 54–55, 68, 140, 317

Acidophilus, 91, 117, 187–191, 319

Acid Redux™ (antacid), 196–200, 313

Acid reflux, 42, 124, 198

Acne, 20, 155, 204, 213. *See also* Skin

Acute stress, 39–40, 45–48, 73

Adaptogenic herbs, 46–48, 287–288

    See also Astragalus (*Astragalus membranaceus*)

Adenosine diphosphate (ADP), 265

Adenosine triphosphate (ATP), 255–256, 265

    coenzyme Q10 (CoQ10) and, 135

    glucose converted into, 77

    pantothenic acid and, 112

    phosphorous, created by, 264

    ribose and, 256

    SAME, creation of, 59

Adenosyl methionine. *See* S-adenosyl methionine (SAMe)

Adolescents

    atherosclerotic plaque buildup in, 108

    bone growth in, 261

    metabolic syndrome in, 102–103

    zinc, use of, 155

ADP (adenosine diphosphate), 265

Adrenal gland, 40, 42, 219

Adrenocorticotropin (ACTH), 67

Advanced glycation end products (AGEs), 78–79

Age-related macular degeneration, 17, 20, 23, 26, 145. *See also* Vision

Age-related memory loss, supplements for

    carotenoids, 17

    DHEA (dehydroepiandrostone), 239

    ginkgo biloba, 70–72

    l-carnitine, 140

    phosphatidyl serine (PS), 66–67

    Vitamin E, 19

AGEs (advanced glycation end products), 78–79

Aging. *See also* Age-related macular degeneration; Menopause

    andropause, 237–244

    benign prostate hyperplasia and, 245

    chronic inflammation and, 152

    oxidative stress and, 49

    pH of body fluids and, 196

Aging, supplements for

    advanced glycation end products (AGEs), 79

    alpha lipoic acid (ALA), 53

    carotenoids, 16

    coenzyme Q10 (CoQ10), 137

    DHEA (dehydroepiandrostone), 239

    grape seed extract, 143, 144

    green tea, 130

    hyaluronic acid (HA), 213

    melatonin, 253, 254

    pomegranate seed extract, 55

    pycnogenol, 128

    quercetin, 169

    s-adenosyl methionine (SAMe), 59–60

    selenium, 27

    superoxide dismutase (SOD), 50–51

    Vitamin C, 23

AIDS, 161

Ajoene, 114–115

ALA. *See* Alpha lipoic acid (ALA)

Alcohol intake

    benign prostate hyperplasia and, 245

    blood pressure, effect on, 106

    carotenoids, use of, 18

    estrogen levels raised by, 237

    HDL cholesterol, effect on, 106

    premenstrual syndrome, effect on, 223

    stomach, alcohol absorbed by, 181

Alcoholism, supplements to treat, 69, 89, 167, 256

Aldosterone, 219, 221, 222

Allergies, causes of, 177

Allergies, supplements for, 166–175

    Eleuthero senticosus, 48

    forskolin, 174

    grape seed extract, 145

    NAC (N-acetyl cysteine), 166–168

    nettle, 172

    pycnogenol, 126, 128, 172–173

    quercetin, 169–171, 175

    spirulina (blue-green algae), 212

    Vitamin C, 23, 171–172

Allicin, 114–115

Alliin, 114

Allium sativum.See Garlic (*Allium sativum*)

Aloe (*Aloe vera*), 299, 323

Alpha-carotene, 14, 16, 17

Alpha glycerylphosphorylcholine (alpha GPC), 68

Alpha linolenic acid (flaxseed oil), 21, 69, 203–205, 320

Alpha lipoic acid (ALA), 13, 316

    for chronic inflammation and autoimmunity, 158

    companion supplements, 22, 51, 54–55, 121, 129, 138, 145, 157

    for oral health, 298

    for oxidative stress and aging, 52–55

347

7-S YNDROME H EALING

Ashwaganda, 48
astragalus, 160
forskolin, 173
n-acetyl cysteine (NAC), 167
quercetin, 170–171
B-sitosterol, 251
Building and maintaining, nutrients for
minerals, 32–34
vitamin D, 29–31
vitamin K, 31–32
Burns, healing. *See* Wound healing
Bursae, 268
Butcher's broom (*Ruscus aculeatus*), 146–148, 323
B vitamins, 6, 36–37, 150, 183, 211, 307, 314–315. *See also*
Choline; Inositol
B-2 (*See* Riboflavin)
B-3 (*See* Niacin)
B-5 (*See* Pantothenic acid)
B-6, 134–135, 192, 224, 227–228, 274–275
B-12, 134, 135, 182, 211, 233, 307, 314
companion supplements, 12, 61–62, 113, 138, 142, 157
magnesium, activated by, 274
metabolism, role in regulating, 34–37
TMG and, 133, 134

C

Calcium, 32, 33, 308, 311
ability to absorb, 30
bone health and, 268–278, 290
cardiovascular function and, 150
companion supplements, 58, 148, 171, 227
in dong quai, 233
in garlic, 115
home test for supplement, 271
magnesium and, 274–275, 282–283, 289
muscle function and, 263
premenstrual syndrome, effect on, 224
Calmness, supplements for, 46, 62, 69, 256–257
Camellia sinensis. *See* Green tea and green tea extract
(EGCG)
Cancer. *See also* Breast cancer; Colon cancer; Prostate
cancer
black cohosh use and, 233
DHEA (dehydroepiandrostone) use and, 241
IGF-1 and, 78
menopause and, 231
stress, effect of, 42
Cancer, supplements to treat
astragalus, 161
bovine colostrum, 166
carotenoids, 16
for chemotherapy, 47, 257
coenzyme Q10 (CoQ10), 136
flaxseed, 203
garlic, 115–116
grape seed extract, 144
green tea, 129–130
indole-3 carbinol, 235–236
lycopene, 247
multiple vitamin/mineral supplement, 6
n-acetyl cysteine (NAC), 167

omega-3 fatty acids, 124
quercetin, 169–170
spirulina (blue-green algae), 212
Vitamin A, 10
Vitamin C, 23
Vitamin D, 30–31
Vitamin E, 20
Candida albicans, 96, 185–186, 189
Cardiovascular syndrome, x, 105–150. *See also* Cardiovascular system
gender issues, cardiovascular disease, 106–108
heart energetics, supplements for, 135–143, 150
homocysteine regulators, 133–135, 150
indicators of, 105
inflammation and protecting arteries, 16, 56, 117–132,
149–150, 153–154, 176
other syndromes affected by, 149–150
peripheral circulation, supplements for, 146–148
restless legs, supplements for, 143–148
risk factors for, 106
varicose veins, supplements for, 143–146
Cardiovascular system, 102, 241. *See also* Atherosclerosis;
Blood lipids; Blood pressure, high; Cardiovascular syndrome; Cholesterol levels; Heart disease; Stroke
gender differences, 106–108, 231
insulin resistance, effect of, 78
menopause and, 231
metabolic syndrome and, 75, 103–104
peripheral veins, 143–148, 150
soluble fiber, role of, 92
stress, effect of, 40
superoxide free radicals, effect of, 50
Cardiovascular system, supplements for
alpha lipoic acid (ALA), 54
artery protection, 126–132
black cohosh, 232
carotenoids, 14–16, 18
CLA (conjugated linoleic acid), 87
coenzyme Q10 (CoQ10), 135–136
DHEA (dehydroepiandrostone), 238, 240
flaxseed, 203–204
forskolin, 173–174
garlic, 114–116
ginkgo biloba, 71–72
grape seed extract, 145
green tea, 130–131
l-carnitine, 140
magnesium, 142
milk thistle, 90
muira puama, 243
n-acetyl cysteine (NAC), 168
omega-3 fatty acids, 122–123
pantethine, 97–98, 112
policosanol, 111
prickly ash bark, 148
pycnogenol, 126–129
quercetin, 170
red Chinese yeast, 120
selenium, 27
TMG, 133
Vitamin E, 19, 125
Carnisine, 317
Carnitine. *See* Acetyl L-carnitine (ACL); L-carnitine
Carotenes, 13, 126, 307

spirulina (blue-green algae), 211
zinc, 156
Fatty acids, 183. *See also* Celadrin®; Essential fatty acids (EFA)
  for arthritis treatment, 278
  for heart muscle energy, 265
  in muira puama, 242–243
  in saw palmetto, 244
  stomach, absorbed by, 181
  transfer to cells of, 139–140
FDA. *See* Food and Drug Administration (FDA)
Federal Trade Commission, 5
Feedback mechanism, 217
Females. *See* Women
Female sex steroids, 221
Fenugreek (*Trigonella foenum-graecum*), 95, 324
Fertility, effect of insulin on, 78
Fertility, supplements for
  carotenoids, 15
  chaste tree, 227
  coenzyme Q10 (CoQ10), 137
  DHEA (dehydroepiandrostone), 238, 240
  flaxseed, 203, 204
  L-arginine, 243
  n-acetyl cysteine (NAC), 168
  Vitamin E, 20
  zinc, 156
Fever, 70
Fever blisters. *See* Cold sores
Feverfew, 57, 58
Fiber, 91–92, 200–202
Fish oils, 121–125, 207, 288–289, 321
Flavonoids, 13, 25, 308. *See also* Isoflavones
  in chaste tree berries, 224
  companion supplements, 24, 25, 132, 146, 148, 229, 250, 276–277
  in garlic, 115
  in ginkgo biloba, 71
  in grape seed extract, 143–144
  in pycnogenol extracts, 172
  quercetin, 169, 175
  in red clover, 232
  silymarin, 88
  in St. John's wort, 63
  in tribulus, 241
Flaxseed (*Linum usitatissimum*), 202–207, 320
Flaxseed oil. *See* Alpha linolenic acid (flaxseed oil)
Flu. *See* Cold and flu symptoms
Fluoride, 32
Fluorine, 33
Foam cells, 118
Folic acid, 37, 134–135, 233, 298, 307, 314
  companion supplements, 61–62, 134
  digestive system, absorption by, 182
Follicle-stimulating hormone (FSH), 219, 221
Food and Drug Administration (FDA), 3–5, 121–122
Food and Nutrition Board, National Academy of Sciences, 6–8, 92, 97
Food factors, 319–322
Foods. *See also* Diet
  acid, neutral, and alkaline, 195–196
  acidophilus in, 188
  for bone health, 269
  calcium in, 270

carotenoids in, 14–15
CLA (conjugated linoleic acid) in, 85
cooking, effect on food enzymes of, 190
dysmenorrhea and, 226
fiber, sources of, 91–02
functional, 3–4
HDL cholesterol and, 106
health foods, development of, 3
indole-3 carbinol in, 235
inflammatory bowel diseases and, 194–195
lycopene in, 247
as multiple base, 308
premenstrual syndrome, effect on, 223–224
quercetin in, 169
sodium in, 276
stress management, role in, 45
vanadium in, 97
Vitamin A in, 9, 10
Vitamin K in, 32
Forskolin, 173–174, 324
FOS (fructooligosaccharides), 206, 320
Fo-ti (*Polygonum multiflorum*), 232, 236, 324
Free radicals, 45, 73, 193, 238. *See also* Antioxidants
  alpha lipoic acid (ALA), effect of, 52, 53
  blood vessels, attacks on, 127, 149 (*See also* Inflammation, of blood vessels)
  CLA (conjugated linoleic acid), effect of, 87
  coenzyme Q10 (CoQ10), effect of, 135–137
  ester-C, effect of, 132
  garlic, effect of, 116
  pycnogenol, effect of, 129
  singlet oxygen radicals, elimination of, 15
  superoxide dismutase (SOD), effect of, 50, 288
Fructooligosaccharides (FOS), 206, 320
FSH. *See* Follicle-stimulating hormone (FSH)

G

GABA. *See* Gamma aminobutyric acid (GABA)
Gall bladder, 181, 182–183, 201
Gamma aminobutyric acid (GABA), 68, 69, 256–257, 317
Gamma globulin, 166
Gamma linoleic acid (GLA), 207–211, 226, 320
Garlic (*Allium sativum*), 114–117, 125, 138, 324
Gastric reflux. *See* Acid reflux
Gastrointestinal gland, 219
Gastrointestinal tract, 186. *See also* Digestion; Malabsorption syndrome
Genistein, 236
GERD. *See* Acid reflux
Germanium, 115
Ginger (*Zingiber officinale*), 138, 325
Gingeval disease. *See* Periodontal disease
Ginkgo flavone glycosides, 71
Ginkgo (*Ginkgo biloba*), 62, 70–72, 309, 325
Ginkgolides, 71
Ginseng (*Panax ginseng*), 325
GLA (gamma linoleic acid). *See* Gamma linoleic acid (GLA)
Glaucoma, 23, 173
Glisodin®, 288
Glucagon, 78

7-SYNDROME HEALING

Isoprenoids, 220
Itchiness, 128

J

Jet lag, 254
Joints, 268. *See also* Arthritis
  inflammatory diseases, 153
    injury and recovery, 284–289
  leaky gut syndrome and, 186
  pain, 278–284
  periodontal disease and, 119
  superoxide free radicals, effect of, 50
Joints, supplements for, 280–289. *See also* Chondroitin;
  Glucosamine
  calcium and magnesium, 282–283
  Celadrin®, 285–289
  green tea, 131
  hyaluronic acid (HA), 283
  manganese, 275, 283
  omega-3 fatty acids, 123, 124
  quercetin, 169
  s-adenosyl methionine (SAMe), 60–62
  TMG, 133
  Vitamin C, 22–23

K

Kellogg, W. K. and John, 3
Kelp, 321
7-keto DHEA. *See* DHEA (dehydroepiandrostone)
  (7-keto)
Kidneys, 219, 249

L

Labels, supplements
  acidophilus, 189
  disclaimer, required, 5
  garlic supplements, 114
  grape seed extracts, 145
  L-carnitine, 141
  omega-3 fatty acids, label claim for, 121–122
  protein powder, sweetened, 101
  U.S. Food and Drug Administration rules, 4–5
Lactobacillus acidophilus, 187
Lactoferrin, 166
Lansoprazole, xii
L-arginine, 243–244, 317
Latin names, herbs, 5
Laurifoline, 148
L-carnisine, 317
L-carnitine, 139–142, 150, 317
  companion supplements, 54–55, 88, 138, 142
LDL cholesterol, 103, 105, 149, 153. *See also* Cholesterol
  levels
  atherosclerosis, role in, 117
  fiber, role of, 91
  guidelines for, 108
  smoking and, 118
  stress, effect of, 47
LDL cholesterol, supplements for
  Ashwaganda, 48

carotenoids, 16
cinnamon, 96
CLA (conjugated linoleic acid), 87
coenzyme Q10 (CoQ10), 135
garlic, 115
green tea, 131
Gymnema sylvestre, 95
omega-3 fatty acids, 123
pantethine, 112
policosanol, 110
pycnogenol, 127–128
quercetin, 170
selenium, 27
Vitamin C, 24, 250
Vitamin E, 19, 125
Leaky gut syndrome, 166, 186–194, 215
Lean body mass, 106, 268–269
Lecithin, 21, 68, 125, 138, 241
Legs, restless, 143–148, 150
L-glutamine, 191, 193–194
Licorice. *See* Deglycyrrhized licorice (DGL)
Ligaments, 267–268, 275
Lignans, 236
Linoleic acid, 225–226
Lipid metabolism, 47, 66, 86, 97, 111
Lipids. *See* Blood lipids; Triglycerides
Lipitor®, 12
Lipoic acid, 13, 126
Lipoproteins, 86
Liver function, 181–183. *See also* Detoxification, liver
  premenstrual syndrome and, 224
  statin drugs, effect of, 109–110
Liver function, supplements for
  alpha lipoic acid (ALA), 52, 54
  astragalus, 161
  garlic, 115
  green tea, 130, 131
  indole-3 carbinol, 235
  milk thistle, 88–89
  pycnogenol, 128, 129
  red yeast rice, 120, 121
  s-adenosyl methionine (SAMe), 61
Lovastatin, 110
L-theanine, 257
Lungs. *See* Respiratory system
Lupus, 124, 165
Lutein, 13, 15–17, 23, 25, 157
Lycopene, 13, 15–17, 247, 316
Lymphatic system, 148
Lysine, 91, 142, 188

M

Maca, 241
Macro minerals, 32
Macrophages, 28, 119, 151, 153, 177
Magnesium, 32, 33, 142, 150, 308, 311
  in dong quai, 233
  in garlic, 115
  for heart muscle energy, 265
  premenstrual syndrome, effect on, 224
  Vitamin D use and, 31
  ZMA, 101–102, 313

stress, effect of, 42, 80, 81
supplements to control (*See* Weight loss)
Ocimum sanctum(holy basil), 287, 325
Octacosanol, 321
Olea europaea(olive leaf extract), 165, 326
Oleuropein, 165
Oligomeric proanthocyanidin complexes (OPCs), 126, 143–145, 172
Olive leaf extract (*Olea europaea*), 165, 326
Omega-3 fatty acids, 69, 158, 202, 203, 321
as blood thinners, 123, 124
companion supplements, 21, 111, 121, 125, 157
DHEA (dehydroepiandrostone), effect of, 241
essential role of, 122
fish oil supplements, 121–125
therapeutic uses of, 122–124
Omega-6 fatty acids
arachidonic acid, 68, 69
CLA (conjugated linoleic acid), 85, 87
companion supplements, 125, 157, 241
Omega-9 fatty acids, 125
Omeprazole, xii
OPCs (oligomeric proanthocyanidin complexes), 126–127, 143–145, 172
ORAC (oxygen radical absorbance capacity), 298–299
Oral health, 211, 262, 291–299. *See also* Periodontal disease; Teeth
Organic foods, sales of, 2
Osteoarthritis. *See* Arthritis
Osteoblasts, 261, 269
Osteocalcin, 277
Osteoporosis, 237, 272, 277. *See also* Bone health
Osteo syndrome, 259–299. *See also* Arthritis; Bone health; Joints
bone thinning, 289–291
muscle, ligament, and tendon power, 263–268
oral health, 262, 291–299 (*See also* Periodontal disease; Teeth)
osteo power, 260–262
Ovaries, 219
Oxidation and oxidative stress, 48. *See also* Antioxidants; Free radicals
aging and, 49, 238–239
artery walls, 115, 136 (*See also* Inflammation, of blood vessels)
Oxygen radical absorbance capacity (ORAC), 298–299
Oxygen utilization, supplements for, 47, 69, 137

P

PABA, 308
Packer, Lester, 13, 52
Pain
from arthritis (*See* Arthritis)
stress, effect of, 42
Pain, supplements for
calcium, 273
carnitines, 55
flaxseed, 203, 204
5-HTP (5-hydroxytryptophan), 56–57
melatonin, 254
ribose, 256
s-adenosyl methionine (SAMe), 61

Panax ginseng(ginseng), 325
Pancreas, 82, 102, 181, 182, 218, 256. *See also* Insulin
Panic attacks, 56, 58, 63
Pantesin®, 113
Pantethine, 36, 111–113, 314
companion supplements, 95, 97–98, 113, 148
Pantothenic acid, 36, 97, 111, 112, 256, 308, 314
Paracrine hormones, 220
Parathyroid gland, 219
Parkinson's disease, 48, 49
Passionflower, 65
Pectin, 321
Pepper, 191–192
Peptic ulcers. *See* Ulcers
Peptides, 46, 193, 317–318. *See also* Cytokines
in enteric nervous system (ENS), 184
PepZin
quercetin, companion to, 171
Periodontal disease, 25, 293–299
calcium, effect of, 273
cardiovascular disease and, 119
coenzyme Q10 (CoQ10), effect of, 137
Periwinkle (*Vinca minor*), 69
Peroxynitrate free radicals, 50
Pfaffia paniculata(suma), 251, 328
pH, 182, 196
Phellodendron amurense,80, 327
Phenolic fruit acids, 172
Phenols, 148
Phosphatidyl choline. *See* Lecithin
Phosphatidyl inositol (IP$_3$), 68
Phosphatidyl serine (PS), 65–70, 316
DHEA (dehydroepiandrostone), companion to, 241
ginkgo biloba, companion to, 72
omega-3 fatty acids, companion to, 125
s-adenosyl methionine (SAMe), companion to, 61, 62
Phospholipids, 65–66. *See also* Phosphatidyl serine (PS)
Phosphorous, 32, 33, 264
bone thinning and, 290
in garlic, 115
vanadium, effect in cellular transfer of, 97
Phytoestrogens, 236
Phytosterols, 233
Pineal gland, 253–255
Piperine, 192
Piper nigrum L.(black pepper), 191–192
Pisperidone, xii
Pituitary gland, 217–218
Plantago psyllium, P. ovata(psyllium), 200–202, 322
Plant enzymes, 321
Plant sterols, 120, 241, 242
Platelet aggregation, 127, 173, 233. *See also* Blood clotting
Policosanol, 109–111, 115, 322
Polygonum multiflorum.See Fo-ti (*Polygonum multiflorum*)
Polymenorrhea, 226
Polyphenols, 13, 16, 25, 129–131, 298–299
Polyunsaturated fats, 15, 106
Pomegranate, 54, 55, 321
Potassium, 32, 33, 150, 312
blood pressure, effect on, 106
companion supplements, 138, 148, 274–276
in garlic, 115
Power surges. *See* Hot flashes
Pravochol®, xii

S-adenosyl methionine (SAMe), xiii, 58–62, 68, 133, 134, 318
Salidrosides, 47
Salivary enzymes, 180, 196
SAMe. *See* S-adenosyl methionine (SAMe)
Samuelson, Michael, M. D., 44
Saponins, 241–242
Sarsparilla, 327
Saw palmetto (*Serenoa repens, Sabal serrulata*), 244–248, 251, 327
Schizophrenic condition, 62
Scordinin, 114
Scurvy, 276
Secretin, 183
Seizures, 69
Selenium, 13, 26–29, 32–34, 157, 192, 211, 308, 312
    coenzyme Q10 (CoQ10), companion to, 138
    DHEA (dehydroepiandrostone), companion to, 241
    in garlic, 115
    garlic, companion to, 117
    grape seed extract, companion to, 145
    n-acetyl cysteine (NAC), companion to, 168
    policosanol, companion to, 111
    Vitamin C, companion to, 24, 25
    Vitamin E, companion to, 21, 126
    zinc, companion to, 157
Semi-essential nutrients, 8, 13, 32, 68
Senile dementia, 48. *See also* Age-related memory loss, supplements for; Alzheimer's disease
Serenoa repens(saw palmetto), 244–248, 327
Serotonin, 253
    allergic reactions, role in, 177
    ginkgo biloba and, 71
    5-5-HTP (5-hydroxytryptophan) and, 56–57, 229, 235
    L-theanine and, 257
    menopause, role in, 235
    premenstrual syndrome, role in, 229, 235
    s-adenosyl methionine (SAMe) and, 59–60
*7-Color Cuisine: Making healthy, colorful foods a lifestyle for nutrition,*45, 79, 184, 196, 214
Sexual function. *See also* Impotence and erectile dysfunction
    andropause and virility, 237–244
    Ashwaganda, effect of, 48
    ginkgo biloba, effect of, 72
    insulin and, 78
    in menopause, 230
Short-term stress. *See* Acute stress
Siberian ginseng (*Eleutherococcus senticosus*), 47–48, 327
Silicon, 32, 33, 313
Silymarin. *See* Milk thistle (*Silybum marianum*)
Simvastatin, xii
Singlet oxygen radicals, elimination of, 15
Sinus, 168, 175
Skin, 237. *See also* Acne; Cold sores; Eczema; Herpes simplex; Psoriasis
    advanced glycation end products (AGEs), effect of, 79
    leaky gut syndrome and, 186
    stress, effect of, 42
Skin, supplements for
    acidophilus, effect of, 189
    aloe, 299
    alpha lipoic acid (ALA), 52, 54

copper, 275
echinacea, 163
flaxseed, 203, 204
GLA (gamma linoleic acid), 207–210
grape seed extract, 144–145
hyaluronic acid (HA), 213
milk thistle, 89
nettle, 172
omega-3 fatty acids, 123
pycnogenol, 126, 128
selenium, 27
spirulina (blue-green algae), 210–214
Vitamin A, 9, 10, 213
Vitamin C, 23
Vitamin D, 30
Vitamin E, 20
zinc, 155, 156
Skullcap, 65
Sleep disturbances, 41, 181
    heart attacks, prior to, 106
    in menopause, 230–233, 236
    stress, effect of, 45
Sleep disturbances, supplements for
    Ashwaganda, 48
    calcium, 273
    Eleuthero senticosus, 47
    5-HTP (5-hydroxytryptophan), 56, 57
    melatonin, 254
    St. John's wort, 62, 64
    vinpocetine, 70
Slow metabolism, 141
Small intestine, 181, 183, 201. *See also* Digestion
Smilax (*Smilax officinalis, S. medica*), 251, 327
Smoking
    cardiovascular disease, role in, 118
    carotenoids, use of, 18
    vision health, role in, 170
    Vitamin C, use of, 23
SOD. *See* Superoxide dismutase (SOD)
Sodium, 32, 33, 106, 150, 223, 275–276
Sorbitol, 170, 294
Sore throat, 155, 156, 232
Soy isoflavones, 232, 234–235
Soy powder, 318
Spirulina (blue-green algae), 210–214, 322
Sports injuries, 43–44
St. John's wort (*Hypericum perforatum L.*), xiii, 61–65, 327
Stamina. *See* Energy
Statin drugs
    liver, effect on, 109–110
    policosanol compared to, 110
Statin-like natural compound, red yeast rice as, 120, 121
Steroid hormones, 220–221, 238
Steroids, 217–219
Steroid saponins, 241–242
Sterols, 244, 251
Stevia (*Stevia rebaudiana*), 95, 102, 327
Stomach, 181–182, 193–194. *See also* Digestion
Streptococcus group A bacteria, 118
Stress
    digestion and, 184, 196
    immune system and (*See* Immune system)
    inflammation and, 42, 151

melatonin, effect of, 253–254
Stress management, 42–55
   acute stress, supplements for, 45–48
   astragalus, effect of, 161
   chronic stress, supplements for, 48–55, 80–81, 161
   diet, healthy, 45
   elimination of stress, 43
   exercise for, 43–44
   green tea, effect of, 129
   mindfulness, meditation, prayer, and relaxation, 44–45
   pantethine, effect of, 112
Stress syndrome, x, 39–73. *See also* Brain function; Chronic stress; Memory; Stress management
   acute stress effects, 39–40, 45–48, 73
   cortisol and, 78, 80
Stroke, 117, 128
   menopause and, 231
   metabolic syndrome and, 75
   supplements for, 19, 71, 114, 123, 133
Sugar alcohols, 294–297
Sulfides, 114
Sulfur, 32, 33, 97, 312
Suma (*Pfaffia paniculata*), 251, 328
Sunburn, 204
Sunlight, sensitivity to, 65. *See also* UV rays
Superoxide anion free radicals, 50
Superoxide dismutase (SOD), 49–52, 54, 55, 288, 316
Supplements. *See also* Labels, supplements; Multiple vitamin/mineral supplement; specific supplements
   brands, 309–328
   combination formulas, xiii
   condition-specific formulations, xiii
   contraindications, tables of, 310–328
   dosages, xii
   prescribed drugs, interactions with, xii, 310–328
   prescribed drugs enhanced by, xiii
   production standards, 4
   reasons for using, 6–7
   regulation of, 3–5
   selection factors, 5, 307–309
   statistics on use of, xi–xii
   testing, 4
   as unregulated, 2
Swallowing, 180–181
Syndromes. *See also* specific syndromes
   biological syndrome categories, x
   defined, ix
Syndrome X. *See* Metabolic syndrome
Systemic hormones, 220

T

Tamoxifen, 233
Tannins, 131, 148
T-cells, 28, 118, 151, 153, 160, 176–177
Tea, green. *See* Green tea
Tea tree oil, 116
Teeth, 30, 97, 262, 292–299. *See also* Periodontal disease
Telemerase, 10
Tendons, 265–266, 275
Terminalia chebuls, T. belerica(triphala), 205–206, 328
Terpene lactones, 71
Testes, 219

Testosterone, 237–239, 242, 244, 246, 251
Tetrahydrofolate. *See* Folic acid
Theanine (L-theanine), 257
Thiamin, 36, 307, 314
Thymus, 219, 256
Thyroid, 217, 218, 240
   DHEA (dehydroepiandrostone) use and, 241
   stress, effect of, 42
   supplements for, 26, 97, 174
Thyroid-stimulating hormone (TSH), 217
TIAs (transitory ischemic events), 118
Tingling, 128
Tinnitis, 70, 233
TMG (trimethylglycine), 111, 133–135, 318
Tocopherols and tocotrienols. *See* Vitamin E (tocopherols and tocotrienols)
Trace minerals, 32, 115–116. *See also* Chromium; Selenium; Zinc
Trans fats, 106
Transitory ischemic events (TIAs), 118
Trans resveratrol, 55, 134, 322
Tribulus (*Tribulus terrestris*), 241–242, 251, 328
Trifolium pratense.See Red clover (*Trifolium pratense*)
Triglycerides, 149
   cardiovascular syndrome and, 106
   guidelines for, 108
   metabolic syndrome, 75
   obesity, effect of, 76
   stress, effect of, 47
Triglycerides, supplements for
   cinnamon, 96
   CLA (conjugated linoleic acid), 87
   garlic, 115
   pantethine, 112–113
   policosanol, 110
   red yeast rice, 120
Trigonella foenum-graecum.See Fenugreek (*Trigonella foenum-graecum*)
Trimethylglycine (TMG). *See* TMG (trimethylglycine)
Triphala (*Terminalia chebuls, T. belerica, Embilica officinalis*), 205–206, 328
Tryptophan, 56, 182. *See also* 5-HTP (5-hydroxytryptophan)
Turmeric (*Curcuma longa*), 91, 279, 287–288, 328

U

Ulcerative colitis, 186, 194–195
Ulcers, 48, 185, 194–200. *See also* Helicobacter pylori (*h. pylori*)
   stress, effect of, 42
   supplements for, 189, 198, 249
Ultra-trace elements, 32
United States Pharmacopoeia (USP), 4
Upper respiratory conditions, supplements for, 11, 16, 160, 169
Uric acid, 103
Urinary tract infections/urination problems, 153, 164, 172, 189, 244, 245, 248–251
Urtica dioica.See Nettle (*Urtica dioica*)
UV rays, 15, 65, 170, 277

V

Vaccium macrocarpon(cranberry extract), 248–251, 319
Vaginal dryness, 230, 232, 240
Valerian, 62, 65
Vanadium, 32, 33, 95, 97, 308, 313
Varicose veins, supplements for, 126, 128, 145, 146–148
Vascular system. *See* Cardiovascular system
Vegetarians
  l-carnitine deficiencies of, 139, 140
  spirulina as protein source, 211
Vertigo, 70
Vinca minor(Periwinkle), 69
Vinpocetine, 68, 69–70
Virility, 237–244
Virus protection, supplements for
  bovine colostrum, 166
  Eleuthero senticosus, 47
  garlic, 115
  St. John's wort, 63, 64
  superoxide dismutase (SOD), 51
Vision, supplements for. *See also* Age-related macular
  degeneration; Cataracts
  alpha lipoic acid (ALA), 53–54
  carotenoids, 14, 15, 17
  Eleuthero senticosus, 47
  forskolin, 173, 174
  grape seed extract, 145
  magnesium, 102
  n-acetyl cysteine (NAC), 167
  quercetin, 170
  superoxide free radicals, 50
  Vitamin A, 9–11, 213
  Vitamin C, 23
  Vitamin E, 20
  zinc, 156
Vitamin A, xiii, 7, 9–13, 17, 307, 310
  bone thinning and, 290
  carotene converted to, 14, 15
  in dong quai, 233
  in garlic, 115
  oral health and, 298
  in spirulina, 213
  stress and, 49
Vitamin A, companion supplements, 12
  coenzyme Q10 (CoQ10), 138
  grape seed extract, 146
  n-acetyl cysteine (NAC), 168
  quercetin, 171
  Vitamin C, 22, 25
  Vitamin E, 21
  zinc, 12, 157
Vitamin B. *See* B vitamins
Vitamin C, 7, 13, 17, 19, 22–26, 53, 171–172, 307, 310
  ester-C, 132
  in garlic, 115
  for herpes simplex treatment, 188
  metabolic syndrome and, 79
  in nettle, 172
  oral health and, 298
  in spirulina, 213–214
  stress and, 49
Vitamin C, companion supplements, 25–26
  butcher's broom, 148

calcium, 276–277
chaste tree, 229
chromium, 84
coenzyme Q10 (CoQ10), 25, 138
cranberry extract, 250
echinacea, 165
forskolin, 174
ginkgo biloba, 72
grape seed extract, 145, 146
n-acetyl cysteine (NAC), 168
pycnogenol, 129
quercetin, 171
vanadium, 97
Vitamin A, 22, 25
Vitamin E, 21, 22, 24, 25, 126, 250
Vitamin D, 7, 159, 282, 291, 310
  building and maintaining, role in, 29–31
  companion supplements, 157, 277
Vitamin D_3, 307
Vitamin D-3 hormone, 258
Vitamin D steroids, 221
Vitamin E (tocopherols and tocotrienols), xiii, 7, 13, 17–21,
  125–126, 307, 310
  in dong quai, 233
  in garlic, 115
  metabolic syndrome and, 79
  oral health and, 298
  in spirulina, 211
  stress and, 49
Vitamin E, companion supplements
  chaste tree, 229
  coenzyme Q10 (CoQ10), 138
  garlic, 117
  grape seed extract, 146
  green tea, 132
  n-acetyl cysteine (NAC), 168
  omega-3 fatty acids, 125
  pantethine, 113
  policosanol, 111
  pycnogenol, 129
  quercetin, 170
  red yeast rice, 121
  selenium, 26, 28
  Vitamin A, 21
  Vitamin C, 21, 22, 24, 25, 126, 250
Vitamin K, xiii, 7, 31–32, 183, 277, 311
Vitamin K_1, 307
Vitamins, 7, 307, 310–311. *See also* Multiple vitamin/min-
  eral supplement; specific vitamins
  essential, 6–8
  labeling requirements, 4–5
Vitexin, 143
Vitex (*Vitex agnus-castus*). *See* Chaste tree (*Vitex*
  agnus-castus)

W

Waist circumference, 75, 106, 237
Walnut, black or green, 202
Wart removal, 116
Weight, 181. *See also* Obesity
  blood pressure, effect on, 106
  menopause, weight gain in, 230